ARISTOTLE:

The Classical Heritage of Rhetoric

edited by

Keith V. Erickson

The Scarecrow Press, Inc.
Metuchen, N. J.   1974

Library of Congress Cataloging in Publication Data

Erickson, Keith, comp.
   Aristotle: the classical heritage of rhetoric.

   Includes bibliographical references.
   1. Aristoteles. Rhetorica. I. Title.
PA3893.R4E7   808.5   74-10775
ISBN 0-8108-0740-8

1820813

For

Michelle Leslie Erickson

TABLE OF CONTENTS

PREFACE

The history of Western civilization records numerous interpreters and practitioners of rhetoric. A meager list of scholars who have contributed a theory of rhetoric includes such luminaries as Plato, Cicero, Quintilian, St. Augustine, Joseph Priestley, George Campbell, Hugh Blair, Richard Whately, Thomas De Quincey, John Quincy Adams, I. A. Richards, Richard Weaver and Kenneth Burke. These and other theorists have applied many and varied interpretations to the principles and functions of rhetoric. Yet, for sheer acumen and understanding, their accounts seldom match or approach Aristotle's treatment as developed in the Rhetoric. The Rhetoric certainly may be argued as the most important classical rhetoric and, perhaps, as the most significant work on the subject ever authored. Even today the Rhetoric influences research in oral communication. One need only examine contemporary theories of rhetoric to discover strong Aristotelian traces; further, the terms "Neo-Aristotelian" and "New Rhetoric" eloquently testify to Aristotle's impact.

The purpose of this book is to provide in a single source contemporary research concerning Aristotelian rhetoric. This book is addressed to the scholar and student interested in advanced studies of the Rhetoric. The delicate line balancing the trade-off between student and scholar interest and the degree to which both may fruitfully read this volume have been taken into account. Two general guidelines, apart from a set of specific criteria, were observed for justifying the inclusion of each selection: first, philological emendations or interpretations of minor passages or concepts were omitted on the ground that they would benefit only the most serious reader of the Rhetoric; secondly, survey or introductory articles aimed at the casual reader were omitted. Specifically, the following standards were observed: (1) relevance to rhetorical theory, (2) overall significance, (3) primary focus upon Aristotelian rhetoric, (4) original scholarly contribution.

The major advances and distinguishing features of Aristotelian rhetoric are explored by the contributing authors. The subjects range from Chroust's analysis of Aristotle's early lectures and lost rhetorics to Solmsen's treatment of the Aristotelian tradition in ancient rhetoric. Detailed interpretations of topoi are advanced by Grimaldi and Ochs, while the enthymeme is explicated by McBurney and Bitzer. In addition, ten other subjects dealing with Aristotle's theories of rhetorical discourse are investigated. Moreover, this anthology is the first English language "commentary" on Aristotle's theory of rhetorical discourse since Cope's monumental three-volume edition of 1877.

The traditional editorial problems of format and selection were encountered. Though the addition or deletion of particular items from this anthology may be argued, the editor believes the selections to be among the best scholarly interpretations of Aristotle's rhetorical theories in the English language; my companion work, A Bibliography of Aristotle's Rhetoric: 1475-1975 (Scarecrow Press, in press), provides further resources for investigation.

An anthology, especially one reprinting essays from journals published in five countries, requires the efforts and cooperation of numerous individuals. I wish to express my gratitude to each author who extended the professional courtesy of granting the right to reprint his work. Without their complete cooperation this project would never have been completed. Thanks are due the editors and publishers of American Journal of Philology, L'Antiquité Classique, Archiv für Geschichte der Philosophie, Laval Théologique Philosophique, The New Scholasticism, Philosophy and Rhetoric, Princeton University Press, Quarterly Journal of Speech, Revue des Etudes Grecques, Speech Monographs, Traditio, and the Transactions of the American Philological Association. Special recognition is extended to the librarians of the University of California (Los Angeles), Houston, Michigan, Pennsylvania, Pennsylvania State, Rice, Southern California, Texas Tech, and the Library of Congress who lent assistance with this project as well as with my aforementioned bibliography. I especially wish to thank Dr. Bruce E. Gronbeck for his thorough criticism and help in initiating this work.

Keith V. Erickson
Texas Tech University

INTRODUCTION

ARISTOTLE: THE CLASSICAL HERITAGE OF RHETORIC

One of the most respected and enduring works of antiquity is Aristotle's Rhetoric. The Rhetoric's numerous contributions to rhetorical theory include the enthymeme, topoi, tria genera causarum, pistis, emotions and the antistrophic relationship of rhetoric to dialectic. Aristotle approaches rhetoric systematically, grounding it upon a philosophical framework; this marks the Rhetoric as unique among classical rhetorics. Other rhetoricians of this period wrote handbooks offering practical advice on the art of oratory. Aristotle saw as his purpose, however, a methodological examination of the subject; not a "how to" description but rather an in-depth study of the phenomena of rhetoric. Crem notes that "Aristotle's treatise is unique, in that it is a properly scientific consideration of the subject."[1]

Outline of the Rhetoric

The Rhetoric is divided into three books which roughly outline the stages of preparing a rhetorical address. Many of the rhetorics of antiquity are developed about the canons or offices of speech. The Latin divisions of inventio, dispositio, elocutio, memoria, and pronuntiatio constitute stages in the process of writing and delivering an oration. The Rhetoric is not bounded by these dimensions, however. Book I establishes the speaker and his functions in the persuasion process, while Book II focuses upon the audience, analyzing the relationship between human nature, emotions, and moral considerations. Book III investigates style and matters apropos to the writing of an oration. Charles Sears Baldwin summarizes the book's design by noting that the "speech itself, the final utterance ... has thus been approached as the art of adjusting the subject-matter of a given case through the intelligence and emotion of the speaker to the intelligence and emotion of the audience."[2] Organized in this fashion the Rhetoric departs from the classical arrangement of partes orationis--the divisions of speech (proem, narration, proofs, and epilogue). Aristotle's schema relegates these divisions to disposition. Friedrich Solmsen concludes that: "This entirely new approach is ... obviously based on Aristotle's conception of a thing's organic unity as implying a principle of structure

1

and being different from a mere accumulation of its parts. "3

The first sentence of Book I philosophically establishes the position of rhetoric to logic: "Rhetoric is the counterpart of dialectic. "4 Aristotle develops his argument by showing the respective provinces of the two arts. We are told that neither rhetoric nor dialectic is superior to the other; rather, they lie in an anti-strophic relationship. Rhetoric and dialectic are similar in that they treat subjects belonging to no particular science whose substance, as a rule, is known to all men. Likewise, they proceed in a rational way, yet unlike the sciences, afford only probable reasons. They differ from one another in that rhetoric often is concerned with moral matters, dialectic with speculative considerations. Dialectic reaches for an audience of logically trained minds while rhetoric adjusts to the common citizen. Rhetorical syllogisms, enthymemes, are the rhetorician's tools, while syllogisms and induction are the dialectician's. Rhetoric, Aristotle continues, is to be seen as yet another way of establishing truth--"the application of proof to people. "5

Book I establishes four functions or purposes of rhetoric. First, should the true and just fall prey to their opposites, a rhetorician, through effective discourse, can set straight the imbalance. Secondly, Aristotle argues, science deals with the instruction of matter the multitude cannot grasp; therefore, rhetoric is obligated to facilitate learning because it relies upon generally accepted principles. Thirdly, by proving opposites rhetoric enables us to counteract false arguments. Finally, the fourth function of rhetoric he identifies as self-defense: "It would be absurd if it were considered disgraceful not to be able to defend oneself with the help of the body, but not disgraceful as far as speech is concerned, whose use is more characteristic of man than that of the body. "6

Aristotle formally defines rhetoric as the "faculty of discovering the possible means of persuasion in reference to any subject whatever. "7 This is the function and province of rhetoric. The process of persuasion is achieved by a judicious use of proofs. The proofs of rhetoric are either artistic or inartistic. Artistic proofs are basically arguments from probability; they stem from the speaker's ability to "invent" or discover lines of argument from a culture's pool of accepted opinions. Inartistic proof is direct evidence such as the testimony of slaves, contracts, and witnesses, external to the speaker's art. Both artistic and inartistic proofs, however, are recognized as members of the Aristotelian inventional process as both must be molded into actual discourse. The proofs, pistis, furnished by the speech are ethos, pathos, and logos. Ethos, or credibility, is a speaker's perceived moral character. Pathos, the arousal of emotion, lies within the listener, while logos (roughly speaking a "logical" rhetorical argument), lies within the structure and form of the address.

Rhetoric as Aristotle defines it is a faculty for providing

arguments of two modes. The first is paradeigma--the example.
The example is an inductive argument supplying probable conclusions to the subject discussed. The second mode is the enthymeme,
a deductive rhetorical syllogism. Aristotle departs here from his
contemporaries by linking rhetorical arguments to dialectic and analytics. Heretofore, orators had conceived of the enthymeme as
simply a clever stylistic device. Aristotle, however, recognized
its logical bases and formulated it as a rhetorical syllogism.
Lloyd Bitzer defines the enthymeme as a "syllogism based on probabilities, signs and examples, whose function is rhetorical persuasion. Its successful construction is accomplished through the joint
efforts of speaker and audience, and this is its essential character."8 While the syllogism is the normal structure of dialectical
arguments, the enthymeme's form is conducive to the purposes of
rhetoric. Generally, enthymemes are concrete while abstract deduction is characteristic of the syllogism.

The enthymeme takes its materials from what Aristotle calls
the "topics." A discussion of "topics" or topoi appear in three
sections of the Rhetoric. Topoi, according to modern interpreters,
means seat or place of an argument. Robert Brake believes Aristotle's topoi are "areas or locales in which ideas are grouped according to their kinds and from which they can be drawn."9 Topoi
have been classified by various schemes, the most comprehensive
being that of material and formal (discussed by Aristotle at the
conclusion of Book II). Material topoi are of two kinds: (1) common (kinoi) and, (2) special (eidê). Common topics concern general principles of probability which apply equally well to all disciplines. The topos of "more or less," an example Aristotle uses,
can furnish enthymemes as easily for physics as for politics. Later in Chapter 18 of Book II, he enumerates the range of the common topics as embracing the possible and impossible, greatness
and smallness, what will or will not occur, and what has or has
not happened. These topoi are especially useful for the three types
of oratory (to be discussed shortly). Special or genera topics draw
their materials from particular disciplines. A special topic involves a proposition habitually associated with specific types of
speeches. The rhetorician employs special topoi when topics of a
universal (common) nature do not apply or fail to expedite his argument. Moreover, Brake concludes: The special topoi embrace
substantive items or propositions found largely in the areas of
ethics and politics and furnish the premises for enthymemes."10
Aristotle observes that speakers as a rule rely more heavily upon
specific or particular topics than common topics.

Aristotle next delineates the types of speaking and their respective special topoi. He divides rhetorical situations into deliberative, forensic, and epideictic speaking--the tria genera causarum.
Deliberative speaking occurs in public assemblies and gathering
places. The orator speaks of those events and circumstances to
come--the future. The topics of deliberative oratory are the ex-
pedient and harmful. The speaker exhorts a course of action and

speaks of the good and bad.   Deliberative oratory is pragmatic, requiring the orator to know and adjust to current events and ideas.
Aristotle concludes by developing an analysis of special topoi (discussed as the constituents of "happiness," "goodness," and "utility") applicable to deliberative speaking--offspring, wealth, honor,
health, strength, beauty, old age, friendship, fortune, virtue, etc.

The second form of oratory is epideictic or ceremonial
speaking.   The epideictic oration, since it deals with praise and/or
blame of existing conditions, directs itself to the present.   It has
as its end the honorable or disgraceful.   The epideictic speaker
must of necessity address himself to considerations of the ethical
and moral: "He will ... speak of virtue and vice, of the noble
and disgraceful, since they constitute the aim of one who praises
and of one who blames."[11]   Aristotle concludes by demonstrating
how the rhetorician employs this line of argument.

Aristotle concludes Book I with an analysis of the modes
and functions of forensic oratory.   Forensic oratory is courtroom
speaking, taking one of two postures--accusatory or defensive.
Forensic speaking addresses issues committed or not committed.
Here Aristotle examines the motives of unjust acts, the criminal
"mind" and the character of those exposed to unjust acts; these
aspects of crime provide lawyers with special topoi.   There are
shortcomings, however, to his discussion of forensic evidence, for
"his division of 'extrinsic proofs' ... is for the modern lawyer
neither scientific or significant."[12]

Book II of the Rhetoric addresses itself to the audience,
which is essentially a study of human emotions and attitudes.
Aristotle predicts that an audience will react positively to a speaker possessing the qualities of wisdom, virtue and goodwill.   Obviously, an orator should exhibit these qualities.   How the rhetorician is perceived depends upon each auditor's judgment which is
affected by his emotions.   In Book II Aristotle defines emotion as
"all those feelings that so change men as to affect their judgments,
and that are also attended by pain or pleasure."[13]   He analyzes
anger and outlines three kinds of slighting--contempt, spite and
insolence.   He concludes that "clearly the orator will have to speak
so as to bring his hearers into a frame of mind that will dispose
them to anger, and to represent his adversaries as open to such
charges and possessed of such qualities as do make people angry."[14]
Similar analysis of the respective emotions and their opposites ensues with their application to rhetorical discourse; with fear, love,
envy, shame, kindness, indignation and emulation examined.   Aristotle then applies the emotions and moral qualities to human character, showing how they correspond to the various ages and for-
tunes of men.

Following the divisions of the common topics (discussed
earlier) Aristotle turns to rhetorical arguments common to all
oratory--example and enthymeme.   The example is divided into

fables and the illustrative parallel. Aristotle advises us that "if
we can argue by Enthymeme, we should use our Examples as subsequent supplementary evidence. They should not precede the Enthymemes; that will give the argument an inductive air, which only
rarely suits the conditions of speech-making."[15] Aristotle next
examines the maxim--a special form of enthymeme. He notes four
varieties of maxims and warns the orator that they are appropriate
only to elderly men: "For a young man to use them is like telling
stories--unbecoming."[16] The maxim renders the advantage of in-
vesting a speech with moral character.

Aristotle divides enthymemes into "elementary classes"--
demonstrative and refutative. "The demonstrative enthymeme draws
conclusions from admitted premises, the refutative draws conclusions disputed by the adversary."[17] These enthymemes are built
upon lines of argument evolving from a list of twenty-eight valid
and nine fallacious topics. These "formal" topics are the third
form of topoi alluded to earlier. The formal topoi, derived from
Aristotle's Topics, serve as lines of argument independent of particular subject-matter and dependent upon abstract analysis. "The
list is a random one of some of the more usual arguments from
cause, sign, and example encountered in speaking."[18] A few examples will illustrate our point. The twenty-eight valid formal
topoi include arguments of time, opposites, definition, correlation,
ambiguity, induction, consequences, antecedents and past action
among others. Generally, they reveal characteristics of the thing,
idea, or person discussed by the orator. The invalid or fallacious
formal topoi are arguments which appear correct but are not.
Aristotle did not discover these topoi but rather catalogued them;
most of these topoi had been employed by the Attic orators. Aristotle concludes Book II with a discussion of how to refute enthymemes. He demonstrates that enthymemes are based upon four
types of alleged fact: (1) probabilities, (2) examples, (3) infallible
signs, and (4) ordinary signs; by diagnosing the weakness of each
Aristotle demonstrates how they may be refuted.

Book III of the Rhetoric examines the process of speech
composition. Because this portion of the work differs in focus
from Books I and II it has been considered by scholars as either
a spurious or separate treatise later appended to the Rhetoric.
There are a number of arguments to support these positions.
Examining the lists of Diogenes Laertus we find no Rhetoric containing three books. Instead a Rhetoric of two books is catalogued
as well as a Style in two books. Solmsen[19] has demonstrated that
two introductions found in Book III link it to earlier and later drafts
of the Rhetoric. This indicates that Aristotle envisioned the three
books as comprising one treatise. Seen in this light, Book III was
not appended to the Rhetoric, but was written in conjunction with
books I and II.

The third book opens with a brief analysis of delivery.
Aristotle exhibits distaste for the matter, as though he were cha-

grined at having to acknowledge the importance of delivery. He
quickly dismisses the concept by noting that "rightly considered it
is thought vulgar,"[20] needing attention because of the sorry nature
of audiences. Baldwin, however, concludes that: "Tantalizing in
its brevity, this passage is nevertheless suggestive; for it sketches
an analytic division of delivery into voice-placing and volume, pitch
and rhythm; it points to the value for public speaking of the arts
of dramatic recital; and, most important of all, it relates delivery
to the whole idea of style as concrete presentation versus abstract
formulation."[21]

Following delivery the Rhetoric discusses style, beginning
with word-choice. There are many virtues of style but chief among
them is perspicuity or clarity, which is achieved by employing
nouns and verbs as they are conventionally found. Ornamentation,
the second virtue of style, is achieved through the judicious use of
metaphors: "This will be secured by observing due proportion;
otherwise there will be a lack of propriety."[22] Chapter 3 discusses
inappropriateness and the vice of excessiveness, while Chapter 4 introduces similes. Having discussed the individual components of
style, Aristotle analyzes sentences and clauses. The final virtue
of style is appropriateness (Chapter 7) which is achieved through
the expression of emotion and character (ethopoiia). Propriety
must be observed in regard to the subject matter: "Style is proportionate to the subject matter when neither weighty matters are
treated off-hand, nor trifling matters with dignity...."[23] Appropriateness is important because it makes one's case or point appear
more credible.

The structure or form of diction is developed next. Rhythm,
Aristotle says, is a vital consideration in rhetorical discourse.
The orator is warned to avoid meter lest his speech ring of poetry;
and, in equal measure, rhythm should avoid excess. Of the types
of rhythm the heroic is found lacking in prose harmony while the
iambic fails to arouse the listener. The trochaic is likewise found
wanting, as it is a skipping rhythm suggestive of "comic dancing."
Aristotle finds the paean most suitable for suasory discourse. The
chief virtue of the paean is its non-metrical yet rhythmical structure: "The paean should be retained, because it is the only one of
the rhythms mentioned which is not adapted to a metrical system,
so that it is most likely to be undetected."[24]

The description of the period in Chapter 9 has often been
misinterpreted. Part of the difficulty lies in the differing interpretations we and the ancients have given the term.[25] At least two
types of periods were known in antiquity. The first type is characteristic of Isocrates (the historical period, long sentences made
up of subordinate clauses), while the second, an earlier form, was
favored by Gorgias and Antiphon (the balanced period, parallelism
or antithesis composed of two divisions). The latter more closely
describes Aristotle's definition: "This is made clear by his comparison of the period to the strophe-Antistrophe structure of the

dithyramb and by his continual reference to the two parts of the
period, the beginning and the end he calls them once. "26 There
are three additional points concerning Aristotle's period. First, a
period, unlike its modern counterpart, need not consist of an entire sentence. Secondly, there is no indication that a period
possesses a rhythmical structure. Finally, the two divisions are
each called a kolon and make up a group of words (which need not
be grammatically independent); the major requirement being only
that it offset equally its sister (i.e., antithetical or parallel) kolon.

Aristotle next discusses the metaphor. The metaphor consists of more than a single word--often whole phrases, sentences
and ideas. He sees the focus or object of the metaphor given life
or action: "They all make the subject moving and living; and actuality is movement. "27 Metaphors, though, should not be obvious and ought to be drawn from appropriate subjects. Various
forms of metaphor, such as proverbs, hyperboles and similes are
discussed.

Distinctions between various style forms are made in Chapter 12. Aristotle reminds the orator of the natural incompatibility
of oral and written styles. Obviously that style best suited for
prose or poetry ill-suits the rhetorician. Because compositions
are written without regard to oral delivery they fall short when
spoken aloud. Likewise, "speeches suited for delivery, when delivery is absent, do not fulfill their proper function and appear
silly. "28

Aristotle completes the Rhetoric with a brief analysis of
dispositio. Unlike the rest of the work, this section appears shallow, echoing rhetorical handbooks of that period. Baldwin dismisses
this section by suggesting that "it has little significance [showing]
little of Aristotelian discernment and suggestiveness. "29 Aristotle
notes that there are four components of a speech--introduction,
proposition, proof, and epilogue. A brief analysis of the appropriate construction and use of each follows. Suddenly, with no
epilogue of his own, he ends the Rhetoric. Using an example of a
suitable conclusion drawn from Lysias, Aristotle seems to have
put double meaning in his last sentence: "I have spoken; you have
heard; you know the facts; now give your decision. "30 This concludes our outline of the Rhetoric.

Overview of Articles

We briefly outlined the Rhetoric to place in perspective
Aristotle's various concepts embodied in the work. The essays reprinted here thoroughly expound upon these concepts. The following is a brief summary of each article.

The purpose of Anton-Hermann Chroust's essay ("Aristotle's
Earliest 'Course of Lectures on Rhetoric'") is to analyze the prob-

able content and circumstances of Aristotle's series of lectures on
rhetoric in the Academy. To support his arguments, Chroust
examines several classical works referring to the lectures, including Aristotle's lost rhetorical work, Theodectea. Chroust affords
us a fascinating picture of the lectures as well as a lost Aristotelian rhetoric.

Philodemus, a critical observer of Aristotle, is the earliest
known source mentioning these lectures. Philodemus states that
Aristotle offered lectures in the afternoon, maintaining it a "scandal to remain silent and let Isocrates speak out." (As is commonly known, Isocrates was the chief rival, antagonist, and competi-
tor of Aristotle and the Academy.) Chroust details Philodemus'
attack upon Aristotle's attention to the study of rhetoric. Briefly,
Philodemus' criticism stems from the belief that Aristotle slighted
natural and moral philosophy when he turned his attention to rhetoric. While Philodemus rebuked Aristotle for attempting to combine rhetoric and philosophy, Cicero later praised him for it. Cicero agreed with Philodemus, however, that Aristotle turned to the
teaching of rhetoric as a countermove against the successes of
Isocrates and his school.

In recent years much debate has centered upon these early
lectures and the conflicting evidence from classical sources.
Chroust examines the arguments of Stahr, Diels, Blass, Rose,
Heitz, Solmsen, and Kantelhardt whose research links these lectures with various rhetorical works of Aristotle. Chroust concludes that the evidence as to the date and doctrinal content of
these lectures is inconclusive, making definitive statements concerning them impossible. We can assume, however, that the lectures arose from Aristotle's personal dislike of Isocrates and his
school of oratory. And, if two assumptions (as detailed in the
text) concerning the Aristotelian Gryllus and Platonic Phaedrus are
correct, then a probable date of 360 to 355 B.C. can be affixed to
the lectures.

Chroust's essay facilitates our understanding of the development of Aristotle's rhetorical theories. Chroust's investigation
sheds light on two heretofore cloudy facts of Aristotle's back-
ground--the early lectures on rhetoric and his Theodectea. Knowledge of the lectures and Theodectea provide a firmer basis for understanding the heritage of the Rhetoric; an appreciation of the
lectures and rhetorics preceding the Rhetoric are important in fa-
cilitating our grasp of Aristotle's maturing opinion concerning
rhetorical discourse.

Chroust's essay ("Aristotle's First Literary Effort: The
Gryllus, A Lost Dialogue on the Nature of Rhetoric") examines
another of Aristotle's lost rhetorics--the Gryllus. Chroust summarizes research reconstructing the Gryllus and theorizes as to
the content and thrust of the work. This book is believed to be
Aristotle's earliest work. Evidence dates the Gryllus' composition

at ca. 360 B.C., probably during Aristotle's eighth year of study under Plato.

The book's title, Gryllus, has generated much speculation among scholars as to its content and purpose. The work takes its name from Gryllus, the son of Xenophon, who died shortly before the battle of Mantinea. The work's unusual title (for Aristotle) suggests Plato's manner of entitling dialogues and also lends confirmation to the general belief that the work was written in dialogue form. More puzzling is the connection between Gryllus and a work of rhetoric. Did Aristotle, as Heitz suggests, merely wish to commemorate a friend (although no evidence of their friendship exists)? Or, as argued by Thillet and Solmsen, was the work primarily a polemical piece which argued that not all rhetoric is art while simultaneously attacking certain rhetoricians (especially those having eulogized Gryllus for the purpose of ingratiating themselves to Xenophon)? The latter explanation is more probable, suggests Chroust. Further, the Gryllus may be viewed as a polemic against Isocrates and his philosophical and educational ideals.

Chroust concludes that the title of the work is incidental, that it was a work on rhetoric written in dialogue form echoing the rhetorical standards of Plato, and attacking the teaching of Isocrates. Unfortunately, the work does not survive; in addition to providing us with a better understanding of Aristotelian rhetoric, it would have given us a clearer picture of the young Aristotle. Chroust's analysis of the Gryllus is useful for extending our knowledge of Aristotelian rhetoric beyond the extant Rhetoric and for providing us with a glimpse of Aristotle's formative thinking in rhetorical theory.

Theresa Crem ("The Definition of Rhetoric According to Aristotle") clarifies Aristotle's definition of rhetoric. Crem examines the Rhetoric's definition in light of Aristotle's avowed aim of authoring a scientific presentation of rhetoric. The article is divided into two parts, "common considerations of the nature of rhetoric" and a "proper treatment of rhetorical method" (wherein is examined the end of rhetoric).

Crem notes initially that Aristotle's Rhetoric is unique among classical rhetorics in that it is a scientific consideration of the subject. Of the many rhetorics preceding the Rhetoric the overwhelming majority were handbooks offering practical advice on public speaking rather than, as is characteristic of Aristotle, a methodological examination of the nature of rhetorical discourse. Aristotle wrote neither as a notable teacher of oratory nor as an experienced rhetorician, but rather as a logician.

Crem clarifies Aristotle's definition of rhetoric by examining the antistrophic relationship of rhetoric to dialectical logic. In Chapter 2 he informs us that the rhetorical

method is concerned with the modes of persuasion--proofs. The
utility of the rhetorical method is also discussed. The rhetorical
method is defined by Aristotle as the faculty of discovering, in any
case, the available means of persuasion. Rhetoric is viewed as a
faculty since it has no determinate subject; it is concerned with observing the available means of persuasion rather than with explicating or defining a particular subject matter. Crem concludes
her article with a discussion of the audience and its importance to
Aristotelian rhetoric.

Robert Price ("Some Antistrophes to the Rhetoric") believes
that the Rhetoric should not be considered, in the words of W. D.
Ross, a "curious jumble of literary criticism with second rate
logic, ethics, politics, and jurisprudence." Price wishes to prove,
moreover, that the Rhetoric is a parallel work to the Topics and
Analytics--not an application of them.

Rhetoric is announced in the opening line of the Rhetoric as
the counterpart or antistrophe to dialectic. Price sees rhetoric
and dialectic as antistrophic arts because both share the structure
of such arts "as are concerned with the production of certain logoi
for certain purposes." Logoi are defined by Aristotle as faculties
for furnishing arguments. Because these logoi differ greatly, Price
examines their similarities in terms of sullogismoi (especially, syllogisms in process.) This distinction may be applied to other
works of Aristotle which are antistrophically related.

Deliberation is the first antistrophe recognized by Price.
He notes that deliberation, although sharing features with the Rhetoric not found in the other antistrophes, is not explicitly identified
by Aristotle. The second antistrophe is evaluation, which is nowhere discussed by Aristotle. Price analyzes this antistrophe in
so far as he sees it a "reworking of the materials of Deliberation
in a manner near to that of both rhetoric and demonstration."
Recollection, the third antistrophe, has as its basis a single passage to be found in Aristotle's Parva naturalia. The fourth antistrophe, demonstration, is characterized by its notions that (1)
within a single mind everything occurs, and (2) the object is to
discover the grounds of a case in order to generate premises lend-
ing themselves to a specific conclusion. Tasks requiring demonstration, however, are limited. Dialectic is the fifth antistrophe
analyzed. The last antistrophic art is Rhetoric. Price demonstrates how rhetoric is one of the sister arts having faculties for
furnishing logoi. He does not consider rhetorical syllogisms to be
inferior or imperfect, nor does he see them as demonstrative syllogisms. Likewise, he does not view Aristotle's inartistic proofs
as logoi but rather as means for producing conclusions; an orator,
rather than invent them, finds such proofs.

Price's article is important because it explores the Rhetoric's similarity of purpose with the other antistrophic arts as a
faculty for furnishing logoi, and as a member of a family of anti-

strophic arts.   Price also justifies the Rhetoric's logoi (enthymemes) as different but not defective syllogisms, for providing arguments.   In addition, Price reaffirms Aristotle's positioning of
rhetoric as a parallel work to the Topics and Analytics.

        As we have already noted, rhetoric "is the counterpart of
dialectic. "   This statement, found in the opening paragraph of the
work, is Aristotle's attempt to relate rhetoric to logic.   There is
disagreement, however, as to how and in what manner rhetoric is
a counterpart or antistrophe of dialectic.   Brother S. Robert's
article ("Rhetoric and Dialectic: According to the First Latin
Commentary on the Rhetoric of Aristotle") details the similarities
and differences between these two concepts.

        Robert employs William of Moerbeke's commentary on Aris-
totle's Rhetoric as commented on by Giles as the basis for his
analysis.   As Giles' commentary played a significant role in early
Aristotelian scholarship and because its essential interpretation
differs little from modern renderings, its distinction of rhetoric
and dialectic is of interest.

        Robert's article is divided into two parts: an examination
of how rhetoric and dialectic differ, and secondly, their common-
alities.   These two concepts are seen to differ across several dimensions.   Alfarabius, for example, commented that dialectic is
concerned with universals, and rhetoric with particulars.   In addition Giles notes that dialectic generates greater probability because
rhetoric is moved by the will.   Also, dialectic is an instrument
for discovering truth while rhetoric is properly the province of
statesmen interested in persuasion.   And too, rhetoric is more
concerned with mortal affairs, dialectic with the speculative realm;
consequently, rhetoric may turn its attention to the arousal of passions while dialectic ordinarily avoids them.

        The similarities of rhetoric and dialectic are likewise de-
tailed.   These two disciplines are seen akin in terms of their prob-
abilistic nature, rationality, and quasi-universality.   Robert considers rhetoric and dialectic alike, finally, in that both are acts
of reason "whereby men attain all that is knowable. "

        Whitney J. Oates (Aristotle and the Problem of Value) notes
that perhaps the most striking characteristic of Aristotle's Rhetoric
is its ambivalence concerning a theory of value.   Oates suggests
the Rhetoric attempts two lines of analysis in explicating rhetoric--
that of aligning rhetoric philosophically with logic, politics, and
ethics, while developing the practical concerns of a rhetorical handbook.   We note, therefore, a moral rhetoric linked to ethics, politics and logic, while an amoral, or indeed immoral, treatment
emerges when matters of rhetorical practicality are discussed.

        Evidence of an amoral theory of rhetoric arises when Aris-
totle advises the political orator in the ways of expediency, effi-

ciency, and advantages over the apparently "secondary" matters of
justice and honor.   Likewise, in the Rhetoric's passage aligning
rhetoric to logic and the ethical branch of politics, suggesting it to
be partly like dialectic as well as sophistical reasoning (dealing
with words), his underpinning for a philosophically grounded rhetoric gives way.   Thus, we are left with the uncomfortable choice of
deciding whether a moral, immoral, or amoral rhetoric is advanced by Aristotle.

Oates suggests Aristotle could not have envisioned the Rhetoric as a handbook for three reasons: first, the Rhetoric is situated
in the corpus primarily with works which treat of or relate to
Aristotle's metaphysics or philosophy.   Secondly, Aristotle makes
clear his intention to relate the work to his other treatises and,
lastly, suggests Oates, Aristotle recognized that rhetoric must be
treated philosophically if it is to transcend the level of a non-
intellectual discipline.   Oates concludes that had Aristotle developed
a more thorough and overriding theory of value the confounding elements of the Rhetoric's ambivalence would not have arisen.   In
short, Oates sees Aristotle's work as an amoral rhetoric.

Oates' analysis is important because it places in proper perspective not only the role of the orator and his justification for
adapting truth to the common man, but for its clarity in determining a value orientation in the Rhetoric.   It is little known that Aristotle envisioned an amoral rhetoric.   In this context Oates provides
us a value oriented framework with which to judge persuasion as it
implies the adjusting of ideas and arguments to individuals for the
purpose of affecting their behavior.

Perhaps chief among Aristotle's contributions to rhetorical
theory is his concept of "enthymeme."   Because Aristotle spoke of
the enthymeme as the "very body and substance of persuasion,"
scholarly attempts at explicating the concept are numerous.   James
H. McBurney's analysis ("The Place of the Enthymeme in Rhetorical Theory") is one of the more valuable studies.

McBurney begins his analysis by contrasting the levels of
knowledge--science, dialectic, rhetoric, and sham reasoning.
McBurney defines the enthymeme by examining pertinent passages
of the Rhetoric.   He analyzes (1) probabilities and signs as the materials of the enthymeme; (2) the example; (3) ethos and pathos;
(4) topoi; (5) the distinction between refutative and demonstrative
enthymemes; (6) passages suggesting the suppression of a proposition.   McBurney, having discussed the enthymeme from these six
viewpoints, concludes that: (1) the enthymeme is to rhetoric as
the syllogism is to logic; (2) probable signs and causes constitute
the premises of an enthymeme; (3) "these premises are drawn
from topics varying in specificity and exactness from the particular facts of a given substantive field to the most general principles
of probability"; (4) language may be phrased to affect ethos, pathos
and probable truth; (5) not all enthymemes can be stated as valid

syllogisms because of deficiencies in the inferential process; (6) rhetorical examples may be reduced to an enthymematic form; and (7) a suppressed premise is characteristic but not necessary to the enthymeme. McBurney concludes by historically tracing the enthymeme after Aristotle and by suggesting its place in contemporary rhetorical theory.

McBurney's analysis of the enthymeme was a pioneering work. The thoroughness and clarity of his arguments, together with his introductory remarks on reasoning, are widely noted. Lloyd Bitzer ("Aristotle's Enthymeme Revisited"), however, disagrees with a number of McBurney's conclusions. Bitzer, like McBurney, notes that the enthymeme as developed by Aristotle is a perplexing concept in that no consistent statement of it is made. Bitzer synthesizes and critically analyzes research investigating the enthymeme.

Bitzer challenges the definitions of many interpreters of the enthymeme. Briefly, he demonstrates that while the enthymeme is a syllogistic form distinguishable from dialectical and demonstrative syllogisms, neither premise probability by itself nor an enthymeme's formal deficiency constitutes its essential feature. Likewise, he suggests, enthymemes by definition are not necessarily concrete while syllogisms are abstract. Thus, while most enthymemes are probable, formally deficient, and concrete, we cannot generalize and say that all enthymemes exhibit such characteristics. Having examined various inadequacies of current interpretations, Bitzer advances his own analysis of the enthymeme.

We are to consider the term "incomplete syllogism" (one or more suppressed premises) in a special sense; an "incomplete syllogism" to Bitzer means that the "speaker does not lay down his premises but lets his audience supply them out of its stock of opinion and knowledge." Premises may or may not be verbalized. The enthymeme, therefore, accomplishes for rhetoric what the question-answer format does for dialectic: "The speaker draws the premises for his proofs from propositions which members of his audience would supply if he were to proceed by question and answer." The resulting syllogism Bitzer calls "enthymeme." Bitzer emphasizes that a speaker and audience jointly must produce enthymemes if they are to occur.

Bitzer's essay is important for several reasons: (1) he summarizes all the research investigating Aristotle's enthymeme; (2) he demonstrates that, contrary to tradition, enthymemes are not incomplete syllogisms; (3) he believes premises are verbalizable; and (4) he suggests a vital commingling effect of enthymemes upon the speaker-listener relationship.

The two forms of logical proof established in the Rhetoric are the enthymeme and example. We have noted McBurney and Bitzer's analyses of the enthymeme and their summaries of research investigating this concept.   They observed that the enthymeme has generated considerable research.   By comparison, the example has received scant attention.   Gerard Hauser's study ("The Example in Aristotle's Rhetoric: Bifurcation or Contradiction") fills this void by examining the example and resolving an internal conflict concerning it.

Aristotle elevates the example in Book I to a place of lofty importance--rhetorical induction.   In Book II, however, we discover disparate statements concerning the example.   Rather than a mode of proof independent yet co-ordinate with the enthymeme, as in Book I, Book II asserts the example to be a special form of enthymeme, subordinate to and serving merely as a source of materials for the enthymeme.   Aristotle's definition is seemingly a contradiction which is never resolved internally.

In attempting to resolve the conflict, Hauser turns to Aristotle's doctrine of induction (as exemplified in his theories of epistemology and metaphysics) to explain the rhetorical example.   Hauser argues, as demonstrated in the Metaphysics and Organon, that Aristotle had a bifurcated concept of induction.   Thus, Hauser suggests, Aristotle may have envisioned a bifurcated theory of example; allowing us to take at face value the description of example found in Book II--the example as a support in enthymematic proof. Thus, the Rhetoric develops not a disparate doctrine of example but rather one consistent with Aristotle's bimodal theory of induction.   Gerard Hauser's essay is important, therefore, for suggesting an answer to a previously confusing riddle concerning the dual-definitions of "example" found in the Rhetoric.

In recent years much investigation has focused upon the concept of pistis; the theories advanced, however, are not always consistent.   Lienhard ("A Note on the Meaning of ΠΙΣΤΙΣ in Aristotle's Rhetoric") attempts to resolve the conflicting interpretations.   He examines in particular the work of Grimaldi and Wikramanayake.

The specific details of each scholar's argument is left for the reader's study.   Basically, however, Grimaldi saw the meaning of pistis in the following relationship: "Pistis as matter (ethos, pathos, pragma) is ordered by pistis as effect."   Consistent with this view, Grimaldi thought it inaccurate to separate ethos and pathos from a third, logical, proof.   It is Wikramanayake's belief that ethos and pathos are proofs independent of other considerations and that parallel to them is another form of proof consisting of the enthymeme and example--logical proof.   In order to determine the efficacy of either position Lienhard turns to the Rhetoric and examines the several senses in which the term pistis is employed.

Lienhard identifies six ways in which Aristotle interpreted pistis, five of which are relevant to rhetorical discourse.   The confusion is tentatively settled with the observation that Aristotle carefully and intentionally changed the meaning of the word depending

upon its context.   The evidence suggests that before Aristotle
changed the context he clearly warned the reader.   Lienhard concludes by noting that "pistis means the state of mind produced, it
occurs in the singular or in a verbal or adjectival form." That
is, each of the five senses of the term applicable to rhetoric refers to the proof which induces belief; and hence pistis is the key
to Aristotle's philosophy of discourse.   Lienhard's analysis is important because he distinguishes the relationship of the forms of
proof to each other and to rhetorical discourse in particular.

   The Aristotelian topoi, the next subject examined, are recognized by Grimaldi as playing a significant role in Western
culture even though, curiously enough, they have not been understood fully ("The Aristotelian Topics").   The topoi have been obscured by a number of factors, including Aristotle's reluctance to
announce forthrightly what he meant by the concept.   A decline of
methodology following Aristotle and Cicero's misdirected emphasis
(which passed to Quintilian and from him into the middle ages and
Western tradition), further facilitated the misinterpretation of topoi.
Grimaldi believes it a genuine loss that this truncated form of the
topics fails to engender the richer form of discourse he sees them
providing.

   Grimaldi critically analyzes the "particular" and "general"
topics as developed by the Rhetoric.   Particular topics are sources
which clarify a subject while general topics are forms of inference
allowing the speaker to develop further conclusions.   Additionally,
general topics concern universal principles of probability that apply
equally well to all disciplines and express a common human ex-
perience--virtue, expediency, or justice.   The general topics embrace the possible and impossible, greatness and smallness, what
will or will not occur, and what has or has not happened.

   Particular topics, however, draw materials from their respective disciplines.   Thus, a special topic would involve a proposition unique to a certain genus.   The particular topoi furnish
premises for enthymemes and are more widely used than general
topics.

   Grimaldi's analysis is especially important for an understanding of material topoi, for he sees them divided into particular
and general topoi.   He shows how these topoi are not commonplaces,
as has often been urged, and demonstrates their capacity to furnish
premises for enthymemes.   Grimaldi does not discuss, however,
the formal topics.

   Donovan J. Ochs ("Aristotle's Concept of Formal Topics"),
unlike Grimaldi who examined the particular and general topics,
analyzes Aristotle's concept of the "formal" topics.   Ochs' specific
purpose is an explanation of the twenty-eight forms of formal topoi
found in Book II of the Rhetoric.   He argues that rhetorical topics
are not to be viewed as a logical system of invention but rather

as primary, indivisible, and inherent elements from which enthymemes are constructed. He proves his thesis by examining the
rhetorical topics along a time-line development of the Rhetoric and
the intervention of the Topics. By designating the various stages
of the Rhetoric we note that Aristotle's theory of topics preceded
the enthymeme. Ochs indicates that not until the first expansion
of the Rhetoric were the genera-materials and "commons" added.

The term "element, " which is equated with a topic both in
the Rhetoric and Topics, is defined as the first "inherent thing out
of which a thing is constructed. " Aristotle conceives of "topic"
and "element" as being synonymous terms. A topic, of course, is
viewed as that under which enthymemes fall. This does not imply,
as Ochs points out, that the twenty-eight topics constitute a logical
system. It is the conclusion of most commentators that these
topics do not provide premises for rhetorical arguments. Rather,
as Ochs concludes, they seem more akin to an amalgam of "miscellaneous molds into which rhetorical arguments usually are cast. "
Formal topoi, therefore, as distinct from general and particular
varieties, are seen as lines of argument rather than means for
furnishing premises. It is obvious, therefore, that formal topoi
are not dependent upon subject matter. In conclusion, the value of
Ochs' essay arises from his analysis of formal topoi, a subject not
developed by Grimaldi.

William W. Fortenbaugh ("Aristotle's Rhetoric on Emotions")
notes with disappointment that many scholars have found the Rhetoric's treatment of the emotions superficial. Fortenbaugh, however,
thinks Aristotle's analysis is neither superficial nor lacking in precision. Rather, he sees the Rhetoric's treatment of the emotions
as important for philosophical psychology, ethical theory and, obviously, rhetorical theory. Fortenbaugh defends his thesis by analyzing the Rhetoric's treatment of happiness and pleasure.

Aristotle, Fortenbaugh suggests, saw value in the study and
application of the emotions to rhetorical discourse. Aristotle believes an orator must understand correctly the individual emotions
and their capacity to affect the judgment of auditors. Further,
should the orator's understanding of them be deficient in any way,
it would preclude achieving the proper emotional response desired
from an audience. Essentially, the means of analyzing the emotions are knowing: (1) the grounds for an individual emotion; (2)
the object of an emotion; and (3) the condition of men which leads
them to a particular emotion.

Fortenbaugh justifies the Rhetoric's account of the emotions
by indicating its significance for rhetorical and ethical theory as
well as for philosophy. While his analysis of the importance of
emotions to rhetorical theory is of particular interest to us, the
application of the emotions to ethical theory and philosophy is
equally revealing. Moreover, Fortenbaugh's analysis of the emotions is very thorough. Fortenbaugh lifts our understanding of the

Rhetoric's treatment of the emotions from the belief that Aristotle merely echoed popular opinions to viewing the emotions as an integral and representative part of his philosophy.

The metaphor is another facet of rhetorical theory developed by Aristotle. William J. Jordan ("Aristotle's Concept of Metaphor in Rhetoric") constructs a verbal model of Aristotle's concept of metaphor. An issue forwarded by Osborn argues that Aristotle's concept is a linguistic as opposed to a psychological approach to metaphor. The thesis of Jordan's essay is that "Aristotle's concept of metaphor is essentially psychological in that it identifies semantic and structural characteristics which affect reader and listener behavior." The model is necessarily a biased one. It emphasizes the psychological dimensions of metaphor and gives little attention to other approaches, such as the aesthetic and poetic, which have been treated extensively elsewhere.

The semantic characteristics identified by Aristotle evolve from perceptual discrepancy on the part of the listener who does not expect a specific metaphor to occur. Metaphor is cognitively discrepant because it is either a more general term, a more specific term, a different specific term or an analogous term compared to the literal or expected term. Further, it may be cognitively discrepant when it refers to a literal referent as expending energy. Metaphor is affectively discrepant because it evaluates the referent in terms which are affectively different from the literal term.

Structurally metaphor may be described in terms of the frequency of occurrence of the words which compose the metaphor. Aristotle recommends that high frequency words are most advantageous for the construction of metaphor.

Because of the semantic and structural characteristics of metaphor, Aristotle views the metaphor as being rhetorically advantageous. Specifically, he holds that metaphor creates liveliness, affects appetence and causes pleasure. Each of these responses may be viewed as effects of metaphor or specific types of behavior in the listener or reader of metaphoric discourse. Because of these psychological or behavioral effects which Aristotle attributes to specific characteristics of metaphor, this essay concludes that Aristotle's concept of metaphor is essentially psychological.

Aristotle treats delivery very briefly in his Rhetoric. Delivery is not given the prominence afforded the functions of invention, arrangement, and style. The perfunctory and obligatory manner in which delivery is mentioned leaves the reader pondering its overall significance. Need an orator concern himself with the probable effectiveness of his delivery when constructing and arranging his speech? It is Sonkowsky's belief that this question should be answered affirmatively.

Aristotle's celebrated and yet tantalizingly brief description of delivery is expanded by Sonkowsky through an analysis of the Rhetoric and other rhetorical tracts. Cicero, Plato, and Theophrastus are analyzed for supportive evidence. Sonkowsky suggests that in the Aristotelian tradition delivery was vitally involved in the process of literary composition. Sonkowsky confirms his thesis by an examination of Aristotelian proofs, emotions, and style. Further, from the "debate" between Aristotle and Plato over the philosophical importance of rhetoric, Sonkowsky demonstrates how the vividness of oral composition clashed with the rhetorical delivery of written speech and how rhetorical delivery was somehow thought to resemble divine inspiration.

Sonkowsky's article is reprinted for two reasons: (1) because delivery is analyzed in terms of its relationship to other concepts embodied in the Rhetoric, and (2) the demonstration of Aristotle's influence on fuller treatments of rhetoric, such as Theophrastus' and Cicero's.

Wayne N. Thompson ("Stasis in Aristotle's Rhetoric") notes that scholars investigating stasis have analyzed numerous works of Aristotle (Categories, Topics, Physics, Generation of Animals). Curiously, the Rhetoric has been studied only slightly for an expressed stasiastic method. Thompson, noting this void, compares Books I and II with Book III; further, he draws comparisons of the Rhetoric's concept of stasis with Hermagoras and other rhetors.

Books I and II, Thompson notes, contain only two passages suggestive of stasiastic elements. "Moreover, in length, position, and content the only two passages that bear important stasis-like characteristics are insignificant when viewed in relation to the total treatment of invention (p270)." Thompson hypothesizes that a theory of stasis was unknown to Aristotle during the writing of the first two books of the Rhetoric. It seems unlikely that Aristotle would have ignored stasis since it is so useful in the preparation of discourse. Nowhere in the first two books does Aristotle indicate stasis being applicable to the inventional process. Book III exhibits Aristotle's awareness of the concept. Six examples of stasis-like elements are developed; too, Book III evolves a system of analysis. Stasis as developed in the Rhetoric is brief and underdeveloped; certainly not a formal system comparable to those of Hermogenes or Hermagoras.

Our final essay, "The Aristotelian Tradition in Ancient Rhetoric," is perhaps the most frequently cited essay on Aristotelian rhetoric in the English language. Friedrich Solmsen, the author, identifies Aristotle's major contributions to rhetoric and his influence upon subsequent rhetorics. Rather than detail every conceivable "contribution" Solmsen takes the wiser course of examining those significant concepts previously ignored or inadequately developed by ancient rhetoricians.

Solmsen identifies five essential differences between Aristotelian rhetoric and those rhetorics developed by his predecessors. The most readily noticed departure of Aristotle from his contemporaries is the manner in which rhetorical materials are organized. Traditionally, rhetoric had been divided under partes orationis, even to the extent of subdividing each section into various species. Generally, however, there were four recognized parts of a speech--proem, narration, proofs, and epilogue. Aristotle attacks the superficiality of this approach and opted for a division into proofs, style, and disposition. Second, the Rhetoric is distinguishable from other texts in its treatment of proofs. It is here that his theories of ethos, pathos, and logos emerge. In addition, the enthymeme is for the first time introduced, and evidence and topoi are seen in new light. Aristotle develops a careful analysis of the emotions, how they play upon the feelings and how a speaker's character affects his success. Fourth, Aristotle recognizes three types of speaking--the epideictic, forensic, and political. Finally, it is Aristotle who formally develops the virtues of style. He sees clarity, ornateness, and appropriateness as qualities a good speech should possess.

Solmsen concludes by detailing extensively how the Rhetoric's unique characteristics left their mark on later rhetorical systems. This article nicely rounds out our scholarly journey into the ancient world's most impressive rhetorical treatise. [31]

NOTES

1. Theresa Crem, "The Definition of Rhetoric According to Aristotle," Laval Théologique et Philosophique, 12 (1956), 233.
2. Charles Sears Baldwin, Ancient Rhetoric and Poetic (New York: Macmillan and Co., 1924), 12.
3. Friedrich Solmsen, "Aristotelian Tradition in Ancient Rhetoric," American Journal of Philology, 62 (1941), 39.
4. Rhet. 1354a1.
5. Baldwin, 1924, 9.
6. Rhet. 1355b1.
7. Rhet. 1355b25.
8. Lloyd Bitzer, "Aristotle's Enthymeme Revisited," Quarterly Journal of Speech, 45 (1959), 408.
9. Robert J. Brake, "A Reconsideration of Aristotle's Conception of Topics," Central States Speech Journal, 16 (1965), 107.
10. Brake, 1965, 108.
11. Rhet. 1366b9.
12. Baldwin, 1924, 17.
13. Rhet. 1378a20-21.
14. Rhet. 1380a1.
15. Rhet. 1394a12.
16. Rhet. 1395a4.
17. Rhet. 1396b15.
18. Brake, 1965, 108.

19. Friedrich Solmsen, Die Entwicklung der Aristotelischen Logik
     und Rhetorik (Berlin, 1929).
20. Rhet. 1404a5.
21. Baldwin, 1924, 22.
22. Rhet. 1405a9.
23. Rhet. 1408a2.
24. Rhet. 1409a5.
25. George Kennedy, "Aristotle on the Period," Harvard Studies
     in Classical Philology, 63 (1958), 283-288.
26. George Kennedy, The Art of Persuasion in Greece (Princeton,
     N. J.: Princeton University Press, 1963), 110.
27. Rhet. 1412a3.
28. Rhet. 1413b2.
29. Baldwin, 1924, 34.
30. Rhet. 1420b6-7.
31. The reader will want to examine additional sources explicating
     the Rhetoric. A very meager list of sources in English include:
     Floyd D. Anderson, "Aristotle's Doctrine of the Mean and its
     Relationship to Rhetoric, " Southern Speech Communication
     Journal 34 (Winter, 1968), 100-07; Robert J. Brake, "The Sub-
     stance of Rhetoric: Good Reasons: Aristotle Re-examined, "
     Quarterly Journal of Speech 50 (1964), 184-85, also "A Recon-
     sideration of Aristotle's Conception of Topics, " Central States
     Journal, 16 (May, 1965), 106-12; Lane Cooper, The Rhetoric
     of Aristotle, New York: D. Appleton and Company, 1932; Ed-
     ward M. Cope, The Rhetoric of Aristotle, with a commentary
     by the late Edward Meredith Cope. Cambridge: Cambridge Uni-
     versity Press, 1877. 3 vols.; Daniel Crimmin, A Dissertation
     upon Rhetoric, tr. from the Greek of Aristotle. London, 1811;
     Benedetto Croce, "Rhetoric: or the Theory of Ornate Forms, "
     Problema di estetica e contributi alla storia dell' estetica Itali-
     ana. 2nd ed., Bari, 1923, 313-26; Otto Alvin Loeb Dieter,
     "Stasis, " Speech Monographs, 17 (November, 1950), 345-69;
     Keith V. Erickson, A Bibliography of Aristotle's Rhetoric:
     1475-1975, Scarecrow Press, in press; Elaine Fantham, "Cice-
     ronian Conciliare and Aristotelian Ethos, " Phoenix, 27 (Autumn,
     1973), 262-75; Edwin Flemming, "A Comparison of Cicero and
     Aristotle on Style, " Quarterly Journal of Speech, 4 (January,
     1918), 61-71; Helen Fleshler, "Plato and Aristotle on Rhetoric
     and Dialectic, " Pennsylvania Speech Annual, 20 (1963), 11-17.
     Reprinted in Keith V. Erickson, Communicative Rhetoric: A
     Workbook, Berkeley, Calif., 1968, 8-12; Lawrence J. Flynn,
     S. J., "Aristotle: Art and Faculty of Rhetoric, " Southern Speech
     Communication Journal, 21 (Summer, 1956), 244-54; John Henry
     Freese, Aristotle, with an English Translation: the "Art" of
     rhetoric, by John Henry Freese. London, 1926; Daniel Gould-
     ing, "Aristotle's Concept of the Enthymeme, " Journal of the
     American Forensic Association, 2 (1965), 104-08; Irving J. Lee,
     "General Semantics and Public Speaking; Perspectives on Rheto-
     ric Compared: Aristotle, Hitler and Korzybski. " in Papers from
     the Second American Congress on General Semantics. Edited by
     M. Kendig. Chicago: Institute of General Semantics, 1943,
     329-34; G. L. Henderson, "The Peripatetic Mean of Style and

Three Stylistic Characters, " American Journal of Philology,
25 (1904), 125-46; Marvin T. Herrick, "The Early History of
Aristotle's Rhetoric in England, " Philological Quarterly, 5
(1926), 242-57; Forbes Iverson Hill, "The Genetic Method in Recent Criticism on the Rhetoric of Aristotle. " Unpublished Ph. D.
dissertation, Cornell University, 1963; W. Stuart Hinman, Literary Quotations and Allusion in the Rhetoric, Poetic and Nicomachean Ethics of Aristotle. Staten Island, New York: Private
Edition, 1935; Laura Virginia Holland, Counterpoint: Kenneth
Burke and Aristotle's Theories of Rhetoric. New York: Philosophical Library, 1959; Wilbur Samuel Howell, "Aristotle and
Horace on Rhetoric and Poetics, " Quarterly Journal of Speech,
54 (1968), 325-339; Everett Lee Hunt, "Plato and Aristotle on
Rhetoric and Rhetoricians, " Studies in Rhetoric and Public
Speaking in Honor of James A. Winans. Edited by A. M. Drum-
mond. 2nd ed. New York: Russell and Russell, 1962, 3-60; Richard Huseman, "Aristotle's Doctrine of the Mean: Implications
for Rhetorical Style, " Western Speech, 34 (1970), 115-21; Edward H. Madden, "The Enthymeme: Crossroads of Logic, Rhetoric, and Metaphysics," Philosophical Review, 61 (1952), 368-
76; D. S. Margoliouth, "On the Arabic Version of Aristotle's
Rhetoric, " Semitic Studies. Edited by George Alexander Kohurt,
Berlin, 1897, 376-87; James H. McBurney, "Some Recent Interpretations of the Aristotelian Enthymeme, " Papers of the Michigan Academy of Science, Arts and Letters, 21 (1936), 489-
500; Richard McKeon, "Rhetoric and Poetic in the Philosophy of
Aristotle, " Aristotle's Poetics and English Literature. Edited
by Elder Olson. Chicago, 1965, 207-36; James J. Murphy, ed.,
A Synoptic History of Classical Rhetoric, New York: Random
House, 1972; also, "The Scholastic Condemnation of Rhetoric in
the Commentary of Giles of Rome on the Rhetoric of Aristotle, "
in Arts libéraux et Philosophie Au Moyen Age. Montreal, 1967,
833-41; Robert Olian, "The Intended Uses of Aristotle's Rhetoric, " Speech Monographs, 35 (1968), 137-48; Georgiana P.
Palmer, The TOPOI of Aristotle's Rhetoric as Exemplified in
the Orators. University of Chicago, 1934; Rhys Roberts, Rhetorica. The Works of Aristotle. Translated into English under
the editorship of W. David Ross. Oxford, 1924; also, New York,
1954; Lawrence Rosenfield, "The Doctrine of the Mean in Aristotle's Rhetoric, " Theoria, 31 (1965), 191-98; also, "Rhetorical
Criticism and an Aristotelian Notion of Process, " Speech Monographs, 33 (1966), 1-16; also, Aristotle and Information Theory:
A Comparison of the Influence of Causal Assumptions on Two
Theories of Communication. The Hague, Netherlands: Mouton,
1972; R. C. Seaton, The Aristotelian Enthymeme, " Classical
Review, 27 (1914), 113-19; Joseph Schwartz, "Kenneth Burke,
Aristotle, and The Future of Rhetoric, " College Composition and
Communication, 17 (1966), 210-16; Friedrich Solmsen, "Aris-
totle and Cicero on the Orators Playing Upon the Feelings, "
Classical Philology, 33 (1938), 390-404; G. H. Wikramanayake,
"A Note on the Pistis in Aristotle's Rhetoric, " American Journal
of Philology, 82 (1961), 193-96; Ross Winterowd, "Aristotle and
Extrapolation, " Rhetoric: A Synthesis, New York, 1968, 18-44.

1. ARISTOTLE'S EARLIEST "COURSE OF LECTURES ON RHETORIC"*

by Anton-Hermann Chroust

Diogenes Laertius reports that "in time the circle [of students] around him [scil., Aristotle] grew larger. He then sat down to lecture [regularly?], observing that, 'It would be base to keep silent and let Xenocrates [should read: Isocrates] speak.' He also taught his pupils to discourse upon a set theme, besides training them in rhetoric. "[1]

Philodemus appears to be the oldest known source attesting to the fact that during the early 'fifties Aristotle delivered a course of lectures on rhetoric in the Academy. [2] Philodemus, who among other matters berates Aristotle for having abandoned philosophy in favor of rhetoric (and "politics"), also claims that Aristotle taught rhetoric primarily for the purpose of antagonizing and discrediting Isocrates, the rival and opponent of the Academy. Philodemus' main arguments, which might go back to Epicurus (a rather persistent foe of Aristotelian philosophy) or to some other Epicurean source or sources equally hostile towards Aristotle, are as follows: Aristotle taught rhetoric in the afternoon (in the Academy), maintaining that "it is a scandal to remain silent and let Isocrates speak out. "[3] He also composed treatises on rhetoric. He insisted that politics constitutes a branch of general philosophy;[4] and he spoke in a confused and obfuscating manner about the difference between rhetoric and politics. He justified the preoccupation with politics by alleging that ignorance of politics keeps a man out of touch with everything that transpires;[5] that philosophy and philosophic culture can flourish only among politically enlightened citizens; and that the performances of contemporary politicians in general were disappointing. [6] But anyone who runs a school of rhetoric primarily for the purpose of gaining popularity among people who actually despise philosophy and exalt rhetoric beyond all measure--especially if on account of his profligate youth that person lacks the bare necessities of life[7]--such a person might obtain some pupils for a short while, until he should decide to return to philosophy.

*Reprinted by permission of the author and publisher from L'Antiquité classique 33 (1964), 58-72.

Philodemus continues: Aristotle did not act the true philosopher when he said that it is a scandal to remain silent and let
Isocrates speak out.   For, if Isocrates' activities were of no consequence, he should have been ignored.   If, on the other hand, the
art of speaking is truly important, Aristotle should have engaged
in rhetoric and the teaching of rhetoric irrespective of what Isocrates did; and, if neither should be the case, Aristotle should not
have devoted himself to rhetoric, unless he should run the risk of
being regarded as an incompetent man, as acting from sheer envy
of Isocrates, as a quarrelsome person, or as having been van-
quished by Isocrates.   But if in his conduct Aristotle was guided
by the popular misconception that it was dishonorable to remain silent and let Isocrates speak out, he certainly did not observe or
understand the proper purpose of rhetoric.   But if he had the
proper purpose in mind, why did he not find it disgraceful to speak
out through his disciples in the lawcourts who acted like hired
forensic orators rather than like divinely inspired philosophers?
Why did Aristotle desert philosophy, why did he cease to urge the
younger men to dedicate themselves to philosophy (and turn to
rhetoric)?[8]   In doing so he certainly exposed himself to much resentment and hatred on the part of Isocrates' disciples or of some
other teachers of rhetoric.

Assuredly, Aristotle implanted in his disciples much admiration for his genius.   As soon as he deserted philosophy and began
to collect, with the assistance of his disciples, all sorts of information in order to impress people with his erudition,[9] he studied
and taught rhetoric, politics, agriculture, cosmetics, mining, and,
worse, the several aphrodisiacs.[10]   In doing so he was less re-
spectable than the ordinary teachers of rhetoric who merely attempted to impart a certain ability and convey the principles of
rhetoric.   But if he was really searching for the truth, why did he
not choose the rhetoric taught by Isocrates (which he ridiculed in
many ways) rather than political rhetoric (which he considered different from that taught by Isocrates)?   If it was political rather
than didactic rhetoric Aristotle was practicing, it was ridiculous
for him to assert that it was a disgrace to permit Isocrates to
speak and teach.   None of Aristotle's disciples made a success in
either kind of rhetoric or became teachers of others.   Isocrates,
as time went on, progressed and after having taught rhetoric returned to philosophy.[11]   By concentrating on rhetoric, Aristotle
neglected to pay attention to natural philosophy and moral philosophy.

This is a brief and eclectic summary of Philodemus' vi-
tuperations of Aristotle and his "fling" at rhetoric.   The remainder
of this account, though perhaps an important and revealing piece
of evidence of Epicurean hostility towards Aristotle and Aristotel-
ianism in general, is of no particular interest to us.

Cicero insists that the combination of elegantia and doctrina
was the prime aim of Aristotle in teaching rhetoric.   When the

latter saw that Isocrates had much success not only on account of
the excellence of his disciples, but also because he abandoned forensic oratory in favor of a shallow type of oratory, he changed
his whole program of instructing students, combining the study of
scientific subjects with the practice of rhetoric.[12] From this it
would appear that while Cicero praises Aristotle for having combined (actually, re-united) philosophy and rhetoric, Philodemus re-
bukes Aristotle for having done so. This, in turn, suggests that
Cicero made use of a source favorable to Aristotle, while Philodemus relied on a source hostile to him.[13] However, both Philodemus and Cicero seem to be guilty of an "anachronism" when
they imply that Aristotle already had taught philosophic subjects
for some time before he decided to include rhetoric in his curricu-
lum.

In Tusculan Disputations I.4.7, however, Cicero insinuates
that Aristotle started to teach rhetoric only in order to compete
with or, perhaps, to outvie Isocrates: "Stimulated by the professional success of Isocrates, the orator, [Aristotle] began to teach
young people to speak [eloquently] and to combine philosophic wisdom with rhetorical elegance."[14] Very similar is Quintilian's version which records that when Isocrates was already very old, Aristotle started to teach the art of oratory in afternoon classes, justifying his doing so with the remark that it would be a shameful
thing to remain silent and let Isocrates speak out;[15] and Syrianus'
report that Aristotle offered "afternoon classes" in which he discussed with his friends problems of rhetoric, insisting that there
are two kinds of oral persuasion, rhetoric and dialectics, and urging on his students by saying that it was shameful to remain silent
and let Isocrates speak out.[16]

In recent times the problem of the early Aristotelian "lectures on rhetoric" was first tackled by A. Stahr, who pointed out
that in some way these lectures were connected with Aristotle's and
the Academy's rivalry with Isocrates and his school.[17] Some time
later H. Diels made the truly important suggestion that these lectures were at the basis of an "early (and, perhaps, the earliest)
draft" of certain parts of the extant Aristotelian Rhetoric.[18] Diels
also insisted that during the lifetime of Plato Aristotle taught a
course in rhetoric in the Academy, and that the Τέχνης τῆς Θεοδέκτου
Συναγωγή (in one book)[19] contains these lectures, which were taken
up and later published by Theodectes after Aristotle had left the
Academy.[20] Six years later, in 1892 to be exact, F. Blass advanced two major theses: first, these lectures were delivered
around 355 B.C., that is, shortly after the composition of the
Aristotelian Gryllus (with which they may be connected); and, secondly, as to their doctrinal or philosophic content they were under
the influence of the Platonic Phaedrus[21]--two far-reaching and, it
would seem, correct assumptions.

Many a scholarly investigation has been made concerning the
exact nature and date of the so-called Τεχνῶν Συναγωγή (in two books)

attributed to Aristotle. [22]   This Συναγωγή, which could also be
called a "florilegium" or "handbook" of the art of oratory, was
credited to Aristotle by Cicero, [23] Quintilian[24] and others. [25]   It
appears to have been a sort of "manual" or "anthology" for the
use in a course of lectures on rhetoric.   To compile such a "florilegium" was fully in keeping with Aristotle's general didactic principle that in the several domains of human knowledge and human
learning it is always of great advantage to know something about
the experiences, achievements, and contributions of others.   Hence,
Aristotle makes it somewhat of a practice to review the views of
his predecessors on the subject he is about to discuss. [26]   But it
cannot be determined with any degree of certainty whether this
particular "florilegium" is related to the course of lectures which
were delivered by the young Aristotle in the 'fifties during his
membership in the Academy, or whether it was connected with a
course of lectures given by Aristotle in the Lyceum at a later date
and of which some traces can be found in Aristotle's extant Rhetoric.   Cicero, who highly praises the suavitas et brevitas dicendi
of its author, observed that on account of these qualities the
Τεχνῶν Συναγωγή by far surpasses all other works of its kind. [27]

        H. Diels related the Τέχνης τῆς Θεοδέκτου Συναγωγή (one
book)[28] rather than the Τεχνῶν Συναγωγή to Aristotle's early course
of lectures on rhetoric. [29]   However, the authorship of the Τέχνης
τῆς Θεοδέκτου Συναγωγή, subsequently quoted here as the Θεοδέκτου,
is much debated.   A number of ancient authors, among them Quintilian, [30] Dionysius of Halicarnassus, [31] and others, [32] have credited
this composition to Aristotle.   Cicero ascribed it to Theodectes. [33]
Aristotle, in Rhetoric 1410 b 2, is said to refer to the Θεοδέκτου,
although it is by no means certain whether he cites his own work
or that of someone else. [34]

        In the light of this conflicting ancient testimony more recent
Aristotelian scholarship has come up with a variety of theses.   V.
Rose first declared that in Rhetoric 1410 b 2 Aristotle refers back
to the Θεοδέκτου (which he considered the authentic work of Theodectes) rather than to the Τεχνῶν Συναγωγή. [35]   But soon he revised
his opinion.   Proceeding on the assumption that all of the so-called
Aristotelian dialogues, including the Θεοδέκτου, were simply spurious and, hence, may not be ascribed to Aristotle, he suggested
that the reference in Rhetoric 1410 b 2 is merely a scholium
added to the Aristotelian text at a later date. [36]   E. Heitz, who
concurred with V. Rose that the reference in Rhetoric 1410 b 2
could very well be a later (and mistaken) scholium, was inclined
to consider the Θεοδέκτου the work of Theodectes. [37]   E. Zeller,
who refused to commit himself on this involved issue, argued that
if the Θεοδέκτου was the authentic work of Aristotle--and there
exists no evidence either to prove or disprove this--then the only
way to explain this curious title is to assume that Aristotle had
dedicated this work to his friend and pupil Theodectes. [38]

        Finally, H. Diels, who relied a great deal on the testimony

of Valerius Maximus, [39] proposed that the θεοδέκτου is an authentic
Aristotelian composition, and that it constitutes the earliest, though
rather inadequate, version of the extant Aristotelian Rhetoric. [40]
In support of his thesis Diels made the following argument: the
θεοδέκτου was written while Plato was still alive and while Aristotle offered a course of lectures in rhetoric at the Academy.
Theodectes, formerly a disciple of Isocrates, came to be the pupil and close friend of Aristotle.   When Plato died in 348/7, Aristotle left Athens.   Theodectes remained behind and took over the
"lectureship" in rhetoric vacated by Aristotle's departure.   He
made full use of the original materials or "florilegium" Aristotle
had used when he taught this course (Τεχνῶν Συναγωγή ?), and later
published them (or had them published by one of his disciples) under his own name.   In 335 Aristotle returned to Athens and discovered that his old "florilegium", in all likelihood greatly en-
larged and fully kept up to date by Theodectes, was a rather effective not to say excellent text.   After the death of Theodectes,
Aristotle resumed the teaching of rhetoric and soon began to work
over and improve upon this "florilegium" which, after many editorial revisions, became the extant Aristotelian Rhetoric. [41]

The hypotheses of H. Diels as well as those advanced by
other scholars were convincingly refuted by F. Solmsen, who maintained that since the ancient "catalogues" of Aristotle's writings
contain a Τέχνης τῆς Θεοδέκτου Συναγωγή ', it follows that Aristotle
simply made a "résumé" of a treatise on the art of rhetoric originally composed by Theodectes. [42]   Solmsen also pointed out that
judging from the few surviving fragments Theodectes' theories about
rhetoric were quite distinct from those advocated by Aristotle.   In
addition, Solmsen insisted that Aristotle, Rhetoric, book III, chapters 13-19, is largely inspired by Theodectes' theories.   Already
some of the ancient authors and critics took notice of this fact,
but due to a tragic misunderstanding they conceived the erroneous
notion that originally the θεοδέκτου was composed by Aristotle. [43]

Some scholars have tried to prove that certain sections of
the extant Aristotelian Rhetoric go back to Aristotle's early course
of lectures on rhetoric.   A. Kantelhardt, for instance, believed
that he had discovered in the extant Rhetoric elements belonging to
different periods in Aristotle's literary activities.   Hence, he
claimed that Rhetoric 1354 a 11 to 1355 b 23 is the oldest part of
this work, dating back to the original Aristotelian course of lectures on rhetoric or, to use W. Jaeger's terminology, to the
"Urrhetorik". [44]   Kantelhardt's generic or evolutionary hypothesis,
on the whole, was accepted and further elaborated by F. Solmsen,
the disciple of W. Jaeger, who added Rhetoric 1354 a 1-11 to the
"Urrhetorik. "   This "Urrhetorik, " Solmsen continues, in essence
dates back to the time when Aristotle gave his first course of lectures in rhetoric in the Academy during the lifetime of Plato. [45]

The theses of Solmsen in the main were accepted by W.
Jaeger, [46] but rejected by P. Gohlke, [47] the disciple of Jaeger's old

antagonist, H. von Arnim.   In a way Gohlke revived the old hypothesis, already announced in the Rhetorica ad Alexandrum, 48
that Aristotle wrote an early treatise on rhetoric which subsequently was published by Theodectes.   This early treatise, Gohlke insisted, reflects Aristotle's teaching of rhetoric during his stay at
the Academy. 49   I. Düring, again, proposed that the greater part
of the extant Rhetoric, namely, books I and II, with the exception
of chapters 23 and 24 of book II, were composed between 360 and
35550--a view which probably will not be widely accepted.   I. Düring suggested nothing less than that the major parts as well as the
dominant doctrines of the extant Rhetoric were shaped while Aristotle was still a disciple of Plato and a member of the Academy.
Only book III and chapters 23 and 24 of book II would be post-
Academic. 51

In view of the fact that scholars apparently have failed to
reach what even remotely might be called an agreement as to the
chronology underlying the evolution of Aristotle's views concerning
rhetoric, it is well-nigh impossible to establish firmly either the
doctrinal content or the exact date of Aristotle's earliest course of
lectures on rhetoric or that of the Τεχνῶν Συναγωγή . 52   Since with
one possible exception none of Aristotle's early dialogues or exoteric writings may safely be related to this "course" with any degree of definiteness, we will have to rely on the somewhat unre-
liable testimonia of ancient biographers and "literary critics" as
well as on some other "circumstantial evidence" in order to learn
something about this "course. "   Judging from these testimonia it
might be maintained that this "course" owed its origin to the general or personal feeling of antagonism and resentment which existed
between the Academy (or Aristotle) and Isocrates and his school of
rhetoric;53 and, perhaps, to Aristotle's or the Academy's conviction that Isocrates both as an orator and a teacher of rhetoric was
worse than disappointing. 54   The "course" might also have been
instituted in order to combine and integrate rhetoric (Isocrates?)
and dialectics (Plato?)55 for the purpose of making rhetoric more
"scientific"56 and dialectics more attractive and persuasive. 57
Perhaps Aristotle was also encouraged to offer this course and,
incidentally, to attack Isocrates by what Plato had said recently
about rhetoric in his Phaedrus (268A ff.).

In addition, around 362-360, 58 Aristotle had composed his
Gryllus which, apart from being influenced by the Platonic Phaedo,
also betrays an acquaintance with Plato's Phaedrus, written after
369 /8. 59   The Gryllus, it has been suggested, already "takes a
slap" at Isocrates and the servile attitude the latter allegedly displayed towards Xenophon on the occasion of the death of Xenophon's
son Gryllus. 60

Hence, the Platonic Phaedrus and the Aristotelian Gryllus
might be considered as the two "pivotal points of reference" with
the help of which we should try to determine the approximate date
as well as the likely doctrinal content of Aristotle's course of lec-

tures on rhetoric: the Gryllus probably became the occasion for
Aristotle's offering (or being permitted to offer) this course in the
Academy, especially since in this dialogue he seems to have demonstrated not only his qualifications as a teacher of rhetoric, but
also his ability and determination to stand up to Isocrates, a man
much disliked by the members of the Academy; and the Platonic
Phaedrus and the notions about the proper use of rhetoric and dialectics expressed there probably furnished the general program of
how rhetoric ought to be taught. 61

        If this be so, then also the technique of writing dialogues
or of arguing philosophically an intricate subject had to change.
To some extent it had to abandon the "old fashioned" rhetoric and
dialectics and develop in accordance with the "new form" initiated
by the Phaedrus: the dialogue from now on depended more on its
internal structure as a whole rather than on the specific character
of its discussants (as it did in the early dialogues of Plato), thus
not only gaining in unity of scientific presentation, but also in real
content.   Lengthy theoretical examinations of the subject under discussion as well as intricate scientific demonstrations conducted in
a methodical fashion take the place of scintillating verbal duels.
Already in his later dialogues Plato had come to realize the necessity of changing over from the "obstetric question and answer
game" to the "dialogue of discussion. " This "dialogue of discussion, " which Aristotle subsequently adopted and perfected in some
of his exoteric compositions, is simply a novel expression of the
fact that the scientific element gradually and inexorably asserted
itself also in the particular form in which scientific discussion was
carried on. 62 It is not impossible and, indeed, is most likely
that in his course of lectures on rhetoric Aristotle also taught this
"new dialectics" or scientific form of argumentation and presentation.

        If we are correct in our assumption that the Platonic
Phaedrus and the Aristotelian Gryllus constitute the "two pivotal
points of reference" in any determination of the approximate date
as well as the probable doctrinal content of Aristotle's course of
lectures on rhetoric and, incidentally, of the Τεχνῶν Συναγωγή, then
it also would be fairly safe to surmise with F. Solmsen63 and I.
Düring64 that this course of lectures offered by Aristotle in the
Academy was first delivered between 360 and 355.   This thesis receives additional support from the fact that the Antidosis of Isocrates, which among other matters also contains some sharp attacks
upon Aristotle and the manner in which he taught rhetoric, 65 was
published around 353--an indication that Aristotle must have taught
this subject for some time.   Hence, it is not impossible, and is
even probable, that the Τεχνῶν Συναγωγή, this "florilegium" or
"manual" designed for the use in a course of lectures on rhetoric,
likewise was composed somewhere between 360 and 355.

NOTES

1. Diogenes Laertius V, 3.
2. Philodemus, De Rhetorica, Volumina Rhetorica, vol. II,
   pp. 50ff. (edit. S. Sudhaus), col. 48, 36-col. 57, 45.--Here
   Philodemus might be following Epicurus (see E. Bignone,
   L'Aristotele Perduto e la Formazione Filosofica di Epicuro,
   vol. II (1936), p. 97) or some other Epicurean or Epicureans. According to frags. 171, 235, and 237 (Usener), and
   Diogenes Laertius X. 25, Epicurus, Metrodorus, and Her-
   marchus did attack Aristotle and his philosophy. Hermar-
   chus, in fact, wrote an Against Aristotle. See here also
   H. M. Hubbell, "The Rhetorica of Philodemus, " in Transactions of the Connecticut Academy of Arts and Sciences, 23
   (1920), pp. 243-382; H. M. Hubbell, "Isocrates and the
   Epicureans, " in Classical Philology, 11 (1916), pp. 405-418;
   I. Düring, Aristotle in the Ancient Biographical Tradition
   (1957), pp. 299-314; E. Berti, La Filosofia del Primo
   Aristotele (1961), pp. 175-185; W. Wieland, "Aristoteles als
   Rhetoriker und die Exoterischen Schriften, " Hermes, 86
   (1958), pp. 323-346.--Wieland also takes issue with the
   opinion, current since the days of J. Bernays, Die Dialoge
   des Aristoteles (1863), passim, that the expression, λόγοι
   ἐξωτερικοί, refers to the dialogues which Aristotle wrote
   while he was still a member of the Academy. See here also F. Dirlmeier, Nikomachische Ethik (1956), pp. 274ff.
   With a few exceptions, ancient authors and critics insist
   that the "exoteric works" of Aristotle are "less scientific"
   than the "esoteric" (intramural) or doctrinal compositions.
   Cicero (De Finibus V. 5. 12), Strabo (XIII. 1. 54), and
   Plutarch (Adversus Coloten XIV. 4) call the exoterica "popular writings" composed for the general public; Gellius
   (Attic Nights XX. 5) calls them compositions which were
   concerned with rhetoric, politics, and "topics. " In any
   event, the problem of the "exoteric" or "esoteric" works
   has never been resolved in a satisfactory manner.
3. See here also Cicero, De Oratore III. 35. 141; Quintilian,
   Institutio Oratoria III. 1; Diogenes Laertius V. 3 (should
   read Isocrates rather than Xenocrates); Syrianus, Scholia in
   Hermogenem IV. 297 (edit. Walz), or, II. 52. 21 (edit.
   Rabe). See also Euripides, Philoctetes frag. 796 (edit.
   Nauck), frag. 785 (Dindorf).--According to Gellius, Attic
   Nights XX. 5, Aristotle gave his "exoteric lectures" in the
   afternoon or evening, while the "esoteric lectures" were
   delivered in the morning. This raises an interesting problem: did the Academy (and later the Peripatus) teach its
   "esoteric" or intramural doctrines in the morning in the
   restricted circle of "initiates" or "advanced students"; and
   its "exoteric, " "introductory, " or "popular" subjects in the
   afternoon before a general public, "non-initiated persons"
   or "undergraduate students, " as the Pythagoreans are believed to have done? See here also notes 15 and 16, infra.

4. That politics is a branch of philosophy is restated in Aristotle,
    Metaphysics 1025 b 22-25; Nicomachean Ethics 1181 b 15;
    et passim.
5. E. Bignone, op. cit., vol. II, at pp. 97-101, maintains that
    this remark probably refers to something Aristotle had said
    in his Politicus.
6. E. Bignone, op. cit., vol. II, at p. 249, believes that this
    particular passage refers to something Aristotle had said in
    his Eudemus (or, On the Soul); I. Düring, Aristotle in the
    Ancient Biographical Tradition (1957), p. 303, suggests that
    it might refer to Aristotle's Politicus.
7. This might be a reference to the many but wholly unsupported
    stories that in his youth Aristotle lived a profligate life.
    See, for instance Diogenes Laertius X. 8 (frag 171 Usener);
    Aristocles, in: Eusebius, Praeparatio Evangelica XV. 2
    (791B-793B Migne).   See also E. Bignone, op. cit., vol. II,
    at pp. 89-91; S. Sudhaus, "Aristoteles in der Beurteilung
    des Epikur und Philodemos," in Rheinisches Museum, vol.
    48 (1893), p. 562; S. Sudhaus, "Noch einmal Nausiphanes
    und Aristoteles bei Philodemos," in Philologus, vol. LIV
    (1895), pp. 80ff.
8. Philodemus might possibly refer here to the Aristotelian
    Protrepticus.   See also E. Bignone, op. cit., vol. I, at
    pp. 125-127.   It should be borne in mind, however, that
    the Aristotelian Protrepticus was written probably after
    353/2 B.C. (it was probably a "reply" to Isocrates' Anti-
    dosis, composed in 353/2), hence, is definitely posterior to
    the "Lectures on Rhetoric." Here as elsewhere, Philodemus
    is guilty of a gross anachronism.
9. This passage might be a reference to Isocrates, Antidosis
    243ff., and ibid. at 258ff. See also Philodemus, op. cit.
    at col. 52, 41-42, where he maintains that together with his
    disciple (Theophrastus?) "he collected the laws, the argu-
    ments of the cities concerning their territorial boundaries,
    the many constitutions, and the laws enacted at times of
    crises...." These "collections" most certainly were made
    after 345 B.C., and possibly much later.
10. Aphrodisiacs are mentioned in Aristotle, Eudemian Ethics
    1225 b 4; [Aristotle], Magna Moralia 1188 b 32-38.
11. See Isocrates, Antidosis, passim.
12. Cicero, De Oratore III. 35. 141. See also Cicero, Orator
    XIV. 46.
13. I. Düring, op. cit. at p. 311, and ibid., at p. 313, suggests
    that Hermippus' Vita Aristotelis is Cicero's main and, per-
    haps, sole source.
14. Cicero seems to avoid here the "anachronism" found in the
    De Oratore III. 35. 141.
15. Quintilian, Institutio Oratoria III. 1. See also Strabo XIV. 1.
    48.
16. Syrianus, Scholia ad Hermogenem IV. 297 (edit. Walz), II. 5.
    21 (edit. Rabe).
17. A. Stahr, Aristotelia: Leben, Schriften und Schüler des

Aristoteles, vol. I (1830), pp. 63-70. Stahr did not realize as yet that the Aristotelian Protrepticus was the result of this rivalry.

18. H. Diels, "Über das Dritte Buch der Aristotelischen Rhetorik," in Abhandlungen der Königlichen Akademie der Wissenschaften zu Berlin, Philologisch-Historische Klasse, vol. IV (1886), pp. 11-16.

19. Diogenes Laertius V. 24 (no. 82); Vita Hesychii, no. 74. Hesychius claims that it contained three books. Also, Hesychius gives a slightly different title. Ptolemy (El-Garib) does not mention it in his "list."

20. H. Diels, loc. cit.

21. F. Blass, Die Attische Beredsamkeit, vol. II (1892), pp. 64-65. Blass refuted also G. Teichmüller's rather fantastic thesis that between 344 and 342 Aristotle re-entered the Academy for a brief spell, and that it was during this period that he delivered these lectures. See G. Teichmüller, Literarische Fehden im Vierten Jahrhundert vor Chr. (1881), pp. 228-232.

22. Diogenes Laertius V. 24 (no. 77); Vita Hesychii, no. 71; Ptolemy, no. 24. Hesychius and Ptolemy claim that this work consisted of one book.--See here also Diogenes Laertius, loc. cit., who also lists a Treatise (Handbook) on the Art of Rhetoric in Two Books (no. 78); a Treatise (Handbook) on the Art of Rhetoric in One Book (no. 79); and an Another Treatise (Handbook, Collection) on the Art of Rhetoric in Two Books (no. 80), which might be a revised version of no. 77. The corresponding numbers in the Vita Hesychius.--With the exception of the hyper-critical V. Rose, no scholar has seriously challenged the authenticity of the Τεχνῶν Συναγωγή.--Τέχνη, as H. Bonitz, Index Aristotelicus 759 a 50ff., has pointed out, signifies here the ratio et doctrina artis (Kunstlehre), or the precipue institutio oratoria. See also Aristotle, Nicomachean Ethics 1140 a 10-14; Metaphysics 981 a 5ff.

23. Cicero, De Inventione II. 2; Cicero, De Oratore II. 38. 160; Cicero, Brutus 12 (Quintilian, Institutio Oratoria III. 1. 8-13).

24. Quintilian, Institutio Oratoria III. 1. 13.

25. Dionysius of Halicarnassus, De Isocrate 18; Anonym., Prolegomena in Isocratem, Scholia in Aeschinem et Isocratem (edit. Dindorf, 1852), p. 105. See V. Rose, Aristotelis qui Ferenbantur Librorum Fragmenta (1886), pp. 118-120, frags. 136-141.

26. See, for instance, Aristotle, Nicomachean Ethics 1181 b 6-12.

27. Cicero, De Inventione II. 2. See here also P. Moreaux, Les Listes Anciennes des Ouvrages d'Aristote (1951), pp. 96-97.

28. Diogenes Laertius V. 24 (no. 82); Vita Hesychii, no. 74. Hesychius entitles it Τέχνης τῆς θεοδέκτου Συναγωγήν (in three books).

29. H. Diels, op. cit. supra note 18, at pp. 11-16.

30. Quintilian, Institutio Oratoria II. 15. 10 (frag. 125 Rose), and

ibid. at IV. 2. 31 (frag. 126 Rose); I. 4. 18 (frag. 127
Rose). Quintilian is not certain whether he should credit
this work to Aristotle or to Theodectes.

31.   Dionysius of Halicarnassus, De Compositione Verborum 2
(frag. 127 Rose); De Vi Demosthenis 48 (frag. 127 Rose).
Dionysius is not at all certain whether he should ascribe
this work to Aristotle or to Theodectes.

32.   Pseudo-Aristotle, Rhetorica ad Alexandrum 1421 a 38 (see V.
Rose, op. cit. at p. 114), where it is not made clear
whether this work of Aristotle was edited by, or addressed
to, Theodectes. Valerius Maximus VIII. 14. 3, who apparently relied on the Rhetorica ad Alexandrum as well as
on Aristotle, Rhetoric 1410 b 2, reports that Aristotle had
entrusted his disciple Theodectes with the editing of this
work, but afterwards discovered to his regret that it was
credited to, and circulated under the name of, Theodectes.
See here also E. Heitz, Fragmenta Aristotelis (1869),
p. 124; V. Rose, op. cit., at p. 114; Anonymus Seguerianus,
"De Orat. Polit.," in L. Spengel, Rhetorici Graeci, vol. I,
p. 454 (frag. 134 Rose), who considers it an authentic
Aristotelian composition; Scholia in Aristotelis Rhetoricam
1410 b 2 (frag. 132 Rose), where it is called an authentic
work of Aristotle dedicated to Theodectes. For additional
sources see V. Rose, op. cit., at pp. 116-118.

33.   Cicero, Orator LI. 172 (frag. 128 Rose), and ibid. at LVII.
19 (Quintilian, Inst. Orat. IX. 4. 88; Rufinus, De Metris
II. 2); LXIV. 218 (frag. 129 Rose).

34.   See here also H. Bonitz, Index Aristotelicus 104 a 33ff.:
suum se citare librum non distincte scribit Aristoteles,
tamen ex formula citandi vero est simillimum.

35.   V. Rose, De Aristotelis Librorum Ordine et Auctoritate
(1854), p. 89.

36.   V. Rose, Aristoteles Pseudepigraphus (1863), p. 137.--Rose
went so far as to doubt the authenticity of the Aristotelian
Rhetoric or, at least, of book III. He based his somewhat
extravagant thesis on the assumption that Aristotle could not
possibly have claimed as his own a work (the θεοδέκτου)
that was authored by someone else.

37.   E. Heitz, Die Verlorenen Schriften des Aristoteles (1865),
pp. 85-87. See also E. Heitz, Fragmenta Aristotelis (1869),
p. 124.

38.   E. Zeller, Die Philosophie der Griechen, vol. II, part 2 (3rd
edit., 1879), p. 76, note 2.

39.   See note 32, supra.

40.   H. Diels, op. cit. supra note 18, at pp. 11-16.

41.   H. Diels, loc. cit. Diels also pointed out that because of its
high reputation Aristotle did not hesitate to refer back to
Theodectes' version in Rhetoric 1411 b 2, thus avoiding the
necessity of having to enlarge upon a point already made by
Theodectes.

42.   F. Solmsen, Drei Rekonstruktionen zur Antiken Rhetorik und
Poetik, II: "Theodektes," in Hermes, 67 (1932), pp. 144-

151.
43. F. Solmsen, loc. cit. See also P. Moraux, op. cit., supra
     note 27, at p. 100.--Of Theodectes' life we know only that
     he was from Phaselis in Lycia; that he taught rhetoric and
     "tragediography"; and that he died in Athens at the age of
     41, not long after the year 340. See F. Blass, Attische
     Beredsamkeit, vol. II (1892), pp. 441-446; F. Solmsen, ar-
     ticle "Theodectes," in RE, 2. Reihe, vol. V (1934), cols.
     1722-1734. According to some sources he was first a
     disciple of Isocrates, then of Plato, and finally of Aristotle.
     Suda, article "Theodectes"; Dionysius of Halicarnassus, De
     Isocrate 19; Epistola ad Ammaeum I. 2; Athenaeus, Deipno-
     sophistae XIII. 566 E; Cicero, Orator LI. 172.   F. Blass,
     loc. cit., surmises that he joined the Academy during the
     time Aristotle lectured on rhetoric. Together with the most
     prominent orators of his day (Naucrates, Isocrates, and
     Theopompus), he was invited to Halicarnassus in 353 on the
     occasion of King Mausolus' death in order to compose a
     eulogy on the deceased. Pliny, Historia Naturalis XXXVI.
     30; Gellius, Attic Nights X. 8. 5ff.; Pseudo-Plutarch, Vita
     Isocratis 838 B; Eusebius, Praeparatio Evangelica X. 3
     (464A Migne); Suda, loc. cit. All this would indicate that
     by 353 his reputation must have been considerable and,
     hence, that by this time he probably was no longer a disci-
     ple of Aristotle. This would also lend support to our con-
     tention that Aristotle taught rhetoric in the Academy prior
     to 353, and in all likelihood much before that time. Suda,
     loc. cit., mentions a Τέχνη ῥητορική ἐν μέτρω. For additional
     detail see P. Moreaux, op. cit., at p. 101.
44. A. Kantelhardt, De Aristotelis Rhetoricis (Doctoral Thesis of
     the University of Göttingen, 1911).
45. F. Solmsen, Die Entwicklung der Aristotelischen Logik und
     Rhetorik (1929), pp. 208-228.
46. W. Jaeger, Paideia, vol. III (1944), pp. 251-252.
47. P. Gohlke, "Die Entstehung der Aristotelischen Ethik, Politik,
     Rhetork," in Sitzungsberichte der Akademie der Wissenschaf-
     ten in Wien, Philologisch-Historische Klasse, 223 (1944),
     fasc. 2, pp. 111-141.
48. See note 32, supra.
49. P. Gohlke, op. cit.--Gohlke also added to the earliest Aris-
     totelian writings on rhetoric the Rhetorica ad Alexandrum,
     now lost but considered spurious by the vast majority of
     scholars, as well as another early Rhetoric, now likewise
     lost. This whole "group of Rhetorica" Gohlke assigned to
     Aristotle's Academic period; it was composed prior to the
     Topics. After the Topics, but prior to the first revision of
     the Analytics, Aristotle made the first revision of what ulti-
     mately became the preserved Rhetoric. After the first re-
     vision of the Analytics he made a second and final revision
     of the Rhetoric, which antedates the final revision of the
     Analytics.
50. I. Düring, Aristotle in the Ancient Biographical Tradition

(1957), pp. 258-259. Düring justified his thesis by showing
that Aristotle did not refer to, or comment upon any passages from Demosthenes' famous speeches. Demosthenes, it
will be remembered, made his first appearance in the law
courts of Athens (on behalf of Leptines) in 354. See also
ibid. at p. 314.

51. Düring, loc. cit., argued as follows: in book I of the Rhetoric (1355 a 21-29, and ibid. at 1356 a 35-1356 b 21), Aristotle quotes the Topics (1355 a 28-29), the Analytics (1356
b 18-19). From this it might be inferred (?) that Aristotle
wrote all these works, or at least their earliest versions
(or parts), before he composed (or revised) the Rhetoric.
Book III of the Rhetoric (1411 a 1-8), which refers to the
War of Olynthus (349/8), as well as chapters 23 and 24 of
book II, which might be a later "insertion," in all likelihood were written after the death of Plato in 348/7.

52. See note 22, supra.

53. See, for instance, Cicero, Tuscul. Disput. I. 4. 7.

54. See, for instance, Philodemus, loc. cit. supra note 2; Cicero,
De Oratore III. 35. 141 (see note 12, supra).--Aristotle's
extant Rhetoric indicates, however, that he had a fairly high
opinion of Isocrates. See, for instance, Rhetoric 1368 a
5ff., which contains a reference to Isocrates' Evagoras 45,
Panathenaicus 32, and, perhaps, Ad Nicoclem 29; ibid. at
1399 a 1ff. (Helen 18-48); ibid., at 1399 a 4ff. (Evagoras
51ff.); ibid. at 1401 a 9-10 (Evagoras 65-69); ibid. at 1414
b 26 ff. (Helen 1ff.); ibid. at 1414 b 33ff. (Panegyricus 1-2);
ibid. at 1418 a 33ff. (Panegyricus 110-114; On Peace 27;
Helen 23-38, 41-48; Busiris 21-29, 38-40; Panathenaicus
72-84); ibid. at 1418 b 27ff. (Philippus 4-7; Antidosis 132-
139, 141-149); ibid. at 1418 b 35 (Archidamus 50); etc.,
etc. As a matter of fact, Aristotle's style in the extant
Rhetoric manifests the influence of Isocrates. This, then,
would suggest that in the course of time Aristotle changes
his views about Isocrates (as did Plato).

55. See, for instance, Syrianus, loc. cit. supra note 16.

56. See, for instance, Quintilian, Institutio Oratoria II. 17. 1,
and ibid. II. 17. 4.

57. See E. Berti, La Filosofia del Primo Aristotele (1962), p. 182.

58. The Gryllus is a eulogy on Xenophon's son Gryllus who died
in the battle of Mantinea in 362.

59. It is held here that the Platonic Phaedrus is one of the "late"
dialogues. See, for instance, O. Regenbogen, Kleine
Schriften (ed. F. Dirlmeier, 1961), pp. 248-269, especially
at pp. 255-256. As to the "new dialectics" employed in the
Phaedrus, see ibid. at pp. 251ff., and 266-269. The late
dating of the Phaedrus has also been suggested by C. Ritter,
W. Lutoslawski, H. Raeder, and many other scholars.

60. See Diogenes Laertius II. 55: "Aristotle mentions [in the
Gryllus?] that there existed a great many authors of ...
eulogies on Gryllus, who wrote in part at least, in order to
ingratiate themselves in a servile manner with Gryllus' father

[Xenophon]. Hermippus ... asserts that even Isocrates wrote an encomium on Gryllus."--See here also F. Solmsen, op. cit. supra, note 45, at pp. 196-198. As a matter of fact P. Thillet, "Note sur le Gryllus, Ouvrages de Jeunesse d'Aristote, " in Revue Philosophique de France et de l'Etranger, 82 (1957), p. 353, suggested that in his Gryllus Aristotle refers to Isocrates (in an uncomplimentary manner?). It should be borne in mind that Isocrates was a disciple, and perhaps the most outstanding disciple, of Gorgias whom Plato had so viciously attacked in his Gorgias; and that in his Gryllus Aristotle probably has fashioned some of his invectives against Isocrates after Plato's Gorgias.-- The thesis that in the Gryllus Aristotle might have "taken a slap" at Isocrates might find some additional support in Cephisodorus, a pupil of Isocrates, who composed an Against Aristotle (in four books) in which he attacked Aristotle. See, for instance, Dionysius of Halicarnassus, De Isocrate 18; Epistola ad Amaeum I. 2; Athenaeus, Deipnosophistae II. 60DE, and ibid. at III. 122B; Themistius, Oratio XXIII 285 AB (p. 345, edit. Dindorf). Among other charges Cephisodorus also chastised Aristotle for having criticized Isocrates' method, educational policy, and philosophic outlook. F. Blass, op. cit. supra note 21, vol. II, at pp. 451-453, believed that the Against Aristotle was written after the death of Isocrates (in 338), while E. Bignone, op. cit. supra note 2, at pp. 58-61, suggested that it was a rebuttal of Aristotle's Protrepticus (composed between 352 and 350), and that it was written after Aristotle's return to Athens in 335/4. I. Düring, op. cit. supra note 50, at pp. 389-391, on the strength of the evidence found in Dionysius of Halicarnassus, Epistola ad Pomp. 1, rightly assumed that the Against Aristotle primarily was meant to "set the record straight." Düring also held that it was written around 360. Should Düring's date prove to be correct, then the Against Aristotle in all likelihood would have been provoked by Aristotle's Gryllus. This then would lend support to the theory that in his Gryllus Aristotle criticized Isocrates and his methods. But, again, if the year 360 should be accepted as the date for the composition of Cephisodorus' Against Aristotle, then this work probably could not have taken issue with Aristotle's course of lectures on rhetoric, unless we were willing to concede either that Aristotle began to teach rhetoric in the Academy some time before 360--a most unlikely assumption; or that the Against Aristotle was composed not much earlier than 355. See here also P. Moraux, op. cit. supra note 27, at pp. 334-337.

61. See E. Berti, loc. cit. supra, note 57.
62. See here W. Jaeger, Aristoteles, Grundlegung einer Geschichte seiner Entwicklung (1923), English translation of 1948 (Oxford Paperbacks, 1962), pp. 28-29.
63. F. Solmsen, op. cit. supra, note 45, at p. 218.

64. I. Düring, op. cit. supra note 50, at pp. 258-259, and ibid.
     at p. 314.   F. Blass, op. cit. supra, note 21, vol. II,
     p. 64, had already suggested this date in 1892.
65. See especially Antidosis 258ff. Aristotle's Protrepticus, which
     is believed to be a rebuttal of the Antidosis, in all likeli-
     hood was written shortly after 353/52.

2. ARISTOTLE'S FIRST LITERARY EFFORT: THE GRYLLUS, A LOST DIALOGUE ON THE NATURE OF RHETORIC*

by Anton-Hermann Chroust

In their "catalogues" of Aristotle's writings, Diogenes Laertius, [1] the author of the Vita Hesychii, [2] and Ptolemy-el-Garib[3] include a composition entitled Concerning Rhetoric or Gryllus. Except for a few relatively insignificant "fragments" or references, this Gryllus[4] has been completely lost in the course of time, as were the other earliest writings of Aristotle. Quintilian, recording the arguments made by people who deny that rhetoric is an art (in the Platonic sense τέχνη), observes that "Aristotle, as was his habit, advanced some tentative arguments of his own in his Gryllus, which are indicative of his mental subtleness and ingenuity."[5] And Diogenes Laertius reports: "[In his Gryllus] Aristotle maintains that there are innumerable authors of epitaphs and eulogies upon Gryllus [the son of Xenophon], who wrote, in part at least, for the purpose of ingratiating themselves to his father."[6]

From these brief remarks it would seem to follow that Aristotle composed a work on rhetoric which he entitled Gryllus. [7] In this composition he insisted that not every form of rhetoric is an "art" (τέχνη). Since in the Gryllus he apparently refers to "a great many epitaphs and eulogies "written in memory of Gryllus, it is reasonable to assume that he composed this dialogue shortly after the death of Gryllus. [8] According to Diogenes Laertius, Gryllus fell in a cavalry skirmish which preceded the battle of Mantinea in the year 362 B.C. [9] Since, in the words of Diogenes Laertius, at the time Aristotle wrote the Gryllus, "a great many epitaphs and eulogies upon Gryllus" already existed, several years must have passed between the death of Gryllus and the composition of the Aristotelian dialogue. Thus it might be surmised that the Gryllus was composed about 360 B.C., or perhaps a little later; and that it is probably the first "published," or major, composition which can be credited to Aristotle. In sum, it was probably written during Aristotle's eighth year of study with Plato in the Academy, that is, when he was approximately twenty-five years of age.[10]

*Reprinted by permission of the author and publisher from Revue des Etudes Grecques 78 (1965), 576-591.

It is commonly, though by no means universally, [11] held that
Aristotle's Gryllus was composed in dialogue form. As shall be
shown presently, it was written in fairly close imitation of those
passages in Plato's Gorgias which denounce certain types of prevailing rhetoric. Hence, it might be expected that the Gryllus
would also imitate the external form of the Platonic Gorgias.
Moreover, tradition has it that the earliest compositions of Aristotle, as they have been listed by Diogenes Laertius, Ptolemy-el-
Garib and in the Vita Hesychii, were dialogues[12]--in a certain
sense "Platonic" dialogues.[13] Finally, the very title of this work
also suggests that it was a dialogue. For this unusual title--unusu-
al for Aristotle--seems to be an imitation of Plato's manner of entitling his dialogues.[14] Significantly, however, as W. Jaeger has
convincingly shown, the Aristotelian dialogues, even the earliest,
appear to have been primarily "expository" rather than "dramatic"
works.[15]

What, then, is the likely connection between the title of this
work, Gryllus, and its ostensible subject, rhetoric? E. Heitz[16]
among others, advances the thesis that, as is the case with Aristotle's lost dialogue Eudemus or On the Soul[17] where the title is a
purely dedicatory title, Aristotle chose the title Gryllus to commemorate and honor one of his personal friends. Heitz argues that
just as the Eudemus, composed shortly after 352 B.C.,[18] com-
memorates Aristotle's close friendship with Eudemus of Cyprus
(who also fell in battle), so also the Gryllus, this dialogue on the
nature of rhetoric, was occasioned by the death of Gryllus in 362
B.C., and written in memory of a dear friend. To justify the
title, Gryllus, for a work on rhetoric, Heitz concludes that Gryllus
must also have been a discussant, and perhaps the main discussant,
in the dialogue bearing his name.[19] P. Thillet points out, however, that Heitz's thesis is highly conjectural, not to say improbable.[20] Moreover, there is no evidence whatever that Aristotle
and Gryllus were personal friends, or that Aristotle wished to
honor Gryllus. Thus, the connection between Gryllus and a discussion of the nature of rhetoric would seem to be purely accidental or, at least, artificial.

P. Thillet and F. Solmsen, on the other hand, have suggested what seems to be a more plausible explanation of this unusual combination of Gryllus' name and rhetoric. On the strength of
Quintilian's remark that "Aristotle ... advances some tentative
arguments of his own in his Gryllus, which are indicative of his
mental subtleness and ingenuity,"[21] Thillet and Solmsen arrive at
the conclusion that the Gryllus is primarily a polemical piece rather
than a constructive or doctrinal work.[22] This seems to follow,
Thillet and Solmsen maintain, from the fact that Quintilian refers
to the Aristotelian Gryllus in the context of his lengthy discussion
of "whether rhetoric is an art." Quintilian recalls that neither the
past teachers of rhetoric nor the rhetoricians themselves ever
questioned the categorization of rhetoric as an art, and that they
were supported in this by many philosophers, among them the ma-

jority of the Stoics and Peripatetics. [23] As regards those philosophers who hold the opposite view--who insist that rhetoric is not
an art--Quintilian continues, it must always be kept in mind that
these particular philosophers did not truly affirm what they actually
believed, but merely disputed involved and difficult issues in order
to display their ingenuity of reasoning and their eristic talents. [24]
Of the several arguments advanced in support of the thesis that
rhetoric is not an art, Quintilian remembers those which had maintained that rhetoric was a "natural gift"; [25] those which insisted
that "nothing that is based upon art can have existed before the
art in question existed, whereas men have always from time im-
memorial spoken in their own defense or in the denunciation of
others, " long before the art or the teaching of rhetoric was invented; [26] and those which claimed that that which a man does or
can do without having first formally learned or studied it cannot
belong to any art--and all men are capable of speaking, even those
who have never (in a technical or formal sense) learned how to
speak. [27]

        Quintilian further notes: although in his Gryllus Aristotle
offers "some tentative arguments of his own" [28] against rhetoric as
an art, the Stagirite "also wrote three books on the art of rhetoric,
in the first of which he not only admits that rhetoric is an art, but
also treats it as a department of politics and of dialectics (or
logic). " [29] From this remark Thillet and Solmsen conclude that
Aristotle's Gryllus must have denied that rhetoric, or at least certain types of rhetoric, constitutes an art (τέχνη). In view of the
change of position which becomes manifest in the first book of the
Aristotelian Rhetoric, Quintilian apparently considers the Gryllus
primarily a polemic against certain rhetoricians or teachers of
rhetoric who were prominent in his day, rather than a doctrinal
work. Now we might also better understand Diogenes Laertius' observation that "Aristotle had insisted that a great many people had
composed epitaphs and encomia upon Gryllus, largely for the purpose of ingratiating themselves (χαρίζόμενοι) with his father Xenophon. " [30] The expression χαρίζεσθαι is frequently used by Plato to
characterize the servility or obsequiousness of certain sophists and
rhetoricians who indulged in abject flattery. [31] Hence, we might
also infer from the fact that Aristotle calls "obsequious"
(χαριζόμενοι) the eulogists of Gryllus (or Xenophon) that he was
hostile towards these rhetoricians, and that in the Gryllus he gave
vent to this hostility. The Gryllus, therefore, must be considered
primarily a polemical work aimed at certain rhetoricians or teachers of rhetoric.

        If all this is true, then the remark of Diogenes Laertius
(II. 55) can be harmonized with the observations made by Quintilian.
The realization that the Gryllus is primarily a polemic against
certain rhetoricians would also explain the otherwise puzzling title
of this dialogue: the Gryllus was not written, as some scholars
insist, to honor the memory of Gryllus, but to chastise those
rhetoricians who, in a spirit of abject flattery, had composed many

epitaphs and eulogies commemorating the heroic Gryllus. [32]   The
death of Gryllus became the occasion for a plethora of obsequious
eulogies.   These eulogies drew the ire of Aristotle and induced
him to attack their composers and the kind of rhetoric they were
employing. [33]   This is the only connection between the title of this
dialogue and its real subject matter--between Gryllus and rhetoric.
Had the Aristotelian Gryllus actually been an epitaph or eulogy
upon Gryllus, it would have implied a serious contradiction: flattering Gryllus (or Xenophon) while condemning Gryllus' flatterers.

    In sum, when composing the Gryllus, Aristotle was moti-
vated not perchance by an admiration for Gryllus or Xenophon, but
rather by his fawning tenor of these eulogies.   Aristotle's ire was
probably the more aroused[34] by the participation of some of the
most prominent rhetoricians of the day, among them Isocrates, in
the praise of Gryllus. [35]   There can be no doubt that some of these
eulogies were abject in tone and over-ingratiating in sentiment.
On the strength of the surviving, though scanty evidence, it could
even be maintained that the Aristotelian Gryllus, as shall be shown
presently, is a polemic aimed at Isocrates in particular. [36]

    The excessive number of prominent eulogists and the ob-
sequious praises they voiced, implied, at least to Aristotle and to
the members of the Academy, that some rhetoricians regarded
rhetoric simply as a means of arousing emotions and passions.
Through the deliberate efforts of certain eulogists, rhetoric had
been degraded to a mere emotional appeal to the irrational part of
the soul (ignoring the rightful demands of the rational part of the
soul)[37] in order to achieve purely emotional reactions.   Hence, it
is not surprising that Aristotle, the disciple of Plato, should object
to such contemptible practices, as well as to the ultimate philosophic outlook underlying them.   In rejecting and denouncing this
type of rhetoric, Aristotle acts in full accordance with the spirit
and tenets of Plato's basic philosophic teachings.   Moreover, in
refuting these eulogists he also wishes to re-establish the undisputed supremacy of reason over passion, the primacy of intellectual integrity (in the Platonic sense) over worldly success, [38] and,
perhaps, the superiority of the Academy over the school of Isocrates.

    It is likely, further, that Aristotle, in formulating his at-
tacks upon the eulogists, availed himself of the invectives with
which Plato had chastised the sophists and rhetoricians in his
Gorgias.   As a matter of fact, it would be reasonable to surmise
that the Gryllus re-iterates in substance--perhaps in a more "expository" and "methodical" manner--certain anti-sophistic and anti-
rhetorical utterances found in the Platonic Gorgias. [39]   Hence, in
order to reconstruct the essential tenor of the Gryllus, it would
be appropriate to turn to this Platonic work.

    In the Gorgias, Plato maintains that rhetoric "is not an art
($\tau\acute{\epsilon}\chi\nu\eta$) at all ... [but] something which, as I was lately reading in

a work of yours [scil., Polus'], you claim having turned into an
art ... [Rhetoric] is a sort of experience ... producing a kind of
emotional delight and gratification.... The whole, of which rhetoric is but a part, is not an art at all, but the habit of a ready
and bold wit which knows how to manipulate men. And this habit
I sum up under the heading of 'flattery'.... "[40] In brief, rhetoric
as practiced by certain sophists and rhetoricians, including probably Isocrates, cannot be, in the opinion of Plato, a τέχνη, because
τέχνη is exclusively concerned with that intellectual activity which
gives a rational account of empirical facts by relating them to ultimate principles or causes. Since, according to Plato, this is
not the case with rhetoric (at least not with the type of rhetoric
promulgated by the sophists), it cannot be a τέχνη. Therefore,
Plato insists, rhetoric, like flattery, is actually something "ig-
noble ... because it aims at pleasure without giving any thought to
what is 'best.' An art I do not call it, " Plato concludes, "but
only an emotional experience, because it is unable to explain or to
offer a reason for the nature of its own application. And I do not
call an irrational (unprincipled) thing a τέχνη. "[41]

It need not be assumed, however, that in his Gryllus Aristotle merely restates the basic theses advanced in the Platonic
Gorgias. From Quintilian's observation that in the Gryllus Aristotle "produces some tentative arguments of his own [that is, not
those of Plato?], which are indicative of his mental subtleness and
ingenuity, "[42] it might be inferred that in the Gryllus Aristotle not
only adopts the basic position held by Plato, but also devises some
original ideas and arguments, as well as an original method of
argument. In so doing he apparently displays considerable acumen,
ingenuity and originality. [43] It is not impossible, as Thillet points
out, [44] that Quintilian actually quotes some of Aristotle's own arguments, such as the statements that "all arts have their own subject matter ... whereas rhetoric has none";[45] that "no art will
acquiesce in false opinions, because a true art must be based on
immediate perceptions ... whereas rhetoric gives its assent to
false conclusions";[46] that "every art has some definite and proper
end towards which it directs its efforts, whereas rhetoric, as a
rule, has no such end, even though at times it claims to have such
an end without, however, succeeding in fulfilling its promise";[47]
that "the arts know when they have attained their proper end, whereas rhetoric does not";[48] that "rhetoric does things which no art
does, namely, makes use of vices that serve its ends, inasmuch
as it proclaims falsehoods and excites passions";[49] that "rhetoricians
speak indifferently on either side of an argument ... [whereas] no
true art is self-contradictory, rhetoric does contradict itself, and
whereas no true art attempts to demolish what it itself has built
up, this does happen in the operations of rhetoric";[50] and that because "rhetoric teaches either what ought to be said or what ought
not to be said, it is not an art, inasmuch as it teaches also what
ought to be said, or because while it teaches what ought to be said,
it also teaches precisely the opposite. "[51] These arguments, some
of which are remarkably acute, could very well have been developed

in Aristotle's Gryllus, independently, though probably under the
influence, of Plato's Gorgias, and used in support of Aristotle's
thesis that rhetoric--or a certain type of rhetoric--is not a τέχνη.
Hence, it may also be maintained that Quintilian's Institutio Oratoria
II. 17. 14-30, contains substantial "fragments" of the lost Aristotelian Gryllus. 52

It has already been pointed out that in all likelihood the
Aristotelian Gryllus is a polemic directed at contemporary rhetoricians in general (or, at least, at those orators who appealed to
emotions and passions through flattering memorials and obsequious
eulogies), and at Isocrates in particular. This latter statement
requires additional substantiation. We know from Diogenes Laertius that "Isocrates likewise wrote an encomium on Gryllus. "53
The fact that Diogenes Laertius mentions this valuable bit of information in the context of his report that "a great many people composed epitaphs and eulogies on Gryllus, " and that Aristotle denounced
these people for doing this, seems to indicate that Aristotle not only mentions Isocrates in the Gryllus, but probably also attacks him
for his obsequiousness. 54 It would plainly be unthinkable for Aristotle to take issue with these rhetoricians without engaging Isocrates,
the most outstanding and most renowned orator of the time, who
had likewise composed an obsequious encomium on Gryllus.

Quintilian relates that Isocrates was the most distinguished
pupil of Gorgias of Leontini. 55 If this was the case, Isocrates'
rhetorical style and standards were probably patterned after those
of his teacher. Gorgias, it will be remembered, was savagely denounced in Plato's Protagoras and Gorgias, after the manner of
which Aristotle, as has been argued, probably patterned some of
his invectives against the rhetoricians (and against Isocrates) in the
Gryllus. 56

The assumption that in his Gryllus Aristotle also denounces
Isocrates finds additional support in the fact that Cephisodorus, a
pupil of Isocrates, attacks Aristotle. In his Against Aristotle, published about 360 B.C., 57 this Cephisodorus reproaches Aristotle
for having criticized (and wholly misunderstood) Isocrates' method,
educational policy and philosophic outlook. 58 This, in turn, impels
the surmise that Aristotle, in his Gryllus, had denounced Isocrates
and the kind of rhetoric or philosophy he propagates. Thus, Aristotle's denial of rhetoric's categorization as an art would seem to
be aimed directly at Isocrates. 59 If this is the case, Aristotle
seems to attach to Isocrates, reputedly the greatest orator of his
day, the label of dilettante. Moreover, in Aristotle's judgment,
Isocrates' brand of rhetoric is emphatically not τέχνη. 60

The question might now be raised as to what the particular
issues were which prompted Aristotle's attack upon Isocrates. It
is known that Plato had made the radical claim that henceforth all
true paideia, including true rhetoric and true intellectual culture,
must be founded exclusively on the rational knowledge of imperish-

able values or principles, and on the exclusive use of phronesis. However, the educational ideas of the sophists, despite Plato's savage denunciations in the Protagoras and in the Gorgias, succeeded in retaining a prominent place in the educational, intellectual and cultural life of Greece. [61] This was due, in no small degree, to the efforts of Isocrates, who pronounced rhetoric--his brand of rhetoric--the sound foundation of all higher education or educational philosophy. More than that, he severely criticized and ridiculed the almost mythical importance which Plato and the Platonists attached to phronesis, and the apparently exaggerated Platonic intellectualism, which held up pure intellectual knowledge as the panacea for all the ills of this world. [62] Isocrates, on the other hand, tried to find certain solutions to man's almost infinite concrete problems--solutions, which could reasonably and effectively be translated into practical action and, at the same time, retain some moral meaning. [63] Isocrates persuasively advocated this approach to life, teaching it in his school, which about the year 360 B.C., had acquired a considerable reputation (and an impressive enrollment) not only throughout Greece, but also beyond the Hellenic orbit.

One is led, therefore, to assume further that in his Gryllus Aristotle discusses and criticizes the very principles (or lack of principles) which Isocrates proposed in his rhetoric and, indeed, in his whole "philosophy of life. "[64] Here Aristotle openly confronts and violently opposes Isocrates' philosophic and educational ideals.[65] The attacks which Aristotle here launches against Isocrates and his whole school also reveal something about the intellectual outlook of the young Aristotle, who in 360 B.C. still professed most enthusiastically the intellectual ideals so eloquently propagated by his teacher Plato, as he would for several years to come. As a faithful and, one might assume, ambitious student of Plato, he was fully convinced that Plato's lofty ideals were infinitely superior to the intellectual and cultural notions advocated by Isocrates, the most successful and, at the same time, the most dangerous rival of Plato and the Platonic Academy.

Finally, Isocrates' eulogy on Gryllus (and Xenophon) probably presented a unique opportunity for Aristotle actively to participate in the "great conflict of ideas" which separated the school of Plato from that of Isocrates, --to enter into the crucial contemporary "dialogue" between the two most outstanding men of the times on problems touching upon the ultimate foundations of the truly intellectual life. [66] Moreover, it was a splendid opportunity to "strike a telling blow" for the Academy and thereby earn the attention, and perhaps the admiration, of his teacher Plato and of the entire Academy. By championing in his Gryllus the Platonic-Academic views in the debate on the constitution of the truly intellectual or philosophic life, Aristotle probably displayed all the uncompromising enthusiasm characteristic of youth. With the sense that he was supporting and furthering the work of his teacher and of his associates in the Academy, Aristotle could not but condemn the cultural and intellectual ideals advocated by Isocrates.

This clash between Aristotle and Isocrates, which in all likelihood was the main theme of the Gryllus, might be reduced to a conflict between an uncompromising "principled philosophy" and a less principled "practical philosophy of life" which takes into account worldly success, practical effectiveness, and the general human condition within an existential rather than ideal world.

It appears that the Gryllus produced certain practical or tangible results--rewards for which Aristotle had perhaps hoped when composing this polemic. Apparently as a consequence or reward for his Gryllus Aristotle was permitted--perhaps even urged-- to offer a course of lectures on rhetoric in the Academy. Certainly this signal honor can at least partially be attributed to this demonstration of his qualification as a teacher and advocate of Platonic rhetoric, --to his loyalty to the Academy in standing up to a man much condemned and much disliked by Plato and the Academy, the mighty Isocrates. [67]

In summation, it may be maintained that Aristotle's Gryllus was not perchance a "memorial" honoring Gryllus, but rather a composition on the nature of rhetoric; that its title, Gryllus, is purely incidental; that it was written in dialogue form; that it adhered in substance to the rhetorical or philosophic standards which Plato had established in the Protagoras and Gorgias (and in the Phaedrus); that it contained a sustained and, presumably, violent attack upon certain contemporary rhetoricians and, especially, on Isocrates; that it denounced Isocrates' alleged indifference or opposition to true--Platonic--philosophy and its attendant rigoristic educational ideals; that it made a strong case in support of a rhetoric (and philosophy) based upon a comprehensive grasp of ultimate and absolute moral and intellectual values; that in the Gryllus the youthful Aristotle already displayed the logical, dialectic and eristic acumen for which he later gained much renown; and that in consequence of the Gryllus Aristotle was judged qualified to lecture on rhetoric in the Academy.

NOTES

1.   Diogenes Laertius V. 22 (no. 5) lists a Περὶ ῥητορικῆς ἢ Γρῦλος (also spelled Γρῦλλος or Γρύλλος) in one book. See P. Moraux, Les listes Anciennes des Ouvrages d'Aristote (Louvain, 1951), passim.

2.   Vita Hesychii (also called Vita Menagii or Vita Menagiana) 10 (no. 5) lists a Περὶ πολιτικῆς ἢ Γρῦλος in three books. See P. Moraux, op. cit. at pp. 195ff.

3.. The "catalogue" of Aristotelian works compiled by Ptolemy-el-Garib (no. 3) lists a Περὶ ῥητορικῆς ἢ Γρῦλος in three books. See P. Moraux, op. cit., passim.

4.   See J. Bernays, Die Dialoge des Aristoteles (Berlin, 1863),

p. 62; V. Rose, Aristoteles Pseudepigraphus (Leipzig, 1863),
pp. 76ff.; E. Heitz, Die Verlorenen Schriften des Aristoteles
(Leipzig, 1865), pp. 189ff.--In keeping with his general,
though wholly erroneous thesis that all of the so-called "exoteric" works credited to Aristotle are spurious, Rose denies
that the Stagirite ever authored a Gryllus. He ascribes the
Gryllus to Theophrastus. Rose's theses were refuted by E.
Heitz, loc. cit.

5. Quintilian, Institutio Oratoria II. 17. 14; frag. 69 Rose (V.
Rose, Aristotelis Qui Ferebantur Librorum Fragmenta,
Leipzig, 1886, p. 76); frag. 2 Ross (W. D. Ross, Aristo-
telis Fragmenta Selecta, Oxford, 1955, p. 7).

6. Diogenes Laertius II. 55; frag. 68 Rose; frag. 1 Ross.

7. It seems probable that in his earliest works Aristotle followed
the Platonic model and, hence, used one-word titles, often
naming these dialogues after some personage. See Diogenes
Laertius V. 22 (Nerinthus, Menexenus, Eudemus and Alexander, or Sophistes, Eroticus, Symposium and Protrepticus).
It might be conjectured that the "sub-title, " On Rhetoric, is
a later addition.

8. While most scholars (see infra) are of the opinion that
the Gryllus was composed shortly after the death of Gryllus in 362 B.C., F. Solmsen, Die Entwicklung der Aristotelischen Logik und Rhetorik (Berlin, 1929), p. 200,
insists that it must have been written several years after
362, because it apparently refers to many existing eulogies
on Gryllus. See also P. Moraux, op. cit. at p. 33, and
ibid. at pp. 323ff.; P. Thillet, "Note sur le Gryllos, ouvrage
de jeunesse d'Aristote, " Revue Philosophique de la France
et de l'Etranger, vol. 147 (1957), pp. 352ff.; O. Gigon,
"Interpretationen zu den Antiken Aristoteles-Viten, " Museum
Helveticum, vol. 15 (1958), pp. 169ff., and note 42.

9. Diogenes Laertius II. 54-55. See also Pausanias I. 3. 4.

10. Aristotle was born in 384 B.C., and according to tradition,
entered the Academy in 367 B.C.

11. See Thillet, op. cit. at pp. 353ff.

12. The fact that Aristotle's earliest compositions were dialogues
is attested by Ammonius, Commentarius in Aristotelis Categorias, in: Commentaria in Aristotelem Graeca (subsequently cited as CIAG), vol. IV, part 4 (edit. A. Busse, 1887),
p. 6, lines 25ff.; Simplicius, Commentaria in Aristotelis De
Coelo, in: CIAG, vol. VII (edit. J. Heiberg, 1894), p. 228,
lines 31ff.; Simplicius, Commentaria in Aristotelis Physicorum Libros Quattuor Priores, in: CIAG, vol. IX (edit. H.
Diels, 1882), p. 8, lines 16ff.; Olympiodorus, Prolegomena
et in Aristotelis Categorias Commentarium, in: CIAG, vol.
XII, part 1 (edit. A. Busse, 1902), p. 7, lines 5ff.; Philo-
ponus (olim Ammonius), Commentarium in Aristotelis Categorias, in: CIAG, vol. XVIII, part 1 (edit. A. Busse,
1898), p. 3, lines 18ff.; Elias (olim David), Commentaria in
Porphyrii Isagogen et Aristotelis Categorias, in: CIAG, vol.
XVIII, part 1 (edit. A. Busse, 1900), p. 114, lines 22ff.,

and ibid. at p. 124, lines 3ff. See also Plutarch, Adversus
Coloten 20; Dio Chrysostom, Oratio LIII. 1.

13. Plutarch, Adversus Coloten 20, calls the early writings of
Aristotle "Aristotle's Platonic works," implying that in form
as well as in content these writings were very similar to
Plato's dialogues. See also Cicero, Ad Atticum IV. 16 2,
and ibid. at XIII. 19. 4; Cicero, De Oratore III. 21. 80;
Cicero, Ad Familiares I. 9. 23; Ammonius, op. cit. at
p. 6, lines 25ff.; Elias, op. cit. at p. 114, lines 15ff.,
and ibid. at p. 115, lines 3ff.; p. 124, lines 3ff.; Simplicius,
Commentarius in Aristotelis Categorias, in: CIAG, vol.
VIII (edit. C. Kalbfleisch, 1907), p. 4, lines 20ff.

14. Cicero, who read some of Aristotle's earliest dialogues, at-
tests to the fact that they were composed in a clear and in-
cisive style; that they were remarkable for their form; and
that they were replete with logical acumen. See Cicero,
De Oratore I. 11. 49; Cicero, Academica Priora II. 38;
Cicero, De Inventione II. 2. 6; Cicero, De Finibus Bonorum
et Malorum I. 5. 14; Cicero, Topica I. 3; Cicero, Brutus
XXXI. 120; Cicero, Lucullus XXXVIII. 119 (edit. O. Plas-
berg); Cicero, Ad Atticum II. 1. 1.   The Ciceronian testimony substantiates the remark of Quintilian, Institutio Oratoria II. 17. 14 (note 5, supra). See also Themistius,
Oratio XXIII. 319C; Quintilian, op. cit. at X. 1. 83.

15. See W. Jaeger, Aristoteles: Grundlegung einer Geschichte
seiner Entwicklung (Berlin, 1923), pp. 29ff. This work has
been translated into English under the title of Aristotle:
Fundamentals of the History of His Development (Oxford,
1934 and 1948).   All subsequent references to Jaeger will
refer to the translation of 1948.--It will be noted that in
his later dialogues Plato changes from a "dramatic" to a
more "expository" treatment of his subject. W. Jaeger also credits Aristotle with having originated a type of dialogue
which is tantamount to a "scientific discussion." W. Jaeger,
loc. cit.

16. E. Heitz, op. cit. at p. 167.

17. See A.-H. Chroust, "Eudemus or On the Soul: A Lost Aristotelian Dialogue on the Immortality of the Soul," published
in Mnemosyne 19 (1966), 17-30.

18. See A.-H. Chroust, op. cit.

19. E. Heitz, loc. cit.

20. P. Thillet, op. cit. at pp. 353ff. Thillet argues that the
Gryllus is a work on rhetoric, which might be referred to
as Gryllus, but which should really be called On Rhetoric.
He assigns great importance to the fact that the proper and
full title of this dialogue is On Rhetoric or Gryllus (and not
merely Gryllus).   To Thillet this particular order or sequence within the title is highly significant.

21. See note 5, supra.

22. F. Solmsen, op. cit. at pp. 196ff.; P. Thillet, op. cit. at
p. 353.

23. Quintilian, op. cit. at II. 17. 2.

24. Ibid. at II. 17. 4.
25. Ibid. at II. 17. 5.
26. Ibid. at II. 17. 7.
27. Ibid. at II. 17. 11.
28. See note 5, supra.
29. Quintilian, op. cit. at II. 18. 14.
30. See note 6, supra.
31. See Plato, Gorgias 462C, and ibid. at 463B; 502E; 413D.
      See also F. Solmsen, op. cit. at pp. 196ff.
32. See F. Solmsen, op. cit. at pp. 196ff.
33. That Xenophon was not exactly a friend of Plato's is attested
      by Diogenes Laertius II. 57: "He [scil., Xenophon] and Pla-
      to were jealous of each other...." See also ibid. at III. 34:
      "And it appears that Xenophon was not on good terms with
      him [scil., Plato]. At any rate, they have written similar
      accounts as if out of rivalry with each other.... And in
      the Laws [694C] Plato declares that the story of Cyrus' edu-
      cation [as reported in Xenophon's Cyropaedia] was a mere
      fiction...." There can be little doubt that Aristotle, then a
      member of the Academy and a pupil of Plato, shared Plato's
      dislike of Xenophon.
34. It is entirely possible that Plato himself should have urged his
      pupil Aristotle to take these flatterers to task, especially
      since Isocrates, Plato's old rival, had also composed an
      epitaph or eulogy on Gryllus. Obsequious eulogies certainly
      violated the canons of rhetoric laid down by Plato in the
      Gorgias and more recently in the Phaedrus.
35. Diogenes Laertius II. 55, on the authority of Hermippus, The
      Life of Theophrastus, reports that Isocrates, the most
      prominent and best known rhetorician of the mid-fourth cen-
      tury B.C., had likewise composed an encomium on Gryllus.
      --It is quite possible that Isocrates (or perhaps Gorgias, the
      teacher of Isocrates) was the originator of this type of eu-
      logy. This may be gathered from certain passages in
      Plato's Gorgias, which seem to be directed against Isocrates.
      It will be noted that Plato, too, discusses the good man and
      father who "had the misfortune to lose his son." The good
      man, Plato insists, will bear the loss with greater equanimi-
      ty than the bad man. "He ... will be moderate in his sor-
      row.... For there is a principle and a dictate of reason in
      him, which commands him to resist [the temptation to give
      vent to his emotions].... This principle would tell him to
      display patience in his sufferings and not to give way to im-
      patience, as there is no way of knowing whether such things
      are good or evil.... He would take counsel about what has
      happened ... and ... not like children ... waste his time
      in setting up a howl, but always accustom his soul forthwith
      to apply a remedy, raising up that which is sickly and fallen,
      banishing the cry of sorrow by the healing art [scil., phil-
      osophy].... This is the true way of meeting the incidents
      of fate." Plato, Republic 603Eff.
36. See P. Thillet, op. cit. at p. 353. F. Solmsen, op. cit. at

p. 198, note 1, suggests that the Gryllus contained three
distinct parts: (1) a critique of the traditional epitaphs or
eulogies; (2) a critique of contemporary rhetoric in general;
and (3) a critique of Isocrates in particular.

37.   Undoubtedly, Aristotle at that time still adhered to Plato's
doctrine of the tri-partite soul.   Hence, rhetoric, as exemplified in some of these eulogies would appeal exclusively
to the appetitive--irrational--part of the soul which, in the
Platonic system, constitutes the lowliest part of the soul.

38.   Plato, it will be remembered, entertained a purely intellectual
notion of τέχνη.   To him τέχνη is that disciplined activity of
the intellect which gives account of the true facts by relating them to their ultimate cause or causes--the Ideas.   See
E. des Places, Lexique de la langue philosophique ... de
Platon (Paris, 1964), s.v. and p. xiii.

39.   This is not the place to discuss in detail the extent to which
the Gryllus was influenced by Plato's Phaedrus.   The Phaedrus, it will be noted, sheds new light on Plato's later
views about the nature of rhetoric (and also on his relationship with Isocrates?).   Modern scholarship insists that the
main theme of the Phaedrus is the connection between philosophy and rhetoric.   See A. Dies, Autour de Platon (Paris,
1927), vol. III, p. 418.--In the Phaedrus Plato maintains
that any form of rhetoric which merely attempts to mislead
the listeners is most certainly not a τέχνη.   See Plato,
Phaedrus 260Eff.   But there exists another kind of rhetoric
which is founded on an understanding of truth and of the one
true reality from which it derives its arguments and methods.
This kind of rhetoric may be called a τέχνη.   Ibid. at 263Bff.
But if rhetoric is the art of persuading the soul so that it
may become virtuous, then the orator must know something
about the nature of the soul.   He "must learn the differences
of human souls, for there are so many souls ... and from
them come the differences between man and man.... [He]
will next divide speeches into their different categories:
'Such and such persons,' he will say, 'are affected by this
or that kind of speech in this or that way,' and he will tell
you why.   The pupil must have a good theoretical notion of
them first, and then he must have experience of them in
actual life, and be able to follow them with all his senses
about him, or he will never get beyond the precepts of his
masters and teachers.   But when he understands what persons are persuaded by what arguments, and sees the person
about whom he is speaking in the abstract actually before
him, and knows that it is he, and can say to himself, 'This
is the man or this is the character who ought to have a
certain argument applied to him in order to convince him of
a certain opinion'--he who knows all this, and knows also
when he should speak and when he should keep silent, and
when he should use pithy sayings, pathetic appeals, sensa-
tional effects, and all the other modes of speech which he
has learned--when, I repeat, he knows the times and the

seasons of all these things, then, and not till then, is he a
perfect master of his art...." Ibid. at 271Eff. --Scholars
disagree as to whether Aristotle was acquainted with the
Platonic Phaedrus at the time he composed the Gryllus.
W. Jaeger, for instance, denies that about the year 360 B.C.
Aristotle knew the Phaedrus. Jaeger's thesis, however,
seems highly conjectural. The Phaedrus, it is widely held,
was written about 370/69 or shortly thereafter, while the
Gryllus is usually dated about 360. It would have been
rather unusual for Aristotle, "the great reader," not to have
known the Phaedrus by 360, or, as seems even more unlikely, simply to have ignored it. But since the Platonic Gorgias, which, judging from Aristotle's lost Nerinthus, made
such an impression on Aristotle (see Themistius, Oratio
XXIII. 356), denounces without compromise or exception the
sophists and orators as well as their peculiar rhetoric, the
Gorgias rather than the more conciliatory Phaedrus supplied
Aristotle with the kind of materials and the form of argument he needed for his Gryllus. This might explain why
Aristotle apparently did not make use of the Phaedrus when
composing his Gryllus. It must also be admitted that in the
Phaedrus Plato discusses a type of rhetoric that is fundamentally different from the kind of rhetoric which he had
condemned in the Gorgias. Hence, Plato could very well
call rhetoric a τέχνη in the Phaedrus, whereas in the Gorgias he denies its categorization as a τέχνη. Finally, it
should also be observed that in the Gryllus Aristotle attacks
only obsequious rhetoric, that is, those orators who attempted to arouse emotions and passions. Here he denies
that theirs is a τέχνη, but he does not denounce rhetoric in
principle, which can, after all, still be a τέχνη, provided
it complies with certain rational principles. See also P.
Kucharski, "La rhétorique dans le Gorgias et le Phèdre, "
Revue des Etudes Grecques, vol. 74 (1961), pp. 371ff.

40. Plato, Gorgias 462Bff.
41. Ibid. at 465A.
42. See note 5, supra.
43. See also F. Solmsen, op. cit. at pp. 198ff.
44. P. Thillet, op. cit. at pp. 353ff. See also F. Solmsen, op.
     cit. at pp. 201ff.
45. Quintilian, op. cit. at II. 17. 17.
46. Ibid. at II. 17. 18.
47. Ibid. at II. 17. 22.
48. Ibid. at II. 17. 26.
49. Ibid.
50. Ibid. at II. 17. 30. This could possibly be a reference to
     Isocrates, who in his younger days was forensic orator or
     logographer taking on clients and arguing "on both sides of
     a case" before the heliastic courts in Athens.
51. Ibid.
52. It is not impossible that some of these arguments might also
     have been advanced by Athenodorus of Rhodes, Critolaus,

Hagnon, Carneades, Diogenes of Babylonia, Clitomachus, Epicurus and others, all of whom were opposed to the rhetoricians and, hence, criticized their methods. See Quintilian, op. cit., at II. 17; Sextus Empiricus, Adversus Rhetoricos, passim; Cicero, De Oratore, passim; Philodemus, Volumina Rhetorica, passim; etc.

53. Diogenes Laertius II. 55. This valuable information is apparently derived from Hermippus' Life of Theophrastus. Ibid.

54. See P. Thillet, op. cit. at pp. 353ff.; P. Moraux, op. cit. at p. 31; F. Solmsen, op. cit. at p. 204.

55. Quintilian, op. cit. at III. 1. 13. Quintilian continues: "Our authorities are not in agreement as to who was his [scil., Isocrates'] teacher. I, however, accept the statement of Aristotle on this subject [namely, that Gorgias was the teacher of Isocrates]...." Frag. 139 Rose; frag. 3 Ross.-- V. Rose lists this passage from Quintilian among the fragments of the Τεχνῶν συναγωγή, but W. D. Ross lists it among the fragments of the Gryllus. J. Bernays, op. cit. at p. 157, already conjectured that this fragment belonged to the Gryllus.

56. See also A.-H. Chroust, "Aristotle's Earliest Course of Lectures on Rhetoric, " Antiquité Classique, vol. 33 (1964), pp. 58-72, especially at pp. 69ff.

57. See, for instance, Athenaeus, Deipnosophistae II. 60DE, and ibid. at III. 122B; Dionysius of Halicarnassus, De Isocrate 18; Themistius, Oratio XXIII. 285AB (p. 354, edit. L. Dindorf); Eusebius, Praeparatio Evangelica XIV. 6; Dionysius of Halicarnassus, Epistola ad Ammaeum I. 2.

58. F. Blass, Attische Beredsamkeit, vol. II (Leipzig, 1892), pp. 451ff., holds that Cephisodorus' Against Aristotle was written after the death of Isocrates (338/37 B.C.); E. Bignone, L'Aristotele Perduto e la Formazione Filosofica di Epicuro, vol. II (Florence, 1936), pp. 58ff., maintains that the Against Aristotle is a rejoinder to Aristotle's Protrepticus (written about 350 B.C.), which, in turn, is a "rebuttal" of Isocrates' Antidosis; and I. Düring, Aristotle in the Ancient Biographical Tradition (Göteborg, 1957) pp. 389ff., on the strength of the evidence found in Dionysius of Halicarnassus, Epistola ad Pompeium 1, assumes that Cephisodorus' Against Aristotle was intended primarily to "set the record straight." Düring also insists that the Against Aristotle was composed about 360 B.C. Should Düring's thesis prove to be correct, and it appears that this is the case, then the Against Aristotle could have been "provoked" by the Aristotelian Gryllus, and hence, might be considered a rejoinder to the Gryllus. This, then, would lend support to the thesis that in the Gryllus Aristotle criticizes Isocrates and his methods.

59. Quintilian, op. cit. at II. 17. 14.

60. Aristotle, Rhetoric 1354 a 11ff., likewise contains a pointed attack on Isocrates.

61. See H. von Arnim, Leben und Werke des Dion von Prusa
    (Berlin, 1898), pp. 4ff.
62. Isocrates, Against the Sophists 20ff.--The Against the Sophists
    is directed primarily against the "Socratics," including Plato.
63. It was probably this particular point of view which became the
    main target of Aristotle's (and Plato's) attacks: Isocrates'
    willingness to come to terms with existential reality, with
    the concrete human existence, and with what is reasonably
    practical--a position, which in the eyes of Plato and the
    young Aristotle was unforgivable "heresy."
64. Judging from Quintilian, op. cit. at II. 17. 30, Aristotle's
    Gryllus also contained the information that in his earlier
    days Isocrates had been a logographer or forensic orator--
    not always a reputable profession--in order to make money.
    See note 50, supra; Dionysius of Halicarnassus, De Isocrate
    18; Cicero, Brutus 28. In later years Isocrates was most
    reluctant to mention this period of his life. In his Gryllus
    Aristotle probably brought to light these early activities of
    Isocrates, noting also that a great many of Isocrates' old
    forensic speeches could be found in Athenian book shops.
    Dionysius of Halicarnassus, loc. cit.
65. The Antidosis of Isocrates, published in 353/52 B.C., might
    well be a "rebuttal" of Aristotle's Gryllus. In the Protrep-
    ticus, published about 350 B.C., Aristotle also takes issue
    with the Antidosis. See A.-H. Chroust, Aristotle: Pro-
    trepticus.--A Reconstruction (Notre Dame, 1964), p. xiv.
    Thus it appears that the Aristotle-Isocrates feud went on for
    some time.
66. In the light of all this, the report of Quintilian becomes com-
    prehensible, namely, op. cit. III. 1. 14: "[Aristotle] ...
    [in the form of a travesty] quoted the well-known line from
    [Euripides'] Philoctetes as follows: 'Isocrates still speaks,
    hence it would be a shameful thing should I remain silent.'"
    The name of Isocrates is substituted for the original term
    "barbarians" in the Philoctetes. See Euripides, Philoctetes,
    frag. 785 Dindorf; frag. 796 Nauck. See also Diogenes
    Laertius V. 3, where Aristotle is credited with having re-
    marked: "It would be a base thing to keep silent and let
    Xenocrates speak out." This, too, is a travesty of Euripi-
    des' line. Some scholars suggest that Xenocrates is but a
    corruption of Isocrates. See also Cicero, De Orat. III. 35.
    141; Synesius, Scholia in Hermogenem II. 59. 21ff. (Rabe);
    Philodemus, De Rhetorica III, p. 50 (Sudhaus), col. XLVIII,
    36.
67. See A.-H. Chroust, "Aristotle's Earliest Course of Lectures
    on Rhetoric," Antiquité Classique, vol. 33 (1964), pp. 70ff.

3. THE DEFINITION OF RHETORIC ACCORDING TO ARISTOTLE*

by Theresa M. Crem

INTRODUCTION

Aristotle's treatise on rhetoric is unique, in that it is a properly scientific consideration of the subject. This characteristic becomes manifest, when we compare it with other rhetorical treatises, such as those of Cicero. The works of this great rhetorician are of high value because of his wide experience in the field; nevertheless, they do not methodically treat of the nature of rhetoric. Rather, they are handbooks of practical advice on public speaking and on the formation of the rhetorician.

On the other hand, Aristotle speaks not as an experienced rhetorician, but as a logician. Rhetoric is a part of logic understood in the broad sense, i.e., taken to include all disciplines which direct the act of reason. In the order of logical treatises, the Rhetoric is placed immediately after the Topics, which is concerned with dialectic. Hence, because he is proceeding from a logical point of view, and since these two parts of logic have a great deal in common, Aristotle very aptly begins his consideration of rhetoric by comparing it to dialectic.

Aristotle's aim in writing this work is a scientific presentation of the rhetorical method. Thus, besides setting down its nature in the first two chapters, he also discusses the many things which the rhetorician must know in order to practice his art successfully. Hence, in the remainder of Book I he divides rhetoric into three genera: deliberative, forensic, and epideictic; and gives the characteristics and special topics proper to each. In Book II he discusses passions, human character, virtues and vices; for without some knowledge of these, the rhetorician would be incapable of constructing a speech proportionate to his audience, and of arousing their passions. After this, he treats of common topics, which are applicable to rhetoric in general. Book III is principally devoted to style and arrangement which, though secondary, obviously must be included in any complete study of rhetoric. It is evident,

*Reprinted by permission of the author and publisher from Laval Théologique et Philosophique XII (1956), 233-250.

then, that although Aristotle was not himself a rhetorician, still
he was far from lacking experience in this domain. For besides
possessing the universality proper to a scientific treatise, his
work contains a wealth of concrete detail.

The commentary which is to follow, however, is limited to
the first and the beginning of the second chapter of Book I, which
is the most important part of the treatise, for it contains a definition of rhetoric and an explanation of the rhetorical method.
Aristotle's text has been incorporated herein, therefore we do not
think it necessary to quote it apart. This article is a literal commentary, based on the principle that the sole function of a commentator is to be an intermediary between the master and the reader, by making the master's thought more explicit and hence more
easily understood. In order to assure greater fidelity, we have
compared various translations[1] of the Greek original.

I. COMMON CONSIDERATIONS ON THE NATURE OF RHETORIC

This first section has four divisions: a quid nominis of
rhetorica utens, the an est of rhetorica docens, a common consideration of what should constitute the rhetorical method, and a
résumé.

1) A "Quid Nominis" of "Rhetorica Utens"

Here Aristotle does three things: he compares rhetoric to
dialectic, gives the reason for this comparison, and substantiates
this reason by examples drawn from common experience.

a) A Comparison of Rhetoric and Dialectic

Aristotle states that rhetoric is the antistrophe of dialectic.
This is an instance of the locutio exemplaris, i. e., the use of a
word having a sole, concrete signification to manifest something
else. There is no new imposition as is the case in analogy; nor
is the word given an improper or figurative sense as in the metaphor. [2]

Aristotle draws his example from the Greeks' everyday life,
using something with which all were familiar, the choral odes.
The antistrophe is that part of the choral ode which alternates with
and answers the strophe. Thus, what is meant by this locutio
exemplaris is that there is a special relation between dialectic and
rhetoric. Just as the strophe and antistrophe are similar in that
they are corresponding parts of the choral ode, so too, dialectic
and rhetoric have certain characteristics in common. In the same
way, just as the strophe and antistrophe are distinct from one
another and ordered in a particular way, inasmuch as the antistrophe is always consequent upon the strophe; so also, rhetoric is

distinct from dialectic, and is in a way consequent upon it. Hence, it is clear that by means of this locutio exemplaris any Greek familiar with dialectic would immediately acquire a fundamental, though common notion of the nature of rhetoric.

It is unfortunate that in English translation, "antistrophe" is usually rendered by another term, such as "counterpart"; for by this departure from the precision of Aristotle's terminology, the principle of manifestation which he intended is lost.

b) The Reason for This Comparison

Aristotle does not now consider the aspects in which rhetoric and dialectic differ, for this presupposes more distinct knowledge. However, he immediately states what they have in common: both dialectic and rhetoric are concerned with matters which are in some way known by all men, and which are proper to no definite science.   These two characteristics are closely related, being effects of the same cause.   Such matter does not belong to any particular science because it is common; i. e., it extends to many things, but in a superficial way.   For this same reason, it falls within the comprehension of all men.   On the contrary, the subject proper to a given science is known only to the initiated in that science, and unknown to the majority of men.   This is obvious from the fact that the multitude cannot understand scientific reasoning.   But dialectic and rhetoric are not limited to any determinate genus of being.   They treat of any subject whatever, arguing not from principles proper to a given thing, but from certain common principles familiar to all.

There are other similarities between rhetoric and dialectic; in fact, they are so closely related that distinct knowledge of rhetoric implies knowledge of the Topics.   However, we are now concerned only with a confused and common knowledge, a quid nominis which will lead us to distinct knowledge.   Therefore, Aristotle restricts himself to mentioning a similarity which is most manifest, one which can be understood even by those having no knowledge of rhetoric.

c) Aristotle Substantiates this Reason

A proof that the matter of rhetoric and dialectic is such things as are known by all men is the fact that all make use of these faculties to some extent: dialectic, when they criticize opinions or seek to uphold them; rhetoric, when they defend themselves or accuse others.

2) The "An Est" of "Rhetorica Docens"

These faculties can be used in two ways, either by chance or by acquired habit.   In either way success is possible; therefore

we can inquire as to the reason for this success. Once this cause
has been found, we can set up principles which will enable the intellect to proceed in a determinate fashion. Such an inquiry obviously is the function of a method, for the very word "method"
means "a short way."[3]

        This rhetorical method is rhetorica docens (τέχνη), which
must not be confused with rhetorica utens (ῥητορική). To clarify
this point it may be useful to manifest the same distinction as
applied to dialectic. Dialectica docens, the doctrine contained in
the Topics, is the speculative art concerned with directing probable
argument. It proceeds demonstratively, and so is a science in the
strict sense. Dialectica utens is the application of dialectica docens
in actual argument. This use of dialectic declines from the mode
of science because its matter is only probable.[4] Thus, when Aristotle describes rhetoric as the antistrophe of dialectic, possessed
by all and having common matter, he is referring to both rhetoric
and dialectic under the aspect of utens. For the matter of dialectica and rhetorica docens, like that of all the other sciences, is
not common but proper; it is not possessed by all, but must be
acquired.

        By proceeding in this fashion, Aristotle also manifests the
priority in time or generation of rhetorica utens over rhetorica
docens. The same doctrine is taught by Cicero: "But to my thinking the virtue in all the rules is, not that orators by following
them have won a reputation for eloquence, but that certain persons
have noted and collected the doings of men who were naturally elo-
quent: thus eloquence is not the offspring of the art, but the art
of eloquence...."[5]

3) In What the Rhetorical Method Should Consist

        Aristotle proceeds to develop the quid, first by a negative
treatment, then by a positive consideration. He does three things:
manifests the errors in the treatises written by his predecessors,
shows by a positive approach what should constitute the method,
and states the utility of such a method.

    a) A Negative Treatment:
        The Errors of Aristotle's Predecessors

        Aristotle begins with a history of the method in order better
to manifest the quid. This is an example of using history to ill-
uminate a question of properly doctrinal import. He says that
those who have written treatises on rhetoric have constructed only
a small part of the method. For proofs are the only true constituents of the method; all else is merely accessory. Now these
authors say nothing about enthymemes, which are the substance of
rhetorical persuasion, but deal principally with non-essentials.
The arousing of prejudice, pity, anger, and other passions has

nothing to do with the essential facts, but is merely a personal appeal to those judging the case.   A sign of the irrelevance of such procedure is that it is forbidden by law in well-governed states. If these laws were applied everywhere, such writers would be left with nothing to say.   Yet this is sound law and custom, and all men agree that it should be so.   For it is wrong to pervert the judge by moving him to anger, envy, or pity.   Aristotle likens this to warping a carpenter's rule before using it.   This is an apt comparison, because the judge is as a rule of justice. [6]   Now since passion can impede reason, it is possible to influence him in favor of one side or another by arousing his passions; but this is to put an obstacle in the way of the exercise of his function.

That passion can be detrimental is easily shown; for example, in anger there is a certain use of reason insofar as the angry man reasons that he must avenge an injury, yet his reasoning is imperfect, lacking determination and order.   Because of the velocity of its movement, anger excludes deliberation. [7]   In the Ethics, [8] Aristotle compares the angry man to hasty servants who start out on an errand before they have heard the entire command, and therefore make mistakes; and to dogs which bark as soon as they hear a knock at the door, before knowing whether it is friend or foe.

However, passion can either precede or follow judgment. If it precedes, it is an obstacle because it impedes deliberation, which is necessary for the formation of the judgment.   But if passion occurs after the judgment has been formed, it is a help rather than a hindrance.   Such passion is a sign of the motion of the will, which in its intensity, overflows into the inferior appetite.   It can also be an instrument aiding execution by enabling one to act more promptly and easily. [9]   For this reason, passion should not precede discourse, but rather, should be its effect.   Hence, Aristotle says that once the rhetorician has clearly stated the facts and evaluated them, then he must arouse the passions of the audience. [10]

The rôle of the litigant is merely to show whether or not a fact is so, whether it has or has not happened.   As to whether a thing is important or unimportant, just or unjust, the judge must not take advice from the litigants, but it is his duty to decide for himself all points which the law does not already specifically define for him.

It is of great importance that good laws should themselves determine as many points as possible and leave very few to the decision of the judges; and this for three reasons.   First, because law-making is restricted to one or to a few public personages having the whole people under their care, [11] and it is easier to find one or a few men who are wise and capable of legislating, than it is to find the large number which would be necessary to judge each particular case.

Secondly, laws are made after long deliberation, whereas court decisions must be given on short notice, a fact which makes it difficult for the judge to satisfy the claims of justice and expediency.

The third and most important reason is that the judgment of the legislator is not particular but universal and concerning future events; whereas the judge must decide actual, particular cases. Laws are universal propositions of the practical reason which are ordered to operation. They hold the same position with respect to operations as propositions of the speculative reason hold with respect to conclusions.[12] Any precept in regard to some particular work is devoid of the nature of law except insofar as it regards the common good.[13]

Since law bears not on the particular, but on the universal and future, it is free from passion. Because men's acts and choices are concerned with singulars, the appetite is affected in relation to the singular. Therefore, from the very fact that the sensitive appetite is a particular power, it has great influence in disposing man so that something seems to him desirable or undesirable in particular cases. For example, that which seems good to a man when angry no longer seems good to him when he is calm. Thus, the intellect is moved to judge in accordance with appetite, for according as a man is, such does the end seem to him.[14] Consequently, reason is said to govern the sensitive appetite with a political rule as opposed to a despotic rule, for the irascible and concupiscible powers can resist the commands of reason, just as free men can act counter to the commands of their ruler.[15] From this we can conclude that the more reason is liberated from passion, the more easily can it judge rightly.

Hence in law courts, where particular and actual issues are under consideration, the judges are often so influenced by feelings of friendship, hatred, or personal interest that they are no longer capable of discerning the truth adequately, and their judgment is obscured by personal pleasure or displeasure. For this reason, the judge should be allowed to decide as few things as possible-- only those particular facts which cannot be foreseen by the legislator, as for example, whether something has or has not happened.

If all this is true, it is evident that those who make rules about such matters, as what must be the contents of the introduction, or the narration, or any of the other divisions of a speech, are treating non-essentials as if they pertained to the method. For they are concerned not with proof, but only with putting the judge into a favorable frame of mind, and they completely ignore what is proper to the rhetorician, namely, the construction of enthymemes.

Consequently, although the method of deliberative and forensic rhetoric is the same, and although the former, being more directly concerned with the common good, is nobler and more befitting a statesman than the latter, which is limited to transactions between private individuals, these authors say nothing about deliberative rhetoric, but all devote themselves to writing treatises on how to plead in court. The reason for this is that in deliberative rhetoric there is less inducement to talk about non-essentials, because since it treats of issues which are of more general interest, there is less opportunity for unscrupulous practices. In a political debate, the man who forms a judgment makes a decision about his own vital interests--the good at stake, being a common good, belongs to him also. Thus, there is no need to prove anything except that the facts are in reality what the supporter of a measure maintains them to be. The fact that Aristotle's predecessors neglected this nobler branch of rhetoric, in which there is little chance of moving the judge, is a sign that their method consisted principally in a consideration of the passions, with moving the judge as the end in view.

On the contrary, in forensic rhetoric merely upholding the facts does not suffice; it is very useful to win over the listeners. For here it is other people's affairs that are to be decided; therefore, the judges, intent on their own satisfaction and listening with partiality, give in to the disputants instead of judging between them. Hence, as we have seen, in many states irrelevant speaking is forbidden in the law courts; but in the public assembly, those who have to form a judgment are themselves able to guard against it.

b) Positive Consideration

Aristotle then manifests in a common way in what the rhetorical method (rhetorica docens) should consist; a proper treatment is reserved for Chapter II. He states that it is now clear that this method, in its strict sense, is concerned with the modes of persuasion, i. e., with proofs. Here it is important to note that rhetorical persuasion is not convertible with persuasion in all its amplitude, but is restricted to persuasion in view of action for the common good. For rhetoric deals with political things, [16] and is therefore subordinated to politics, [17] which is concerned with the highest common good operable by man. [18]

Now it is evident that persuasion is a kind of demonstration, since we are most completely persuaded when we consider a thing to have been demonstrated. Here, by "demonstration" Aristotle does not mean the ratio propria as given in the Posterior Analytics, which is verified only in demonstration propter quid, but the ratio communis taken to include all kinds of proofs. Rhetorical demonstration consists principally in the enthymeme which is, in general, the most effective of the modes of persuasion. The term "enthymeme" (ἐνθύμημα) is derived from ἐνθυμεῖσθαι which means "to keep in mind, " "to consider"; and a rhetorical syllogism is so-called from the fact that only one of its propositions is expressed, whereas the other is merely understood or kept in the mind.

Hence, the enthymeme is nominally defined as "an argument consisting of only two propositions, an antecedent and its consequent;
a syllogism with one premiss omitted."[19]

Thus, the enthymeme is a kind of syllogism, and the consideration of every kind of syllogism pertains to logic--either to
logic as a whole, or to one of its parts. Since the end of logic
is to direct the act of reason, so that man may be able to proceed with order, facility, and without error,[20] it is concerned with
the act of reason as with its proper matter.[21] But the syllogism,
being a kind of discourse from the known to the unknown, is proper
to the third operation of the mind; consequently, it is evident that
logic must treat of every kind of syllogism. Aristotle distinguishes
between "logic as a whole" and "one of its parts," because the
syllogism can be considered either as to form alone, or as to both
matter and form. The study of the syllogism as to form, prescind-
ing from determinate matter, pertains to a part of logic, namely,
to the Prior Analytics. Since the principles laid down in this
treatise apply to all syllogisms regardless of their determinate
matter, this part of logic can be said to consider every kind of
syllogism.[22] If, however, we consider also the matter of the
syllogism, then different parts of logic are devoted to different
kinds: the Posterior Analytics, to the demonstrative syllogism
having necessary matter; the Topics and the Sophistics, to the dialectical syllogism, which has probable matter; and the Rhetoric,
to the enthymeme. Thus, if we consider the syllogism as to both
matter and form, the study of every kind of syllogism pertains to
the whole of logic.

It is to be noted that both "syllogism" and "logic" are understood in a broad sense. "Syllogism" is not restricted to the
true syllogism, i.e., to one having perfect syllogistic form, but
is taken to include the enthymeme, which is imperfect, and which
therefore can be called a syllogism only secundum quid. In the
same way, "logic" is taken to include all disciplines which direct
the act of reason, and therefore also rhetorica docens, whose
function it is to direct the act of reason in forming enthymemes.[23]

Some thought that even logic in the broad sense was concerned only with the true syllogism, thus determining the common
subject of logic from the principal subject. This position is un-
tenable because logic, being the mode of all science, must have a
subject equally applicable to them all. But the true syllogism requires a universal, and therefore cannot always be used, as is the
case in rhetorica utens.[24]

By comparing the enthymeme to the syllogism, Aristotle
relates the method of rhetoric fundamentally to logic. He who
possesses logic and is proficient in constructing syllogisms will
also be skillful in forming enthymemes, once he has learned what
the subject of the enthymeme is, and how the enthymeme differs
from the logical syllogism. Furthermore, although it is principally

ordered to science, logic must also consider probable knowledge,
for the true and the apparently true are apprehended by the same
faculty.   Men have a certain natural capacity for truth, and therefore usually do attain it. [25]   This applies to the probable also, for
the same power which enables us to arrive at truth, also enables
one to recognize the probable.

c) The Utility of the Rhetorical Method

Next, Aristotle gives four reasons why such a method is
useful:

1) The true and the just have a natural tendency to prevail
over their opposites; therefore, if decisions are not what they
should be, the defect must be due to the speakers themselves.
Rhetorica docens can remedy this.

2) In dealing with some audiences, not even the possession
of the most distinct knowledge will make it easy for us to persuade
them.   For argument based on such knowledge implies instruction,
and there are people whom one cannot instruct.   In fact, under
such circumstances, the use of distinct or scientific knowledge would
actually impede persuasion.   For although man is by nature proportionate to truth in a common way, this does not extend to particulars.   Consequently, confused knowledge is more certain than distinct knowledge, because its object is common, and therefore more
proportionate to our intellect, which proceeds from potency to act.
Because our intellect must operate in this fashion, we first know
things in a general way and under a certain confusion before knowing them distinctly; for confused knowledge is intermediate between
pure potency and perfect act.   It is important to note that confusion
is opposed not to certitude, but to distinctness.   For example, we
can know with certitude that man is animal, but this is confused
rather than distinct knowledge, for it is not a complete knowledge
of man up to his ultimate difference, since "animal" contains "rational" only in potency. [26]

Hence, the rhetorician must use as modes of persuasion
and argument, notions already possessed by all; as Aristotle states
also in the Topics, [27] where he speaks of the utility of dialect for
handling a popular audience: "[Dialectic] is useful because when
we have considered the opinions held by most people, we shall
meet them on the ground not of other people's convictions, but of
their own, while we shift the ground of any argument that they
appear to us to state unsoundly."

3) We must be able to employ persuasion, just as strict
reasoning can be employed, on opposite sides of a question, not
in order that we may in practice employ it in both ways (for we
must not make people believe what is wrong), but in order that we
may see clearly what the facts are, and that if another person argues unfairly, we on our part may be able to refute him.   Of the
arts, only rhetorica and dialectica utens draw opposite conclusions.

In commenting on Aristotle's Topics, St. Albert states that because dialectica docens enables us to find common appearances, it enables us to argue probably about any problem with ease from either side of a contradiction. [28]

Both of these arts draw opposite conclusions impartially; yet the facts do not lend themselves equally well to the contrary views. Rather, things that are true and things that are better are, by their very nature, almost always easier to prove and easier to believe.

4) It is absurd to hold that a man should be ashamed of being unable to defend himself by physical strength, but not of being unable to defend himself by speech and reason, when the use of speech is more proper to man than the use of his limbs.

If it is argued that one who uses such power of speech unjustly may do great harm, this is an objection which applies equally to all good things except virtue (for virtue, understood in its primary sense, i.e., moral virtue, by its very definition implies a perfecting of the agent and an assurance of good operation), [29] especially to those things which are most useful, such as strength, health, wealth, or military power. For as a man can confer the greatest benefit by using these properly, so can he inflict the greatest injuries by abusing them.

4) Résumé

It is clear then, that rhetorica utens does not deal with a particular genus of things, but that like dialectica utens, it is universal. It is also evident that it is useful. Furthermore, its function is not simply to succeed in persuading, but rather, to discover the means of persuasion available in each particular case.

The rhetorician does not always succeed in persuading, for there are three possible impediments: a bad case, perverse judges, and weakness of argument due to the contingency of the matter. Yet, if he operates well according to the principles of his art, we say that he has sufficiently attained his end, even should he fail to persuade. [30] For in any discipline we cannot seek more than its principles warrant. [31] In this, rhetorica utens resembles all the other arts. For example, the function of medicine is not simply to restore the patient to health, but to promote this end as far as possible; for even those who will never recover can be given proper treatment.

Moreover, it is evident that it pertains to rhetoric to discover the real and the apparent means of persuasion, just as it is the function of dialectic to discern the real and the apparent syllogism. This does not make the dialectician a sophist, for the sophist is defined not by his knowledge, but by his moral purpose--

he is morally perverse.   An argument can be sophistic without its
proponent's being a sophist.   Dialectic is ordered to truth; bad
intention is completely extrinsic to it.   Thus a man is a dialectician because of his knowledge or faculty; he is a sophist because
of his evil intention.[32]   However, in rhetoric there is no such
distinction, for the rhetorician may be denominated either from his
faculty, or from his intention.

        Aristotle brings his first chapter to a close with a state-
ment of what is to follow in the next chapter.   He says that we
shall now treat of the rhetorical method itself to see how we can
attain our goal.   But first, we must make a fresh start, and before going further, define rhetoric anew.

        In this chapter, Aristotle began with a quid nominis of
rhetorica utens, which gave us only a vague notion of its nature.
Next he proceeded to the an est of rhetorica docens, and finally,
by means of first a negative and then a positive approach, he en-
abled us to acquire further insight into what rhetoric is--principal-
ly, that the substance of the method consists in proofs.   However,
this does not as yet give us the distinct quid; it is still confused
and common knowledge.

        In Chapter II, Aristotle will incorporate our newly acquired
knowledge into a new definition, thus furnishing us a fresh point of
departure.   From there, he will continue in a proper way the positive treatment of the rhetorical method.

II. A PROPER TREATMENT OF THE RHETORICAL METHOD

        This section has two divisions: the quid rei of rhetorica
utens, and a consideration of the end of rhetoric.

1) The "Quid Rei" of "Rhetorica Utens"

        Aristotle begins by defining rhetoric as the faculty of dis-
covering, in any given case, the available means of persuasion.
Rhetoric is a faculty, because it has no determinate subject.   For
every art and science can instruct or persuade about its own particular subject: for instance, medicine deals with health and sick-
ness; geometry, with the properties of magnitudes; and arithmetic,
with numbers.   But rhetoric is the power of observing the means
of persuasion on any subject which presents itself, and this is why
we say that it is not concerned with any particular or definite
genus of things.

2) The End of Rhetoric: Persuasion

        This definition makes it clear that rhetorica utens aims at

effecting persuasion.[33] Now, persuasion implies the presentation
of an object as an operable good.[34] But the good is said in relation to appetite,[35] and furthermore, it is envisioned by the rhetorician as operable. Therefore, persuasion is not a purely speculative assent, but it also involves appetite, and is ordered to moving
the will.[36]

Because of this, it is of capital importance that the rhetorician should consider the dispositions of his audience; for according
as men are differently disposed, so will different things seem good
to them. Since the passions play an essential rôle in disposing
man, St. Thomas holds that rhetoric, unlike demonstration, is not
restricted to the domain of reason; but that in order to attain its
end, it must also arouse the passions of the audience.[37] It is
evident then, that persuasion involves two elements, one which is
appetitive, and the other which is properly rational.[38] The latter
consists in a partial inclination to reason to one side of a contradiction which is known as suspicion.[39]

Suspicion can be said to be a mean between doubt and opinion. It is opposed to doubt and resembles opinion, in that it involves inclination to one side of a contradiction. Yet, it differs
from opinion, inasmuch as this inclination is not total, and is therefore not a true adherence.[40] To make these differences more explicit: in doubt, the intellect is completely undetermined; for there
is no greater inclination to one side of a contradiction rather than
to the other. Opinion involves a total inclination, or a true adherence to one side of a contradiction which, however, does not
result in complete assent; for there remains a fear that the other
side may be true.[41] This adherence constitutes a determination of
reason, albeit incomplete, inasmuch as the inclination is totally to
one side.[42] But in suspicion, the inclination of reason is only pre-
dominantly, and not totally to one side of a contradiction.[43]

Thus, we can assign two reasons for the necessity of arousing the passions in rhetoric: the weakness of rhetorical argumentation, which renders it incapable of effecting a true assent of reason, and the fact that mere presentation of truth is insufficient to
move men to action. St. Augustine very aptly explains the latter
aspect:

> Verum quoniam plerumque stulti homines ad ea quae
> suadentur recte, utiliter et honeste, non ipsam sincerissi-
> mam quam rarus animus videt veritatem, sed proprios
> sensus consuetudinemque sectantur, oportebat eos non
> doceri solum quantum queunt sed saepe et maxime commo-
> veri. Hanc suam partem quae id ageret, necessitatis
> pleniorem quam puritatis, refertissimo gremio deliciarum,
> quas populo spargat, ut ad utilitatem suam dignetur adduci,
> vocavit rhetoricam.[44]

A further insight into the rôle played by the dispositions of the audience can be had by examining the words of Cicero:

> This indeed is the reason why, when setting about a
> hazardous and important case, in order to explore the
> feelings of the tribunal, I engage wholeheartedly in a
> consideration so careful, that I scent out with all possible
> keenness their thoughts, judgments, anticipations and
> wishes, and the direction in which they seem likely to be
> led away most easily by eloquence.... If however an
> arbitrator is neutral and free from predisposition, my
> task is harder, since everything has to be called forth
> by my speech, with no help from the listener's character.
> But so potent is that Eloquence, rightly styled by an ex-
> cellent poet, "soulbending sovereign of all things," that
> she can not only support the sinking and bend the upstand-
> ing, but, like a good and brave commander, can even
> make prisoner a resisting antagonist. [45]

Is this contrary, then, to the position maintained by Aristotle when he criticizes his predecessors? Not at all, for his
criticism is aimed at those who give no thought to argumentation,
but make rhetoric consist entirely or principally in moving the passions. That Aristotle does not underestimate the importance of the
dispositions of the audience is evident from the fact that he devotes
the greater part of Book II to a study of the various passions and
types of human character. Also, of the three modes of persuasion,
only the third is based on argumentative proof. The difference
lies in that Aristotle holds argumentation to be essential: "enthymemes ... are the substance of rhetorical persuasion";[46] arousing
the passions, though necessary, is only secondary. Hence, they
are not to be aroused at the outset, when they could impede judgment, but only in the epilogue. "Next, when the facts and their
importance are clearly understood, you must excite your hearers'
emotions."[47] By then, the rhetorician has proceeded as far as
possible in the line of argumentation, i.e., he has aroused suspicion. But because the matter is too contingent to merit assent,
he must bridge the gap by an appeal to the emotions.[48] Thus, the
foundation of judgment is laid by means of an exposition of the facts
of the case, but judgment is completed and assured through movement of the passions.

Once it has been understood that rhetoric is ordered to persuasion, we have the key to the entire rhetorical method. For the
end is the cause of causes,[49] inasmuch as all else is intended for
the sake of the end, and must therefore be proportionate to it.

NOTES

1.   Rhetoric, trans. W. Rhys Roberts, ed. Solmsen, N.Y., Ran-
        dom House, 1954; The Art of Rhetoric, trans. John Henry
        Freese, The Loeb Classical Library, Cambridge, Mass.,

Harvard University Press, 1939; Art Rhétorique, trans.
Jean Voilquin et Jean Capelle, Paris, Librairie Garnier,
1944.

2. The locutio exemplaris and the metaphor resemble each other
    and are opposed to analogy inasmuch as they are not new
    impositions of a word. However, they differ in that the
    metaphor implies a new and figurative sense, whereas the
    locutio exemplaris does not. In constructing a metaphor,
    a word which properly signifies a certain object is applied
    to something else bearing some resemblance to that object.
    But despite this resemblance, the word cannot properly sig-
    nify the new object; therefore, it must do so only in a figu-
    rative or improper sense. This figurative sense then be-
    comes the principle of manifesting a characteristic of the
    new object. Thus, the metaphor is a kind of discourse
    notable for its brevity, for in one word it signifies a thing
    and that to which the thing is compared. In the locutio
    exemplaris, however, there is no question of a new and im-
    proper sense, for it is not the application of a name to a
    new object. Rather, it is merely the comparison of an ob-
    ject relatively unknown, to another which is better known,
    in order to attain a more complete knowledge of the former.
    The principle of manifestation lies in the proper sense of
    the words used.

3. "Est autem quod dicimus methodum metaphorice: dicitur
    enim methodus brevis via, quae via est compendii, et
    vulgariter vocatur summa. Per similitudinem ergo trans-
    fertur ad istam scientiam proprie et artem: quia cum
    speculabilia et operabilia multa offerantur, sua multitudine
    et longitudine, distantiae quidem ipsorum dispendere faciunt,
    nisi per formam scientiae et artis ad compendium redigantur:
    et ab hae similitudine nomen methodi ad artem et scientiam
    transfertur" (St. Albert, in I Topicorum, Prooemium,
    cap. 2).

4. "Dialectica enim potest considerari secundum quod est docens,
    et secundum quod est utens. Secundum quidem quod est
    docens, habet considerationem de istis intentionibus, institu-
    ens modum, quo per eas procedi possit ad conclusiones in
    singulis scientiis probabiliter ostendendas; et hoc demonstra-
    tive facit, et secundum hoc est scientia. Utens vero est
    secundum quod modo adiuncto utitur ad concludendum aliquid
    probabiliter in singulis scientiis; et sic recedit a modo
    scientiae" (St. Thomas, in IV Metaphysicorum, lect. 4,
    edit. Marietti, n. 576). Cf. also St. Albert, in I Topicorum,
    Prooemium, cap. 1.

5. De Oratore, I, cap. 32, n. 146; trans. E. W. Sutton, The
    Loeb Classical Library, Cambridge, Mass., Harvard Univ.
    Press, 1942.

6. "...Sic cum debemus uti judice tanquam regula rectitudinis,
    non debemus illum ad hanc vel illam partem inflectere, ex-
    citando in eo iram, misericordiam, invidiam, etc...."
    (Sylvester Maurus, in I Rhetoricorum, cap. 1, a. 2, n. 5).

7. St. Thomas, in III Ethicorum, lect. 5, edit. Marietti, n. 442.
8. VII, chap. 6, 1149 a 25-31.
9. St. Thomas, Q. D. de Veritate, q. 26, a. 7, c. and ad 3; in
    IV Ethicorum, lect. 8, n. 805.
10. Rhetoric, III, chap. 19, 1419 b 24.
11. St. Thomas, Ia IIae, q. 90, a. 3.
12. Ibid., a. 1, ad 2.
13. Ibid., a. 2.
14. St. Thomas, Ia IIae, q. 9, a. 2, c. and ad 2.
15. "Invenitur enim inter partes hominis quod anima dominatur
    corpori, sed hoc est despotico principatu in quo servus in
    nullo potest resistere domino ... et hoc videmus in mem-
    bris corporis, scilicet manibus et pedibus quod statim sine
    contradictione ad imperium animae applicantur ad opus.
    Invenimus etiam quod intellectus seu ratio dominatur appe-
    titui, sed principatu politico et ragali qui est ad liberos,
    unde possunt in aliquibus contradicere: et similiter appeti-
    tus aliquando non sequitur rationem. Et hujusmodi diversi-
    tatis ratio est, quia corpus non potest moveri nisi ab anima,
    et ideo totaliter subjicitur ei; sed appetitus potest moveri
    non solum a ratione, sed etiam a sensu; et ideo non totali-
    ter subjicitur rationi" (St. Thomas, in I Politicorum, lect.
    3, Laval Univ. Edit., p. 22). Cf. also Ia IIae, q. 9, a. 2,
    ad 3; Ia Pars, q. 81, a. 3, ad 2.
16. St. Thomas, in I Ethicorum, lect. 3, n. 36.
17. Ibid., lect. 2, n. 28.
18. "Tertio possumus accipere dignitatem et ordinem politicae ad
    omnes alias scientias practicas. Est enim civitas princi-
    palissimum eorum quae humana ratione constitui possunt.
    Nam ad ipsam omnes communitates humanae referuntur.
    Rursumque omnia tota quae per artes mechanicas constitu-
    untur ex rebus in usum hominum venientibus, ad homines
    ordinantur, sicut ad finem. Si igitur principalior scientia
    est quae est de nobiliori et perfectiori, necesse est politi-
    cam inter omnes scientias practicas esse principaliorem et
    architectionicam omnium aliarum, utpote considerans ulti-
    mum et perfectum bonum in rebus humanis. Et propter hoc
    Philosophus dicit in fine decimi Ethicorum quod ad politica
    perficitur philosophia, quae est circa res humanas" (St.
    Thomas, in I Politicorum, Prologus).
19. Webster's New International Dictionary of the English Language,
    the word "enthymeme."
20. St. Thomas, in I Posteriorum Analyticorum, Prooemium, edit.
    Marietti, n. 1.
21. Ibid., n. 2.
22. "... Vel per dialecticam totam vel per aliquam ejus partem,
    puta per illam, quae traditur in libris Priorum, habemus
    facultatem conficiendi syllogismos universim et varias species
    syllogismorum...." (Sylvester Maurus, in I Rhetoricorum,
    cap. 1, a. 3, n. 10). Here "dialectic" means "logic":
    "... Nomine dialecticae intelligendo non solum Topicam,
    sed logicam universam, quae agit de omni syllogismo" (Ibid.).

"Secundum autem quod simpliciter dicitur simplex formale
a sua acceptum simplicitate formali, non tractat de syllogismo simpliciter tota logica, sed determinatur in uno
librorum ejus...." (St. Albert, in I Priorum Analyticorum,
tract. 1, cap. 1).

23. "... Logica generaliter dicta totum comprehendit trivium vel
quatrivium secundum Aristotelem.... Haec ergo comprehendit ... rhetoricam...." (St. Albert, in I Topicorum,
tract. 4, cap. 2).

24. "Inter species autem argumentationis praecipua est syllogismus. Propter quod quidam dixerunt quod logica tota est de
syllogismo et partibus syllogismi: determinantes commune
subjectum logicae secundum id quod est subjectum principale.
Non enim de omnibus fides esse poterit per syllogismum,
propter hoc quod discursus syllogisticus non est nisi ab universali universaliter accepto: quod in multis scientiis esse
non poterit, ut in rhetoricis. Propterea quod in illis prae-
cipue locales habitudines attenduntur, a quibus per enthy-
memata concluditur id quod quaesitum est. Cum igitur
logica, ut dicit Aristoteles, det omni scientiae modum dis-
serendi, et inveniendi, et dijudicandi quod quaesitum est:
oportet quod de tali sit ut de subjecto, quod omnibus in
omni aequaliter applicabile est.... Propter quod syllogismus commune subjectum logicae esse non potest" (St. Albert, De Praedicabilibus, tract. 1, cap. 4).

25. This statement must not be taken in an absolute way, for as
regards proper, scientific knowledge man is usually in
error. (Aristotle, On the Soul, III, chap. 3, 427 b 1; St.
Thomas, in III de Anima, lect. 4, edit. Marietti, n. 624).
It must be understood in its context, taking into consideration that this is a rhetorical treatise. Now, the matter of
rhetoric is common and concerned with civil things, and as
regards such communia man usually does arrive at truth.
That rhetorical matter is proportionate to the masses may
be seen from the fact that a rhetorical proposition is called
an opinion held by the common people: "In tertio autem
ordine est propositio opinabilis opinione plurimum non
sapientum: et argumentatio ex his composita vocatur ratio
vel argumentatio rhetorica" (St. Albert, in I Posteriorum
Analyticorum, tract. 1, cap. 2).

26. St. Thomas, in I Physicorum, lect. 1, edit. Marietti, n. 7;
in II Metaphysicorum, lect. 1, nn. 282, 285; Ia Pars, q. 85,
a. 3.

27. I, chap. 2, 101 a 30-34; trans. W. A. Pickard-Cambridge,
ed. McKeon, N.Y., Random House, 1941.

28. "... Hanc methodum ... (quae docet communia invenire) ...
conferens ad facile de proposito arguendum de utraque parte
contradictionis, valet ad exercitationes..." (in I Topicorum
tract. 1, cap. 5).

29. "... Virtutes sunt principia actionum quae non transeunt in
exteriorem materiam, sed manet in ipsis agentibus. Unde
tales actiones sunt perfectiones agentium. Et ideo bonum

harum actionum in ipsis agentibus consistit" (St. Thomas,
in II Ethic., lect. 4, n. 282).

"... Omnis virtus subiectum cuius est, facit bene habere,
et opus eius bene se habens ... secundum virtutem propriam
unaquaeque res et bona sit, et bene operetur" (Ibid., lect.
6, nn. 307-308).

"... Per virtutem aliquis non solum potest bene operari,
sed etiam bene operans: quia virtus inclinat ad bonam
operationem, sicut et natura" (Ibid., n. 316).

"... Virtus, ex ipsa ratione nominis, importat quamdam
perfectionem potentiae..." (St. Thomas, Ia IIae, q. 55, a. 2).

"... Virtus humana, quae est habitus operativus, est
bonus habitus, et boni operativus..." (Ibid., a. 3).

"Virtus autem humana ... secundum perfectam rationem
virtutis dicitur, quae requirit rectitudinem appetitus; huiusmodi enim virtus non solum facit facultatem bene agendi,
sed ipsum etiam usum boni operis causat. ... Constat
autem quod perfectum est principalius imperfecto. Et ideo
virtutes quae continent rectitudinem appetitus, dicuntur
principales. Huiusmodi autem sunt virtutes morales..."
(Ibid., q. 61, a. 1).

30. "Neque enim rhetoricus advocatus omnino et universaliter
persuadebit, impedimento triplici impeditus: malitia causae,
perversitate judicis, et debilitate allegationis suae.... Sed
si unusquisque ... ex contingentibus secundum suae artis
facultatem nihil omiserit, dicemus disciplinam et disciplina-
bilem finem habere sufficenter secundum artis contingentiam,
quamvis non semper habeat finem sufficenter in alio secundum effectum persuasionis..." (St. Albert, in I Topicorum, tract. 1, cap. 5).

31. "... Nemo quaerat in scientia quod ex principiis ejusdem non
poterat" (Ibid.).

32. "A sophista vero differt philosophus 'prohaeresi,' idest elec-
tione vel voluptate, idest desiderio vitae. Ad aliud enim
ordinat vitam suam et actiones philosophus et sophista.
Philosophus quidem ad sciendum veritatem; sophista vero
ad hoc quod videatur scire quamvis nesciat" (St. Thomas,
in IV Metaph., lect. 4, n. 575).

33. "... Per rhetoricam, quae componit ad persuadendum, ut sc.
supra dixit, quod non fuit intentionis quod sua praedicatio
niteretur philosophicis rationibus; ita nunc dicit non fuisse
suae intentionis niti rhetoricis persuasionibus (St. Thomas,
in I ad Corinthios, lect. 4, cap. 2).

34. "Per modum quidem persuasionis, sicut cum proponitur
aliquid virtuti cognoscitivae ut bonum" (St. Thomas, Q. D.
de Malo, q. 3, a. 4).

"Nulla igitur substantia creata potest movere voluntatem
nisi mediante bono intellecto. Hoc autem est inquantum
manifestat ei aliquid esse bonum ad agendum: quod est
persuadere. Nulla igitur substantia creata potest agere in
voluntatem, vel esse causa electionis nostrae, nisi per
modum persuadentis" (St. Thomas, Summa Contra Gentiles,

III, cap. 88).

"Tertio modo, ille qui persuadet objectum propositum
habere rationem boni: quia et hic aliqualiter proponit
proprium objectum voluntati, quod est rationis bonum vel
apparens" (St. Thomas, Ia IIae, q. 80, a. 1).

35. "Ex parte quidem obiecti, movet voluntatem et ipsum bonum
quod est voluntatis obiectum, sicut appetibile movet appetitum; et ille qui demonstrat obiectum, puta qui demonstrat
aliquid esse bonum. Sed sicut supra dictum est, alia
quidem bona aliqualiter inclinant voluntatem; sed nihil sufficienter movet voluntatem, nisi bonum universale quod est
Deus.... Angelus ergo non sufficienter movet voluntatem
neque ut obiectum, neque ut ostendens obiectum. Sed inclinat eam, ut amabile quoddam, et ut manifestans aliqua
bona creata ordinata in Dei bonitatem. Et per hoc inclinare
potest ad amorem creaturae vel Dei, per modum suadentis"
(St. Thomas, Ia Pars, q. 106, a. 2).

36. "... Voluntas ad aliquid inclinari dicitur dupliciter: uno
modo ab exteriori; alio modo ab interiori. Ab exteriori
quidem, sicut ab obiecto apprehenso; nam bonum appre-
hensum movere dicitur voluntatem; et per hunc modum dicitur movere consilians vel suadens, in quantum scilicet facit
apparere aliquod esse bonum.... Obiectum non ex necessitate movet voluntatem; et ideo nulla persuasio ex necessitate
movet hominem ad agendum" (St. Thomas, De Malo, q. 3,
a. 3).

"Et mediante hoc obiecto potest aliqua creatura inclinare
aliquatenus voluntatem, non tamen necessario immutare;
sicut patet cum aliquis persuadet alicui aliquid faciendum
proponendo ei eius utilitatem et honestatem; tamen in po-
testate voluntatis est ut illud acceptet vel non acceptet, eo
quod non est naturaliter determinata ad id" (St. Thomas,
Q. D. de Veritate, q. 22, a. 9).

37. "Cuius ratio est, quia consideratio huius libi directe ordinatur
ad scientiam demonstrativam, in qua animus hominis per
rationem inducitur ad consentiendum vero ex his quae sunt
propria rei; et ideo demonstrator non utitur ad suum finem
nisi enunciativis orationibus, significantibus res secundum
quod earum veritas est in anima. Sed rhetor et poeta in-
ducunt ad assentiendum ei quod intendunt, non solum per ea
quae sunt propria rei, sed etiam per dispositiones audientis.
Unde rhetores et poeta plerumque movere auditores nituntur
provocando eos ad aliquas passiones, ut Philosophus dicit in
sua Rhetorica" (St. Thomas, in I Peri Hermeneias, lect. 7,
edit. Marietti, n. 87).

38. "Unde secundum quod aliquis est causa quod aliquid appre-
hendatur ut bonum ad appetendum, secundum hoc movet
voluntatem. Et sic solus Deus efficaciter potest movere
voluntatem; angelus autem et homo per modum suadentis, ut
supra dictum est. Sed praeter hunc modum, etiam aliter
movetur in hominibus voluntas ab exteriori, scilicet ex pas-
sione existente circa appetitum sensitivum; sicut ex concu-

piscentia vel ira inclinatur voluntas ad aliquid volendum.
Et sic etiam angeli, inquantum possunt concitare huiusmodi
passiones, possunt voluntatem movere. Non tamen ex
necessitate quia voluntas semper remanet libera ad consentiendum vel resistendum passioni" (St. Thomas, Ia Pars,
q. 111, a. 2, c).

"Dicitur tamen diabolus incensor cogitationum, inquantum
incitat ad cogitandum, vel ad appetendum cogitata, per
modum persuadentis, vel passionem concitantis" (Ibid., ad
2).

39.   We have thought it best to use the English word "suspicion"
to translate the Latin suspicio. However, a few precisions
must be made to clarify its meaning in this context. The
first meaning of "suspicion" is "... imagination or apprehension of something wrong or hurtful, without proof, or on
slight evidence...." (Webster's New International Dictionary
of the English Language, the word "suspicion"). But suspicion, as an effect produced by rhetorical argumentation,
does not necessarily imply "something wrong or hurtful."
Rather, it should be understood in the sense in which it is
synonymous with "surmise" and "conjecture." The second
meaning given for "surmise" is "suspicion"; the third meaning is "a thought or idea based on scanty evidence; a conjecture; a random conclusion..." (Ibid., the word "surmise").
"Conjecture" is defined as "... to form opinions concerning,
on grounds confessedly insufficient to certain conclusion";
and "suspect" is given as a synonym (Ibid., the word "conjecture").

40.   "Quandoque vero, non fit complete fides vel opinio, sed suspicio quaedam, quia non totaliter declinatur ad unam partem
contradictionis, licet magis inclinetur in hanc quam in illam.
Et ad hoc ordinatur Rhetorica" (St. Thomas, in I Posteriorum Analyticorum, Prooemium, edit. Marietti, n. 6).

41.   "Quandoque vero intellectus inclinatur magis ad unum quam
ad alterum; sed tamen illud inclinans non sufficienter movet
intellectum ad hoc quod determinet ipsum in unam partium
totaliter; unde accipit quidem unam partem, tamen semper
dubitat de opposita. Et haec est dispositio opinantis, qui
accipit unam partem contradictionis cum formidine alterius
(St. Thomas, De Veritate, q. 14, a. 1).

42.   "... Quandoque quidem etsi non fiat scientia, fit tamen fides
vel opinio propter probabilitatem propositionum, ex quibus
proceditur; quia ratio totaliter declinat in unam partem contradictionis, licet cum formidine alterius, et ad hoc ordinatur Topica sive Dialectica" (St. Thomas, in I Post. Anal.,
Prooemium, n. 6).

"Licet opinans non sit certus, tamen iam determinavit se
ad unum..." (St. Thomas, in VI Ethicorum, lect. 8, edit.
Marietti, n. 1221).

"Et dicit, quod omne illud de quo habetur opinio, iam
est determinatum quantum ad opinantem, licet non sit determinatum quantum ad rei veritatem" (Ibid., n. 1226).

43. "Quidam vero actus intellectus habent quidem cogitationem in-
     formem absque firma assensione: sive in neutram partem
     declinent, sicut accidit dubitanti; sive in unam partem magis
     declinent sed tenentur aliquo levi signo, sicut accidit sus-
     picanti; sive uni parti adhaereant, tamen cum formidine al-
     teris, quod accidit opinanti" (St. Thomas, IIa IIae, q. 2,
     a. 1).
44. De Ordine, II, cap. 13, n. 38: Oeuires de saint Augustin, éd.
     Bénédictine, Paris Desclée de Brouwer, 1948, Vol. IV.
45. Orator, II, cap. 44, n. 186; trans. H. M. Hubbell, The Loeb
     Classical Library, Cambridge, Mass., Harvard Univ. Press,
     1939.
46. Rhetoric, I, chap. 1, 1354 a 14.
47. Aristotle, Rhetoric, III, chap. 18, 1419 b 24, trans. W. Rhys
     Roberts, ed. Solmsen, N. Y., Random House, 1954.
48. "The emotions are all those feelings that so change men as to
     affect their judgments, and that are also attended by pain or
     pleasure" (Ibid., II, chap. 1, 1378 a 20).
49. St. Thomas, in V. Metaphysicorum, lect. 3, n. 782.

4. SOME ANTISTROPHES TO THE RHETORIC*

by Robert Price

Aristotle opens his account of the art of rhetoric with the claim that it is an antistrophe to dialectic.[1] On the assumption that this metaphor has the choral ode as its source we must understand him to be maintaining that these arts are formally or structurally similar despite some variation in detail or in specific subject matter. We might therefore expect him to make out his claim by pointing to the formal similarities between the two arts. That he seems to point to material similarities here and afterwards[2] when he informs us that "both have to do with matters that are in a manner within the cognizance of all men and not confined to any special science"[3] need not dissuade us from this view. The balance of the section makes clear that our attention is to center on the manner in which all men deal with these matters "for all ... endeavor to criticize or uphold an argument." Furthermore, they sometimes do so "with a familiarity arising from habit" and so it is possible for us to make our way (hodopoiein) in "investigating the cause" (ten aitian theorein) of their doing so.[4] The work of these arts, then, lies in the fact that they are the (efficient) cause operative in argument and so "proofs [pisteis] are the only things in (Rhetoric) that come within the province of the art; everything else is merely accessory."[5] Aristotle is still more explicit later when he locates the positive likeness between Rhetoric and Dialectic in the fact that both are "faculties for furnishing arguments [logoi]."[6]

This of course fits in well with Aristotle's general characterization of the arts. At VI, 4, of the Ethics we find:

> Now architectural skill, for instance, is an art, and it is also a rational quality [hexis] concerned with making [poietike]; nor is there any art which is not such.... All art deals with bringing something into existence [peri genesin]; and to pursue an art means to study [theorein] how to bring into existence a thing ... the efficient cause of which lies in the maker and not in the thing made....

*Reprinted by permission of the author and publisher from Philosophy and Rhetoric 1 (1968), 145-164.

The peculiarity of our antistrophic arts is merely that the things made are logoi, in particular reasons (sullogismoi) and inductions (epagogai).[7] What these various logoi have in common is that each produces in the hearer (who may also be the speaker) a certain conviction; indeed it is in roughly this way that Aristotle defines sullogismos on three separate occasions:

> Sullogismos is a logos in which, certain things having been laid down, something other than these necessarily results through [dia] them. [8]

Rhetoric and Dialectic are antistrophic arts because both share the structure of such arts as are concerned with the production of certain logoi useful for certain purposes. The study of these arts will then consist in theorizing about the objects made as well as about the tasks for which they are the appropriate instruments. Although the logoi, the instruments fashioned, are to be at the center of attention we may expect attention to shift from art to objects to task precisely because this progression is that which is normally encountered in process; it is after all the progression from efficient cause to ousia (substance) to final cause (telos). Although these objects can be examined in a quasi-scientific manner we will need throughout to make such qualifications as stem from the fact that we will here be dealing with artifacts and so with objects whose efficient cause and telos lie outside themselves.

There are of course a number of further arts which share this structure and so may be thought of as antistrophes to Rhetoric on the same grounds. The most striking case is Demonstration;[9] Deliberation, although no treatise is devoted to it, is another case; so, too, is Evaluation which I will distinguish from Deliberation below; the last case which I will discuss is Recollection whose candidacy depends upon a single hint from Aristotle.[10] Before I turn to a detailed discussion of these arts and the casual processes into which they enter I want to make clear why I wish to discuss the Rhetoric in this context.

1. The Place of the Rhetoric in the Corpus

There is a tendency in the literature to regard the Rhetoric as a "curious jumble of literary criticism with second rate logic, ethics, politics, and jurisprudence."[11] When we do so the Rhetoric is no longer thought of as a parallel treatise to the Topics and Analytics as I have implied but is instead a (peculiar) application of these works such that the rhetorical syllogism, for example, stands to the syllogism proper as (defective) practical argumentation to (perfected) theoretical argumentation. Much of this attitude is reflected in Bekker's 1831 arrangement of the corpus; whether the arrangement is related to the attitude as efficient or final cause I do not know. His principle of arrangement was, of course, Aristotle's division of the arts and sciences into theoretical, practical, and productive, supplemented for the theoretical sciences by the material hierarchy of Metaphysics Zeta[12] and for the practical sciences by their architectonic. In addition the works known at least since Alexander Aphrodisias as the Organon were grouped at the front, ostensibly because they had no subject matter. The effective result, which did not reflect the earliest tradition, [13] was to place the principal antistrophic treatises at opposite ends of a corpus arranged in part in terms of the generality and presumptive philosophical significance of its subject matter.

An important by-product is the tendency to detach the Analytics, the "logical" writings, [14] from the treatment of the productive arts and so to emphasize what was to become formal logic to the neglect of those aspects of the syllogism which depend on its being a logos produced in process. Certainly Aristotle never forgets these aspects. He can, for example, summarize the more "formal" sections of the Prior Analytics as having theorized about "coming-into-being" (genesis) of syllogisms and introduce what follows with the remark that "we ought ... also to have the capacity [dunamis] to make them [poiein]."[15] Since it is just these aspects of the syllogism which are useful in understanding Aristotle's procedure in the Rhetoric I will in the following section return to the syllogism in process in order later to emphasize the parallel nature of the Rhetoric and the Analytics.

What we have in effect are a number of sister arts concerned with the production of logoi each of which makes use of some counterpart of the syllogism of the Analytics. None of them is an application of that work; rather all are applications of the lost work on methodology.[16] Such differences as are present in the purposes of the various arts influence the aspects of the syllogism under discussion but none of the treatises is a treatise on syllogism per se; rather all the arts count syllogisms among their instruments and so all the handbooks study them. When we view Rhetoric in this light we will find that, instead of it being the "curious jumble" in which the remaining arts are applied, it is of central interest because it contains the more interesting features of all the arts. Aristotle would not have inferred from the absence of complexity in some of the antistrophic arts that he was in the presence of the exemplar from which Rhetoric was to be fashioned; neither should we.

2. Syllogisms in Process

The syllogism is not the only logos produced in process but it is the one to which Aristotle most frequently returns and the one (together with induction) which he cites when comparing Rhetoric and Dialectic.[17] In this section I will give an account of the causal processes underlying its use in Demonstration as Aristotle presents the matter in the Prior Analytics; this is of course not an account of the syllogism but of one of its varieties because the

Prior Analytics is not about syllogistic but about demonstration.
The process is, however, both fairly typical and frequently misunderstood; so it provides a useful beginning to a survey of the
antistrophic arts.   The scope of this essay will not permit much
defense of the interpretation offered.

The first thing to note about the demonstrative syllogism is
that Aristotle does not treat it as it might occur in a scientific
debate or even an instructional context although it could no doubt
be adapted to such contexts.   It is instead described in terms of a
single individual's search for scientific knowledge; accordingly, as
is markedly not the case in the Rhetoric and Dialectic, all the
elements occur within a single mind.   What happens within that
mind is that the investigator forms, presumably from his own observations, a certain belief as to how things are, and desires to
know that this is the case.   Suppose he believes that A belongs to
all C (i.e., that all C is A).   He will then attempt to make a
syllogism which will yield the knowledge that A belongs to all C.
He crafts this syllogism by finding a middle, say B, such that he
knows that A belongs to all B and knows that B belongs to all C.
These latter bits of knowledge will be the results either of previous acts of the same sort or of previous epagogai (inductions) of
the sort discussed in the Posterior Analytics.   When he has lo-
cated two such premisses they in him combine and the resultant
demonstrative syllogism, demonstrative because the premises are
known, brings-into-being the knowledge that A belongs to all C.
In summary he obtains the knowledge that A belongs to all C by
making in himself the logos which produces that knowledge in him
out of (psychological?) necessity.   This logos and not some complex implication or inference is what Aristotle for the most part
and I throughout count as the (demonstrative) syllogism.   The
logos might, for example, be

A belongs to all B and B belongs to all C.

In effect the syllogism is to its conclusion as the speech is to the
audience's response.

With this paradigm at hand we can now describe the causal
processes which underlie all the antistrophic arts.   Aristotle himself gives a general description of such a process (with a different
art in mind) in the Physics:

> Why does he exercise, we ask.   And the answer because
> he thinks it good for his health satisfies us.   And there
> are all the intermediary agents which are set in motion
> by the primary agent and make for the goal as means to
> the end.   Such are the reduction of superfluous flesh and
> purgation, or drugs and surgical tools, as means to
> health.   For both action and tools may be the means
> through which the efficient cause reaches the end aimed
> at.[18]

What is implicit here and elsewhere is a causal chain which
reaches back from the end, or final cause, of an activity through
the arts which provide the means to the primary agent who desires the end. In our case the scientist's telos is knowledge, the
remote efficient cause his desire for that knowledge, and the proximate efficient cause, the means, which he employs, is the syllogism which in turn is furnished by him as user of the art of Demonstration which in its turn is an intermediate efficient cause. In
brief his desire causes him to engage in Demonstration which
causes him to make the syllogism which is the efficient cause of
the knowledge which is what he desired in the first place.

Note here that if we could distinguish an Art of Syllogistic
from an Art of Demonstration the latter would be architectonic to
the former because the "[demonstrator] knows what are the distinctive characteristics of the [syllogism] as such--that is to say, its
form,--and gives his orders accordingly; while what the other
knows is out of what [terms or premisses] and by what manipula-
tions the [syllogism] is produced."[19] This relationship between
the architectonic art, the user's art, and the subsidiary or manufacturer's art will reappear in our discussion. Most frequently
the antistrophic arts will be the manufacturing art, and ethics and
politics the user's art,[20] although the antistrophic arts themselves
sometimes call upon ethics and politics for their materials. Whatever may be the particular architectonic relationship the sequence
in process will be made up of an end laid down and a series of
means, among them a logos, provided by the subsidiary arts.

We have then a clear progression from efficient to final
cause; the logoi produced (here the demonstrative syllogism) stand
as the quasi-substance at the center of the analysis; the effect
produced (here the conclusion of the demonstrative syllogism)
stands as the proximate final cause; and the remote efficient and
final causes are supplied by the art which is architectonic to the
antistrophic art in the particular application. Since we do not have
proper substances or even artifacts here it is of course possible
to locate that which is to be explained somewhat further along in
the process, e.g., at the conclusion. Aristotle seems to do so in
the Posterior Analytics when he enumerates four kinds of causes:

> There are four kinds of cause: the essence, the neces-
> sitating conditions [to tinon onton anangke tout' einai],
> the efficient cause which started the process, and the
> final cause.[21]

If we apply this division of causes to the syllogism the necessitat-
ing condition[22] can only be the premisses combined, which in turn
are efficient cause of the conclusion.[23]

To complete this causal account we need only give a brief
account of the formal and material causes operative in the antistrophic arts: I will once again use the relatively simple case of

the demonstrative syllogism as my example. Here the situation is
somewhat confused by a passage in the Physics which has often
been taken to assert that the premisses are the material cause and
the conclusion the formal cause, a claim which suggests that Aristotle pays little heed to the temporal process so far described.
The passage reads:

> For letters are the causes of syllables, and the material
> is the cause of the manufactured articles, and the fire
> and the like are the causes of physical bodies, and the
> parts are causes of the whole, and the premisses are
> causes of the conclusion [sumperasmatos] in the sense of
> that out of which [to ex hou] these respectively are made;
> but of these some are causes in the sense of substratum
> (e.g., the parts stand in this relationship to the whole),
> and others in the sense of essence--the whole or the
> synthesis or the form. 24

Let me say first of all that it is the premisses taken separately
which are the material cause. The matter of the syllogism should
be the parts of which the whole is made and into which it passes
away; this cannot be the premisses taken together but must be the
premisses taken separately. One clear way in which syllogisms
pass away is after all by decomposition into their parts as when
the beginning student in mathematics or the drunkard now sees the
proof and now doesn't, now sees how the premisses hang together
and now sees them only separately. Ethics VII, 3, after discussing
the ways in which we sometimes have one premiss only potentially
(in the practical syllogism) and so cannot combine the two, makes
the point:

> ... when a single [mia] opinion results from the two
> [premisses] the soul must in the case [of the demonstra-
> tive syllogism] affirm the conclusion, while in the case
> of opinions concerned with production it must immediately
> act.

The same point is made in the Prior Analytics:

> Nothing prevents a man who knows both that A belongs
> to the whole of B, and that B again belongs to C, think-
> ing that A does not belong to C, e.g., knowing that
> every mule is sterile, and that this is a mule, and think-
> ing that this animal is with foal: for he does not know
> that A belongs to C unless he considers the two together
> [me sunteoron to kath' hekateron.]25

The relation of the premisses to the syllogism is as part to whole,
as matter to form, in somewhat the same way in which the finger
and liver are parts of man or, better, the blade and handle are
parts of a cutting instrument. When separate they are the matter;
when together they are the man or cutting instrument. What is

peculiar about premisses is that being only ousia-like in character
they may be assembled, disassembled, and reassembled, without
loss of potency. [26]

     I should add that Aristotle does not refer to the conclusion
as whole or form here (assuming that sumperasma means conclusion in this context) because he counts it as the formal cause.
The formal cause of the syllable was not the syllable; rather the
whole there was just the quasi-ousia under study; and the whole in
the present case is but the premisses combined, referred to, as
is natural with a tool, by means of that which they were made to
produce, in much the same way as I referred to the knife by its
purpose in the previous example.   There is no reason to doubt
that Aristotle accepts his standard view of the formal cause in art,
i. e., counts as formal cause the art of demonstration.   The only
plausible alternative would be to take his use of schema as suggesting that the arrangement of terms within the logos is to be the
formal cause.

     We have now at hand the means to box the syllogism's
causal compass and so to provide a paradigm for the analysis of
the logoi produced by the various antistrophic arts within process.
Basically we have a logos, either a string of words or the thoughts
it reflects, as the central entity made: its matter is the logoi, or
thoughts, of which it is composed; its form is its scheme or the
art which produces it; its proximate efficient cause the art in the
possession of its manufacturer; its more remote efficient cause the
desire for the conclusion or outcome for which it is produced; its
final cause the conclusion or outcome of which it in turn is the
efficient cause; its remote final cause the goal of the architectonic
art which invokes it.   That the analysis of the logos can be conducted in this fashion is indicative of the degree to which it falls
between art and nature.   The briefest way of expressing this point,
and the reason why Aristotle uses the language of nature as well
as of art in his description, is to note that the fashioning of the
syllogism is a matter of art but what the premisses do when combined is a matter of nature.   That is why we investigate how to
make (poiein) syllogisms but when A belongs to all B and B belongs
to all C a syllogism will come-into-being (genesei).

3.   The First Antistrophe: Deliberation

     The first antistrophe to Rhetoric which I will describe is
Deliberation.   Although Aristotle does not explicitly so identify it--
he does not even call it an art--it shares a number of features
with Rhetoric which are present in no other antistrophe.   Of these
the principal feature is that the premisses and conclusion of the
deliberative syllogism need not be explicitly stated.   To see why
this is so, and to locate some of the differences between Deliberation, Demonstration, and Rhetoric, requires a brief outline of the
causal context in which this feature arises.   Two rather lengthy

passages from Aristotle provide the necessary detail:

> Does goodness decide the end or the means to it? Well,
> our position is that it decides the aim because this is not
> a matter of logical inference [syllogism] or rational prin-
> ciple [logos] but in fact this must be assumed as a start-
> ing point. For a doctor does not consider whether his
> patient ought to be healthy or not, but whether he ought
> to take walking exercise or not, ... and similarly no
> other art either deliberates about its end. For as in the
> theoretic sciences the assumptions are primary principles
> (i. e. reached by induction) so in the productive sciences
> the end is a starting point and assumption.... There-
> fore the end is the starting point of the process of thought,
> but the conclusion of the process of thought is the start-
> ing point of the action.
>
> Eudemian Ethics 1227^b

> But why is it that thought sometimes results in action
> and sometimes does not? Apparently the same thing
> happens as when one thinks and forms an inference about
> immovable objects. But in the latter case the end is
> speculation (for when you have conceived the two premisses
> you immediately conceive and infer the conclusion); but in
> the former case the conclusion conceived and drawn from
> the two premisses becomes the action. For example
> when you conceive that every man ought to walk and that
> you yourself are a man, you immediately walk.... Again,
> I need a covering, and a cloak is a covering, I need a
> cloak. What I need I ought to make; I need a cloak, I
> ought to make a cloak. And the conclusion "I ought to
> make a cloak" is an action. The action results from the
> beginning of the train of thought.... That the action is
> the conclusion is quite clear; but the premisses which
> lead to the doing of something are of two kinds through
> the good and through the possible.

> And as those sometimes do who are eliciting conclu-
> sions by questioning, so here the mind does not stop and
> consider at all one of the two premisses, namely the ob-
> vious one; for example if walking is good for a man one
> does not waste time over the premiss "I am myself a
> man." Hence such things as we do without calculation
> [logidzesthai], we do quickly. For when a man acts for
> the object which he has in view from either perception
> or imagination or thought, he immediately does what he
> desires; the carrying out of his desire takes the place of
> inquiry or of thought. My appetite says, I must drink;
> this is drink says sensation or imagination or thought,
> and one immediately drinks.
>
> De Motu Animalium, 701^a

A number of things need to be noticed here.   (1) One of the premisses of action comes from desire or the good; this may be
reached or produced in thought through induction; it may also simply be there as it always is in animals in the form of desire; in
effect Aristotle will speak of syllogism here even when we have
no more than what some would call a "preconscious" or "uncon-
scious" motive.   (2) The second premiss (the minor in traditional
terminology) comes from perception or intellect; these are the
ranges of faculties[27] involved in induction; and here too the result
of an induction need not be "consciously" expressed--"the mind
does not stop at all and consider the obvious premiss."   (3) All
that is necessary for this syllogism to come-into-being is that the
mind receive at some level the stamp of desire associated with the
major and the stamp of information associated with perception and
then that it do that which it does at once--"make the two into one."
This last act or constructed object is the syllogism and the end of
this process of thought is action; no "mental" conclusion need be
drawn at all.   (4) Note also the parallels Aristotle draws with the
theoretical syllogism; there both premisses are formed by percep-
tion-intellect through induction, the two are combined, and the end
of the process is the reasoned fact.

It is clear, too, that Aristotle here describes deliberation
in terms appropriate to natural processes.   Indeed in its context
the passage from De Motu Animalium is just Aristotle's explanation of how the soul moves the body.   Aristotle gives the remote
final cause--the goal of the action; he gives the remote efficient
cause--the goal acting as desire, he gives the proximate final
cause--the action; and he gives the proximate efficient cause--the
inductions, or perhaps, although implicitly, the art of deliberation.
And at the center of the analysis is the produced ousia-like entity,
the practical syllogism.

What is not present in this passage or in any other in which
Aristotle describes the practical syllogism is even more important:
(1) There is no attempt to reduce the practical syllogism to the
demonstrative syllogism by exhibiting it as some mood or figure
(to use later terminology) of that logos.   That this cannot be done
has frequently been a matter of despair for later logicians.   Whether Aristotle had a clear enough grasp of the matter to see that it
could not be done is uncertain; that he saw no need to do it is however still another indication that he did not regard Deliberation as
an application of the syllogistic of the Prior Analytics but rather
as a parallel art.   (2) There is no hint that the practical syllogism
is in any way defective or inferior because its conclusions and
more obvious premisses are unexpressed; indeed, because the conclusion is an action, it is an essential feature of the art of deliberation that its conclusions sometimes remain unspoken.

We have then an antistrophic art, a faculty for furnishing
logoi, whose concern is in part the production of logoi which bring
something else into being, here actions.   The art itself is somewhat

different from that of Demonstration and Rhetoric because of the
purposes for which it is enlisted.   I will close discussion of it by
noting similarities and differences with Demonstration to the extent
that these involve syllogistic.   Similarities: (1) Everything occurs
within a single mind.   (2) The faculties which yield the premisses
of Demonstration yield some of the premisses of Deliberation.
Differences: (1) In Demonstration the object is to discover the
grounds (cause, middle term, or premisses) of a given fact and so
to create premisses which will yield a given conclusion; in Deliberation the object is to determine what to do and so to discover the
conclusion which follows from premisses ready at hand if not always under attention.   (2) The conclusions and premisses of Deliberation need not always be attended to and they need not be
necessary.

4.   The Second Antistrophe: Evaluation

        This antistrophe is nowhere discussed by Aristotle although
the third book of the Nicomachean Ethics appears to presuppose it;
I include it because it is a reworking of the materials of Deliberation in a manner nearer to that of both Rhetoric and Demonstration.
Suppose we wish to determine whether a person who commits a particular act is to be praised or blamed.   A part of our problem is
to determine the principle (if any) under which he acted.   What we
do is to begin with that act as conclusion and search for a middle
term which would in the circumstances produce that act; the middle
term is then the principle under which he acted.   E.g., a man is
seen to obtain a cloak; so we entertain the premisses "He needs
a covering and a cloak is a covering"; we then see that these premisses produce that action and so have uncovered a middle (the
need for covering) which could have produced that action.   Much as
the demonstrative syllogism moves from a fact to premisses which
provide the reasons for the fact and so establish it as knowledge,
we move from an act to premisses which provide perhaps the reasons for the act and so enable us to praise or blame.   We do not
of course know that this reason was his reason, nor even, when
we do what is known as rationalizing, that it was our reason.

        There is presumably no reason why minor or even conclu-
sion cannot go unstated here as in the normal Deliberative syllogism; both Enthymeme and Example are as appropriate here as in
the rhetorical situation.   The particular interest of the situation
lies in the fact that we are here converting a form of argument to
a different causal context than that in which we originally found it.
I count this as Aristotle's standard move throughout the antistrophic
treatises; we do not have an application of the Deliberative syllogism but rather a further use which depends in part on the features
which made possible the application in which we found it.   Clearly
the situation which yields the evaluative syllogism is typical of
many rhetorical situations.   The rhetor knows what has been done,
or knows what he would have us do; his problem is to find reasons

which we will accept as compelling.

5.   The Third Antistrophe: Recollection

The claim that Recollection is an antistrophic art depends
on a single passage in the Parva Naturalia:

> ... none of the known animals can recollect except man.
> This is because recollecting is, as it were, a kind of in-
> ference [sullogismos]; for when a man is recollecting he
> infers that he has seen or heard or experienced some-
> thing of the sort before, and the process is a kind of
> search [dzetesis]. This power can only belong by nature
> to such animals as have the faculty of deliberation; for
> deliberation too is a kind of inference [sullogismos].
>   "On Memory and Recollection, " 2, 453a10

His earlier description of this process makes clear why this language is appropriate.   Like any kind of syllogizing recollecting consists in locating a logos or (as in Deliberation and Rhetoric) the
corresponding perception which is naturally succeeded by one which
we wish to have brought into being.   Here Aristotle suggests that
the succession may be of necessity (as when we recollect the conclusion of a mathematical proof by beginning with the premisses)
or by habit (ethos) (as when we recollect a line of a poem by beginning again).   Whatever may be the connection between the various thoughts or perceptions, however, Aristotle's notion is that we
recollect by entering into a chain of thoughts somehow connected
and follow through on them until we reach the desired thought; i. e. ,
the one we wished to recollect.   The process here is rather like
Demonstration and Evaluation; we begin with a characterized conclusion and search for a premiss (the starting point of a chain)
which will re-produce that conclusion in the desired way; here with
an indication that it is a re-experience.

The interesting thing here is that that this "search for a
mental picture" is characterized as syllogistic despite the fact that
the connections between the terms are most typically those of as-
sociational psychology (contrariety is the only Aristotelean connection not in the Humean canon.)   Although I will not stop to box the
causal compass in this case, Aristotle's language makes clear here
as elsewhere that this syllogistic art makes basic use of causal
processes.   I note in this connection that chains of recollection are
likened to chains of temper and fear in that either, once started up,
is not happily interfered with. 28   Still more convincing is the following passage:

> Dwarfish people and those who have large upper extremi-
> ties have poorer memories than their opposites, because
> they carry a great weight on their organ of perception,
> and their impulses cannot, from the first, keep their di-

rection, but are scattered, and do not easily travel in a
straight course in their recollecting.
                    "On Memory and Recollection, " 2, 453^{b}1

If recollecting is a kind of syllogizing it is hard to see how anyone
could suppose that the author of this passage thought of the Prior
Analytics as a study in formal logic.

6. The Fourth Antistrophe: Demonstration

I have already said most of what needs to be said concerning Demonstration. Here I want only to bring out a feature of it
which was not easily put at the outset of this paper.

The architectonic enterprise which enlists Demonstration as
its instrument is normally a science. Since science in Aristotle
deals characteristically with necessary connections, with that which
is always, and since it deals officially with essential connections,
relations between genus and species, the tasks in which Demonstration are enlisted are quite limited. Indeed there are only two:
the recognition of necessary relationships of inclusion and perhaps
exclusion between kinds through induction, and the derivation of
other such relationships from these. This being so, it is hardly
surprising that the syllogistic invoked is of a highly restricted sort
and is of itself exclusively concerned with inclusion and exclusion
between kinds.

In so far as Aristotle regarded contemplation and science as
especially valuable human activities, that part of the art of syllogistic to which Demonstration and Science are architectonic no
doubt has a certain priority; to the extent that the creation of the
syllogistic was perhaps the younger Aristotle's most difficult and
original accomplishment he no doubt remained inordinately fond of
it; it is not clear that he thought it had any other priority. No
passage in Aristotle attempts the derivation of the other forms of
syllogistic from the syllogistic of Demonstration although many passages draw parallels between the other forms and the demonstrative
forms; in effect there is nothing in the Prior Analytics or anywhere
else which requires us to suppose that Aristotle's selection of topics
was influenced by a belief in the logical priority of the syllogistic
of the Prior Analytics; the selection, although it was not entirely
determined by the Posterior Analytics, was clearly the result of
his interest in demonstrations and so in the relations between genus
and species.

7. The Fifth Antistrophe: Dialectic

I include under the heading Dialectic a grab-bag of antistrophic arts as seems to be Aristotle's practice. Dialectic in the
Rhetoric seems sometimes to include Demonstration; as described

in the Topics (Book VIII) it seems to include or be equated with
Examination and Questioning (Erotetics): as described in the On
Sophistical Refutations it seems to exclude these two. The only
anchor in Aristotle's treatment is perhaps his notion that dialectical syllogisms are those which have generally accepted opinions as
their starting point. [29] Whatever may be the accurate division of
this and related arts--I doubt that Aristotle had any need to settle
on one--a kind of genetic origin in eristic debate is clear. [30] Here
I will limit myself to extracting from the opening and design of the
Topics a number of features relevant to the Rhetoric.

         Dialectic, in contrast with Deliberation, Demonstration, and
Recollection, is like Rhetoric in that the situation in which it occurs involves more than one party. The typical situation is that
of a kind of contest between questioner and answerer of the sort
depicted in Plato's Gorgias and Protagoras in which a kind of
mental gymnastics occurs which will hopefully prove of use in
philosophy or other arts. Book VIII of the Topics is therefore devoted to the question of arrangement of premisses so as to conceal
our aims in order to draw our opponent-answerer along with us.
As such it provides a kind of parallel to Book III of the Rhetoric
in that both are required because we have an observer-participant.
Equally well the bulk of the Topics as of the Rhetoric is given over
to the collecting of methods of arguing which will guide the questioner toward those premisses which will produce in his opponent
the desired conclusion or contradiction. These are of course the
Topoi and they run the range from what we would count as logical
advice to what we would count as substantive advice. E.g.,

> Furthermore we can judge things from their inflected
> forms, uses, actions and deeds, and also vice versa;
> for they follow one another. For example if 'justly' is
> preferable to 'courageously' then 'justice' is preferable
> to 'courage';....
>
>   Topics III, 3, 118a35

> Another commonplace is that what is more conspicuous
> is preferable to what is less conspicuous, also that
> which is more difficult; for we value more highly the
> possession of such things as are not easy to obtain.
>
>   Topics III, 2, 117b28

However we analyze these provisions for argument Aristotle keeps
before himself at all times the notion that choice of argument depends on the situation of the two participants. We are never permitted to forget that we are in a concrete situation:

> Against a young man you should apply your training in
> inductive methods; against an expert your training in de-
> ductive methods [sullogistikon].
>
>   Topics, VIII, 14, 164a13

8.   The Last Antistrophe: Rhetoric

We come at last to Rhetoric itself.   Here, too, the character of the art is fixed by the purposes for which it is enlisted.
The location of the rhetorician in process provides in effect the
guide to Aristotle's choice of subjects and emphases.   Note first
that the rhetorician must confront an audience of more than one
and that the logoi he constructs in his speech are expected to bring
something like into being in each of them regardless of age, political attitude, or education.   This produces two demands immediately and Aristotle responds to both.   1) He must cut his argument to
suit his audience and so must know how to argue to their respective kinds.   2) If the desired conclusion is to come-into-being in
them the premisses must be accepted by them.   Clearly they must
either be in them before the rhetorician speaks, in which case he
must begin from their opinions, or they must be transferred from
him to them.   In the latter case he, as Aristotle notes, must in
manner and character be his own proof.

Two further points are by now quickly made:

(1) There is no reason to expect rhetorical reasons (syllogisms) to be instances of demonstrative syllogisms.   The variety
of syllogism present in the Analytics was present because of the
interest of the Demonstrator in genus-species relationships; other
varieties should be expected in these quite different circumstances
and these expectations are borne out by the Dialectic-like set of
Topoi.

(2) The enthymeme is too often regarded as a degraded or
imperfect syllogism.   In a superficial way this is true since an
enthymeme is by definition a syllogism with a premiss (perhaps)
supplied by the audience and so unexpressed (although not unthought)
by the rhetorician.   But this does not obviously make it a defective
demonstrative syllogism; where we do not have both premisses supplied by the same party we have something much different than
Demonstration as I have described it.   That a premiss is implicit
is no mark of defectiveness either.   Rather it reminds us that we
are dealing with something nearer to the deliberative syllogism
than the demonstrative syllogism.   No one, after all, criticizes an
animal's reasoning ability if he, lusting after his mate, sees her,
and goes to it.

(3) It is now clear enough why Aristotle speaks of the
"artless" modes of persuasion. [31]   Witnesses, evidence given under
torture, and such things are of course part of the Art of Advocacy
and are properly thought of as instruments for producing conclusions.   They are not however logoi fashioned by the orator but are
rather found by him.   Selection may be involved but construction
is not, so, although no descriptions of the situation in which the
forensic orator finds himself is complete without making reference
to them, Aristotle must distinguish them from the speech proper.

(4) In Chapter III Aristotle distinguishes three kinds of
Rhetoric drawing the division in terms of the audience the speaker
is appealing to although the distinction amounts to a division of the
speaker's purpose.   The types are of course, deliberative, forensic, and epideictic.   Here we can see that the rhetorical syllogism
is nearer to both the deliberative and evaluative syllogism than it
is to the demonstrative.   In so far as a speech is an exhortation
to action it is like the premisses of a deliberative syllogism; in so
far as it is forensic it is like the evaluative.   In either case since
the desires of our audience and matters of fact--will exercise make
you healthy?--are needed in practical syllogisms, a study of human desires and of accepted information and modes of argument in
the various subject matters is required and this the Topoi and Book
II readily provide.

The scope of this essay prevents further detail but enough
has been said, I hope, to make clear that what binds the Rhetoric
to the antistrophic arts is not the extent to which it is an application of them but rather the extent to which it and they are concerned with concrete enterprises whose causal analysis demands
that they display parallel features.   The Rhetoric is like Demonstration, Deliberation, and Dialectic, because the purposes of the
Rhetorician are in some respects like the purposes of the practitioners of the other arts.

9.   The Arts Collected

We have now displayed Rhetoric as one among many sister
arts all of whom may properly be described as faculties for furnishing logoi.   These logoi are of course very diverse; our description here has been limited for the most part to the sullogismoi
among them, and even these range from the premisses of the
demonstrative syllogism to the starting points of recollective chains.
That which comes-into-being through nature from them, whether
out of necessity or habit, is even more diverse; the range is from
knowledge to opinion and from actions through attitudes to memories.   But all may reasonably be thought of as conclusions because
all are forced upon us by thoughts fashioned for that purpose;
whether the argument achieves its force through its logic or our
psychologic is a matter of great importance in post-Aristotelian
philosophy but not one which, after all, matters much in practice
or, I think, in Aristotle.

Still there is a difference here.   We may rank the arts in
terms of the mental faculties involved.   These may be graded in
terms of the degree of abstraction involved, i.e., in Averroistic
terms, in terms of the layers of matter contaminating the noetic
core.   Here clearly the sensual memories of recollection, the desires and perceptions of animal deliberation will rank low, and the
completed inductions of the Posterior Analytics and those to the
first principles of Ethics will rank high, with the opinions and atti-

tudes which make up the bulk of Rhetoric and Dialectic falling
somewhere in between.   On such a view then abstract Demonstration is the superior art and the merely sensible contents of the
De Motu Animalium and "On Memory and Recollection" are inferior
and the Rhetoric is indeed a "curious jumble" falling somewhere
in between.   But note well that this ranking neither presupposes
nor entails that the lower arts are in any sense an application of
the higher arts.   The Analytics on this view does not provide the
theory for which the Rhetoric is the practice; the arts remain applications of some common methodology.   All that can be said is
that the elements which they fashion are of varying degrees of abstraction: we have in effect a reaffirmation of their independence
because we have specified a difference.

But if anything has been gained from this inquiry it is not
the recognition that Rhetoric is different from the remaining arts;
we knew this before we started.   Rather it is the recognition that
Rhetoric is one of a family of arts with no apparent ancestry.
To cast the Prior Analytics for the role and so to force analyses
of speeches onto a syllogistic rack is clearly a mistake.   The
source of the mistake is, I suspect, the belief that the less complex is suited to be paradigm for the more complex; the roots of
this belief in Platonism and before need not be discussed here.   It
is certainly the case that Demonstration exhibits some features of
the antistrophic arts in an especially clear way.   It is for this
very reason that it altogether fails to exhibit other features; it is
not concerned with action; it is not concerned with opinion; it is
not concerned with attitude; it is not concerned with things that may
or may not come into being; it has no concerns beyond truths about
the inclusion and exclusion of kinds; above all it is not concerned
with time and other minds.   It is therefore simple but not because
it is a paradigm for Rhetoric but because it omits what is of interest in Rhetoric.   But, to Aristotle's credit, this is not because
he has failed to conceive of Demonstration as an art exercised in
process whose products are causally explicable but because he construed its function in a narrow--doubtless too narrow--way.

NOTES

1.   Rhet., I, 1, 1354^{a}1.   References to Aristotle are to the Loeb
     Classical Library editions; approximate Bekker references
     are added as needed.
2.   Rhet., I, 2, 1355^{b}27.
3.   Rhet., I, 1, 1354^{a}2.
4.   Rhet., I, 1, 1354^{a}9.   "Investigate the cause" suggests science
     rather than art; why Aristotle can use this phrase here and
     in similar contexts (e.g., Top., I, 4, 101^{b}11) will become
     clear as we proceed.
5.   Rhet., I, 1, 1354^{a}13.   When these proofs are found rather
     than made Aristotle describes them as an artless (atechnikos)
     part of the art of (forensic) oratory.   Rhet., I, 2, 1355^{b}36

and I, 15.

6. Rhet., I, 2, 1356ª35. The "artless" proofs of the previous
note do not have this property in an obvious way.

7. "Sullogismos" is normally translated "reasoning" or "syllogism." The reason (i.e., that which produces) for my
translation will be found below. Aristotle sometimes uses
"sullogismos" in the narrow sense of demonstrative or dialectical syllogism as opposed to rhetorical syllogism and
sometimes in a sense wide enough to include at least these
three. I will always use it in the wider sense.

8. Top., I, 1, 100ª25. Cp. Pr. Anal., I, 1, 24ᵇ19 and Rhet.,
I, 2, 1356ᵇ13.

9. The lost Peri Sumboulias may have been such a treatise. Cf.
Diogenes Laertius, V, 24.

10. Memory and Recollection, 2, 453ª10.

11. W. D. Ross, Aristotle, New York, 1959, p. 267. The context leaves unclear whether this is Ross's own view.

12. Meta., VII, 10.

13. The Arabic tradition, for example, counted the Rhetoric and
Poetics as part of the Organon. Even the Arabs were somewhat puzzled by the Poetics in this context although a case
can be made for its also being an antistrophic art.

14. Aristotle himself refers to the demonstrative syllogism in this
way at Rhet., I, 1, 1355ª13.

15. Pr. Anal., I, 27, 43ª23.

16. The well-attested Methodica would be this work if there was
such a work. Cf. Bonitz, Index Aristotelicus, 101ᵇ39, and,
e.g., Diogenes Laertius, V. 23.

17. Rhet., I, 2, 1354ª13.

18. Phys., II, 3, 194ᵇ33.

19. Physics, II, 2, 194ᵇ5. The following substitutions were made:
"demonstrator" for "helmsman"; "syllogism" for "helm";
"terms or premisses" for "wood."

20. Rhet., I, 2, 1356ª116ff. Here Rhetoric is architectonic to
Politics which provides the materials of persuasion. Rhet.,
I, 3, makes clear the more obvious sense in which politics
is the architectonic art.

21. Post. Anal., II, 11, 94ª20.

22. The Greek here is reminiscent of Aristotle's definition of the
syllogism.

23. On such a reading we have proximate efficient cause where
we typically expect to find the material cause. The inclusion of two efficient causes, proximate and remote, at the
expense of the more "passive" material cause occurs elsewhere in early Aristotle. Cp., e.g., Metaphysics Lambda,
5, 1071ª15.

24. Phys., II, 3, 195ª16. "That out of which" is Aristotle's
standard formula for the material cause. Here it seems
to be extended to the whole or formal component as well.

25. Pr. Anal., II, 21, 67ª33.

26. Aristotle nowhere offers this as an explicit criteria for ousia-
hood but the idea is perhaps implicit in his handling of

spontaneous generation. De Gen. Anim. I, 1.

27. Post. Anal., II, 19 has the briefest statement.
28. Mem. et Rem. 453a26.
29. Cf., e.g., Top. I, 1, 100a30.
30. Gilbert Ryle, Plato's Progress, Cambridge, 1966, has the most interesting version of the development.
31. Rhet., I, 2, 1355b36 and I, 15.

5. RHETORIC AND DIALECT: ACCORDING TO THE FIRST LATIN COMMENTARY ON THE RHETORIC OF ARISTOTLE*

by Brother S. Robert, F.S.C.

Great attention has been paid to the decline of rhetoric in the middle ages and its replacement by a form of speaking which was closer to dialectic.[1] According to one view almost all forms of public speaking except preaching had largely ceased to exist, and the one remaining form, preaching, began to be characterized by a dialectical mode sometime in the twelfth century.

A particularly interesting study of one example of this change is made by Jean Paul Bonnes, in an article he wrote on the preaching of Geoffrey Bebion, a distinguished prelate of the twelfth century.[2] The author quotes a sermon written by this apparently very holy man on the text "God has stood in the assembly of the gods, and in their midst He has judged amongst them." As Fr. Dumont, commenting on the article in question, says, this might well have been written anywhere in either eastern or western Christendom from the time of the fathers on.[3] The preacher restricts himself to expounding the text as a guide to life for priests --the "gods" of the text--and to bringing out those points and those "rapprochements" that nourish a deeply felt piety.

In the concluding part of the article another sermon on the same text is quoted. It was written a generation later by an author called Petrus Comestor. Here we see the completion of a transition to the new form of preaching inspired by a general enthusiasm, at least in university circles, for the dialectical approach. The text is given a tripartite division in answer to the questions, "Quis stetit? ubi stetit? ad quid stetit?" Each of these questions is answered by reference to relevant parts of Scripture, and in terms of all the various meanings of each part of the text. This is a direct result of the growth of exegesis according to a dialectical method, from the time of Abelard on. The exigencies of an intellectual exposition, rather than the need to arouse the adherence of the heart, are the primary criteria for the choice and the de-

*Reprinted by permission from The New Scholasticism XXXI (1957), 484-498.

velopment of these points.   This is the great change in orientation.

Several questions necessarily arise if one grants the substantial correctness of this sermon as an example of a new kind
of preaching and its substantial difference from what had been
characteristic of the Christian approach previously.   That this
is the case has been demonstrated, to the satisfaction of most, by
more general studies of medieval preaching, especially the collection of treatises on preaching edited by Fr. Charland.   It is not
necessary for our present purposes to go into this question in any
detail or to decide absolutely about its solution.

There is also another question which, despite its importance,
we need not go into here; that is, the relationship between rhetoric
and preaching.   It is sufficient for our present purpose to entertain
the general hypothesis that something of the ancient heritage of
rhetoric was transferred into the Christian tradition of preaching
and of the teaching of theology, and that some modification of this
tended to be introduced by a greater vogue of the dialectical method.   It would also be well to reflect upon the possibility that there
is truth in the assertion that other forms of rhetoric, especially political and judicial oratory, had fallen into disuse during the middle
ages.

If this much be granted, and it is certainly a minimum, then
it is important to call attention to another doctrinal development of
the Aristotelian tradition certainly known within the lifetime of St.
Thomas and developed shortly after his death by one of his pupils,
Giles of Rome.   I refer to the Rhetoric of Aristotle as translated
by William of Moerbeke and commented on by Giles. [4]

This work is important, if only for the reason that it is the
first work of its kind, and the first to use as its text the recently
made translation of William of Moerbeke, who made so many other
translations from Aristotle for the use of St. Thomas. [5] Both the
translation and the commentary seem to have been made around
1280, [6] that is to say, within a very short time after the death of
St. Thomas.   Giles, as we all know, was a pupil of St. Thomas,
and this work was written before the slight backing away from
Thomist positions was forced upon our author because of the opposition of the University of Paris, and long before the subsequent
development of independent and sometimes not completely Thomistic
positions by the Augustinian doctor. [7]

Anyone who is familiar with the humanists' rejection of
scholasticism will remember how much they insist on the need to
pay attention to human affairs and human values, instead of passing
one's life in sterile word-chopping and in talking about bloodless
abstractions.   Consequently, it is not without importance to point
out that Aristotle's Rhetoric as well as his Poetics are a genuine
part of the Aristotelian and the Thomist tradition.   It may be that
too great an emphasis was placed on the dialectical approach and

that dialectics permeated activities like preaching, that are essentially different and really unsuited to it. This, of course, would explain also a neglect of history, since one of the most serious reasons for reflection on history is the sometimes despised, but usually merely misunderstood, purpose of supplying valid examples for rhetorical discourse.

For a real understanding, then, of the Aristotelian tradition as inherited by the middle ages, it is important to consider the difference between rhetoric and dialectic as expounded in a full blown medieval commentary on the relevant part of the Aristotelian corpus. What emerges concerning the difference between the two disciplines, according to Giles, is that, though the two have some elements in common, they are fundamentally irreducible. We shall see that even when they use instruments that have the same name, these two disciplines are generally different and there is only an analogy between what may seem to a careless observer to be the same thing. Anyone who had fully grasped the truth of such statements would certainly not have needed any humanist reaction to arouse him to the claims of rhetoric for independence from dialectic.

The considerations that concern us seem to me to be in accord with what St. Thomas says on the relations between dialectic and rhetoric. [8] It must be added that Giles states that his purpose in the work is not to give his own opinion but to explain what he believes to be that of Aristotle. [9]

How this work on the Aristotelian tradition of rhetoric affected the practice of public speaking is beyond the scope of this paper, and beyond my competence as well. Nevertheless, it is to be pointed out that the Commentary appeared quite shortly after the reintroduction of the full Aristotelian corpus to the west and that it continued to attract enough attention to merit at least six editions within the eighty years that followed the invention of printing. [10]

The immediate occasion for the discussion of the relationship between dialectics and rhetoric by our author is, of course, the opening sentence of Aristotle's Rhetoric. In the William of Moerbeke text this reads, "Rhetorica assecutiva dialectica est, " ("Rhetoric reaches to dialectic"). In the Bekker text of the rhetoric we read the more rhetorical statement, Ἡ ῥητορική ἐστιν ἀντιστροφος τη διαλεκτικη, "rhetoric is an antistrophe to dialectic. " Either statement is sufficient to raise the moot point of the relationship between the two disciplines.

Our commentator deals with the problem first in a prologue which he writes for the whole work, and secondly, as part of the more limited task of explaining the letter of the text as it touches on the question that concerns us. This applies not only to the opening words of the text but to several other passages in the first two chapters of the work.

We will be concerned mainly with the first of these sets of considerations, namely those contained in the Prologue, because they are more profound and deal more thoroughly with the main problem.

The first and most obvious solution to the problem is to say that dialectic, in the opening sentence of the rhetoric, is to be taken generally as including all logic, and that consequently rhetoric is one of the <u>artes</u> <u>sermocinales,</u> that is to say, one of the logical disciplines too.[11] In other words, rhetoric reaches toward dialectic in the way that any part reaches toward a whole. Our commentator gives this easy solution short shrift by remarking that it is too easy.[12] It is true that dialectic is a name sometimes applied to all the logical disciplines, but it is also the proper name of one of the parts of the logic. It is still necessary to show how rhetoric is related to dialectic as taken in this more restricted sense.

The solution of this more special problem rests on the answer to two questions.

> We must first investigate how (since all sciences are rational, because they all proceed by reason) logic is distinguished from the other rational sciences.... Secondly, we must say why logic and rhetoric are said to be rational simply, since other sciences proceed through firmer and more stable reasons than do either dialectic or rhetoric.[13]

In answering the first of these questions we shall see how rhetoric differs from dialectic, while the second enables us to know what they have in common.

Let us, then, try to see in what way rhetoric differs from dialectic. There are really five <u>artes</u> <u>sermocinales</u>--grammar, poetry, rhetoric, dialectic and demonstration. Grammar can be left aside as being in a certain sense <u>ad libitum,</u> that is, free in the sense that it depends on a conventionally arrived at use of words. Poetry can be passed over also since it leans on stories and representations.[14]

Science, unlike either rhetoric or dialectic, gives reasons which compel the assent of the mind, and thus it is easily distinguished from either of them. We can say of the last three mentioned disciplines that they each result in a different disposition of mind. Science is produced by the use of demonstrative reasons; the dialectician uses probable reason to generate opinion; lastly, the rhetorician uses persuasive reasons to produce faith or credulity.[15] As we have said, it is easy to see how science differs from the other two, but we still have the task of distinguishing faith or credulity from opinion.

There are several inadequate opinions concerning the way in
which these two differ from one another. Some say, for example,
that faith differs from opinion because we adhere more certainly
to those things about which we have an opinion than we do to those
we believe. These people say that belief and especially that
brought about through rhetoric ought to be called a kind suspicion. [16]

St. Thomas, himself, uses this term when he is designating
the disposition generated by rhetoric. [17]

Another opinion is that of Alfarabius, who, in his summary
of the Rhetoric, asserts that rhetoric persuades people about particular things, while dialectic is concerned about universals. [18]

To the first of these opinions it may be answered that it
well may happen that people hold beliefs, especially about political
matters, far more firmly than they hold some opinions. Thus,
the degree of force of these respective kinds of adherence to a
proposition is accidental to the arguments themselves. [19] This,
however, is not the final view of our commentator, for, as he
says, dialectical arguments are per se more convincing than are
rhetorical ones.

Secondly, in reply to Alfarabius, we can say that dialectics
may sometimes concern itself with particular truths, as for instance the relative size of the earth and the sun. [20]

A more profound answer to our question is arrived at by
reflecting on the fact that some things belong to the powers of the
soul taken in themselves, while others belong to one power only as
it depends on some other power. [21] For example, to desire an end
belongs to the will in itself, since it is ordered to the good, but to
choose belongs to the will only in dependence on the reason, for
choice is not of the end, that is of the good in itself, but of things
which are ordered to the end, and the perception of order belongs
to the reason. Consequently, Aristotle, in defining choice, says
it is either an intellective appetite or an appetitive intellect. [22]

The same diversity also holds for acts of the intellect as
such. The acts of the speculative intellect are those to which it
is moved by its own proper object, while the acts of the practical
intellect are those toward which it is moved under the impulse of
appetite. Consequently, in the formal sense, it is malice which
makes us tell a lie and not a speculative error. Malice is an evil
appetite, that is, one directed toward particular things which can
arouse passion, and not toward universals. [23]

In other words, assent brought about through propositions
that in themselves are suited to intellectual assent is a proper mo-

tion of the intellect as such. Agreement caused by propositions suited to direct the mind as moved by the appetite is an action of the practical intellect. [24]

This is the key to solving our problem. The assent of faith (credulity, suspicion) belongs to the intellect according as it is open to being moved by the appetite. Scientific or probable assent of the intellect through demonstrative or probable reasons respectively belongs to the intellect moved by its own object. [25]

The belief that the rhetorician tries to generate is brought about by arguments and it concerns matters about which the appetite is aroused and so tends to move the will. This does not imply necessarily that the will is in fact always moved through rhetorical argument, but only that the proper subject of such discourse is of the kind that tends to move the will. [26]

This also affects the intrinsic probability proper to rhetorical discourse as distinguished from that proper to the dialectician. Since dialectical arguments proceed from what belongs to the intellect according to its own motion, it generates greater probability than does a form of discourse directed toward the intellect as moved by the will. [27]

This, too, is the ground for Alfarabius' opinion that rhetorical persuasion is directed toward particular things, while dialectics is directed toward the universal. The will is moved toward things as they are in themselves, that is to say, particularly, while the intellect grasps them as they are within the intellect, in other words, universally. [28] When we know the diameter of the sun relative to the earth, it is the nature of that body that we are trying to study.

This reason touches upon what is most fundamental in understanding the difference between rhetoric and dialectic. In the Ethics, Aristotle distinguished between two fundamental kinds of human happiness, each caused by a special kind of activity. [29] The highest kind of human happiness comes from the use of the intellect for the discovery of truth, since this pursuit is the proper object of the highest of the human powers. Beneath this pursuit in dignity is the activity of the practical man who uses his reason to discover and to promote practically the common good of society. Consequently, rhetoric will be the proper instrument of the statesman in carrying out his task of persuading those under his direction to perform those actions that are for the common good. On the other hand, dialectics is an instrument for exploring the truth, and so it serves man in the pursuit of the highest kind of happiness.

From what has been said it becomes possible to point out a sixfold difference between the discipline of dialectics and that of rhetoric. Because of their diverse objects, each must turn the at-

tention of its students to different aspects of reality.   First, rhetoric descends more deeply into moral matters, while dialectic tends
to concern itself more with speculative matters.   A practical
science like ethics is obviously concerned with moral matters, but
in comparison to ethics rhetoric must train a man to deal directly
with the most particular practical issues, and especially to defend
the speaker's point of view with a greater finality than an uncertain science like ethics can permit in most cases.[30]   Secondly,
the rhetorician must concern himself with disposing arguments so
as to arouse the passions.   This is precisely legitimate for him
and not for the dialectician.[31]

The rhetorician must arrange his speech so that it can meet
the judgment even of the most simple and uncultivated hearer.   The
dialectician on the other hand must shape his argument so that it
will be accepted by men with deeper and subtler minds.[32]

The arguments used by the rhetorician take as their main
form that of enthymemes and examples, which are precisely inferi-
or versions of syllogisms and inductions, the arguments proper to
the dialectician.[33]

We must go even further than saying that the one kind of
syllogism is inferior to the other.   Not only is this true, but it
must also be said that the two differ in kind generically, or, even
better, that they are only analogously alike, though the two kinds
of argument share the same name.[34]

The rhetorician tends, as we have remarked, to persuade
us concerning singulars, rather than universals, while the dialectician aims at the reverse.[35]

Lastly, the topics from which the rhetorician draws his
arguments are, as one would imagine, such as will bring about
the faith, the belief, proper to political argument, while the dialectician uses those suitable to generate opinion.[36]

We can see, then, how these disciplines differ and what a
distinct task it is to acquire these respective arts.   It remains
now to see in what way rhetoric and dialectic are alike, and thus,
we will be fully able to grasp the reason that lies behind Aristotle's choice of words in the opening lines of the text.

Although the statements that set forth these differences are
succinct, as one would expect in a work in the Aristotelian tradition, yet the essential is there.   The rest of the work considers
the forms of rhetorical argument, the topics useful for each kind
of discourse, and the language adapted to the different forms.   A
reading of the whole work would be necessary for a complete understanding of what kind of discipline rhetoric is, and how completely and wisely it enters into a domain that may be thought by
some to be beyond the purview of the committed Aristotelian of

the middle ages. Obviously such a complete summary of Giles'
work is beyond the limits of this brief article.

It remains now to see in what ways rhetoric is akin to dialectic. This is the second part of our task.

We find the key to their similarity in the description often
applied to both of them, that they are rational disciplines. [37]

In one sense of the term, it seems false to attribute reason
to them in a special way. It is obvious that other disciplines,
mathematics for example, give better reasons than those offered
by either the dialectician or the rhetorician. However, the subject
of these other disciplines is not reason itself but some real object,
some aspect of the real world. They deal with this object rational-
ly, especially when it is well within the human grasp, as is the
case for mathematics. [38]

Rhetoric and dialectic, on the other hand, not only proceed
in a rational way like the other sciences but they concern the acts
of reason itself. Thus, they are rational in a double sense.

Since sciences take their species from their objects rather
than from their mode of proceeding, this claim to be rational belongs in an absolute way to rhetoric and dialectic, since the whole
object studied by rhetoric is that which is calculated to effect per-
suasions, and that of dialectic what will help form opinion. [39]

Another similarity between rhetoric and dialectic is that they
do not proceed by reasons that compel the intellect as do the other
sciences, but rather they give only probable or persuasive reasons
neither of which put the intellect completely at rest. [40]

This is a point which is later developed more fully in connection with kinds of topics used by rhetoric and dialectics.

Another point of similarity between the two is the quasi-
universality of the respective objects of these disciplines. Since
the object of both the speculative and the practical intellect is in
some way coextensive with being, these disciplines, which concern
those acts whereby the mind considers all kinds of things, are in
a way universal. They are, of course, different from metaphysics
which considers real being as being, since rhetoric and dialectic
as sciences are concerned only with acts of the reason.

Thus, we can see the justification of Aristotle's remark
that rhetoric reaches unto dialectic. What reaches unto something
else is not identical with that other thing, but the fact that one
reaches the territory occupied by the other means that the extension of one somehow is that of the other. The two disciplines are
distinct, as we have seen, primarily in that one serves the ends
of the practical intellect, while the other is an instrument of specu-

lation.   They are alike because in a certain way both are disciplines that extend to the whole universe since each is concerned
in its own way with the acts of reason whereby man attains to all
that is knowable.

NOTES

1.   Amongst works on this subject we should mention especially
     the Artes Praedicandi, Th-M. Charland, O. P. (Paris and
     Ottawa, 1936).   The author was inspired particularly, as
     he says, by E. Gilson, "Michel Minet, et la technique du
     sermon médiéval" in Les idées et les lettres (Paris, 1932)
     pp. 93-154.
2.   J. P. Bonnes, "Un des plus grands prédicateurs du XI siècle,
     Geoffre de Loroux, " in Revue Bénédictine, 56 (1945-46)
     174-215.
3.   Père Dumont, L'Eglise et les églises, 1054-1954, Lambert
     Beauduin, editor (Editions de Chevetogne, 1955) I, 44.
4.   For this article use has been made of the 1498 edition of
     Venice from a copy in the British Museum.   Acknowledg-
     ment is hereby made to the Museum for permission to quote
     from it, and to my confrere, Brother T. Michael, for help-
     ing to make the work available to me.   These pages of the
     text have a number for only the second of any two facing
     pages.   I have, for the purpose of these notes, arbitrarily
     added a letter (A, B, C, D) to designate each of the four
     columns sharing the same page number.
5.   Sarton, Introduction to the History of Science (Cambridge Uni-
     versity Press, 1941) II, 922-926.
6.   Sarton, loc. cit.
7.   Thonnard, Précis de l'histoire de Philosophie (Paris, 1945)
     pp. 347, 407.
8.   For example, Summa Theol., II-II, 48, I; in I Post. Anal.,
     1 medio.
9.   "Ubi quod onus expositoris assumpsi, nolo mihi ascribi, quod
     proferam, sed talem promulgabo sententiam qualem credam
     Aristotelem intendisse. " Op. cit., IC.
10. Sarton, op. cit., p. 923.   These editions were between 1481
     and 1555.
11. "... rhetorica est pars dialecticae, sive pars logicae ... est
     ergo rhetorica sermonicativa vel rationalis scientia. " Ibid.,
     IC.
12. "Sed sie dicendo valde modicum praecognitionem haberemus
     de ipsa. " Ibid., IC.
13. The translation of the text is my own.   The original reads as
     follows, "Primo enim investigandum est cum omnes scientiae
     sint aliquo modo rationales, eo quod singulae per rationes
     procedunt, quo distinguitur logica ab aliis scientiis rationali-
     bus....   Secunda declarandum occurrit quare logica et
     rhetorica simpliciter rationales dicantur cum tamen magis
     per rationes firmas et stabiles procedunt huiusmodi scientiae

quam dialectica et rhetorica." Ibid., IC.

14. "Propter primum advertendum quod dimissa grammatica quae
quodammodo est ad libitum et poetica quae innititur aliis
gestibus et repraesentationibus; dicere possummus rhetorica
differre a caeteris scientiis ratiocinativs quia non eodem modo procedat per rationes ut illae." Ibid., IC-D.

15. "Possumus autem assignare differentiam inter ista genera ra-
tionum secundum differentias eorum quae generantur ex illis.
Per rationes probabiles generatur opinio, per persuasivas
fides aggeneratur sive credulitas; per demonstrativas vero
efficitur scientia." Ibid., 1D.

16. "Dixerunt autem aliqui credulitatem sive fidem differant ob
opinione secundum certitudinem quia certius adhaeremus his
quae opinamur quam his quae credimus. Nam huiusmodi
credulitas et potissime quae generatur per rhetoricam
quaedam suspicatio debet dici." Ibid., 1D.

17. In I Anal. Post., 1.

18. "Alfarabius in quibusdam suis praeambulis quae condidit super
rhetoricam vult quod per rhetoricam fiat persuasio in una-
quaque rerum particulariam. Ex quo dicere possumus, cum
opinio fiat circa universalia, differe opinionem a fide sicut
id quod fit circa particularis ab eo quod circa universalia
debet fieri." Ibid., 1D.

19. "Istae autem differentiae vel non videntur verae vel radicalem
differentiam non attingunt. Contingit autem aliquem ad-
haerere firmius his quae credit quam his quae opinatur."
Ibid., 1D.

20. "Rursus autem quia de his singularibus potest esse aliquod
modo opinio, opinamur non enim solem maiorem tota terra,
quem sensus indicat unius pedis." Ibid., 1D.

21. "Aliqui competunt potentiae animae secundum se acceptae,
aliqui competunt uni potentiae in comparatione ad aliam."
Ibid., 1D in medio.

22. "Velle competit voluntati secundum se consideratae, eligere
vero competit ei ut habens ordinem ad rationem. Nam
electio non est finis, sed eorum quae ordinantur in finem;
cum ergo ordinate ad rationem pertinet, eligere non potest
competere voluntati nisi in ordine ad rationem. Propter
quod scribitur 6. Ethicorum quod electio vel est appetitus
intellectivus vel intellectus appetitivus." Ibid., 1D.

23. "Actio vero, intellectus speculativi vocatur intellectus secundum quod est intellectus. Actio vero intellectus practici
magis vocatur intellectum prout habet ordinem ad appetitum:
et ideo facit malicia mentiri circa principium non propter
comparationen ad cognitionem speculativam: sed magis ad
cognitionem praeticam cum propter passiones et maliciam
in affectu exercemur in particulari non in universali."
Ibid., 1D.

24. "Et sicut est in actionibus ita est in assensu: quod aliquis
assentit intellectus secundum motum proprium: aliquis vero
ut motus a voluntate: vel aliquis assentit propositionibus
quibus secundum se est aptus natus assentire. Aliquando

vero assentit aliquibus quibus potest fieri assensus ut habet
ordinem ad appetitum. " Ibid., 1D.

25. "Assensus credulitatis per rationes persuasivas competit in-
tellectui secundum quod est aptus natus moveri ab appetitu.
Assensio vero scientificus et operativus, sive assentire per
propositiones demonstrativas et probabiles competit intellec-
tui ut est aptus natus moveri secundum motum proprium. "
Ibid., 1D.

26. "... aliquando assentit propositionibus quibus secundum se
est aptus natus assentire; aliquando vero assentit aliquibus
quibus potest fieri assensus ut habens ordinem ad appetitus. " Ibid., 1D.

27. "Sed quia non fit persuasio in materia rhetorica nisi fiat in
talibus secundum quod intellectus ab appetitu moveri potest;
propter quod patere potest quod veritatis ... illorum, fidem
ab opinione differre secundum certitudinem, quia non est
tanta certitudo in credulitate rhetorica, cum sit quaedam
suspicatio quanta est in opione.   Nam si loquuntur de certi-
tudine speculationis, veritatem habet quam maior certitudo
speculativa habet in eis circa quam negotiatur intellectus
secundum quod huiusmodi est in opinione quam sit in illis
in quibus est aptus natus moveri ab appetitu, quod fit in
credulitate rhetorica. " Ibid., 2A.

28. "Nam res sunt cognitae secundum modum quo habent esse in
intellectu; sunt vero volitae prout in seipsis.   Nam verum
et falsum sunt in anima.   Bonum et malum sunt in rebus....
Sunt ergo res magis intellectae secundum esse universale,
volitae vero secundum particularem existentiam. " Ibid., 1A.

29. Ethics, X, 7, 8.

30. Ethics, I, 1.

31. "Spectat ad rhetorem determinare de passionibus, non autem
ad dialecticum. " Op. cit., 2A.

32. "Judex locutionis rhetoricae et eius auditor est simplex et
grossus.   Auditor vero locutionis dialecticae debet esse in-
geniosus et subtilis. " Ibid., 2A.

33. "Instrumenta rhetoricae sunt enthimeme et exempla, dialecticae vero syllogismus et inductio. " Ibid., 2A.

34. "Habet se diversitas praedicta secundum intentionem materiae,
sicut corpora supercoelestia differunt a corporibus existenti-
bus in sphaera activorum et passivorum.   Est enim talis diversitas ex ipsa materia, sed non solum ex extensione eius,
ut quod materia sit extensa ex diversis partibus materiae
suscipiantur diversae formae, sed etiam diversa ratione
materiae.   Nam materia supercoelestium et inferiorum cor-
porum non secundum eamdem rationem suscipiunt formas,
cum illa suscipiat formam non habentem contrarium, et
complentem totum appetitum materiae.   Haec autem suscipiat
formam habentem contrarium non terminantem materiae appetitum.   Et sicut diversitas sumitur ex parte materiae una
propter extensionem, alia propter rationem diversam, sicut
diversitas ex parte materiae dupliciter accipitur secundum
genus et secundum numerum.   Nam cum materia causat di-

versitatem propter sui extensionem, facit diversitatem
numeralem, ideo diversi annuli aurei solo numero distingu-
untur, sed cum materia diversitatem propter rationem diversam, sic causat differentiam generis.   Unde supercoelestia corpora et inferiora genere differant quia corruptibilia
non sunt in eodem genere ut potest habere ex decimo Metaphysicorum quae omnia, si bene intellecta sunt, satis osten-
dunt syllogysmum simpliciter non esse genus ad syllogysmum
demonstrativum et dialecticum sed vel est analogum, vel
species respectu eorum.   Nam materia necessaria et probabilis faciunt differentiam propter rationem diversam quia
dictae materiae non secundum eamdem rationem suscipiant
formam syllogysticam.   Sic praedicti syllogysmi differant
genere et syllogysmus absolute sumptus non est genus ad ista
sed analogum, sicut corpus est analogum ad supercoelestia
et inferiora.   Sed si dicta diversitas est propter extensionem
materiae sicut syllogysmus demonstrativus et dialecticus
sunt eamdem speciei, sicut homo masculus et homo mulier
quae non different nisi secundum differentias materiales
sumptas ex extensione materiae, sicut est syllogismo demon-
strativo, et dialectico.   Quia si diversitas inter ea sumitur
ex extensione materiae solum, sic syllogismi dialectici et
rhetorici sunt eiusdem speciei; cum vero hoc est propter
aliam et aliam rationem, sic differunt genere.
       "Sed si quaeratur quid istorum sit, absque dubitatione
dicendum est hoc esse propter rationem diversam.   Nam
materia persuasibilis est ex qua habet esse enthimema, et
probabilis ex qua habet esse syllogysmus dialecticus, non
secundum eamdem rationem recipit formam syllogisticam.
Unde dictum est supra enthimema a syllogismo differre
quantum ad materiam et quantum ad forman." Ibid., 13C.

35.   See note 30 above.
36.   "Tam dialectica quam rhetorica utantur locis.   Loci tamen
       hic et ibi non sumuntur eodem modo.   Haec autem et alia
       quae diligens rhetor investigare potest sumunt originem ex
       differentia quae assignata est inter opinionem et fidem."
       Ibid., 2A, in fine.
37.   "Dialectica et rhetorica simpliciter rationales dicantur."
       Ibid., 2A, in fine.
38.   Ibid., 2B, in principio.
39.   "Nam convenit rhetorica cum dialectica quantum ad id de quo
       est, cum ambae sint de actibus rationis, non autem cum
       aliis scientiis, cum artes aliae sint de rebus." Ibid., 2A,
       in medio.
40.   "Aliae artes procedunt per rationes cogentes et determinantes
       intellectum; dialecticae vero et rhetoricae rationes modo
       persuasivo et probabili." Ibid., 2A, in medio.

6. ARISTOTLE AND THE PROBLEM OF VALUE*

by Whitney J. Oates

The most striking characteristic of Aristotle's Rhetoric, from our point of view, is its ambivalence. On the one hand, it attempts to tie itself in with Aristotelian logic, ethics, and politics, while on the other it is a practical handbook for the instruction of public speakers in all the techniques and tricks of the trade. So far as the question of value is concerned, we can see in the Rhetoric, when the author has foremost in his mind his thought in logic, ethics, and politics, a reflection of the views expressed therein towards matters of value. But when he is in the mood of an author of a practical handbook, [1] any concern for value seems in some places to vanish, leaving us in a realm of amoralism, if not immoralism. Or, in other places, the point of view towards value reflects the most banal type of conventionalism. Perhaps the point about ambivalence can best be made by looking at Aristotle's definition of rhetoric submitted early in the work: "Let rhetoric then be the potentiality, i.e., as a capacity to produce change, involved in observing concerning each particular that which is capable of being persuasive." [2] No one can read this without thinking of the famous passage in Plato's Gorgias where Socrates offers the following terse definition of rhetoric which is immediately accepted by his interlocutor of the moment, the great Gorgias himself: "Rhetoric is the artificer of persuasion." [3] As is well known, the whole argument of the dialogue is devoted to revealing the latent immoralism inherent in this definition. The Aristotelian definition, though it is slightly more extensive, really differs not at all in substance from the Platonic version, and therefore is vulnerable to the same kind of attack which is mounted by the Socrates of the dialogue.

That Aristotle does not wish to be vulnerable to such an attack is evident in a number of passages. He opens the treatise by announcing that rhetoric is the "counterpart" (ἀντίστροφος) of dialectic. As he takes pains to point out, as rhetoric in the field of oratory is akin to dialectic and not to scientific demonstration, so

---

*"Evidence from the Rhetoric," in Whitney J. Oates, Aristotle and the Problem of Value (copyright (c) 1963 by Princeton University Press), pp. 333-351. Reprinted by permission of Princeton University Press.

it is concerned not with certainties but with probabilities about which it is possible to deliberate. Also rhetoric is not confined to any one subject, but can be employed anywhere, no matter what the subject. As Ross observes, rhetoric in argument uses example, the rhetorical counterpart of induction, and enthymeme, the rhetorical counterpart of syllogism. [4] To take an example where Aristotle is clearly attempting to dignify rhetoric, one could cite the following: "The true and the approximately true are apprehended by the same faculty; it may also be noted that men have a sufficient natural instinct for what is true, and usually do arrive at the truth. Hence the man who makes a good guess at truth is likely to make a good guess at probabilities. "[5] Or again, he tries to insist upon the natural affiliation of rhetoric for what is true when he says: "Further, we must be able to employ persuasion, just as strict reasoning can be employed, on opposite sides of a question, not in order that we may in practice employ it in both ways (for we must not make people believe what is wrong), but in order that we may see clearly what the facts are, and that, if another man argues unfairly, we on our part may be able to confute him.... Nevertheless, the underlying facts do not lend themselves equally well to the contrary views. No; things that are true and things that are better are, by their nature, practically always easier to prove and easier to believe in. "[6] Notice how he protests that, though rhetorical persuasion may be used on either side of an argument, we should never do this in practical fact--"We must not make people believe what is wrong. " After all, he insists, it is a fact of nature that the truth and the better are "easier to prove and easier to believe in. " It does not seem wrong to detect in this passage a note of uneasy defensiveness, just as though Aristotle felt the presence of Aristophanes looking over his shoulder as he wrote and saying something about making the worse appear the better reason.

Another passage throws further light on Aristotle's attempt to make his conception of rhetoric philosophically grounded, and perhaps to answer in some measure the Platonic attacks upon the sophists and the rhetoric of a Gorgias. Aristotle's treatise, as is well known, owes much to the analysis of rhetoric in the Phaedrus of Plato, but Aristotelian metaphysics cannot provide the basis for a version of or an adaptation of Plato's "dialectical" rhetoric as "psychagogy" as developed in the Phaedrus. In brief, this Platonic conception holds rhetoric to be the instrument whereby the "soul" of man (i. e., the totality of his inner being, including his cognitive faculties) is turned about, oriented towards, is "converted" to the "truth. " In Platonic terms, this "truth" is the panoply of the Ideas or Forms dominated by the Idea of the Good. Because rhetoric can effect the reorientation of the soul, its awareness and comprehension of the eternal verities will be enhanced. As has been pointed out, since the Aristotelian metaphysics has denied the existence of these objective entities, the Ideas, it is plain that Aristotle's rhetorical theory is forced to be far vaguer with respect to the nature of truth, with which, so he says, the craft of persuasion has some concern.

But let us examine the passage which now perhaps can be better understood in the light of the foregoing remarks on the theory of the Phaedrus. "Furthermore, it is plain that it is the function of one and the same art to discern the real and the apparent means of persuasion, just as it is the function of dialectic to discern the real and the apparent syllogism. What makes a man a 'sophist' is not his faculty, but his moral purpose. In rhetoric, however, the term 'rhetorician' may describe either the speaker's knowledge of the art or his moral purpose. In dialectic it is different: a man is a 'sophist' because he has a certain kind of moral purpose, a 'dialectician' in respect, not of his moral purpose, but of his faculty."[7] It is perfectly obvious that here Aristotle does not wish the term "sophist" to have the unfavourable meaning which it has in the pages of Plato. For Aristotle here a "sophist" is a learned, "wise" man, someone whose distinction depends upon something more than his technical skill, let us say, as a dialectician, this something more being his προαίρεσις, his "moral purpose."[8] Aristotle apparently is disturbed by the fact that no such term as "sophist" is available to him in the field of oratory. The only word that can be used is "rhetorician," which can be applied both to the technically skilled speaker and to the speaker who has "moral purpose." In any event, the clear purport of the passage is to indicate, at least in the present circumstance, that Aristotle wishes us to see moral purpose as basic in his rhetorical theory.

There are other places where Aristotle appears to be attempting to relate rhetoric or persuasion to some form of accepted goodness. For example, when he asserts that in oral discourse, there are three ways in which belief is produced--by the character of the speaker, by his capacity to get his hearers into a proper frame of mind, and by the demonstration or apparent demonstration provided in his argument--Aristotle goes on to say: "Persuasion is achieved by the speaker's personal character when the speech is so spoken as to make us think him credible. We believe good men more fully and more readily than others.... It is not true, as some writers assume in their treatises on rhetoric, that the personal goodness revealed by the speaker contributes nothing to his power of persuasion; on the contrary, his character may almost be called the most effective means of persuasion he possesses."[9] And the same general spirit is evident, when a few lines later Aristotle remarks: "There are, then, these three means of effecting persuasion. The man who is to be in command of them must, it is clear, be able (1) to reason logically, (2) to understand human character and goodness in their various forms, and (3) to understand the emotions--that is, to name them and describe them, to know their causes and the way in which they are excited."[10]

Now we may turn to the other side of the ambivalence of the Rhetoric, as a practical handbook for the public speaker, in order

to discover, if we can, the attitude towards value therein disclosed.
Actually, Aristotle gets down to practical matters in the third chapter of the first book. After having distinguished between the three
types of rhetoric or oratory, viz., political, legal, and epideictic,
or declamatory, he makes the following statement which gives us a
clue as to what we may expect so far as the question of value is
concerned: "Rhetoric has three distinct ends in view, one for each
of its three kinds. The political orator aims at establishing the
expediency or the harmfulness of a proposed course of action; if he
urges its acceptance, he does so on the ground that it will do good;
if he urges its rejection, he does so on the ground that it will do
harm; and all other points, such as whether the proposal is just
or unjust, honourable or dishonourable, he brings in as subsidiary
and relative to this main consideration. Parties in a law case aim
at establishing the justice or injustice of some action, and they too
bring in all other points as subsidiary and relative to this one.
Those who praise or attack a man aim at proving him worthy of
honour or the reverse, and they too treat all other considerations
with reference to this one."[11] The main point to observe in this
passage is that there is an increasing emphasis upon the tactics of
the orator as he engages in the activity of persuasion. The political speaker is advised to concentrate upon the expediency or ad-
vantageousness, τὸ συμφέρον, or the harmfulness "of a proposed
course of action" and to regard as secondary matters of justice,
injustice, honour, or dishonour. The situation is similar in the
case of the trial-lawyer. Admittedly there is some lack of clarity
in the advice, but the disturbing element is that nowhere is the
speaker urged to say what is true about the point at issue. Perhaps we may be accused of being overly-sensitive on this question,
but we are, I believe, justified in so feeling because of the numerous other places in which this practical "eristic" attitude is pat-
ent.[12]

The fourth chapter of the first book of the Rhetoric provides
a good illustration of the point we are trying to make. Aristotle
starts out bravely by suggesting that a political orator must be
concerned with values. "First, then, we must ascertain what are
the kinds of things, good or bad, about which the political orator
offers counsel."[13] But he immediately drops the "good or bad, "
leaving it in the realm of conventional response, and proceeds to
make several analytical and practical distinctions. He then makes
the following very revealing admission: "The truth is, as indeed
we have said already, that rhetoric is a combination of the science
of logic and of the ethical branch of politics; and it is partly like
dialectic, partly like sophistical reasoning. But the more we try
to make either dialectic or rhetoric not, what they really are,
practical faculties, but sciences, the more we shall inadvertently
be destroying their true nature; for we shall be refashioning them
and shall be passing into the region of sciences dealing with definite subjects rather than simply with words and forms of reasoning."[14] In this curious statement, we are justified in applauding
Aristotle's effort to see rhetoric as he thought it truly to be, but

at the same time, in so doing he reduces it to be nothing more
than a matter of words.   It is in this way that Aristotle in effect
divorces rhetoric from any firm philosophical undergirding, despite
the fact that he made the efforts to establish such an interrelation
in the passages we discussed at the outset of the present chapter.
Rhetoric thus becomes nakedly the study of that which will practically produce persuasion.   "Anything goes, " if only persuasion
emerges.

        We can almost rest our case by presenting a somewhat
lengthy passage which brings out crystal clear the value "climate"
in which Aristotelian rhetoric operates.   In the fifth chapter of the
first book of the treatise, he introduces the subject of happiness.
"We may define happiness as prosperity combined with virtue; or
as independence of life; or as the secure enjoyment of the maxi-
mum of pleasure; or as a good condition of property and body, together with the power of guarding one's property and body and making use of them.   That happiness is one or more of these things,
pretty well everybody agrees.

        "From this definition of happiness it follows that its con-
stituent parts are: good birth, plenty of friends, good friends,
wealth, good children, plenty of children, a happy old age, also
such bodily excellences as health, beauty, strength, large stature,
athletic powers, together with fame, honour, good luck, and virtue, [or also the parts of it, practical wisdom, bravery, justice,
and moderation].   A man cannot fail to be completely independent
if he possesses these internal and external goods; for besides these
there are no others to have.   (Goods of the soul and of the body
are internal.   Good birth, friends, money, and honour are external.)   Further, we think that he should possess resources and
luck, in order to make his life really secure.   As we have already ascertained what happiness in general is, so now let us try
to ascertain what each of these parts of it is. "[15]   Very little is
needed by way of comment on this quotation.   The definition of
happiness is totally lacking in any kind of philosophical or critical
discrimination.   Aristotle seems rather to have lumped together
most of the conventional views of men with respect to the nature
of happiness.   And the list of the components of happiness which
follows contains practically every worldly "good" that anybody
could think of.   A nod, to be sure, is given to the notion that in
some sense happiness must be attended by virtue, but this idea is
to all intents and purposes buried in the recital of conventional
goods--good birth, friends, wealth, many good children, and so on
and on, even to a mention of stature and athletic capability.   Where,
oh, where is the contemplative philosopher of the Nicomachean
Ethics ?   Perhaps he might not be handsome enough, or tall enough,
to qualify for the value climate of the Rhetoric.

        Aristotle devotes the remainder of the fifth chapter to more
extended descriptions of each of the constituents of happiness, and
in the following chapter he continues in much the same vein.   The

argument is introduced in these words: "Now the political or deliberative orator's aim is utility: deliberation seeks to determine not ends but the means to ends, i.e., what it is most useful to do. Further, utility is a good thing. We ought therefore to assure ourselves of the main facts about Goodness and Utility in general."[16] Then there ensues a popular or conventional discussion of what is good and useful, along with a virtual repetition of the list of all those things which people regard as good, these being in effect the "parts" of happiness already submitted in the preceding chapter. But at the conclusion of the list, Aristotle again makes clear the unrelievedly practical, or nonphilosophical, atmosphere in which he proposes to carry forward his analysis of rhetoric, when he observes: "The above are pretty well all the things admittedly good. In dealing with things whose goodness is disputed, we may argue in the following ways: That is good of which the contrary is bad. That is good the contrary of which is to the advantage of our enemies; for example, if it is to the particular advantage of our enemies that we should be cowards, clearly courage is of particular value to our countrymen. And generally, the contrary of that which our enemies desire, or of that at which they rejoice, is evidently valuable."[17] It seems scarcely necessary to point out the essential amoralism of this passage, as well as the striking want of philosophical rigour. For example, a value is determined by its being the opposite of what an enemy values. What a strange defence of the moral value courage is herewith offered. We could not be more clearly in the milieu of the worldly.

It has often been argued that such criticisms as we have been making against the Rhetoric are not justified on the ground that the treatise is a practical handbook, a "book of directions" for practical public speakers, and therefore its author is not obligated to face the problem of the philosophical prior assumptions upon the basis of which the rhetorical theory is being developed. Such a defence can hardly stand examination. In the first place, the Rhetoric is found in the corpus of Aristotle in which all the various treatises are in one way or another related to the central view or views of Aristotelian philosophy or metaphysics. Secondly, such an effort to attempt to relate the Rhetoric to the basic Aristotelian position is made at the outset of the treatise, but, as we have tried to indicate, this effort tends to fall out of sight as the claims of the mode of the practical handbook move to the fore, and hence the ambivalence we noted has arisen. And finally, like any other subject or discipline, rhetoric demands to be philosophical. Certainly this must be the case if a study of rhetoric is to transcend the limits of a mere collection of the technical tricks of the trade. That rhetoric should be more than a study of techniques, in other words, that rhetoric must be related to philosophy, is the ground of Plato's critique of the Sophists' view of rhetoric in the Gorgias and the Phaedrus. Therefore, there is legitimate ground to hold that, if Aristotle had equipped himself with a more thoroughgoing theory of value, it would have been impossible for him to have compounded such a worldly and conventional treatise as his Rhetoric proves to be.[18]

No real purpose would be served by a detailed examination
of the remainder of the first book of the Rhetoric.   It will suffice
to point to two or three passages where the conventionality of the
work may be illustrated.[19]   For example, in the seventh chapter,
Aristotle sets out to study "relative goodness and relative utility."[20]
There follows an analysis of comparative values, a "consideration
of degree--the lore of 'less and more,' " as Roberts describes
it.[21]   Typical of the way in which Aristotle develops his argument
is this remark: "Again, that which would be judged, or which has
been judged, a good thing, or a better thing than something else,
by all or most people of understanding, or by a majority of men,
or by the ablest, must be so; either without qualification, or in so
far as they use their understanding to form their judgement."[22]
As is obvious, here we meet again the phronimos, the human being
who possesses practical wisdom, as a sanction for value, as well
as the "majority of men."   To mention the latter as a sanction is,
of course, nothing more than to raise conventional opinion to a
position of over-riding importance.

Let us cite another example.   "The most important and effective qualification for success in persuading audiences and speaking well on public affairs is to understand all the forms of government and to discriminate their respective customs, institutions,
and interests.   For all men are persuaded by considerations of
their interest, and their interest lies in the maintenance of the established order."[23]   While it is perfectly laudible on Aristotle's
side to urge that public counselors should be well versed in the
various forms of government, one cannot help but be slightly dis-
tressed by the latent amoralism involved in the emphasis upon successful persuasion.   In other words, the orator, as Aristotle goes
on to point out, must find out what the goal of a given form of
government is, deduce from it the interest of a citizen under that
government, and in the light of these data persuade the citizen to
believe that his interest lies in the preservation of the form of
government.   So, if an orator is addressing an audience in an oligarchy, he must know that the goal of an oligarchy is money.
Therefore the citizen in an oligarchy has as his goal money also.
The orator then will be successful in his persuasion if he convinces
the citizen that he will achieve his goal, money, only so long as
the established oligarchical order is maintained.   Note that the
orator is not invited to raise any question with respect to the worth
of oligarchy as a form of government, and, furthermore, he is
tacitly invited not to intrude his own convictions on political matters.   And in addition to our point about latent amoralism, we must
observe again that the discussion is carried forward on the strict
level of conventional value thinking.

For another example, there is a passage which we should
have before us where the latent amoralism or even immoralism is
not so latent.   It occurs in Aristotle's treatment of epideictic or

display oratory and it runs as follows: "Since we praise a man
for what he has actually done, and fine actions are distinguished
from others by being intentionally good, we must try to prove that
our hero's noble acts are intentional.   This is all the easier if we
can make out that he has often acted so before, and therefore we
must assert coincidences and accidents to have been intended.
Produce a number of good actions, all of the same kind, and
people will think that they must have been intended, and that they
prove the good qualities of the man who did them."[24]   The deception invited by this passage is clear.   The orator is instructed to
say that the actions of the object of his praise, which in fact were
not done as a result of moral purpose, προαίρεσις, were so done.
It is his task to make his "hero's" coincidental and accidental actions appear to have been undertaken purposefully.   The suggestion
is offered that this palpable untruth can be made plausible to the
audience by referring to the subject's previous history of purpose-
ful action.   It may be urged that this particular illustration is
trivial, but, no matter how trivial it may be, it still makes plain
Plato's contention that rhetoric, defined as the artificer of persuasion, is a producer of "seeming, " and not of truth.

An even more decisive illustration to support the point we
have been trying to establish occurs at the very end of the first
book of the Rhetoric, where Aristotle is treating the question of
oaths.   "If you have already sworn an oath that contradicts your
present one, you must argue that it is not perjury, since perjury
is a crime, and a crime must be a voluntary action, whereas
actions due to the force or fraud of others are involuntary.   You
must further reason from this that perjury depends on the intention
and not on the spoken words.   But if it is your opponent who has
already sworn an oath that contradicts his present one, you must
say that if he does not abide by his oaths he is the enemy of society, and that this is the reason why men take an oath before ad-
ministering the laws."[25]   There is no escaping the fact that the
orator is here advised to operate on an egregious moral double
standard.   If he is caught in a situation involving perjury, i.e.,
having sworn two oaths that contradict each other, he is urged to
wriggle out of his trouble by employing rather dubious means such
as denying that it was really perjury, by hinting that the first oath
was taken under duress, and hence was involuntary, and hence not
a crime.   And it is even suggested further that in fact "perjury
depends on the intention and not on the spoken words. " Whereas,
if his opponent on the other hand is discovered in an identical situation, our good orator is exhorted to assume a lofty moral line by
asserting that anyone who breaks an oath is a subverter of society
--"He destroys everything. " No further comment is needed.

The opening chapter of the second book of the Rhetoric gives
further evidence that Aristotle's view of persuasion is based ultimately upon it as an instrument to produce "seeming. " Since
rhetoric has to do with the making of decisions, Aristotle argues,
"The orator must not only try to make the argument of his speech

demonstrative and worthy of belief; he must also make his own character look right and put his hearers, who are to decide, into the right frame of mind. Particularly in political oratory, but also in lawsuits, it adds much to an orator's influence that his own character should look right and that he should be thought to entertain the right feelings towards his hearers; and also that his hearers should be in just the right frame of mind. "26 The elements of "seeming" or "appearance" are obvious. The orator must make his own character "look right. " He should carefully calculate how he may put his hearers into a proper attitude of mind. He must then believe that he is rightly disposed towards them, or in other words he must "appear" to be so disposed. Perhaps Aristotle would answer this criticism by insisting that in the context of rhetoric it is not necessary to raise the question whether the orator does in fact possess a good character or is in fact rightly disposed towards his audience. He might even add that it would not be too easy for a man to make his character "look right" unless actually his character was good. Such an answer may mitigate the criticism to a degree, but the fact remains that the text itself emphasizes "seeming" and "appearance, " and again it must be recalled that it is exactly this type of rhetoric against which Plato inveighs in the <u>Gorgias</u>.

The same tone of amoralism is apparent when Aristotle turns to the topic of the emotions. "The Emotions are all those feelings that so change men as to affect their judgements, and that are also attended by pain or pleasure. Such are anger, pity, fear, and the like, with their opposites. We must arrange what we have to say about each of them under three heads. Take, for instance, the emotion of anger: here we must discover (1) what the state of mind of angry people is, (2) who the people are with whom they usually get angry, and (3) on what grounds they get angry with them. It is not enough to know one or even two of these points; unless we know all three, we shall be unable to arouse anger in any one. "27 This indeed sounds like an excerpt from a manual for demagogues. One might suppose that Aristotle would defend himself by referring to the rather mundane doctrine of the <u>Nicomachean Ethics</u> which honours an angry man in these words: "The man who is angry at the right things and with the right people, and, further, as he ought, when he ought, and as long as he ought, is praised. "28 But, on the other hand, the element of calculation urged upon the orator so that he can successfully play upon the emotions of his hearers, as in the case of anger seems to be open to question. The spirit of calculation is best seen in the analysis of how to arouse the emotion under the "three heads, " without a complete grasp of which a speaker will be powerless "to arouse anger in any one. " Aristotle, be it noted, does not ask the question here whether it is right or justifiable for the speaker to arouse anger or whether the indulgence in anger is a meritorious action. Without such questions, the advice suggested could well be used by the most unscrupulous rabble-rouser in order to defend himself. It might be added that the underlying ethical position of this quotation cannot be acceptable either to Platonic or Christian feeling, and we can recall as well that the Christian position may even question the validity of "righteous indignation, " particularly if an individual is obviously luxuriating in it.

Two more quotations, taken almost at random, should suffice to bring our discussion of the element of deception, amoralism, immoralism--call it what you will--in Aristotelian rhetorical theory. The first occurs in a discussion of the use of maxims, or gnomic sayings, "To declare a thing to be universally true when it is not is most appropriate when working up feelings of horror and indignation in our hearers; especially by way of preface, or after the facts have been proven. Even hackneyed and commonplace maxims are to be used, if they suit one's purpose: just because they are commonplace, everyone seems to agree with them, and therefore they are taken for truth. "[29] All we need note is the approval of Aristotle given to a bare-faced prevarication, if only it achieves the desired effect among the hearers. We cannot refrain from mentioning one of the illustrations offered, which even for a fourth-century Greek is rather grisly. "Or, if he (i. e. , the orator) is urging people to destroy the innocent children of their enemies, (sc., he may quote), 'Fool, who slayeth the father and leaveth his sons to avenge him. ' "[30] Perhaps we may be wrong to expect moral elevation in a practical handbook on rhetoric, but it does not seem unreasonable to ask that Aristotle exhibit a little more ethical sensitivity than he does in this passage.

Our second quotation is taken from the treatment of the spurious or apparent enthymeme. "Among the lines of argument that form the Spurious Enthymeme the first is that which arises from the particular words employed. One variety of this is when-- as in dialectic, without having gone through any reasoning process, we make a final statement as if it were the conclusion of such a process, 'Therefore so-and-so is not true, ' 'Therefore also so-and-so must be true'--so too in rhetoric, a compact and antithetical utterance passes for an enthymeme, such language being the proper province of enthymeme, so that it is seemingly the form of wording here that causes the illusion mentioned. In order to produce the effect of genuine reasoning by our form of wording it is useful to summarize the results of a number of previous reasonings: as 'some he saved--others he avenged--the Greeks he freed. ' Each of these statements has been previously proved from other facts; but the mere collocation of them gives the impression of establishing some fresh conclusion. "[31] One need only call attention to the words which emphasize the production of "seeming" and appearance.

There remains but to consider briefly the eleventh chapter of Rhetoric I, in which Aristotle discusses the topic of pleasure. It is not necessary to examine it in detail save to note how broadly important pleasure seems to be in his eyes in the context of rhetoric. Take his opening definition: "We may lay it down that Pleasure is a movement, a movement by which the soul as a whole is conscious-

ly brought into its normal state of being; and that Pain is the opposite."32 This definition is bound to be somewhat surprising in
the light of the assertion of the Nicomachean Ethics that pleasure
is an activity, and hence not a "movement."33 In any event, this
eleventh chapter attempts to establish an equivalence between
pleasure and "what is natural" and proceeds to list in conventional
terms almost everything which can in any way be regarded as
pleasurable. The range is imposing as it covers the areas of the
intellect, the body, and the emotions. Anger is called pleasant,
for example, as is revenge. Victory also is designated as a
pleasure, and should even be so regarded in games like "knuckle-
bones, ball, dice, and draughts."34 The purport of it all is that
pleasure must be regarded as an important value or sanction for
value by the rhetorician as he practices his craft of producing persuasion.

It is our hope that we have been able to delineate the
Rhetoric as basically ambivalent, which opens with an attempt to
fix philosophical grounds for the theory about to be offered but
which as it moves forward becomes detached from its philosophical
base and is transformed into a technology of persuasion. We hope
also to have shown in this latter aspect that the treatise gives frequent evidence of amoralism or even on occasion immoralism when,
as Cicero might have put it, the orator is advised to throw dis-
honest "dust in the eyes of the jury." And we should like to repeat our contention that Aristotle might not have been guilty of this
amoralism, had he been able to be guided by a firm theory of
value of his own construction.

NOTES

1. Cf. Ross, Aristotle, pp. 275-276.
2. Rhetoric I, 1355 b 25-26. Ἔστω δὴ ἡ ῥητορικὴ δύναμις περὶ
     ἕκαστον τοῦ θεωρῆσαι τὸ ἐνδεχόμενον πιθανόν. Ross's text.
     The translation is mine, in a somewhat expanded form. Cf.
     above, Chapter IV, note 8, where the definition was quoted, and
     where also may be found the translations of Roberts and Cooper.
3. Plato, Gorgias, 453 a 2. πειθοῦς δημιουργός ἐστιν ἡ ῥητορική.
     Burnet's text.
4. Cf. Ross, Aristotle, pp. 270-271. In general, an enthymeme
     has the basic form of a syllogism. Its premises are prob-
     abilities, and in argument one of them may be suppressed.
5. Rhetoric I, 1355 a 14-18. τό τε γὰρ ἀληθὲς καὶ τὸ ὅμοιον τῷ
     ἀληθεῖ τῆς αὐτῆς ἐστι δυνάμεως ἰδεῖν, ἅμα δε καὶ οἱ ἄνθρωποι
     πρὸς τὸ ἀληθὲς πεφύκασιν ἱκανῶς καὶ τὰ πλείω τυγχάνουσι
     τῆς ἀληθείας, διὸ πρὸς τὰ ἔνδοξα στοχαστικῶς ἔχειν τοῦ ὁμοίως ἔχοντος
     καὶ πρὸς τὴν ἀλήθειάν ἐστιν. Ross's text.
6. Rhetoric I, 1355 a 29-38 (omitting 33-36). ἔτι δὲ τἀναντία δεῖ
     δύνασθαι πείθειν, καθάπερ καὶ ἐν τοῖς συλλογισμοῖς, οὐχ ὅπως
     ἀμφότερα πράττωμεν (οὐ γὰρ δεῖ τὰ φαῦλα πείθειν), ἀλλ' ἵνα μὴ
     λανθάνῃ πῶς ἔχει, καὶ ὅπως ἄλλου χρωμένου τοῖς λόγοις μὴ δικαίως

αὐτοὶ λύειν ἔχωμεν. . . . τὰ μέντοι ὑποκείμενα **πράγματα οὐχ ὁμοίως ἔχει, ἀλλ' ἀεὶ τἀληθῆ καὶ τὰ βελτίω τῇ φύσει εὐσυλλογιστότερα καὶ πιθανώτερα** ὡς ἁπλῶς εἰπεῖν. Ross's text.

7. Rhetoric I, 1355 b 15-21. πρὸς δὲ τούτοις ὅτι τῆς αὐτῆς τό τε πιθανὸν καὶ τὸ φαινόμενον ἰδεῖν πιθανόν, ὥσπερ καὶ ἐπὶ τῆς διαλεκτικῆς συλλογισμόν τε καὶ φαινόμενον συλλογισμόν· ἡ γὰρ σοφιστικὴ οὐκ ἐν τῇ δυνάμει ἀλλ' ἐν τῇ προαιρέσει· πλὴν ἐνταῦθα μὲν ἔσται ὁ μὲν κατὰ τὴν ἐπιστήμην ὁ δὲ κατὰ τὴν προαίρεσιν ῥήτωρ, ἐκεῖ δὲ σοφιστὴς μὲν κατὰ τὴν προαίρεσιν, διαλεκτικὸς δὲ οὐ κατὰ τὴν προαίρεσιν ἀλλὰ κατὰ τὴν δύναμιν. Ross's text. The reader should be aware that "dialectic" in this passage has a different meaning from the "dialectic" of Plato's Phaedrus, to which we have just referred.

8. Given the context, Roberts appears to be justified in translating **προαίρεσις** as "moral purpose." The primary meaning is simply "choice."

9. Rhetoric I, 1356 a 4-13 (omitting 7-10). διὰ μὲν οὖν τοῦ ἤθους, ὅταν οὕτω λεχθῇ ὁ λόγος ὥστε ἀξιόπιστον ποιῆσαι τὸν λέγοντα· τοῖς γὰρ ἐπιεικέσι πιστεύομεν μᾶλλον καὶ θᾶττον. . . . οὐ γάρ, ὥσπερ ἔνιοι τῶν τεχνολογούντων, ‹οὐ› τίθεμεν ἐν τῇ τέχνῃ καὶ τὴν ἐπιείκειαν τοῦ λέγοντος. ὡς οὐδὲν συμβαλλομένης πρὸς τὸ πιθανόν, ἀλλὰ σχεδὸν ὡς εἰπεῖν κυριωτάτην ἔχει πίστιν τὸ ἦθος. Ross's text.

10. Rhetoric I, 1356 a 20-25. ἐπεὶ δ' αἱ πίστεις διὰ τούτων εἰσί, φανερὸν ὅτι ταύτας ἐστὶ λαβεῖν τοῦ συλλογίσασθαι δυναμένου καὶ τοῦ θεωρῆσαι περὶ τὰ ἤθη καὶ περὶ τὰς ἀρετὰς καὶ τρίτον [τοῦ] περὶ τὰ πάθη, τί τε ἕκαστόν ἐστιν τῶν παθῶν καὶ ποῖόν τι, καὶ ἐκ τίνων ἐγγίνεται καὶ πῶς. Ross's text. Other passages which might be cited in this connection are: Rhetoric III, 1404 b I-4 [Style, or the "virtue of speaking," λέξεως ἀρετή, must be marked by clarity and by appropriateness, being neither too mean nor beyond what the subject merits.]; 1417 a 24-28 [the importance of moral purpose]; 1418-a 38-bI.

11. Rhetoric I, 1358 b 20-29. τέλος δὲ ἑκάστοις τούτων ἕτερόν ἐστι, καὶ τρισὶν οὖσι τρία, τῷ μὲν συμβουλεύοντι τὸ συμφέρον καὶ βλαβερόν· ὁ μὲν γὰρ προτρέπων ὡς βέλτιον συμβουλεύει, ὁ δὲ ἀποτρέπων ὡς χείρονος ἀποτρέπει, τὰ δ' ἄλλα πρὸς τοῦτο συμπαραλαμβάνει, ἢ δίκαιον καὶ τὸ ἄδικον, ἢ καλὸν ἢ αἰσχρόν· τοῖς δὲ δικαζομένοις τὸ δίκαιον καὶ τὸ ἄδικον, τὰ δ' ἄλλα καὶ οὗτοι συμπαραλαμβάνουσι πρὸς ταῦτα· τοῖς δ' ἐπαινοῦσιν καὶ ψέγουσιν τὸ καλὸν καὶ τὸ αἰσχρόν, τὰ δ' ἄλλα καὶ οὗτοι πρὸς ταῦτα ἐπαναφέρουσιν. Ross's text.

12. We have in mind, or course, Plato's conception of eristic as the method in argument which justifies the use of any and all means in order to beat an opponent quite irrespective of the merits or "truth" of the case.

13. Rhetoric I, 1359 a 30-31. **Πρῶτον μὲν οὖν ληπτέον περὶ ποῖα ἀγαθὰ ἢ κακὰ ὁ συμβουλεύων συμβουλεύει.** Ross's text.

14. Rhetoric I, 1359 b 8-16. ὅπερ γὰρ καὶ πρότερον εἰρηκότες τυγχάνομεν ἀληθές ἐστιν, ὅτι ἡ ῥητορικὴ σύγκειται μὲν ἔκ τε τῆς ἀναλυτικῆς ἐπιστήμης καὶ τῆς περὶ τὰ ἤθη πολιτικῆς, ὁμοία δ'

ἐστὶν τὰ μὲν τῇ διαλεκτικῇ τὰ δὲ τοῖς σοφιστικοῖς λόγοις. ὅσῳ
δ' ἄν τις ἢ διαλεκτικὴν ἢ ταύτην μὴ καθάπερ ἂν δυνάμεις
ἀλλ' ἐπιστήμας πειρᾶται κατασκευάζειν, λήσεται τὴν φύσιν αὐτῶν ἀφα-
νίσας τῷ μεταβαίνειν ἐπισκευάζων εἰς ἐπιστήμας ὑποκειμένων τινῶν
πραγμάτων, ἀλλὰ μὴ μόνον λόγων. Ross's text. Roberts
may have over-translated when he renders
as "simply with words and forms of reasoning."

15. Rhetoric I, 1360 b 14-30. ἔστω δὴ εὐδαιμονία εὐπραξία μετ'
ἀρετῆς, ἢ αὐτάρκεια ζωῆς, ἢ ὁ βίος ὁ μετὰ ἀσφαλείας ἥδιστος, ἢ
εὐθενία κτημάτων καὶ σωμάτων μετὰ δυνάμεως φυλακτικῆς τε καὶ
πρακτικῆς τούτων· σχεδὸν γὰρ τούτων ἓν ἢ πλείω τὴν εὐδαιμονίαν
ὁμολογοῦσιν εἶναι ἅπαντες.

εἰ δή ἐστιν ἡ εὐδαιμονία τοιοῦτον, ἀνάγκη αὐτῆς εἶναι μέρη
εὐγένειαν, πολυφιλίαν, χρηστοφιλίαν, πλοῦτον, εὐτεκνίαν,
πολυτεκνίαν, εὐγηρίαν· ἔτι τὰς τοῦ σώματος ἀρετάς (οἷον ὑγίειαν,
κάλλος, ἰσχύν, μέγεθος, δύναμιν ἀγωνιστικήν), δόξαν, τιμήν, εὐτυχίαν,
ἀρετήν [ἢ καὶ τὰ μέρη αὐτῆς φρόνησιν, ἀνδρείαν, δικαιοσύνην,
σωφροσύνην]· οὕτω γὰρ ἂν αὐταρκέστατός <τις> εἴη, εἰ ὑπάρχοι
αὐτῷ τά τ' ἐν αὐτῷ καὶ τὰ ἐκτὸς ἀγαθά· οὐ γὰρ ἐστιν ἄλλα παρὰ
ταῦτα. ἔστι δ' ἐν αὐτῷ μὲν τὰ περὶ ψυχὴν καὶ τὰ ἐν σώματι, ἔξω δὲ
εὐγένεια καὶ φίλοι καὶ χρήματα καὶ τιμή, ἔτι δὲ προσήκειν οἰόμεθα
δυνάμεις ὑπάρχειν καὶ τύχην· οὕτω γὰρ ἀσφαλέστατος ὁ βίος.
λάβωμεν τοίνυν ὁμοίως καὶ τούτων ἕκαστον τί ἐστιν.   Ross's text.
I have added a rendering for the bracketed section in 23-24,
which is omitted in the Oxford version.

16. Rhetoric I, 1362 a 17-21. ἐπεὶ δὲ πρόκειται τῷ συμβουλεύοντι
σκοπὸς τὸ συμφέρον (βουλεύονται γὰρ οὐ περὶ τοῦ τέλους, ἀλλὰ
περὶ τῶν πρὸς τὸ τέλος, ταῦτα δ' ἐστὶ τὰ συμφέροντα κατὰ τὰς
πράξεις, τὸ δὲ συμφέρον ἀγαθόν), ληπτέον ἂν εἴη τὰ στοιχεῖα περὶ
ἀγαθοῦ καὶ συμφέροντος ἁπλῶς. Ross's text.

17. Rhetoric I, 1362 b 29-35. ταῦτα μὲν οὖν σχεδὸν ὁμολογούμενα
ἀγαθά ἐστιν· ἐν δὲ τοῖς ἀμφισβητησίμοις ἐκ τῶνδε οἱ συλλογισμοί · ᾧ
τὸ ἐναντίον κακόν. τοῦτ' ἀγαθόν. καὶ οὗ τὸ ἐναντίον τοῖς ἐχθροῖς
συμφέρει· οἷον εἰ τὸ δειλοὺς εἶναι μάλιστα συμφέρει τοῖς ἐχθροῖς,
δῆλον ὅτι ἀνδρεία μάλιστα ὠφέλιμον τοῖς πολίταις. καὶ ὅλως δ οἱ
ἐχθροὶ βούλονται ἢ ἐφ' ᾧ χαίρουσι, τοὐναντίον τούτου ὠφέλιμον
φαίνεται. Ross's text.

18. It should be remembered, however, that in the second book
of the Rhetoric where Aristotle is more explicitly concerned
with the techniques of argument, the sections involving the
enthymeme (especially chapter 22) do exhibit his effort to
connect formally rhetorical theory with logic.

19. Our only exception will be a brief discussion below of the attitude towards pleasure found in the eleventh chapter of
Rhetoric I.

20. This is Robert's rendering for περὶ τοῦ μείζονος ἀγαθοῦ καὶ τοῦ
μᾶλλον συμφέροντος, Rhetoric I, 1363 b 7.

21. Cf. Roberts, analytical Table of Contents, p. viii, in the Oxford translation.

22. Rhetoric I, 1364 b 11-14. καὶ ὃ κρίνειαν ἂν ἢ κεκρίκασιν οἱ
φρόνιμοι ἢ πάντες ἢ οἱ πολλοὶ ἢ οἱ πλείους ἢ οἱ κράτιστοι ἀγαθὸν
μεῖζον, ἀνάγκη οὕτως ἔχειν, ἢ ἁπλῶς ἢ ᾗ κατὰ τὴν φρόνησιν ἔκριναν.

Ross's text.

23. Rhetoric I, 1365 b 21-25. *Μέγιστον δὲ καὶ κυριώτατον ἁπάντων*
    πρὸς τὸ δύνασθαι πείθειν καὶ καλῶς συμβουλεύειν ‹τὸ› τὰς πολιτείας
    ἁπάσας λαβεῖν καὶ τὰ ἑκάστης ἤθη καὶ νόμιμα καὶ συμφέροντα
    διελεῖν. πείθονται γὰρ ἅπαντες τῷ συμφέροντι, συμφέρει δὲ τὸ
    σῶζον τὴν πολιτείαν. Ross's text.

24. Rhetoric I, 1367 b 22-27. *ἐπεὶ δ' ἐκ τῶν πράξεων ὁ ἔπαινος, ἴδιον*
    δὲ τοῦ σπουδαίου τὸ κατὰ προαίρεσιν, πειρατέον δεικνύναι πράττοντα
    κατὰ προαίρεσιν, χρήσιμον δὲ τὸ πολλάκις φαίνεσθαι πεπραχότα· διὸ
    καὶ τὰ συμπτώματα καὶ τὰ ἀπὸ τύχης ὡς ἐν προαιρέσει ληπτέον· ἂν
    γὰρ πολλὰ καὶ ὅμοια προφέρηται, σημεῖον ἀρετῆς εἶναι δόξει καὶ
    προαιρέσεως. Ross's text.

25. Rhetoric I, 1377 b 3-9. *ἐὰν δὲ ᾖ γεγενημένος ὑφ' αὑτοῦ καὶ*
    ἐναντίος, ὅτι οὐκ ἐπιορκία· ἑκούσιον γὰρ τὸ ἀδικεῖν, τὸ δ' ἐπιορκεῖν
    ἀδικεῖν ἐστι, τὰ δὲ βίᾳ καὶ ἀπάτῃ ἀκούσια. ἐνταῦθα οὖν συνακτέον
    καὶ τὸ ἐπιορκεῖν, ὅτι ἔστι τὸ τῇ διανοίᾳ ἀλλ' οὐ τῷ στόματι. ἐὰν δὲ
    τῷ ἀντιδίκῳ ᾖ ὑπεναντίος καὶ ὀμωμοσμένος, ὅτι πάντα ἀναιρεῖ
    μὴ ἐμμένων οἷς ὤμοσεν· διὰ γὰρ τοῦτο καὶ τοῖς νόμοις χρῶνται
    ὁμόσαντες. Ross's text. The Oxford translation is rather
    free, but nonetheless it seems to preserve accurately the
    meaning of the original. In connection with the phrase *ὅτι*
    ἔστι τὸ τῇ διανοίᾳ ἀλλ' οὐ τῷ στόματι, one cannot fail to be re-
    minded of the famous line in Euripides' Hippolytus, "It was
    not my heart but my tongue that swore" (*ἡ γλῶσσ' ὀμώμοχ',*
    ἡ δὲ φρὴν ἀνώμοτος, 612). Cf. Aristophanes' satiric use of
    the line, Frogs, 101-102, and 1471.

26. Rhetoric II, 1377 b 22-28. *ἀνάγκη μὴ μόνον πρὸς τὸν λόγον*
    ὁρᾶν, ὅπως ἀποδεικτικὸς ἔσται καὶ πιστός, ἀλλὰ καὶ αὑτὸν ποιόν
    τινα καὶ τὸν κριτὴν κατασκευάζειν· πολὺ γὰρ διαφέρει πρὸς πίστιν,
    μάλιστα μὲν ἐν ταῖς συμβολαῖς, εἶτα καὶ ἐν ταῖς δίκαις, τό τε
    ποιόν τινα φαίνεσθαι τὸν λέγοντα καὶ τὸ πρὸς αὑτοὺς ὑπολαμβάνειν
    πως διακεῖσθαι αὑτόν, πρὸς δὲ τούτοις ἐὰν καὶ αὐτοὶ διακείμενοί
    πως τυγχάνωσιν. Ross's text.

27. Rhetoric II, 1378 a 19-26. *ἔστι δὲ τὰ πάθη δι' ὅσα μεταβάλλοντες*
    διαφέρουσι πρὸς τὰς κρίσεις οἷς ἕπεται λύπη καὶ ἡδονή, οἷον ὀργὴ
    ἔλεος φόβος καὶ ὅσα ἄλλα τοιαῦτα, καὶ τὰ τούτοις ἐναντία. δεῖ δὲ
    διαιρεῖν περὶ ἕκαστον εἰς τρία, λέγω δ' οἷον περὶ ὀργῆς πῶς τε
    διακείμενοι ὀργίλοι εἰσί, καὶ τίσιν εἰώθασιν ὀργίζεσθαι, καὶ ἐπὶ
    ποίοις· εἰ γὰρ τὸ μὲν ἓν ἢ τὰ δύο ἔχοιμεν τούτων, ἅπαντα δὲ μή),
    ἀδύνατον ἂν εἴη τὴν ὀργὴν ἐμποιεῖν. Ross's text.

28. Nicomachean Ethics IV, 1125 b 31-32. *ὁ μὲν οὖν ἐφ' οἷς δεῖ*
    καὶ οἷς δεῖ ὀργιζόμενος, ἔτι δὲ καὶ ὡς δεῖ καὶ ὅτε καὶ ὅσον χρόνον,
    ἐπαινεῖται. Bywater's text.

29. Rhetoric II, 1395 a 8-12. *καθόλου δὲ μὴ ὄντος καθόλου εἰπεῖν*
    μάλιστα ἁρμόττει ἐν σχετλιασμῷ καὶ δεινώσει, καὶ ἐν τούτοις ἢ
    ἀρχόμενον ἢ ἀποδείξαντα. χρῆσθαι δὲ δεῖ καὶ ταῖς τεθρυλημέναις
    καὶ κοιναῖς γνώμαις, ἐὰν ὦσι χρήσιμοι· διὰ γὰρ τὸ εἶναι κοιναί, ὡς
    ὁμολογούντων πάντων, ὀρθῶς ἔχειν δοκοῦσιν. Ross's text.

30. Rhetoric II, 1395 a 17-18. *καὶ ἐπὶ τὸ ἀναιρεῖν τῶν ἐχθρῶν τὰ*
    τέκνα κα μηδὲν ἀδικοῦντα
    νήπιος ὃς πατέρα κτείνας παῖδας καταλείπει. Ross's text.
    Robert's translation. The line of poetry is from the Cypria,

Fragment 22.   Cf.   Kinkel,   Epicorum Graecorum Fragmenta
(Leipzig, Teubner, 1877).
31.   Rhetoric II, 1401 a 1-13.   τόποι δ' εἰσὶ τῶν φαινομένων
ἐνθυμημάτων εἰς μὲν ὁ παρὰ τὴν λέξιν, καὶ τούτου ἓν μὲν μέρος,
ὥσπερ ἐν τοῖς διαλεκτικοῖς, τὸ μὴ συλλογισάμενον συμπερασματικῶς
τὸ τελευταῖον εἰπεῖν, ''οὐκ ἄρα τὸ καὶ τό, ἀνάγκη ἄρα τὸ καὶ τό'',
ἐν τοῖς ἐνθυμήμασι τὸ συνεστραμμένως καὶ ἀντικειμένως εἰπεῖν
φαίνεται ἐνθύμημα (ἡ γὰρ τοιαύτη λέξις χώρα ἐστὶν ἐνθυμήματος)·
καὶ ἔοικε τὸ τοιοῦτον εἶναι παρὰ τὰ σχῆμα τῆς λέξεως. ἔστι δὲ
εἰς τὸ τῇ λέξει συλλογιστικῶς λέγειν χρήσιμον τὸ συλλογισμῶν
πολλῶν κεφάλαια λέγειν, ὅτι τοὺς μὲν ἔσωσε, τοῖς δ' ἑτέροις
ἐτιμώρησε, τοὺς δ' Ἕλληνας ἠλευθέρωσε· ἕκαστον μὲν γὰρ
τούτων ἐξ ἄλλων ἀπεδείχθη, συντεθέντων δὲ φαίνεται καὶ ἐκ τούτων τι
γίγνεσθαι. Ross's text.   The quotation in 10-11 is from
Isocrates, Evagoras, 65-9.
32.   Rhetoric I, 1369 b 33-35. Ὑποκείσθω δὴ ἡμῖν εἶναι τὴν ἡδονὴν
κίνησίν τινα τῆς ψυχῆς καὶ κατάστασιν ἀθρόαν καὶ αἰσθητὴν εἰς τὴν
ὑπάρχουσαν φύσιν, λύπην δὲ τοὐναντίον.   Ross's text.
33.   Cf. above, Chapter VII, pp. 299-301.
34.   Rhetoric I, 1371 a 2-3.   ἀστραγαλίσεις καὶ σφαιρίσεις καὶ
κυβείας καὶ πεττείας.   Ross's text.

7. THE PLACE OF THE ENTHYMEME
IN RHETORICAL THEORY*

by James H. McBurney

1. Some Introductory Considerations

Aristotle has defined rhetoric as "the faculty of discovering in the particular case what are the available means of persuasion."[1] Interpreting this definition for our purposes we may say that rhetoric is the art of discovering and using in those situations in which speaking and writing play a part, what are the most desirable means of oral and written persuasion. The term persuasion is here used in the broad sense to mean the influencing of human behavior through the use of written and oral symbols. The theory of rhetoric may be understood as the science which underlies this art, and to consist of a more or less organized system of concepts and principles, mostly philosophical and methodological in nature. These concepts and principles have been studied by countless scholars for many centuries as generalizations from examples of speaking and writing designed to improve practice in these arts.

Classical rhetoricians commonly divided their subject into five parts which they called inventio, dispositio, elocutio, memoria, and pronuntiatio. Inventio, the phase with which we shall be primarily concerned here, is the art of exploring the material to discover the lines of reasoning suitable for discussion in any given case. It includes the study of kinds and methods of reasoning, refutation, and fallacies; and is that part of rhetoric most closely related to logic. Says Clark, "In the practice of rhetoric inventio was thus the solidest and most important element. It included all of what today we might call 'working up the case.'"[2]

The enthymeme is a concept developed in this field of inventio and has specific reference to the problem of reasoning in speaking and writing. Ever since Aristotle the term "enthymeme" has been associated in some manner or other with the syllogism, the concept adduced by Aristotle to explain the nature of all reasoning and proof.[3] For Aristotle the enthymeme was the focal concept or

*Reprinted by permission of the author and of the Speech Communication Association, from Speech Monographs III (1936), 49-74.

element of all reasoned discourse.   He speaks of it as "the very
body and substance of persuasion. "[4]   Lane Cooper asks,

> How for example shall we know what our author (Aris-
> totle) means by the term Enthymeme?   This question
> goes to the very heart of the Rhetoric since Aristotle
> tells us that enthymemes are the essential instruments
> of oratorical persuasion. [5]

J. Barthelemy Saint-Hilaire says of the Aristotelian enthymeme in an appendix on the subject included with his French
translation of the Rhetoric:

> ... it occupies in the art of speaking essentially the
> place that the syllogism holds in logic.   If one does not
> know how to make Enthymemes, he can hardly flatter
> himself as being an orator. [6]

It is the purpose of this study to determine the place of the
enthymeme in rhetorical theory.   In the way of a justification of
the inquiry, if such is necessary, I invite your attention to three
propositions: (1) Contemporary rhetorical theory is essentially
Aristotelian; (2) the enthymeme is the focal concept in the rhetoric
of Aristotle; and (3) the enthymeme is seriously misunderstood
today.   For good or evil, depending upon one's point of view, our
ideas about reasoned discourse in speaking and writing remain essentially Aristotelian.   Even those who complain against the Aristotelian influence in this field, and seek new canons for these arts,
will recognize the importance of this influence and should welcome
interpretations.   We have Aristotle's own word for the central
place of the enthymeme in his rhetorical system.   The respects in
which this concept has been misunderstood, while the system of
which it is a part remained relatively intact, will be developed as
our study progresses.   Suffice it to say here that the prevailing
conception of the enthymeme as an elided syllogism is not the
sense in which Aristotle used this term.   As Saint-Hilaire puts it:

> Aristotle attached great importance to the use of the
> Enthymeme, without which the art of rhetoric seemed to
> him almost impossible.   Today the Enthymeme is rele-
> gated to a very secondary position; and this difference
> enables us to see the enormous interval which separates
> the point of view of the ancients from ours. [7]

2.   The Enthymeme in Aristotle

The works of Aristotle which set forth his logical and rhetorical system are Categoriae, De Interpretatione, Analytica Priora,
Analytica Posteriora, Topica, De Sophisticis Elenchis, and Rhetorica.   Aristotle is attempting in these treatises to set forth a system by which truth and certainty, in respect to human knowledge,

may be ascertained and demonstrated verbally; by which truth may be sought through discourse; and by which people may be convinced and persuaded.

A.   The Enthymeme as a part of Aristotle's Logical and Rhetorical System as a Whole: The diagram on the following page may be helpful in following the discussion in this section.   It is of first importance to notice the fundamental distinction which Aristotle makes between two great provinces of knowing, that of scientific knowledge or apodeictic certainty and that of reasoning in the realm of probabilities or opinion.   As Professor John Dewey puts it:

> All philosophies of the classic type have made a fixed and fundamental distinction between two realms of existence.   One of these corresponds to the religious and supernatural world of popular tradition, which in its metaphysical rendering became the world of highest and ultimate reality....   Over against this absolute and noumenal reality which could be apprehended only by the systematic discipline of philosophy itself stood the ordinary empirical, relatively real, phenomenal world of everyday experience.   It was with this world that the practical affairs and utilities of men were connected.   It was to this imperfect and perishing world that matter of fact, positivistic science referred. [8]

Aristotle distinguishes three separate but related methodologies for knowing and persuading, scientific demonstration, dialectic, and rhetoric.   Scientific demonstration is developed in the Prior and Posterior Analytics as the method of discovering and demonstrating truth; dialectic is explained in the Topics as a method of discovering what is probable truth through special forms of dialogue; and rhetoric is understood as the method of discovering what are the available means of persuasion.   Both dialectic and rhetoric are differentiated from scientific demonstration in the fact that they deal with probabilities and do not attempt apodeictic proof in the sense that it appears in scientific demonstration.

Special forms of the syllogism are explained as the methodological instrument in each of these fields and the distinction between induction and deduction introduced in each case.   In the Prior Analytics Aristotle analyzes the several figures and modes of the syllogism, explaining the first figure as the means of scientific demonstration par excellence.   It is the only figure in which the syllogism is perfect without conversion or reduction; it is the only figure in which every variety of conclusion can be proved; and the only one in which the universal affirmative can be proved--the great aim of scientific research. [9]   While Aristotle repeatedly contrasts deduction and induction, he does take the position that induction can be reduced to the syllogism. [10]   He believes further that induction "proceeds through an enumeration of all the cases. "   In

A DIAGRAM OF ARISTOTLE'S LOGICAL AND RHETORICAL SYSTEM

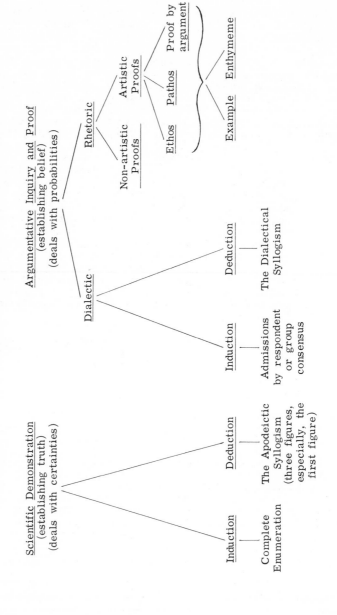

another connection Aristotle discusses induction as an intuitive process or an act of intellectual insight by which the particulars of
our experience suggest to us the principles which they exemplify.[11]

The peculiar characteristic of scientific reasoning consists
in its investigation of <u>causes</u> understood as <u>rationes essendi,</u> or
<u>the reasons for the being of a fact</u> as distinguished <u>from rationes</u>
<u>cognoscendi or reasons for acknowledging its being.</u>[12] Aristotle
states:

> We suppose ourselves to possess unqualified scientific
> knowledge of a thing, as opposed to knowing it in the ac-
> cidental way in which the sophist knows, when we think
> that we know the cause on which the fact depends, as the
> cause of that fact and of no other, and, further, that the
> fact could not be other than it is.[13]

> Assuming then that my thesis as to the nature of scientific
> knowledge is correct, the premises of demonstrated knowl-
> edge must be true, primary, immediate, better known
> than and prior to the conclusion, which is further related
> to them as effect to cause.... The premises must be
> the causes of the conclusion, better known than it, and
> prior to it; its causes, since we possess scientific knowl-
> edge of a thing only when we know its cause....[13]

> Where demonstration is possible, one who can give no
> account which includes the cause has no scientific knowl-
> edge.[13]

Dialectic constituted the art of discussion by question and
answer, of attacking and defending a given thesis from principles
of probability, such as the opinions of men in general, or of the
majority, or of certain eminent authorities. For this purpose,
Aristotle collected topics, or general principles of probability from
which appropriate premises might be drawn. Nearly two hundred
such topics are listed in his work of this name. Aristotle explains
that so far as the forms and rules of the syllogism are concerned,
these are alike applicable to both demonstration and dialectic. "In
both the formal conditions are the same, and the conclusion will
certainly be true, if the premises are true; in both the axioms of
deductive reasoning are assumed," says Grote.[14] Mansel points
out that Aristotle would at least regard logical or formal accuracy
as "salutary" in dialectical discussion.[15]

Concerning the method of dialectic it is important to notice
that Aristotle specifically recognizes its function as an agency for
inquiry and investigation. Its purposes are listed as "intellectual
training, casual encounters, and the philosophical sciences."[16] He
adds that "it has a further use in relation to the ultimate bases of
the principles used in the several sciences ... for dialectic is a
process of criticism wherein lies the path to the principles of all

inquiries. "[16] He distinguishes between dialectic as a competition
and "those who discuss things together in the spirit of inquiry, "[17]
and urges the importance of co-operative effort toward consensus.
He states:

> The principle that a man who hinders the common busi-
> ness is a bad partner, clearly applies to argument as
> well; for in arguments as well there is a common aim
> in view, except with mere contestants, for these cannot
> both reach the same goal; for more than one cannot pos-
> sibly win. [18]

Without pausing to recapitulate at this juncture, we now turn
to rhetoric, which, like dialectic, is differentiated from scientific
demonstration in the fact that it draws its premises from probabilities.   Rhetoric is concerned primarily with long, continuous discourse both spoken and written rather than the short question and
answer method of dialectic.   Cope emphasizes the additional point
that while theoretically rhetoric is as universal as dialectic in the
field of probabilities, practically it is limited for the most part to
a particular class of phenomena with which its two most important
branches, the deliberative and the judicial, almost exclusively deal,
namely human actions, characters, motives, and feelings; and so
it becomes closely associated with the study of Politics (including
Ethics) which treats of moral, social, and political phenomena, of
man as an individual and as a member of society. [19]

Aristotle distinguishes two great types of rhetorical proof,
artistic and non-artistic; the non-artistic proofs, roughly comparable to what contemporary writers in argumentation call 'evidence, '
are explained as "such as are not supplied by our own efforts, but
existed beforehand, such as witnesses, admissions under torture,
written contracts, and the like. "[20] By 'artistic' proofs [means of
persuasion] are meant those that may be furnished by the method
of Rhetoric through our own efforts. "[20] Three modes of persuasion are explained in connection with artistic proof.   "The first
kind reside in the character [ethos] of the speaker; the second consist in producing a certain [the right] attitude in the hearer; the
third appertain to the argument proper, in so far as it actually or
seemingly demonstrates. "[20]

In rhetoric, as well as scientific demonstration and dialectic,
induction and deduction are introduced as the methods of reasoning.
Here, however, the term "example" is assigned to induction and
the term "enthymeme" to deduction.   Aristotle states:

> 'Enthymeme' is the name I give to a rhetorical syllogism,
> 'example' to a rhetorical induction.   Whenever men in
> speaking effect persuasion through proofs, they do so
> either with examples or enthymemes; they use nothing
> else.   Accordingly, since all demonstration (as we have
> shown in the Analytics) is effected either by syllogism

[that is, deductively] or by induction, it follows that induction and syllogism [deduction] must be identified respectively with example and enthymeme. 21

In the following section we shall investigate the relations of
the enthymeme to the various types of rhetorical persuasion and to
the syllogisms of scientific demonstration and dialectic.   Thus far,
it has been our purpose to present a broad perspective of the logical and rhetorical system of which the enthymeme is a part.   This
larger view will be found helpful, if not indispensable, in interpreting the enthymeme.   The diagram on page 120 may be taken as a
summary of the present section.

B.   An examination of the Aristotelian passages in which
Enthymeme is given special treatment: The several passages in
which the enthymeme is given special treatment in Aristotle's
works present six points for investigation as follows: (1) The passages in which Aristotle explains that the materials of the enthymeme are probabilities (εἰκότα) and signs (σημεῖα); (2) the passages
in which Aristotle declares example to be a form of the enthymeme;
(3) the passages in which he discusses the relationship of the enthymeme to the topics or topoi; (4) those in which we may see the
relation of the enthymeme to ethos and pathos; (5) the passages in
which demonstrative and refutative enthymemes are distinguished;
and (6) the passages relating to the suppression of a proposition in
the enthymeme.

1.   The Enthymeme and Probabilities (εἰκότα) and signs
(σημεῖα):   The passages with which we are here concerned are
those in the Prior Analytics II. 27, and the Rhetoric I. 2.   While
these passages are admittedly difficult to interpret, 22 it is my conclusion that Aristotle meant by probabilities (εἰκότα) what we have
previously referred to as rationes essendi, and by signs (σημεῖα),
rationes cognoscendi.   We may say again that by a ratio essendi
we mean an argument which attempts to account for the fact or
principle maintained, supposing its truth granted: it assigns a
cause or a reason for the being of a fact.   The ratio cognoscendi,
on the other hand, is a reason for acknowledging the being of a
fact; it attempts to supply a reason which will establish the existence
of a fact without any effort to explain what has caused it.   When
Aristotle defines an enthymeme as "a syllogism starting from probabilities or signs, " this, then, is the distinction he appears to have
in mind.

The greatest difficulty arises in understanding what Aristotle
means by a probability or εἰκός.   His discussion is obscure and
he does not give us a complete example.   From the description
given, however, we can collect the following information concerning
an εἰκός: (1) It is a generally approved proposition or ὡς ἐπί τό
πολύ;23 (2) It is "already probable" as distinguished from a sign
which "affects to be, would be if it could, " Βούλεται εἶναι;24 (3) as
the probable it bears the same relation to that of which it is prob-

able as a universal statement to a particular; (4) it is dichotimized
with sign; and (5) examples are "the envious hate" and "love attends the objects of affection. "

　　　In other words εἰκός is a proposition expressing a general
principle of probability which when applied in argument does not
attempt to prove the existence of a fact, but rather (assuming its
existence) attempts to account for the fact.　　It is a ὡς ἐπί τό
πολύ (meaning "to happen generally and fall short of necessity")
already probable, whose application to particular phenomena accounts for their probability.　　By supplementing the fragmentary
examples which Aristotle gives us of εἰκός we can see that when
one concludes that Orestes loves his mother, because "love (usually) attends the objects of affection, " the argument does not attempt to prove (to give a sign) that Orestes actually does love his
mother; but rather (assuming it probable that he loves his mother)
attempts to account for or explain this phenomenon.　　Similarly
with the other proposition Aristotle cites, "the envious hate"--if
one concludes that John hates by virtue of the εἰκός, "the envious
hate, " it has not been proved that John actually does hate; but rather, assuming that he hates, it has suggested a possible cause of
his hating.

　　　Aristotle fortunately is much clearer in his definition of
signs.　　He distinguishes three types and gives us examples of
each, the certain sign in the first figure, the fallible sign in the
second figure, and the "example" in the third figure.[25]　　He states,
"a sign affects to be, would be if it could, a demonstrative proposition necessary or probable:　for anything that accompanies an
existing thing or fact, or precedes or follows anything that happens
or comes into being, is a sign either of its existence or of its
having happened. "　　This statement is in itself an excellent definition of a ratio cognoscendi, and that this is in fact what Aristotle
means by σημεῖον we can conclude with considerable assurance
from his three examples.　　His example of a certain sign
(τεκμήριον) which "bears toward the statement it is to prove the relation of a universal to a particular" and which appears in the first
figure, viz. that a woman is with child, because she has milk, is
clearly a ratio cognoscendi (even if the physiology is bad).　　The
having of milk is proof of the fact that a woman is with child (or
has recently given birth to a child), but it can hardly be construed
to be the cause of the pregnancy or the child.　　The same can be
said of the other examples of sign given in the Prior Analytics and
the Rhetoric.　　Those in the second figure, concluding from the observation that a woman is pale that she is pregnant, and that a man
has a fever because he breathes hard, are just as clearly cases of
rationes cognoscendi.　　In these instances both "paleness" and "hard
breathing" are plainly signs as distinguished from causes.　　The
cases cited of "example" in the third figure are also good instances
of signs as we have interpreted the term.

　　　Even in the absence of conclusive affirmative evidence that

Aristotle means to define εἰκός as a ratio essendi (and I think the evidence is fairly conclusive here), we can be reasonably safe in implying from his clear definition of sign as a ratio cognoscendi, that he meant so to define εἰκός; and especially is this true, since the same distinction is made in the case of the scientific syllogism as we have previously noticed.[26] An enthymeme, then, may be defined as a syllogism, drawn from probable causes, signs (certain and fallible) and examples. As a syllogism drawn from these materials, it is important to add here, the enthymeme starts from probable premises (probable in a material sense) and lacks formal validity in certain of the types explained. We shall have more to say about this later. It may also be well to notice here that the interpretation we have placed on εἰκότα and σημεῖα has an important bearing on the contemporary division of argument into antecedent probability, sign, and example.

2. Example as a form of Enthymeme: The second group of passages which help us to understand the enthymeme are those which explain "example" as a species of enthymeme. We have already noticed that Aristotle usually contrasts enthymeme and example, comparing the former to the syllogism and the latter to induction. We have also noted that in the Prior Analytics Aristotle takes the position that induction can be reduced to syllogistic form. Thus, he is altogether consistent in likewise reducing example to an enthymematic form. The passages bearing on this point are Prior Analytics II, 24, and Rhetoric II, 25. The most complete discussion of example as a form of argument without direct reference to its relation to the enthymeme is Rhetoric II, 20. Here Aristotle distinguishes two kinds of example, "one consisting in the mention of actual past facts, the other in the invention of facts by the speaker. Of the latter, again, there are two varieties, the illustrative parallel and the fable." The cases of example which Aristotle cites in this connection are instances of what we today understand as analogical reasoning. The reasoning in these cases, as is always true of analogy if analyzed completely, consists in generalizing from one or more instances and then making a deduction concerning the case in question. Aristotle says here, "Enthymemes based upon Example are those which proceed by induction from one or more similar cases, arrive at a general proposition, and then argue deductively to a particular inference."[27] In actual speaking, I might add, this "general rule" of which Aristotle speaks is rarely stated, thus giving the appearance of arguing directly from one particular case to another particular case. Aristotle recognizes this point when he states:

> Clearly then to argue by example is neither like reasoning from part to whole, nor like reasoning from whole to part, but rather reasoning from part to part, when both particulars are subordinate to the same term and one of them is known. It differs from induction, because induction starting from all the particular cases proves that the major term belongs to the middle, and does not apply the

syllogistic conclusion to the minor term, whereas argument by example does make this application and does not draw its proof from
all the particular cases.[28]

   3.   The Enthymeme and Topics: The passages in which
Aristotle discusses the relation of the enthymeme to the topoi or
topics are especially helpful in clarifying the relations between dialectical and rhetorical reasoning on the one hand and scientific
demonstration on the other.   Topoi, understood roughly as sources
or places from which arguments may be obtained, is a conception
which appears all through classical and mediaeval rhetoric.   While
the several lists of topics given in the Rhetoric are difficult to interpret,[29] it appears that Aristotle meant to distinguish three kinds
of topics as indicated in the following diagram:

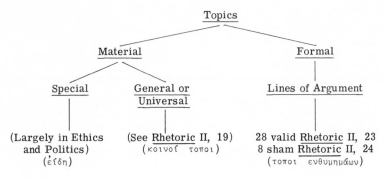

Topics

Material   Formal

Special   General or   Lines of Argument
                 Universal

(Largely in Ethics   (See Rhetoric II, 19)   28 valid Rhetoric II, 23
  and Politics)   (κοινοί τόποι)   8 sham Rhetoric II, 24
    (εἴδη)   (τόποι ενθυμημάων)

Provide premises for enthymemes   Provide "line of argument"
                                                 for enthymeme

          It is the distinction between special and general topics which
helps to explain the relationships between the various specialized
fields of knowledge, and that of rhetoric and dialectic.   Aristotle
makes the point that the special topics may be looked upon as substantive items or propositions peculiar to the special discipline to
which they belong; the general topics on the other hand, are general
principles of probability, understood in a propositional sense, with
application in all fields of knowledge.   While he states that arguments drawn from the general topics are typically rhetorical (or
dialectical, as the case may be) because of this universal application, he nevertheless makes the point that "enthymemes are mostly
formed from these particular and special topics."[30]   This seemingly paradoxical position may be explained as follows.   Aristotle recognizes the autonomy of the various special disciplines and makes
no claim that their subject matter is rhetorical or dialectical data
per se.   At the same time he feels strongly that so far as possible
the speaker and the writer should draw their premises from the
special data of whatever field they are discussing.[31]   His conviction

on this last point is evidenced, as every student of the Rhetoric knows, in his long treatment of politics and ethics in the Rhetoric, the two special disciplines with which the speaker is chiefly concerned.   In other words, while rhetoric as a science is concerned generically with those broad principles of probability which can be adduced to lend cogency to an argument in any field, and, as a methodological science, cannot be expected to be conversant with the special topics of the various substantive fields with which it deals, nevertheless it is important that any speaker be as thoroughly informed as possible in the particular substantive area in which he chooses to speak; and especially is it important that a skilled speaker "have a thorough and detailed knowledge of the special sciences which mainly concern the art of rhetoric--that is, Ethics and Politics, above all, since they have to do with the conduct of men as individuals, and with men in groups."[32]

The topics as "lines of argument" we interpret as methods of reasoning rather than material propositions.   Aristotle makes his transition to this list from a few concluding remarks which he has been making about special and general topics as follows:

> Here, then, we have one principle, and the first for selecting enthymemes; and it refers to the choice of materials for them.   Let us now pass on to their elementary forms: and by "elementary form" I mean the same thing as a class to which an enthymeme belongs.[33]

I think there is little question that we do have a list of methods of reasoning or types of inference in the topics discussed in Rhetoric II, 23-24.   Aristotle appears to have intended that this long enumeration of lines of argument be correlated, roughly at least, with the causes, signs and examples which he discusses in another connection.   The latter may be viewed as a careful, scientific statement of the kinds of enthymematic argument; the former, as a more or less random list of some of the more usual arguments from cause, sign, and example encountered in speaking and writing.[34]

In summary, then, we may say that whereas the speaker goes to the special or general topics for his premises, he may call upon these "lines of argument" for his mode of reasoning. The premises and the line of argument selected will together constitute an enthymeme.   If the enthymeme combines these elements in such a way as to constitute a ratio essendi, it is then an εἰκός; if it combines them in such a way as to constitute a ratio cognoscendi, it is then an argument from sign, which may, as we have seen, appear in the first, second, or third figure of the syllogism.

4.   The Enthymeme and Ethos and Pathos: A very common, and perhaps the usual interpretation of the Rhetoric is that enthymeme and example are the instruments of "rhetorical demonstration," and as such, are to be contrasted with those appeals which

are evinced through the personality of the speaker (ethos) and
those which make an emotional appeal (pathos). I wish to raise
the question here: Does Aristotle mean to bring out this contrast
to the extent of excluding the enthymeme from the realm of ethos
and pathos? The answer to this question is of considerable importance because upon it hinges the relationship of logical and non-
logical or emotional factors in speaking and writing. Are we to
consider the logical structure of an argument something that is
separate and distinct from the so-called emotional appeals? In
other words, what part if any does the enthymeme play in that
mode of persuasion which depends upon the personal character of
the speaker and that which attempts to affect the emotional state
of the listener?

To begin with we must recognize that the enthymeme is a
rhetorical device and as such is dependent, so to speak, upon language symbols, i.e., terms and propositions in significant combinations. Persuasion arising from the personality of the speaker
and other kindred factors (except as it finds its expression in terms
and propositions) is therefore clearly outside the realm of the enthymeme. But what about the personality appeal and attempts to influence the emotional state of the listener (or reader) which are expressed in words and sentences? Here we have the real question:
Is the enthymeme the controlling unit of expression in such persuasion, or is it a purely "logical" instrument of proof?

A careful analysis of Aristotle's system will reveal the
superficiality of attempting to separate the enthymeme from these
"non-logical" methods of persuasion. I submit that in Aristotle's
rhetorical system the enthymeme is the element or unit of all persuasive discourse. The admission of "emotionally loaded" terms
and propositions is in fact one of the important characteristics of
the enthymeme; the premises which compose an enthymeme are
usually nothing more than the beliefs of the audience which are
used as causes and signs to secure the acceptance of other propositions. These premises, as we have seen, are drawn from the
general and special topics or topoi. It is organized around lists
of these topics that Aristotle gives us his semi-popular discussion
of ethics and politics, virtues, vices, and emotions. In other
words, Aristotle presents what he has to say about both ethical
and pathetical persuasion in the form of topics, and we are explicitly told that these topics are the sources to which we may turn
for the propositions to compose our enthymemes. [35]

The order of treatment or sequence of the Rhetoric sus-
tains the position here taken on the enthymeme in relation to ethos
and pathos. Aristotle begins the Rhetoric by proclaiming the enthymeme to be the body and substance of all persuasion. In I, 2
he distinguishes among the three forms of artistic persuasion and
explains the enthymeme in terms of causes and signs. He concludes the same chapter by explaining his topics or topoi as the
places to which we turn for the premises of our enthymemes. Then

in I, 3 he distinguishes the three great divisions of oratory, political, forensic or judicial, and epideictic or ceremonial, and states that he will organize his discussion of topics around this division of the kinds of oratory. This he does and he concludes I, 3 just before taking up this discussion by saying,

> It is evident from what has been said that it is these three subjects, more than any others, about which the orator must be able to have propositions at his command. Now the propositions of Rhetoric are Complete Proofs, Probabilities, and Signs. Every kind of syllogism is composed of propositions, and the enthymeme is a particular kind of syllogism composed of the aforesaid propositions.

From I, 4 to I, 9 Aristotle gives the reader some practical politics designed to help the political orator in the selection of his enthymemes. In I, 9 he gives a discussion of virtues and vices designed to help the speaker in epideictic oratory. In I, 10 he turns to the topics of forensic oratory, stating: "We have next to treat of Accusation and Defense, and to enumerate and describe the ingredients of the syllogisms used therein." This discussion continues to I, 15 where we then are given a discussion of non-artistic proofs, with which Book I is closed.

Aristotle begins Book II by pointing out the importance of ethical and pathetical persuasion in the three types of oratory and from II, 1 to II, 19 gives us some practical psychology concerning human motives and emotions. It is with this that Aristotle concludes his discussion of special topics begun in I, 4. Having concluded his discussion of special topics, he devotes II, 19 to general topics. It will be remembered that the distinction between special and general topics in relation to the enthymeme was made in I, 3.

Upon concluding this discussion of the special and general topics from which the premises of our enthymemes must be drawn, he then in II, 20 takes up the study of the enthymeme in its various forms and concludes Book II in Chapter 26 with this material. Book III, of course, is devoted to style and delivery.

This view of the Rhetoric makes the organization of the work entirely logical and understandable. Aristotle first introduces us to the enthymeme as the element of rhetorical persuasion and gives us some preliminary definitions and classifications; second, he discusses the topics from which enthymemes are to be drawn, explaining that ethical, pathetical, and logical persuasion will be projected through these enthymemes depending upon our choice of propositions; and third the enthymeme is carefully analyzed in its several forms. Books I and II treat inventio and Book III considers mainly elocutio, to a limited extent, pronuntiatio and dispositio, with little or no mention being made of memoria. My point is that if we view the enthymeme as the "body and substance of rhetorical persuasion" as

Aristotle tells us to, we have no difficulty in understanding the organization of the Rhetoric.   On the other hand, if the enthymeme
is to be considered the instrument solely of logical proof with ethical and pathetical persuasion existing outside this concept, it is
exceedingly difficult to understand the organization of the Rhetoric.
There seems to me, however, to be no justification for this latter
position except as we accept superficial impressions which might
be gotten from a failure really to analyze and understand Aristotle's
system of rhetorical invention.

     5.   Demonstrative and Refutative Enthymemes: Aristotle
distinguishes between demonstrative and refutative enthymemes in
Rhetoric II, 22 and 25.   He discusses the two methods of refutation, "counter-syllogism" and refutation by "bringing an objection,"
and explains that refutative enthymemes are constructed from the
same topics from which demonstrative enthymemes are built.   Of
special interest here, however, is his discussion of refutation in
relation to probable causes and signs.[36]   The point is clearly
brought out that an argument drawn from probabilities cannot be
refuted by showing that the conclusion is not necessary and that
formal defects in an enthymematic argument do not necessarily
destroy its claim to cogency.   The probable nature of the enthymeme and its formal inconclusiveness are emphasized.   One does
not properly refute an enthymeme which reasons from a probable
cause by showing that its premises are merely probable, because
it is impossible to make these premises anything other than probable and probability is all that is claimed for the conclusion.   Likewise to show that an argument from sign (in the second or third
figures) is formally deficient does not necessarily refute the enthymeme; such an enthymeme "knows that it is formally deficient,"
so to speak, and it does not contemplate apodeictic certainty for
its conclusion.

     Perhaps no other passages in Aristotle bring out more forci-
bly the point that several forms of the enthymeme are formally deficient than these explanations dealing with the refutation of enthymemes.   This is an exceedingly important point that is almost universally overlooked.   Many rhetorical arguments which are perfectly legitimate in reasoned discourse and which may establish high
degrees of probability, are formally deficient; i.e., they cannot be
thrown into a formally valid syllogism.   Many enthymemes which
are wholly acceptable from the standpoint of cogent speech are formally deficient from the point of view of the apodeictic syllogism.
As Mansel puts it:

          In the Prior Analytics II, 27 Aristotle admits a sign in
          the second figure....   The logical value of two affirma-
          tive premises in the second figure is absolute zero....
          For rhetorical purposes, however, the second figure is
          admissible; an accumulation of Enthymemes, all logically
          worthless, may amount to a moral certainty.[37]

6. A Consideration of the Suppression of a Proposition in the Enthymeme: We know from our examination of Aristotle's works thus far that the identification of the enthymeme with probable causes and signs is a necessary part of the definition of this concept. A cursory examination of the Rhetoric, to say nothing of almost any sample of reasoned discourse, will show that the enthymeme very often appears with one (or more) of the propositions of a complete syllogism suppressed. The only question raised here, therefore, is whether or not the omission of one or more of the propositions of a complete syllogism is necessary in the enthymeme. This question assumes considerable importance because of the almost universal tendency among recent writers to define the enthymeme as an elided syllogism and to make this elision the only differentiation between the syllogism and the enthymeme. Hamilton points out that "the enthymeme was used by the oldest commentators on Aristotle in the modern signification, as a syllogism of one suppressed premise."[38] Jebb states:

> A misapprehension of Aristotle's meaning had, as early
> as the first century B.C., led to the conception of the
> enthymeme as not merely a syllogism of a particular sub-
> ject matter, but also a syllogism of which one premise is
> suppressed.[39]

Most of those who object to the contemporary notion of the enthymeme merely as a truncated syllogism hold that the characteristic thing about the enthymeme is its identification with probable causes and signs, and that the omission of a proposition is purely accidental. De Quincey enunciates this position as follows:

> The enthymeme differs from the syllogism, not in the
> accident of suppressing one of its propositions; either
> may do this or neither; the difference is essential, and
> in the nature of the matter; that of the syllogism proper
> being certain and apodeictic; that of the enthymeme simply
> probable, and drawn from the province of opinion.[40]

The commentator who has contended for this conception most vehemently and argued the point most convincingly is Sir William Hamilton. He contends (1) that the enthymeme as a syllogism of a defective enouncement constitutes no special form of reasoning; (2) that Aristotle does not consider a syllogism of such a character as such a special form; and (3) that admitting the validity of the distinction, the restriction of the enthymeme to a syllogism of one suppressed premise cannot be competently maintained.[41]

There appears to be no place in Aristotle's writings where he defines the enthymeme as an elided syllogism, nor is there any satisfactory evidence that he so understood it. In his discussion of maxims and in many other places, Aristotle recognizes the enthymeme with one or more of its propositions suppressed; as a matter of fact, I think we can safely interpret Aristotle to mean that the

enthymeme usually lacks one or more of the propositions of a complete syllogism.   On the other hand, it seems equally clear that
there is no justification in interpreting him to mean that this is a
necessary characteristic of the enthymeme.   A syllogism drawn
from probable causes and signs is an enthymeme without regard
to the omission of a proposition.

        From this study of the enthymeme as a part of Aristotle's
logical and rhetorical system as a whole and our examination of
the Aristotelian passages in which the enthymeme is given special
treatment, I think that we can draw the following conclusions concerning the enthymeme in Aristotle: (1) The enthymeme is the
syllogism of rhetoric, occupying in rhetoric essentially the same
place that the syllogism occupies in logic; (2) the premises of the
enthymeme are probable causes and signs; (3) these premises are
drawn from topics varying in specificity and exactness from the
particular facts of a given substantive field to the most general
principles of probability; (4) these premises may be phrased in
language designed to affect the emotional state of the listener, to
develop in the audience a confidence in the speaker, or to establish a conclusion as being a probable truth; (5) the inferential
process is formally deficient in several of the enthymematic types,
and many enthymemes cannot therefore be stated in valid syllogisms; (6) the rhetorical example may be reduced to an enthymematic form just as scientific induction may be stated syllogistically;
and (7) the enthymeme often (but not necessarily) appears with one
or more of its three propositions suppressed.

        For Aristotle the enthymeme is the element of reasoned dis-
course, constructive or refutative, demonstrative or "sham"; its
persuasive force may be ethical, pathetical, or logical.   In any
case it draws its premises and line of argument from topics which
combine to enunciate a ratio essendi or ratio cognoscendi; these
take the form of probable causes, signs, and examples, and are
usually expressed by a proposition with a reason, although they may
appear in the complete syllogistic form.

3.   The Enthymeme After Aristotle

        We know from our examination of the enthymeme in Aristotle
that there have been substantial deviations from the Aristotelian
meaning of this concept in the many centuries which separate contemporary rhetorical invention from that of Aristotle.   These
changes assume considerable importance in view of the central
place which the enthymeme occupies in Aristotle's system and the
persistence of Aristotle's system as the essential basis of contemporary rhetorical theory.   In this section, therefore, we shall attempt to see where, when, and why these changes took place.

        A.   The Stoics: The more important philosophical school
following Aristotle, at least from the point of view of this study, is

that of the Stoics.   The accuracy with which Aristotle's successor,
Theophrastus, and the other early leaders of the Peripatetic school
"passed on" Aristotle's teaching, and the availability of reliable
Aristotelian manuscripts even to these early students of the school
appears to be questionable.[42]   In any event the early Stoic philosophers, Zeno (c. 336 B.C.), Cleanthes (331-232 B.C.) and Chrysip-
pus, head of the stoic school from 232-206 B.C., either because
they lacked ready access to Aristotle's writings or because they
sought to develop an original logical and rhetorical system, do not
appear to have maintained the enthymematic conception.   The extant fragments of these writers reveal no reference to the enthymeme[43] despite the fact that they are known to have written treatises on rhetoric.   Such information as we have concerning these
treatises seems to indicate that the stoics were concerned with establishing truth rather than probability and devoted themselves,
even as rhetoricians, to the subtleties of the logical syllogism.[44]
While this predilection for logic can doubtless be explained by the
very nature of the stoic philosophic creed, it seems certain that
rhetorical invention suffered by their disposition to replace the enthymeme with the logical syllogism.

The most renowned rhetorician in the stoic school was Hermagoras (c. 110 B.C.) who, confining himself almost entirely to invention as opposed to style, elaborated on the basis of previous
treatises a system of rhetoric which remained a standard work
throughout the Graeco-Roman period.   The rhetorical system of
Hermagoras we must glean from a few fragments and the many
references to him by later rhetoricians, especially Cicero and
Quintilian, who are known to have been influenced profoundly by
his work.[45]   The influence of Hermagoras on Cicero, as reflected
in Cicero's early work De Inventione (c. 85 B.C.), is in my opinion a factor of great importance in explaining the subsequent tendency to confuse the enthymeme and the logical syllogism.   We
shall examine the De Inventione with this point in mind.

B.   The Roman Doctrine: Cicero devides argument into induction and ratiocination in the De Inventione and then subdivides
ratiocination (deduction) into five parts, propositio, propositionis
approbatio, assumptio, assumptionis approbatio, and complexio.
These five parts are related to the syllogism in the following manner: (1) Proposition (Major premise of syllogism); (2) Proof of
Proposition; (3) Assumption (Minor premise of syllogism); (4) Proof
of assumption; and (5) Summation (Conclusion of syllogism).[46]
Thiele argues at some length that Cicero's five-part ratiocination
(epicheirema), and the explanation which he gives of it, represents
an attempt to accommodate the logical syllogism to the needs of
rhetoric which fails to recognize the enthymeme and seriously per-
verts the purposes and methods of rhetorical invention.[47]   Thiele
traces this influence to Hermagoras.

Briefly, the chief objection to the logical syllogism as a
rhetorical instrument lies in its apodeictic nature and formal rigid-

ity.   The materials with which the speaker and writer must constantly deal, and the type of reasoning in which they must engage,
strongly militate against the application of the demonstrative forms
of the logical syllogism.   If an argument is considered unaccept-
able rhetorically because it falls short of material certainty or
fails to achieve formal validity, the inevitable result must be a
tremendous limitation of the lines of reasoning open to the speaker, to say nothing of the unfortunate effects on the style of the
discourse.   Cicero himself decries this mixing of logic and rhetoric
in his later work De Oratore, 48 and Quintilian makes a point of it
in his Institutio Oratoria. 48

Both Cicero and Quintilian deal with the enthymeme; Cicero
refers to it in his short work Topica, where he assigns a very
special type of matter to this concept and appears not to have the
Aristotelian meaning;49 Quintilian observes the confusion which
surrounds the enthymeme in his day and reviews some of the different meanings assigned to it. 50 While Quintilian does not take a
final position on the form of the enthymeme, he appears to favor
the idea that it is an elided syllogism.   His discussion of the kinds
and methods of rhetorical argument is comprehensive and generally
Aristotelian although some departures traceable mainly to Cicero
are noticeable. 51

C.   The Mediaeval Doctrine: Of first importance so far as
rhetorical invention is concerned in the middle ages is the influence of Cicero's De Inventione throughout this period.   This work,
together with the Rhetorica ad Herennium (c. 85 B.C.), 52 is followed very closely by nearly every mediaeval rhetorician.   As
might be expected the confusion between the enthymeme and the
syllogism which we found to exist in Cicero's epicheirematic conception is thereby transmitted to the middle ages.   Unfortunately
Aristotle's Rhetoric, Cicero's De Oratore, and Quintilian's Institutio Oratoria were almost wholly unknown during this period and
were not recovered until the fifteenth century.

Examples of the influence of the De Inventione with respect
to the applications of the syllogism in the field of rhetorical invention may be seen in the work of the fourth and fifth century writers, Fortunatianus, Victorinus, Julius Victor, and Cassiodorus. 53
All of these writers define the enthymeme as an "incomplete syllogism" and the epicheirema as a "broader following up of the rhetorical syllogism, differing by its breadth and extensiveness from
dialectical syllogisms."

Two other important influences may be noted in the middle
ages, that of Christian rhetoric with its beginnings in St. Augustine's (354-430) De Doctrina Christiana, and the writings of Boethius (c. 480-525).   Rhetoric applied to the art of preaching constituted a strong current through this entire period.   As Caplan puts
it:

Were the modern student, fortified by a knowledge of
Aristotle's Rhetoric, to contend that the rhetorical enthymeme, not the syllogism, is proper to the art of rhetoric,
the mediaeval preacher would perhaps reply that sacred
eloquence differs from secular in that its subject matter
lies not in the realm of opinion and probability, but in
truth and divine science; that it is as sound a procedure
to use a dialectical method in the demonstration of truth
as in the investigation of it; and further, that in Aristotle
and Cicero and Quintilian he had precedents for the policy
of adapting to rhetorical purposes the methods of the allied
arts of dialectic. [54]

Suffice to say here that the emphasis of these mediaeval
"arts of preaching, " in so far as they were concerned with the form
of argument, was on the dialectical or logical syllogism.   Furthermore, both the translations of Aristotle's Organon by Boethius and
his own original writings carried forward the conception of the enthymeme as an elided syllogism.   Boethius translates the controversial passage concerning the enthymeme in the Prior Analytics
II, 27, "Enthymeme ergo est syllogismus imperfectus ex elcotibus
et signis";[55] and states in his De Differentiis Topicis, "The enthymeme is an imperfect syllogism, that is, a form of speech in
which a hurried conclusion is arrived at before all the propositions
have been established.... "[56]   Sir William Hamilton and others
point out that ἀτελής (imperfectus) as found in this and other similar versions of the Analytics "is a manifest interpolation made to
accommodate the Aristotelic to the common doctrine of the enthymeme. "

With the authority of Aristotle thus apparently given to the
conception of the enthymeme as an elided syllogism by his chief
interpreter for the middle ages, it is not surprising that this doctrine persisted.   Isidore of Seville (c. 570-636), following Cassiodorus almost word for word, discusses the enthymeme as "an incomplete syllogism" and the epicheirema as "a broader syllogism
also in use among the rhetoricians, "[57] and Alcuin (735-804) adds
nothing in his dialogues on rhetoric and dialectic.   With the revival
of Aristotle's logical works in the scholastic period we find much
fuller discussions of syllogistic doctrine in such writers as Hugh
of St. Victor, John of Salisbury, and Vincent of Beauvais, but little
development is seen in the theory of the enthymeme.   The concept
is identified with probabilities somewhat more confidently and rea-
listically, but it remains "the incomplete syllogism of the rhetoricians. "   Erasmus and Melancthon later discuss the enthymeme in
much the same way.

In the sixteenth century, following the recovery of Aristotle's
Rhetoric, [58] there appeared a large number of commentaries and
reworkings of this treatise done chiefly by Italians.   The first English work of any consequence, that of Leonard Cox (1530), remained largely in the mediaeval tradition and did little with inven-

tion. By the middle of the seventeenth century, however, Aristotle's Rhetoric was well known in England and Whately's Elements
of Rhetoric and Elements of Logic, appearing at the turn of the
eighteenth century, display a scholarly grasp of the best classical
tradition.   Whately's influence in the field of rhetorical invention
is prominent in American writers, especially Henry Day and later
writers on rhetoric and argumentation.   Throughout this development to this day, however, the momentum gained by the conception
of the enthymeme as an elided syllogism during the many centuries
preceding has been sufficient to sustain this conception with but
scattered dissent.   While the rhetorical trilogy, antecedent probability, sign, and example, the basis of most contemporary classifications of argument, preserves Aristotle's conception of the materials of the enthymeme with considerable accuracy, the formal
relation of these arguments to the syllogism is very generally misunderstood.

4.   The Place of the Enthymeme
     in Contemporary Rhetorical Theory

        The necessary limitations of this abstract will not permit
me to discuss this subject in any detail.   I do think that we can
conclude with considerable assurance from the investigations here
reported that to the extent that syllogistic logic is accepted as the
basis of apodeictic proof, and Aristotle's system of rhetorical invention is retained as the essential basis of our theory of argument in speaking and writing, these interpretations of the enthymeme should be given serious consideration.   On the other hand,
to the degree that the syllogism is repudiated as an adequate concept in logical theory, there is at least a presumption established
against the enthymeme which should lead to further investigations
of its adequacy.   Needless to say, however, a correct version of
the enthymeme will be the necessary starting point of any significant attempt to evaluate this concept and the theory of argument
of which it is a part.

        Objections to the syllogism and its rhetorical applications
have been raised as far back as Francis Bacon, John Locke, and
George Campbell.   These have continued to appear sporadically
with growing frequency in recent years.   The arguments of such
writers as John Dewey, F. C. S. Schiller, Alfred Sidgwick, and
Boris B. Bogoslovsky, while not generally rhetorical in the traditional sense, should be considered.   I have argued in another connection that the conception of the enthymeme here set forth adapts
the syllogism to the problems of ordinary speaking and writing in
such a way as to remove, at least in part, what I understand to
be some of the more important objections of these writers.

NOTES

1. Cooper, Lane. The Rhetoric of Aristotle, New York: D. Appleton and Company, 1932, 7. References to The Rhetoric, unless otherwise indicated, are taken from Professor Cooper's translation.

2. See Clark, D. L., Rhetoric and Poetry in the Renaissance, New York, Columbia University Press, 1922, 27-28.

3. While the term "enthymeme" was used before Aristotle by Isocrates and others to indicate rather loosely and generally the thoughts or sentiments with which a speaker embellishes his work, as a definitive logical and rhetorical concept in the sense in which we are investigating the term it originated with Aristotle. See Octave Navarre, Essai Sur La Rhetorique Grecque Avant Aristote, Paris, 1900, 255; Mansel, H. L., Artis Logicae Rudimenta from the Text of Aldrich (third ed.) Oxford, 1856. Appendix, note F, "On the Enthymeme, " 216.

4. Rhetoric I, 1.

5. Op. cit., xxv.

6. Saint-Hilaire, J. Barthelemy. Rhetoricae d'Aristote. Paris, 1870, Tome Second, 348.

7. Op. cit., 376.

8. Dewey, John. Reconstruction in Philosophy, New York: Henry Holt and Company, 1920, 22-23.

9. See Prior Analytics (in The Works of Aristotle, vol. I, translated into the English under the editorship of W. D. Ross), Oxford: Clarendon Press, 1928, I, 4-7; also I, 14, 79^a. All references to the Prior Analytics, Posterior Analytics, and Topics in this study are to the Ross edition, vol. I, The Works of Aristotle.

10. Prior Analytics II, 23, 68^b.

11. Posterior Analytics II, 19, 100^b.

12. See Joseph, H. W. B., An Introduction to Logic (Second edition revised), Oxford, 1916, 305.

13. Posterior Analytics I, 2, 71^b and I, 6, 74^b. On this point see also Mansel's Aldrich, op. cit., note K. "On the Demonstrative Syllogism, " 241-242; Grote, George, Aristotle (ed. Alexander Bain and G. C. Robertson), London, 1872, vol. I, 315; and Joseph, H. W. B., op. cit., 398-399.

14. Grote, George, op. cit., 383.

15. Mansel, H. L., op. cit., 213.

16. Topics, I, 2, 101^a and 101^b.

17. Ibid., VIII, 5, 159^a.

18. Ibid., VIII, 11, 161^a.

19. Cope, E. M., An Introduction to Aristotle's Rhetoric, London: Macmillan and Co., 1867, 9.

20. Rhetoric, I, 2, 1355^b and 1356^a.

21. Rhetoric, I, 2, 1356^b; see also Prior Analytics II, 23, and Posterior Analytics I, 1, and I, 18; also II, 19.

22. See Ernest Havet, De La Rhetorique D'Aristote. Paris, 1843, 64.

23. See Prior Analytics I, 13, 32^b: also Freidrich Solmsen,
     "Die Entwicklung Der Aristotelischen Logik und Rhetorik"
     (in Neue Philologische Untersuchungen), Berlin, 1929, 13-14.
24. See Cope, E. M., op. cit., 161.
25. It may be noted here that Aristotle reduces "example," or
     what he has previously discussed as rhetorical induction, to
     a form of the enthymeme just as he explains scientific in-
     duction in terms of the syllogism.
26. For authorities on this point see especially Richard Whately,
     Elements of Rhetoric (Reprinted from seventh edition),
     Louisville, Ky.: Morton and Griswold, 1854, 47; also
     Douglas Maeleane. Reason, Thought, and Language, Lon-
     don: Oxford University Press, 1906, 418-419.
27. Rhetoric II, 25, 1402^b.
28. Prior Analytics II, 24, 69^a.
29. Friedrich Solmsen, in his "Die Entwicklung Der Aristotelis-
     chen Logik und Rhetorik," op. cit., argues that Aristotle's
     logical thought underwent a change or development and that
     this change may be seen in two conflicting enthymematic
     theories in the Rhetoric.   The two theories which he finds
     conflicting are the enthymeme defined as a syllogism drawn
     from causes and signs, and the enthymeme developed in re-
     lation to the topics in Rhetoric II, 22-24.   This latter topi-
     cal treatment Solmsen believes to be a remnant of Aristotle's
     earlier logical theory; the enthymeme as a syllogism he holds
     to be indicative of a later development in Aristotle's logical
     thought.   Without arguing the point here, I wish merely to
     say that while this development in Aristotle's logical theory
     does appear to have taken place, I do not find it impossible
     to reconcile the allegedly inconsistent theories of the enthy-
     meme in the Rhetoric.   I have attempted in this section to
     unify the references to the enthymeme in relation to the
     topics and the passages in which it is defined as a syllo-
     gism drawn from probable causes and signs.   See also in
     this connection Stocks, J. L., "The composition of Aris-
     totle's Logical Works," in the Classical Quarterly, vol. 27,
     1933, 115-124.
30. Rhetoric I, 2, 1358^a.
31. See ibid., II, 22, 1396^a and 1396^b.
32. Ibid., II, 22, 1395^b.
33. Ibid., II, 22, 1396^b.   See also on this point Edward Poste,
     Aristotle on Fallacies or the Sophistici Elenchi, London,
     1866, Appendix D, 204-207, especially 206.
34. See Chaignet, A. E., La Rhetorique et Son Histoire, Paris,
     1888, 134-5. See also Eng. Thionville, De La Theorie des
     Lieux Communs dans les Topiques d'Aristote et des Princi-
     pales modifications qu'elle a subies jusqu'a nos jours, Paris
     1855.
35. See Rhetoric I, 2, 1356^a; I, 9, 1366^a; II, 12, 1388^b.
36. Rhetoric II, 25, 1403^a.
37. Mansel, H. L., op. cit., 214.
38. Hamilton, Sir William, Discussions on Philosophy, 154.

39. Jebb, R. C., Attic Orators, London: Macmillan and Co.,
    1876, vol. II, 291.
40. De Quincey, Thomas. Essays on Style, Rhetoric and Lan-
    guage (edited by Fred N. Scott). Boston: Allyn and Bacon,
    1893, 145-146.
41. See Sir William Hamilton, Lectures on Metaphysics and Logic,
    New York: Sheldon and Co., 1876, vol. II, 276-278; ibid.,
    "Discussions on Philosophy," 151-154; ibid., "Recent Publi-
    cations on Logical Science," in The Edinburgh Review, CXV,
    April, 1833, 221-222. See also Cope, E. M., An Intro-
    duction to Aristotle's Rhetoric, op. cit., 102-103, especially
    the footnote; H. L. Mansel's Aldrich, op. cit., 211-212;
    Joseph, H. W. B., Introduction to Logic, op. cit., 350-351;
    Jacobi Facciolati, Orationes XII (Acrases and Patavii, 1729),
    227; Chaignet, A. E., La Rhetorique et Son Histoire, op.
    cit., 113-114.
42. See Shute, Richard. An Essay on the History of the Process
    by Which the Aristotelian Writings Arrived at Their Present
    Form. Oxford: Clarendon Press, 1888, 19-45.
43. Arnim, Joannes ab, Stoicorum Veterum Fragmenta (Lipsiae
    MCMV) four volumes; see also Pearson, Alfred C., The
    Fragments of Zeno and Cleanthes, London: C. J. Clay and
    Sons, 1891.
44. Arnold, E. Vernon. Roman Stoicism, Cambridge: University
    Press, 1911, 73; Sandys, J. E., A History of Classical
    Scholarship (Second ed.), Cambridge: University Press,
    1906, 149; Davidson, William L., The Stoic Creed, Edin-
    burgh: T. and T. Clark, 1907, 63; Zellar, E., The Stoics,
    Epicureans, and Sceptics (tr. by O. J. Reichel, Longmans,
    Green and Co.), London, 1870, 118-119; Stock, St. George,
    Stoicism, London: Archibald Constable and Co., 1908, 31-
    34. See also Laertius, Diogenes, Lives of Eminent Philoso-
    phers (tr. by R. D. Hicks, in Loeb Class. Lib.), London:
    William Heinemann and New York: G. P. Putnam's Sons,
    1925, VII, 42-43; Ciceronis, M. Tulle, De Finibus Bonorum
    et Malorum, Libi Quinque (tr. by James S. Reid), Cam-
    bridge: University Press, 1885, IV, III, 7-10; Dionysius of
    Halicarnassus, On Literary Composition (tr. by W. Rhys.
    Roberts), 95-97.
45. See Thiele, George, Hermagoras: ein Beitrag zur Geschichte
    der Rhetorik, Strassburg, 1893, for an attempted recon-
    struction of the rhetoric of Hermagoras.
46. Cicero's De Inventione (included with Cicero's Orations, tr.
    by C. D. Yonge, vol. IV, Bohn Class. Lib.), London, 1852,
    241-380.
47. Thiele, George, op. cit., 131-137.
48. Cicero's De Oratore II, 28; Quintilian's Institutio Oratoria V,
    32.
49. Cicero, Topica (included with Cicero's Orations, tr. by C. D.
    Yonge, vol. IV, Bohn Class. Lib.). London, 1852, 458-
    486. See also Saint-Hilaire, J. Barthelemy, op. cit., 368.
50. Quintilian's Institutio Oratoria V, 8, 9, and 10; V, 14.

51.   The enthymeme is treated by a number of the later Greek
       rhetoricians, Hermogenes (c. 170 A. D.), Apsines, Minuci-
       anus, Neocles and others in the second, third, and fourth
       centuries.   Hermogenes assigns a wholly new meaning to
       the concept and the others make no contribution of note.
       While Hermogenes was followed by some later writers, for
       example, Georgius Trapezuntius in his Rhetorica (c. 1470),
       I shall not attempt to discuss the point here.   See the
       several volumes of Leonardi Spengel's Rhetores Graeci,
       Lipsiae, 1885, and Christianus Walz, Rhetores Graeci, Lon-
       dun and Lutetiae, 1832, for these later Greek rhetoricians.
52.   The authorship of the Rhetorica ad Herennium, long attributed
       to Cicero, is unknown.   The work resembles the De In-
       ventione very closely, and was widely used as a text and
       reference.   The author of the Ad Herennium explains a five
       step ratiocinative form which resembles that of the De In-
       ventione superficially, but is in fact closer to the Aristo-
       telian conception; like Cicero, he calls this form an
       epicheirema.   The five parts are: propositio, ratio,
       rationi confirmatio, exornatio, and complexio.   Cicero's
       epicheirema is the form which was almost universally cited
       by mediaeval rhetoricians, however.   It should be noted
       that the Ad Herennium exerted a strong influence during the
       latter part of the middle ages and the early renaissance.
53.   See Halm, Carolus, Rhetoris Latini Minores, Lipsiae, 1863,
       118-119, 242-243, 408-413, 498-500.
54.   Caplan, Harry, "Classical Rhetoric and the Mediaeval Theory
       of Preaching, " in Classical Philology, vol. 28, No. 2,
       April, 1933, 87.
55.   See Migne, Patralogia Latina, vol. 64, col. 711.
56.   Ibid., vol. 64, col. 1184; see also col. 1050.
57.   Halm, Carolus, op. cit., 511-512.
58.   The complete manuscript of Quintilian's Institutio Oratoria
       was found at St. Gaul by Poggio in 1416, Cicero's De Ora-
       tore and Brutus, at Lodi in 1421, and Aristotle's Rhetoric
       was published in the Latin version by George of Trebizond
       as early as 1478 and in the Greek in 1508; see Clark, D.
       L., op. cit., 66.

8. ARISTOTLE'S ENTHYMEME REVISITED

by Lloyd F. Bitzer

Aristotle has said that enthymemes are "the substance of rhetorical persuasion."[1] In view of the importance he has given the enthymeme, we might reasonably expect to find it carefully defined. However, although there are many hints as to its nature, the reader of Aristotle's Rhetoric will find no unambiguous statement defining the enthymeme. The problem is perplexing to one of the ablest of Aristotelian scholars, W. D. Ross, who writes, "The enthymeme is discussed in many passages in the Rhetoric, and it is impossible to extract from them a completely consistent theory of its nature."[2]

The problem is no less perplexing to scholars in rhetorical theory. Some of them have attempted to formulate clear definitions of the enthymeme, based on Aristotle's descriptions. The most notable recent attempt of this sort is James H. McBurney's.[3] Other attempts include definitions by Lane Cooper,[4] Charles Sears Baldwin,[5] Thomas De Quincey,[6] and E. M. Cope.[7] With the exception of Cooper, each attempts to define the enthymeme by showing how it differs from the dialectical or the scientific syllogism. My purpose in this paper is to point out some difficulties in the interpretations given by these men and to suggest a possible definition which does not run counter to Aristotle's descriptions. Since Aristotle's statements, however, seem to permit some variety of interpretation of the enthymeme, further criticism and exploration seem justified.

Consider first Lane Cooper's remarks about the enthymeme. He notes the difficulty of determining Aristotle's meaning and suggests that we simply look at good speeches in order to understand what an enthymeme is. "The arguments good speakers actually use in persuasion are enthymemes," he says, and that "is the answer to our question, 'What is an enthymeme?'"[8] Cooper defines the enthymeme, not by stating its characteristics and telling how it differs from other kinds of arguments, but by pointing to where it may be found--in persuasive speeches actually made by good speak-

*Reprinted by permission of the author and of the Speech Communication Association, from Quarterly Journal of Speech 45 (1959), 399-408.

ers. This notion is important in a respect I will try to indicate
later; for the moment, however, Cooper's definition is put aside
because it does not help us understand precisely what the enthymeme is. It does not tell what characteristics make the enthymeme
the substance of rhetorical persuasion.

Baldwin is more specific. He approaches definition of the
enthymeme by contrasting it with the syllogism. He holds that by
enthymeme Aristotle

> means concrete proof, proof applicable to human affairs,
> such argument as is actually available in current discus-
> sions. The enthymeme is not inferior to the syllogism;
> it is merely different. [9]

Baldwin later says that "abstract deduction is summed up in the
syllogism; concrete deduction, in the enthymeme."[10] Apparently
he believes that the enthymeme is quite different from the syllogism and that the mark of difference is its concreteness.

Both Cope and De Quincey argue that the essential feature
of the enthymeme is its foundation in probability and that this feature separates it from the regular syllogism. De Quincey writes:

> An enthymeme differs from a syllogism...; the difference
> is essential, and in the nature of the matter: that of the
> syllogism proper being certain and apodeictic; that of the
> enthymeme simply probable, and drawn from the province
> of opinion. [11]

In An Introduction to Aristotle's Rhetoric, Cope rather cautiously
says the same: "It appears ... that the only essential difference
between the two is that the one leads to a necessary and universal,
the other only to a probable conclusion."[12] Later, however, it
will be noted that Cope changes his opinion in a startling way.

McBurney defines the enthymeme

> as a syllogism, drawn from probable causes, signs (cer-
> tain and fallible) and examples. As a syllogism drawn
> from these materials ... the enthymeme starts from
> these materials ... the enthymeme starts from probable
> premises (probable in a material sense) and lacks formal
> validity in certain of the types explained. [13]

The essential part of this definition is the statement that enthymemes are drawn from probabilities and signs. [14] McBurney emphasizes two other important features of enthymemes--the basis of
the premises in probability and the lack of formal validity in many
enthymematic types. On these two points, he says:

Both dialectic and rhetoric are differentiated from scientific demonstration in the fact that they deal with probabilities and do not attempt apodeictic proof in the sense that it appears in scientific demonstration. [15]

Perhaps no other passages in Aristotle bring out more forcibly the point that several forms of the enthymeme are formally deficient than these explanations dealing with the refutation of enthymemes.   This is an exceedingly important point that is almost universally overlooked. Many rhetorical arguments which are perfectly legitimate in reasoned discourse and which may establish high degrees of probability, are formally deficient; i. e., they cannot be thrown into a formally valid syllogism.   Many enthymemes which are wholly acceptable from the standpoint of cogent speech are formally deficient from the point of view of the apodeictic syllogism. [16]

Thus, except for Cooper, these writers among them hold that the enthymeme is distinctive on account of (1) its basis in probability, (2) its concreteness, and (3) its usual formal deficiency. Too, they hold that the definition of the enthymeme usually found in textbooks on logic is totally inadequate.   That definition, which will be discussed later, makes the enthymeme simply a syllogism having a suppressed premise or conclusion.   The task now is to show how the definitions offered by Cope and De Quincey, Baldwin, and McBurney may not adequately distinguish the enthymeme from the other kinds of syllogism (demonstrative and dialectical), although the definitions do undoubtedly name characteristics which enthymemes usually possess. [17]

Cope and De Quincey try to distinguish between the syllogism and the enthymeme on the grounds that the enthymeme always must be probable, whereas the syllogism always must be certain and necessary.   But a major fault attends these definitions.   They fail to take account of those descriptions of the enthymeme in which Aristotle expressly states that sometimes the enthymeme does begin with certain and necessary propositions and that sometimes the conclusion is necessary.   At 1357a30-32 Aristotle says,

It is evident, therefore, that the propositions forming the basis of enthymemes, though some of them may be 'necessary,' will most of them be only usually true. [18]

And at 1356b14-17 he writes,

When it is shown that, certain propositions being true, a further and quite distinct proposition must also be true in consequence, whether invariably or usually, this is called syllogism in dialectic, enthymeme in rhetoric. [Italics mine.][19]

Also, at 1396ª2-4 he says, "We should also base our arguments
upon probabilities as well as upon certainties."[20]   From these
statements, it seems clear that there is no sharp distinction between syllogism and enthymeme on the basis of probability since
the propositions of enthymemes may be certain and necessary.[21]

McBurney recognizes as the essential part of the enthymeme's
definition the same description Aristotle gives in the Prior Analytics: "Now an enthymeme is a syllogism starting from probabilities
or signs."[22]   He shares with Cope and De Quincey the view that
the premises of enthymemes are merely probable;[23] in addition,
he seems to hold that the usual formal deficiency of most enthymemes is an important identifying feature.   Yet I think it can be
shown that neither of these features absolutely distinguishes the
enthymeme.

First, McBurney correctly observes that both dialectic and
rhetoric deal with probabilities, with the contingent.   As Aristotle
often repeats, neither discipline deals with "things that could not
have been, and cannot now or in the future be."[24]   Neither do
these disciplines treat subjects which are invariable.[25]   Therefore,
McBurney is correct in his statement, "Both dialectic and rhetoric
are differentiated from scientific demonstration in the fact that
they deal with probabilities...."[26]   But he infers (without sufficient warrant, I believe) that the premises upon which enthymemes
are built must therefore be probable.   He says, for example (continuing the sentence just quoted), that dialectic and rhetoric "do
not attempt apodeictic proof in the sense that it appears in scientific demonstration."   However, Aristotle indicates that there is
one kind of enthymeme that meets the conditions for scientific
demonstration.   At 1402ᵇ18-19 he says, "Enthymemes based upon
Infallible Signs are those which argue from the inevitable and invariable."   Further, at 1403ª10-17 he says:

> It will be impossible to refute Infallible Signs, and En-
> thymemes resting on them, by showing in any way that
> they do not form a valid logical proof....   All we can
> do is to show that the fact alleged does not exist.   If
> there is no doubt that it does, and that it is an Infallible
> Sign, refutation now becomes impossible: for this is
> equivalent to a demonstration which is clear in every
> respect. [Italics mine.][27]

Therefore, whenever we find enthymemes based on infallible signs,
we have before us truly demonstrative arguments, resting on inevitable and invariable premises.   Such arguments, proper in both
rhetoric and science, are (or may be) both materially certain and
formally valid.

Further, there is some doubt about the belief, implicit in
McBurney's interpretation, that scientific demonstration must always begin with universal and necessary premises.   Ross points

out that Aristotle is willing to construct a science upon premises
that are "for the most part true." He writes:

> It is noteworthy that, while Aristotle conceives of dem-
> onstration in the strict sense as proceeding from prem-
> ises that are necessarily true to conclusions that are
> necessarily true, he recognizes demonstration (in a less
> strict sense, of course) as capable of proceeding from
> premises for the most part true to similar conclusions. [28]

It is clear, then, that scientific syllogisms may be constructed out
of highly probable premises and that enthymemes may be constructed out of certain and necessary premises. From this it follows that we cannot claim probability of premises or probability of
conclusions as the essential characteristic of enthymemes.

McBurney's second point of emphasis is that many enthymemes are formally invalid, but that they still constitute rhetorical proof. He finds this significant as a distinguishing feature between enthymemes and scientific syllogisms. His point loses its
significance, however, when we note that a great many scientific
syllogisms are also invalid. For example, of the sixty-four possible first-figure syllogisms, only four are valid. Yet in ordinary
talk we often infer successfully from several of the invalid forms.
If it is true that enthymemes are usually formally deficient, it is
equally true that many dialectical and scientific syllogisms, as
used in ordinary discourse, are formally deficient. Hence, formal
deficiency may characterize both the enthymeme and the syllogism.

Baldwin's treatment of the enthymeme--the enthymeme is
concrete whereas the syllogism is abstract--is also questionable.
Many syllogisms have particulars as the subjects of their conclusions, and many enthymemes have abstract ideas as the subjects
of their conclusions. The classic example of the syllogism has
"Socrates is mortal" as its conclusion. It could hardly have a
more concrete subject. Also, an enthymeme with "Let justice be
done" as its conclusion could hardly have a less concrete subject.

Perhaps Baldwin's statement that enthymemes are concrete
means that such arguments, when successful, always require a
specific human commitment or action. But concreteness in this
sense is not peculiar to the enthymeme alone, since dialectical
syllogisms sometimes require commitment to conclusions and action in accordance with those conclusions. Indeed, Aristotle says
that dialectical inquiry "contributes either to choice and avoidance,
or to truth and knowledge."[29] If the conclusions of dialectical arguments contribute to truth and knowledge, then intellectual commitment to conclusions is required of those who accept premises.
If the conclusions contribute to choice and avoidance, then acts of
choice and avoidance are logically required. Therefore, concreteness is not an essential feature of the enthymeme, although, as
Baldwin suggests, most enthymemes probably are concrete.

   In summary, the following points may be made about the enthymeme. (1) The enthymeme is a species of syllogism which differs in some way from the demonstrative and the dialectical syllogism. (2) The essential difference is not to be found in the probability of its premises, because Aristotle's statements indicate that (a) some enthymemes have as their premises propositions based on "the inevitable and invariable," and (b) some scientific syllogisms may have as their premises propositions that are "for the most part true." (3) Neither is the essential difference to be found in the formal deficiency of enthymemes, because (a) Aristotle holds that some enthymemes (those based on infallible signs) are equivalent to strict demonstrations. Furthermore, (b) in ordinary discourse we often infer successfully by using formally deficient dialectical or demonstrative syllogisms. (4) Finally, the essential difference is not to be found in the concreteness of enthymemes, because (a) this feature does not always characterize enthymemes and (b) it sometimes characterizes other kinds of syllogism.

   It is no doubt true that most enthymemes are probable, formally deficient, and concrete. Since not all enthymemes exhibit these features, however, it is impossible to claim any or all of them as the distinctive mark of the enthymeme. Precisely what, then, is the difference between the enthymeme and the demonstrative or dialectical syllogism? If we answer this question, we may be in a good position to formulate a consistent definition of the enthymeme. In the following paragraphs I wish to suggest an interpretation which I believe is in agreement with Aristotle's statements.

   In the Prior Analytics Aristotle distinguishes between two kinds of premises--the demonstrative and the dialectical. Because his distinction provides an important clue to interpretation of the enthymeme, I quote the passage in full.

          The demonstrative premiss differs from the dialectical,
          because the demonstrative premiss is the assertion of one
          of two contradictory statements (the demonstrator does
          not ask for his premisses, but lays them down), whereas
          the dialectical premiss depends on the adversary's choice
          between two contradictories. But this will make no dif-
          ference to the production of a syllogism in either case;
          for both the demonstrator and the dialectician argue syllo-
          gistically after stating that something does or does not
          belong to something else. Therefore, a syllogistic prem-
          iss without qualification will be an affirmation or denial
          of something concerning something else in the way we
          have described; it will be demonstrative, if it is true and
          obtained through the first principles of its science; while
          a dialectical premiss is the giving of a choice between
          two contradictories, when a man is proceeding by ques-
          tion, but when he is syllogizing it is the assertion of that
          which is apparent and generally admitted, as has been

said in the Topics. 30

In this passage there are two features which distinguish demonstrative premises and syllogisms from dialectical premises and syllogisms. First, the demonstrator asserts, or lays-down, his premises without regard to the wishes of any opponent. On the other hand, the dialectician asks for his premises. Instead of laying them down, he seeks the consent of his adversary about them; he gives his adversary "a choice between two contradictories." The first and most important distinction, then, is that the demonstrator lays down his premises, whereas the dialectician asks for his premises. 31 Second, the main requirement for demonstrative syllogizing is that a premise be "true and obtained through the first principles of its science." On the other hand, the main requirement for dialectical syllogizing is that a premise be apparent and generally admitted.

We should note here that, although the premises of dialectic and rhetoric need not be true and need not be obtained through the principles of some science, it is quite possible that some of them are of this character. Scientific propositions--such as Newton's laws--are often popularized and made part of the class of statements from which the orator draws his premises--the class of statements which are apparent and generally admitted. Also, the orator may use special lines of argument which properly belong to other disciplines, including the sciences. 32

Several statements in the Rhetoric indicate that enthymemes differ from demonstrative syllogisms in the same way that demonstrative premises differ from dialectical premises. At 1355a27-28 Aristotle says, "We must use as our modes of persuasion and argument, notions possessed by everybody." Also, at 1395b31-1396a4 he writes:

> We must not, therefore, start from any and every accepted opinion, but only from those we have defined--those accepted by our judges or by those whose authority they recognize.... We should also base our arguments upon probabilities as well as upon certainties.

And at 1402a33-34 he says: "The materials of [rhetorical] syllogisms are the ordinary opinions of men." The practitioner of rhetoric, then, does not lay down premises, but like the dialectician he asks for them. The premises he asks for are notions already possessed by his audience.

We have, then, two kinds of syllogism, demonstrative and dialectical-rhetorical. One important difference--perhaps the essential difference--between the two lies in how premises are secured. In demonstration they are laid down; in dialectic and rhetoric they are asked for. We need now to distinguish between the dialectical syllogism and the enthymeme.

The difference between the dialectical syllogism and the enthymeme is partly the consequence of a difference in the functions or purposes of the arts. Dialectic, says Aristotle, "is a process of criticism," and criticism is its chief function.[33] On the other hand, rhetoric discovers the available means of persuasion, and persuasion is the chief function of rhetorical discourse. Both dialectic and rhetoric ask for their premises (which may or may not be certain and necessary); but they ask for premises with different ends in view. Dialectic must ask for premises because criticism cannot begin until the parties involved agree on some propositions. Rhetoric must ask for premises--must begin with premises held by the audience--because persuasion cannot take place unless the audience views a conclusion as required by the premises it subscribes to.

The dialectical syllogism differs from the enthymeme also according to the kind of response made by the respondent and by the audience when each is asked for premises. The nature of this difference will be noted shortly. For the moment, let us distinguish among the three species of syllogism in the following way: (1) Demonstrative syllogisms are those in which premises are laid down in order to establish scientific conclusions; (2) Dialectical syllogisms are those in which premises are asked for in order to achieve criticism; (3) Rhetorical syllogisms, or enthymemes, are those in which premises are asked for in order to achieve persuasion.

It was stated near the beginning of this paper that recent theorists, including E. M. Cope, have tended to reject the definition of the enthymeme as a syllogism having one or more suppressed premises. In his Introduction to Aristotle's Rhetoric, Cope holds that the essential difference between the syllogism and the enthymeme is that the former "leads to a necessary and universal, the other only to a probable conclusion." He holds also that the definition of the enthymeme as a syllogism having a suppressed premise, is totally inadequate, since the suppression of a premise is not essential to the enthymeme. These views are presented in the text on pages 102 and 103. In a lengthy footnote on page 103, however, Cope alters his view drastically:

> The view of the distinctive characteristic of rhetoric
> given in the text was adopted mainly in deference to the
> decided opinion expressed by Sir W. Hamilton. I am
> now however convinced that he is wrong, and return to
> the opinion which I have myself previously formed upon
> the question. If the only difference between the rhetori-
> cal enthymeme and the syllogism lay in the probability
> of the one and the certainty of the other, it would leave
> no distinction remaining between the dialectical syllogism
> and the rhetorical enthymeme: besides which the posi-
> tion is not true of the dialectical syllogism, whose ma-
> terials and conclusions are all probable and nothing more.

Plainly the difference between the two latter is one of form.   The syllogism is complete in all its parts; the enthymeme incomplete; one of the premisses or the conclusion is invariably wanting.

Thereafter, in the text, Cope refers to the enthymeme as an "imperfect syllogism"[34] and reiterates the view expressed in the footnote quoted above.   For example, at one place he writes:

The enthymeme is deduced from a few premisses ... and often (always, I believe; else what remains to distinguish it from the dialectical syllogism?) consists of fewer propositions (including the conclusion) than the primary or normal syllogism.[35]

Cope's change of opinion seems to have been prompted chiefly by his recognition that, given his earlier definition, he could not distinguish between the dialectical syllogism and the enthymeme.   Earlier he had said that the enthymeme leads to a probable conclusion, whereas the syllogism leads to a necessary conclusion.   However, he observed that the dialectical syllogism also leads to probable conclusions.   Therefore, the enthymeme is confounded with the dialectical syllogism.   In order to separate the two, he returned to the position he had previously repudiated-- that the enthymeme is an incomplete syllogism.   In justifying this latter view, he writes that there is no need for the rhetorician to state all his premises,

because if any of these is already well known--and the propositions of the rhetorician are well known, being popular and current maxims and opinions, and generally accepted rules and principles, which he uses for the major premises of his arguments--there is no occasion to state it at all; the listener will supply it for himself.[36]

There are two difficulties in Cope's revised definition of the enthymeme, provided we consider the enthymeme as the chief instrument of rhetorical persuasion.   First, if we understand the enthymeme as simply a syllogism having one or more suppressed premises or a suppressed conclusion, then we have to maintain that whenever Socrates omits a premise or whenever he lets his adversary draw the necessary conclusion, he is at that moment practicing rhetoric instead of dialectic, regardless of how concise and rigorous his argument.   We must also maintain that whenever an orator fully states his premises and conclusion, he is at that moment practicing something other than rhetoric.[37]   Because of these difficulties, it seems to me that the definition of the enthymeme as an incomplete syllogism must be rejected, unless we use the term "incomplete syllogism" in a special sense.

The second difficulty in Cope's definition is the inadequacy of the reason he gives to support it.   He holds that the orator need not state all his premises because the listener already knows most of them and will supply them for himself. Undoubtedly this is a good practical reason which adequately explains why most enthymemes do in fact have suppressed premises. But is this reason strong enough to explain Aristotle's claim that the enthymeme is the substance of rhetorical persuasion? It seems to me that the reason is not strong enough, because rhetorical persuasion can occur whether an orator vocalizes both or only one of his premises. The success or failure of rhetorical persuasion does not turn upon the suppression of a premise but upon something more fundamental, which I will try to point out shortly.

If we use the term, "incomplete syllogism" in a special sense, however, I believe it expresses very nearly what Aristotle means by the enthymeme and avoids the difficulties which attend Cope's definition. Let us understand the term in this sense: To say that the enthymeme is an "incomplete syllogism"--that is, a syllogism having one or more suppressed premises--means that the speaker does not lay down his premises but lets his audience supply them out of its stock of opinion and knowledge. This does not mean that premises are never verbalized, although to verbalize them often amounts to redundancy and poor rhetorical taste. Whether or not premises are verbalized is of no logical importance. What is of great rhetorical importance, however, is that the premises of enthymemes be supplied by the audience.

The same thought may be expressed in a different way. An orator or a dialectician can plan a rhetorical or dialectical argument while sitting at the desk in his study, but he cannot really complete it by himself, because some of the materials from which he builds arguments are absent. The missing materials of rhetorical arguments are the premises which the audience brings with it and supplies at the proper moment provided the orator is skillful. The missing materials of dialectical arguments are the premises which the respondent supplies when he chooses between contradictories. The relationship of practitioner of rhetoric to audience and of practitioner of dialectic to respondent is precisely the same: In either case, the successful building of arguments depends on co-operative interaction between the practitioner and his hearers.

But we must note an important difference between the forms of interaction which occur in rhetoric and in dialectic--a difference which further clarifies the distinction between the dialectical syllogism and the enthymeme. In dialectic, the interaction between speaker and respondent takes the form of question and answer, and the respondent vocally contributes premises for the construction of dialectical syllogisms. The aim of dialectic is criticism--often the aim is criticism of the respondent's own position; since arguments are formed from premises supplied by the respondent, dialectical arguments have the virtue of being self-critical. Probably there is no more effective way of appraising one's own opinions than the activity of dialectic, because when one assumes the role of respondent and answers the dialectician, one supplies premises from which damaging conclusions may be drawn. The respondent in fact builds a case for or against his own position; he criticizes himself.

The interaction between speaker and audience must have a different form in rhetoric, however, because continuous discourse by the speaker does not allow him to obtain premises from his audience through question and answer. The speaker uses a form of interaction which has its "counterpart" in dialectic, but instead of using question and answer to achieve interaction, he uses the enthymeme, which accomplishes for rhetoric what the method of question and answer accomplishes for dialectic. The speaker draws the premises for his proofs from propositions which members of his audience would supply if he were to proceed by question and answer, and the syllogisms produced in this way by speaker and audience are enthymemes.

The point to be emphasized, then, is that enthymemes occur only when speaker and audience jointly produce them. Because they are jointly produced, enthymemes intimately unite speaker and audience and provide the strongest possible proofs. The aim of rhetorical discourse is persuasion; since rhetorical arguments, or enthymemes, are formed out of premises supplied by the audience, they have the virtue of being self-persuasive. Owing to the skill of the speaker, the audience itself helps construct the proofs by which it is persuaded. I believe this is the reason Aristotle calls enthymemes the "substance of rhetorical persuasion, " and it may be the reason for Lane Cooper's remark that we will find enthymemes in the actual speeches of good speakers. [38]

In this paper I have examined three common interpretations of the enthymeme. One interpretation emphasizes the content of its propositions and holds that the distinctive feature of the enthymeme is the material probability of premises and conclusions. A second interpretation emphasizes its formal structure and holds that the enthymeme is distinctive because usually it is formally deficient. The third interpretation emphasizes its relationship to human affairs and holds that the distinctive feature of the enthymeme is its concrete relationship to human thought and conduct. These interpretations were rejected because each failed to separate the enthymeme from other kinds of syllogism. Each failed to name a truly distinguishing feature.

I have suggested a fourth interpretation which emphasizes the manner of construction of the enthymeme rather than content, form, or relation. In addition to avoiding the difficulties which attend the other interpretations, I think this view succeeds in focusing upon the unique function of the enthymeme in rhetorical persuasion. This view holds that the enthymeme succeeds as an instrument of rational persuasion because its premises are always drawn from the audience. Accordingly, I offer the following as a tentative and exploratory definition. The enthymeme is a syllogism based on probabilities, signs, and examples, whose function is rhetorical persuasion. Its successful construction is accomplished through the joint efforts of speaker and audience, and this is its essential character.

NOTES

1. Rhetorica 1354ª14-15. Unless otherwise indicated, references are to the Rhys Roberts translation of Aristotle's Rhetorica in Vol. XI of The Works of Aristotle, ed. W. D. Ross (Oxford, 1946).

2. W. D. Ross, Aristotle's Prior and Posterior Analytics (Oxford, 1949), p. 409.

3. James H. McBurney, "The Place of the Enthymeme in Rhetorical Theory," SM, III (1936), 49-74.

4. The Rhetoric of Aristotle, translated and with Introduction by Lane Cooper (New York, 1932).

5. Charles Sears Baldwin, Ancient Rhetoric and Poetic (New York, 1924).

6. Thomas De Quincey, "Rhetoric," The Collected Writings of Thomas De Quincey, ed. David Masson (Edinburgh, 1890), X.

7. Edward M. Cope, An Introduction to Aristotle's Rhetoric (London, 1867).

8. Cooper, p. xxvii.

9. Baldwin, p. 9.

10. Baldwin, p. 13.

11. De Quincey, p. 90.

12. Cope, p. 102.

13. McBurney, p. 58.

14. McBurney, p. 66.

15. McBurney, p. 52.

16. McBurney, p. 65.

17. It is important to note that these authors recognize that the enthymeme is a species of syllogism. When they contrast the enthymeme and the "syllogism," they mean by the latter either the dialectical or demonstrative syllogism. Therefore, the question is not, How does the enthymeme differ from the syllogism? Properly speaking, the question is, How does the enthymeme, which is one type of syllogism, differ from the dialectical and the demonstrative syllogism? Aristotle clearly holds that the enthymeme is a kind, or species, of syllogism. At 1355ª6-8 he refers to the enthymeme as "a sort of syllogism"; and at 1356ᵇ3-5 he says, "the enthymeme is a syllogism, and the apparent enthymeme is an apparent syllogism. I call the enthymeme a rhetorical syllogism."

18. Lane Cooper translates this passage as follows: "Let us grant that only a few of the premises of rhetorical deduction are necessarily admitted, and that the majority of cases ... may lie this way or that." The translation by Freese

(Aristotle, The "Art" of Rhetoric, Cambridge, Mass.,
1939) reads as follows: "Few of the propositions of the
rhetorical syllogism are necessary, for most of the things
which we judge and examine can be other than they are."

19. Cope's translation of this passage may account for his view
that probability of premises and conclusion is the essential
feature of the enthymeme. Cope's understanding of the
passage is substantially different, commencing with the
italicized portion: "... either universal or general and
probable, is called in the former case a syllogism, in the
latter an enthymeme." He follows immediately with: "So
that it appears from this ... that the only essential difference between the two is that the one leads to a necessary
and universal, the other only to a probable conclusion" (Cope,
102). Translations by Cooper, Freese, and Jebb agree with
Roberts, however. "To conclude from certain assumptions
that something else follows from those assumptions (something distinct from them, yet dependent upon their existing)
either universally or as a rule--this in Dialectic is called
a syllogism, and in Rhetoric an enthymeme."--Cooper.
"When, certain things being posited, something different results by reason of them, alongside of them, from their
being true, either universally or in most cases, such a
conclusion in Dialectic is called a syllogism, in Rhetoric
an enthymeme."--Freese. "When certain things exist, and
something else comes to pass through them, distinct from
them but due to their existing, either as an universal or as
an ordinary result, this is called in Dialectic, a Syllogism,
as in Rhetoric it is called an Enthymeme."--Jebb, The
Rhetoric of Aristotle (Cambridge, 1909).

20. Cooper's translation reads: "And he must argue not only
from necessary truths, but from probable truths as well."
Freese's translation reads: "Conclusions should not be
drawn from necessary premises alone, but also from those
which are only true as a rule."

21. Grote's explanation of the enthymeme indicates that some
rhetorical arguments may begin with propositions which are
universal and necessary and may produce conclusions which
are universally true: "The Enthymeme is a syllogism from
Probabilities or Signs; the two being not exactly the same.
Probabilities are propositions commonly accepted, and true
in the greater number of cases; such as, Envious men hate
those whom they envy, Persons who are beloved look with
affection on those who love them. We call it a Sign, when
one fact is the antecedent or consequent of another, and
therefore serves as mark or evidence thereof. The conjunction may be either constant, or frequent, or merely oc-
casional: if constant, we obtain for the major premise of
our syllogism a proposition approaching that which is universally or necessarily true.... The constant conjunction
will furnish us with a Syllogism or Enthymeme in the First
figure.... We can then get a conclusion both affirmative

and universally true." See George Grote, Aristotle (London, 1880), pp. 202-203.

Cope's position remains a puzzle. At several places he recognizes that enthymemes sometimes include universal and necessary propositions, yet he holds that the probability of premises and conclusion is the essential feature of the enthymeme. For example, in The Rhetoric of Aristotle (ed. John Edwin Sandys, Cambridge, 1877), he says, "The certain sign, the necessary concomitant, is the only necessary argument admitted in Rhetoric: its ordinary materials are ... only probable." (See p. 225; also p. 271, Introduction.) We will note later that Cope removes some confusion by altering his position substantially.

22.   Prior Analytics 70^{a}9-11.   Aristotle expands this definition in the Rhetoric (1402^{b}12-14) to include examples along with probabilities and the two kinds of signs, fallible and complete proofs.

23.   Walter J. Ong, S.J., has recently expressed a similar view. In Ramus, Method, and the Decay of Dialogue (Cambridge, Mass., 1958), Father Ong writes that Aristotle always understands the enthymeme as a "syllogism defective in the sense that it moves from premises at least one of which is only probable, to a merely probable conclusion" (p. 187).

24.   Rhetoricia 1357^{a}1-7.

25.   Topics 104^{a}3-8.

26.   McBurney, p. 52.

27.   Jebb's translation of this passage reads: "Infallible Signs, and the Enthymemes taken from them, will not admit of refutation on the ground that the reasoning is not strict.... It remains to show that the alleged fact does not exist. If it is shown that it does exist, and that it is an Infallible Sign, then there is no further possibility of refutation; for this amounts to a manifest demonstration."

28.   Ross, p. 74. See also Posterior Analytics, Book II, Ch. 30.

29.   Topics 104^{b}1-3.

30.   Prior Analytics 24^{a}21-24^{b}12.

31.   Cope writes that the philosopher, or investigator, proceeds without regard to any respondent; "the man of science is not allowed to choose which side of an alternative he will take." However, the dialectician "depends upon the concessions of his opponent" (Introduction, pp. 75, 78).

32.   "In proportion as a speaker uses specific arguments, he is deserting the province of rhetoric; but in view of the comparatively small number of general arguments available Aristotle allows the speaker to use specific arguments as well" (Ross, Aristotle, p. 271).

33.   Topics 101^{b}2-4.

34.   Cope, Introduction, p. 105.

35.   Cope, Introduction, pp. 157-58.

36.   Cope, Introduction, p. 158.

37.   Cope's position leads him directly to this consequence. Note especially the last line of this quotation from his Rhetoric

of Aristotle, p. 221: "I will repeat here, that the enthymeme differs from the strict dialectical syllogism only in
form.   The materials of the two are the same, probable
matter, and of unlimited extent.... The difference between
the two is simply this, that the dialectician rigorously maintains the form of the syllogism, with its three propositions,
major and minor premiss and conclusion: the rhetorician
never expresses all three--if he did, his enthymeme would
become a regular syllogism."

38. It may be worthwhile to note that this interpretation of the
enthymeme--and of the whole sphere of rhetorical discourse--
provides a sound theoretical justification for that kind of
speech criticism which studies the audience and relevant aspects of its context as carefully as it studies the speaker
and his preserved speeches.   According to this interpretation, a recorded speech is only partially a speech.   The
complete speech is the actual speech which occurs when
speaker and audience interact, either cooperatively or not.
Therefore, a sound speech criticism of past speeches must
reconstruct the actual speech, and this requires detailed
study of the particular audience to determine the premises
it would or would not have supplied.

9. THE EXAMPLE IN ARISTOTLE'S RHETORIC:
    BIFURCATION OR CONTRADICTION?*

by Gerard A. Hauser

Students of Aristotle are familiar with the emphasis he placed upon the doctrine of logical proof and its two great instruments, enthymeme and example. Although scholars have devoted considerable attention to this doctrine, their inquiries have virtually ignored example, while pursuing enthymeme with great energy.[1] This is particularly strange in light of the almost enigmatic quality pervading Aristotle's discussion of example.

We may focus on the difficulty attending example by contrasting Aristotle's position in Book I with that in Book II. In Book I he maintains:

> With regard to the persuasion achieved by proof or apparent proof: just as in dialectic there is induction on the one hand and syllogism or apparent syllogism on the other, so it is in rhetoric. The example is an induction, the enthymeme is a syllogism, and the apparent enthymeme is an apparent syllogism. I call the enthymeme a rhetorical syllogism, and the example a rhetorical induction. Every one who effects persuasion through proof does in fact use either enthymemes or examples: there is no other way. And since everyone who proves anything at all is bound to use either syllogisms or inductions (and this is clear to us from the Analytics), it must follow that enthymemes are syllogisms and examples are inductions.[2]

And then:

> When we base the proof of a proposition on a number of similar cases, this is induction in dialectic, example in rhetoric....[3]

Finally, he instructs:

*Reprinted by permission of the author and publisher, from Philosophy and Rhetoric 1 (1968), 78-90.

> The 'example' has already been described as one kind of
> induction; and the special nature of the subject-matter
> that distinguishes it from the other kinds has also been
> stated above.   Its relation to the proposition it supports
> is not that of part to whole, nor whole to part, nor whole
> to whole, but of part to part, or like to like. [4]

The discussion in Book I raises example to a position of considerable importance.

In Book II, however, Aristotle presents what appears to be
an altered view, suggesting that either he changed his mind concerning the function of example or he contradicted himself.   He
argues:

> Enthymemes are based upon one or other of four kinds
> of alleged fact: (1) Probabilities, (2) Examples, (3) In-
> fallible Signs, (4) Ordinary Signs. [5]

Then he tells us:

> Enthymemes based upon Example are those which proceed
> by induction from one or more similar cases, arrive at
> a general proposition, and then argue deductively to a par-
> ticular inference. [6]

The treatment in Book II lowers example from its former position
of importance.

As this brief review indicates, Aristotle apparently lays
down two seemingly disparate and, in fact, opposite doctrines on
example.   Book I presents example as an independent mode of
proof, as co-ordinate with enthymeme, as moving from part to
part.   At swords' points with this is Book II which presents example as merely a source of materials for proof, as subordinate
to enthymeme, as moving from part to whole.   Further, the
Rhetoric provides insufficient grounds for explaining this seeming
disparity in doctrine, for resolving it, or for choosing one doctrine
over the other.   Unless we are willing to assume, without substantial internal warranty, that Aristotle does not mean the same thing
by example in Book I and example in Book II, then we are left in
a quandary when interpreting this concept.

While the Rhetoric presents a knotty picture of example,
Aristotle does imply that examining his other works may uncover
lines of reasoning which will facilitate discerning his meaning in
these troublesome passages.   My purpose in this essay is to resolve these difficulties by following Aristotle's most obvious lead--
the relation between induction and example.   I will examine his
doctrine of induction from the perspective of logic, discuss the
particulars composing induction from the perspective of metaphysics
and epistemology, and apply Aristotle's reasoning on these notions

to their rhetorical counterpart of example.

I

In the Metaphysics[7] Aristotle divides intellectual activity into three categories: practical, productive, and speculative reasoning. Were logic entered into one of these categories, it would
come under the speculative. In actuality Aristotle classes only
mathematics, physics, and metaphysics under this head; omitting
logic because it is not a substantive science. Rather, as Ross
states, it is "a part of a general culture which everyone should
undergo before he studies any science, and which alone will enable
him to know for what sorts of propositions he should demand proof
and what sorts of proof he should demand for them."[8]

The primary concern of the Organon is establishing a method whereby the individual may systematically conduct this investigation of propositions. Syllogism and induction are the two vehicles
Aristotle proposes as best suited for operationalizing these inquiries. The Organon is, in no small measure, centered about
explicating the former of these tools. Discussion of induction is
not only skimpy but also presented in the context of syllogism--an
unfortunate treatment which has led to some confusion in interpreting the significance and operation of epagogé.[9] Moreover, the various contexts in which epagogé or induction is used suggest an in-
consistency in application. At times induction appears in the role
of supplying confirmation for universal premises to be used in syllogisms. At other points it assumes the role of arriving at universal premises unknown prior to induction. Yet close examination of the uses Aristotle ascribes to this movement of thought indicates that it may be interpreted in two senses. In both senses
the movement is from particular to universal, but the function of
the movement differs.

In its first sense, what I will call its "independent" sense,
induction is a method whereby a person is led to "see a universal
truth with the eyes of his own soul."[10] When experiencing particulars sharing the same genus, man's mind moves inductively to abstract a knowledge of the universal principle contained within the
particulars. As Aristotle puts it:

> We learn either by induction or by demonstration. Now
> demonstration proceeds from universals and induction
> from particulars; but it is impossible to gain a view of
> universals except through induction (since even what we
> call abstraction can only be grasped by induction, because,
> although they cannot exist in separation, some of them in-
> here in each class of objects, in so far as each class has
> a determinate nature)....[11]

Abstractions of the universal contained in the particulars through "independent" induction leads one to knowledge of an arché: an immediate and primary premise "which has no other premiss prior to it."[12] That is not to say that "independent" induction proves a primary premise. Indeed, the primary premise is beyond proof. But "independent" induction is necessary to lead one to the point where he can "see" for himself the universal contained in the particular.[13] Likewise, it is necessary to acquire the indubitable knowledge without which demonstration is impossible.[14] When this type of induction occurs the individual passes from what is prior and better known to him to what is prior and better known in nature.[15] He passes from knowledge of an object as it appears to him to knowledge of the object as it really exists in the universe, as it is in itself.

The second sense of induction, what I will call its "supportive" sense, is used by Aristotle to describe induction or proof by induction or syllogism by induction.[16] Regardless of the context in which it appears, "supportive" induction functions to verify contentions already put forth.[17] For instance, if one were to argue from opposition, he may look to the contradictories involved, establishing or securing the contradictories through induction.[18] "Supportive" induction would enumerate the particulars involved to determine if, in fact, there were any exceptions.[19] In this way it would support an argument for or against the universal at issue.

On the basis of evidence in the Organon we may conclude that Aristotle treats epagogé as a bifurcated term. "Independent" induction functions as a method whereby universal premises are discovered. "Supportive" induction functions as a method whereby universal premises are verified.

While this distinction indicates the perimeters of induction as a logical notion, a more microscopic view of that term may be had by examining the nature of particulars as the basic units of induction. Here my interest is in ferreting out that segment of the metaphysical nature and psychological function of particulars germane to example. My argument will be that Aristotle's epistemology is founded on the capacity of sense organs and mind to accurately perceive and know (or understand) particulars, and, moreover, that these capacities can, based on the doctrine of form, abstract the universal shared by particulars similar in kind.

At the close of Posterior Analytics Aristotle argues that knowledge begins with the act of sense perception. While perception lasts only as long as the object is present to the senses, something of the percept remains in the soul after the sense act is over. Thus:

> The sense-perception gives rise to memory, as we hold; and repeated memories of the same thing give rise to experience; because the memories, though numerically many, constitute a single experience. And experience,

that is in the universal when established as a whole in
the soul--the One that corresponds to the Many, the unity
that is identically present in them all--provides the starting point of art and science.... [20]

For such a process to lead man to knowledge, the sensory
organs and intellective powers must be capable of accurately relating phenomena from the physical world to man's mind.   Aristotle
is aware of this requirement, and he argues that the sense organs
and intellective powers may be trusted.   He holds, on the basis of
potency and act[21] that each sense organ has in potency the same
quality as the object it perceives has in actuality. [22]   When the potency existing in the sense organ is actualized by the sense object,
the organ becomes identical in quality with the object. [23]   This actualization is one of form. [24]   So that:

In a sense even that which sees is coloured; for in each
case the sense-organ is capable of receiving the sensible
object without its matter.   That is why even when the
sensible objects are gone the sensings and imaginings
continue to exist in the sense organs. [25]

Finally, since each sense organ relates but one kind of object to
the soul, and since the sense organ may become identical in quality
with that object by virtue of actualized form, it follows for Aristotle that the sense organs cannot err in reporting sensory phenomena to the soul. [26]

Aristotle develops a similar argument with nous.   It, like
the sense organs, possesses in potency the form of the object of
perception. [27]   His reasoning is:

If thinking is like perceiving, it must be either a process
in which the soul is acted upon by what is capable of being thought, or a process different from but analogous to
that.   The thinking part of the soul must therefore be,
while impassible, capable of receiving the form of an object; that is, must be potentially identical in character
with its object without being the object.   Mind must be
related to what is thinkable, as sense is to what is sensible. [28]

Hence, the particular actualizes the form in the sense organ
which in turn affects the soul by moving it from the potential form
of "this-here-thing" to the actualized form of "this-here-thing. "[29]
The soul becomes actualized in terms of inceiving the form of the
particular object, the "this, " through sense perception without taking in the matter of the "this" it now knows.   Consequently, the
soul literally may be referred to as being "informed. "[30]   The informed soul qua "in-form" "sees" or recognizes or grasps or in-
tuitively knows the principle of the particular "this, " i. e., its form.

Examining the psychological movement as a whole, Aristotle observes that in the process by which sense perception comes to be memory and repeated memories come to form experience, "what is achieved at each step, whether by sense or by induction, is the grasp and stabilization of the universal."[31] Mind moves from what is prior and better known to us to what is prior and better known in nature. Nous comes to know the universal that resides in the particular. Significantly, it arrives at this knowledge through induction of particulars:

> As soon as one individual percept has 'come to a halt' in the soul, this is the first beginning of the presence there of a universal (because although it is the particular that we perceive, the act of perception involves the universal, e.g., 'man,' not 'a man, Callias'). Then other 'halts' occur among these [proximate] universals, until the indivisible genera or [ultimate] universals are established. E.g., a particular species of animal leads to the genus 'animal,' and so on. Clearly then it must be by induction that we acquire knowledge of the primary premisses, because this is also the way in which general concepts are conveyed to us by sense-perception.[32]

By virtue of the fact that particulars produce knowledge in the soul and are the source of the universal which the soul comes to know, they may be said to act as a cause producing that knowledge. For Aristotle maintains:

> That which is potentially possessed of knowledge becomes actually possessed of it not by being set in motion at all itself but by reason of the presence of something else; i.e., it is when it meets with the particular object that it knows in a manner the particular through its knowledge of the universal.[33]

Particulars, as the source from which the soul comes to know the universal, serve as the material cause of universal knowledge, since universals are abstracted from particulars. And we may see particulars contained within induction as the efficient cause of the knowledge of universals, since universals are abstracted through the agency of induction.

We may conclude that, first, the particular exists as act and actuates the form existing potentially in the sense organ. As such the particular serves as the agent of activity. Second, the particular as form eventually actuates the corresponding form which is in potency in the soul. The actualized form in the soul and the actualized form in the particular are identical in quality. Third, the universal is present in every particular. It is the universal existing as form that is shared in common by the soul and the particular. Finally, we may conclude that the particular serves as the material cause of the universal and, when incorporated under induction, is part of the efficient cause of universal knowledge.

II

At this point we seem to have drifted far from considerations properly rhetorical. However, it appears to me that there is a definite link between these philosophical considerations and Aristotle's doctrine of example. For the remainder of this paper I will attempt to show how the foregoing may aid in resolving the difficulties attending that rhetorical concept.

As previously noted, Aristotle lays down two doctrines of example. While these positions seem to indicate a shift in posture, they do share one point in common. In both cases example is related to induction as its rhetorical form. If we may take Aristotle at his word, his doctrine of example should somehow correspond to his doctrines of induction. More specifically, on the level of their respective functions, one would expect to find a bifurcation of example similar to that of induction. Aristotle's posture, discussed at the beginning of this paper, at least supplies sufficient warranty for the possibility of such a case.

In Book I Aristotle presents example as an independent mode of proof co-ordinate with enthymeme. This seems to correspond to his notion of "independent" induction which stands as a method co-ordinate with syllogism in leading man to knowledge.[34] In Book II example is a support for or reduced to enthymeme. This seems to correspond to "supportive" induction which stands as a support for or is reduced to syllogism. If we apply to example the lines of reasoning Aristotle uses on induction, we find that these seemingly disparate doctrines need not be disparate at all. In fact the rhetorical and logical doctrines may be perfectly consistent. Just as he has a bifurcated concept of induction, so too he may have a bifurcated concept of example.

In order to verify this hypothesis we must determine whether example's movement from part to part is really different from part to whole to part. If it is not--if part to part is merely shorthand for part to whole to part[35]--then example is reduced to enthymeme and the doctrines of Book I and Book II concerning the position of example in Aristotle's theory of proof remain disparate.

I will approach the problem via Aristotle's chapter on example in Prior Analytics,[36] for his illustrations parallel those given in the Rhetoric when example is discussed as a mode of proof. In addition, Aristotle's logical analysis brings the difficulties involved into clearer focus.

Three aspects of the discussion in Prior Analytics are worthy of note. First, example is presented in a context of syllogism--that is, in terms of major and minor extremes and con-

clusions. Second, the treatment immediately follows that of syllogism via induction and bears striking resemblance to that concept.
Together these suggest that example, likewise, is reduced to syllogism.   Third, the discussion concludes with the claim that example differs from induction and syllogism since it moves from
part to part.   Here the implication is that it is not reducible to
syllogism.

How, then, are we to interpret example?   Two possible interpretations suggest themselves.   We may approach example from
a purely logical position or we may approach it from the nature of
particulars as described above.

In terms of the logical relationship required for constructing
argument from example, Aristotle's treatment in Prior Analytics
indicates that example's movement requires more than a single step
from part to part.   Unfortunately his discussion is too long to be
cited in full.   However, the paradigm Aristotle analyzes can be
quoted and will aid in the exegesis of the arduous and complex
treatment he gives example:

> Then if we require to prove that war against Thebes is
> bad, we must be satisfied that war against neighbours is
> bad.   Evidence of this can be drawn from similar ex-
> amples, e. g., that war by Thebes against Phocis is bad.
> Then since war against neighbours is bad, and war against
> Thebes is against neighbours, it is evident that war
> against Thebes is bad. [37]

Given the facts of the prospective argument, Aristotle proceeds to analyze in terms of syllogism the logical relationships ob-
taining in argument from example.   His analysis indicates that the
speaker depicted wishes to convince his audience that war between
his city (Athens) and a neighboring city (Thebes) is bad.   To prove
this he must first get his audience to agree that war among neighbors is bad.   He will prove this point through an example showing
that the major extreme of the argument (bad) applies to the middle
term of the argument (war against neighbors) by means of a term
similar to the third (war between Thebes and Phocis is similar to
war between Athens and Thebes).   It must be known by the audience
that the middle term applies to the third (war between Athens and
Thebes is war against neighbors) and that the major extreme applies to the term similar to the minor extreme (war between Thebes
and Phocis is bad).   Therefore, in order to prove that we should
not make war against the neighboring city, the audience must first
see that war with a neighbor is bad.

Aristotle's discussion in terms of syllogisms, premises and
conclusions resulting from the relating of premises clearly points
out that, on the logical level, examples are being used to form a
generalization.   As his illustration shows, particular cases of a
similar genus are reviewed with the object in mind of forming a

generalization. This generalization is then applied to the exemplified case and, finally, the conclusion is drawn. In fact, in Prior
Analytics when Aristotle distinguishes example from induction, he
never says a generalization is not formed. Rather, he distinguishes the total compass of example's movement from induction's
by contending, albeit in an inferential manner, that induction stops
at the generalization while example continues on to apply the generalization to a particular case. For instance, we review the
parallel cases of warring neighbors and conclude that such wars
are bad. Then, significantly, the generalization is applied in the
argument to reach the conclusion that our city fighting a neighboring city is, likewise, bad. Whether or not this generalization is
formally expressed is irrelevant. The very fact that it is being
formed (either implicitly or explicitly) and, more importantly, must
be formed for the argument to be concluded--for the audience to
arrive at the conclusion desired--indicates that the movement is
not that of a single step from part to part.

This interpretation places example closer to the movement
of syllogism or a combination of induction and syllogism. In the
fact of Aristotle's differentiation of enthymeme and example as two
independent modes of proof, such a position serves only to increase
example's already puzzling nature. [38]

However, a second and, perhaps, more satisfying interpretation is possible if we approach example via the consideration
given the particulars used in induction. To recapitulate, Aristotle
considers the particular to exist as a combination of matter and
form. Man's soul contains potentially the form of objects in the
phenomenal world. As similar particulars pass before the individual, the process of sense-perception actualizes the corresponding
form in the soul so that the actualized form in the particular and
in the soul are identical in quality. By virtue of its actualization
in terms of inceiving the form of the particular, the soul literally
becomes "informed." It recognizes the principle of the "this." It
comes to know the universal that resides in the particular. In so
doing the individual passes from knowledge prior and better known
to him to knowledge prior and better known in nature. Most importantly, this process precludes the necessity of a generalization
to arrive at a conclusion about the particular. The process is
such that once the individual recognizes X and Y and Z as identical in form he has reached the conclusion. When the problem is
approached metaphysically and epistemologically the psychological
movement becomes one of immediate apprehension and instantaneous recognition that a series of particulars are one in kind in
terms of their form.

Taking the cues Aristotle gives while illustrating argument
from example, this approach seems applicable. He says, first,
examples are used "in order to show what is not yet known." Second, its movement is from part to part. [39] Examples, which are
particulars, serve as the efficient cause which actuates the form

in the soul. The actuated soul in turn can now understand what it
did not previously know. It can know that the exemplified is identical in form with the examples. In arriving at this conclusion it
does not have to form a generalization and then apply the generalization. The process is a simultaneous one, an act of recognition
rather than criticism.

That the general exists is true. That the general may show
the exemplified to be of the same genus as the examples is also
true. But that the movement of example is through the general,
that it is from part to whole to part (a position which we must
posit in direct opposition to Aristotle's position if we view example
as reaching its conclusion through the generalization), is not true.
If the example and exemplified are identical in form, they are related to each other simultaneously or in a one-step process. This
interpretation views the movement to be simply what Aristotle says
it is--an unmediated inference which moves from part to part in an
instantaneous single step.

If this formulation is correct, then there is a real difference
between example in Book I and Book II. Now we may take what
Aristotle says in Book II at its face value. In its supportive sense
example provides the materials for enthymematic argument. Moreover, we may view this as supporting the hypothesis that Aristotle
does not have two disparate doctrines of example, but rather a
single, albeit bifurcated, doctrine which is consistent with his doctrine of induction. In sum, the foregoing supplies warranty for interpreting Aristotle's example as being used in two distinct senses.
It may function as an independent method of proof or it may function as a support in enthymematic proof.

In light of this distinction, the following tentative definitions
are offered: When example functions as an independent mode of
proof: it is a rhetorical induction based on the comparison of previously known occurrences of a like genus to present or predicted
occurrences whose genus is unknown to the audience and whose
genus may be directly apprehended by the audience from comparison with the known occurrences. It is an unmediated inference
from part of a genus to another part of a genus. When example is
used as a basis for enthymematic proof: it is a rhetorical induction based on the review of previous occurrences of a known genus
for the purpose of establishing a premise or support for a premise
to be used in a rhetorical proof. [40]

NOTES

1. For a sampling of modern scholarship on the enthymeme see
    Lloyd F. Bitzer, "Aristotle's Enthymeme Revisited," Quar-
    terly Journal of Speech, XLV (December 1959), 399-408;
    Walter R. Fisher, "Uses of the Enthymeme," The Speech
    Teacher, XIII (September, 1964), 197-203; James H.

McBurney, "The Place of the Enthymeme in Rhetorical
        Theory," Speech Monographs, III (1936), 47-74; Edward H.
        Madden, "The Enthymeme: Crossroads of Logic, Rhetoric
        and Metaphysics," Philosophical Review, LXI (1952), 368-
        376; Edward D. Steel, "Social Values, The Enthymeme, and
        Speech Criticism," Western Speech, XXVI (Spring, 1962),
        70-75; Earl W. Wiley, "The Enthymeme: Idiom of Persua-
        sion," Quarterly Journal of Speech, XLII (February, 1956),
        19-24.

2.   Rhetoric 1356^a-36^{b}10.   All references to the Rhetoric are
        from the translation by W. Rhys Roberts in The Works Of
        Aristotle, Vol. XI, ed. W. D. Ross (Oxford: Clarendon
        Press, 1924).

3.   Ibid., 1356^{b}13-14.

4.   Ibid., 1357^{b}25-28.

5.   Ibid., 1402^{b}13-14.

6.   Ibid., 1402^{b}16-18.

7.   Metaphysics 1025^{b}25.

8.   Sir David Ross, Aristotle (New York: Barnes and Noble,
        1964), p. 20.

9.   For a sampling of views toward Aristotle's notion of induction
        see George Grote, Aristotle (London: John Murray, 1872)
        Vol. I, 256ff.; Ernst Kapp, Greek Foundations of Traditional
        Logic (New York: Columbia University Press, 1942),
        pp. 79-84; John Randall, Jr., Aristotle (New York: Colum-
        bia University Press, 1960), pp. 40ff.; Ross, pp. 39-41;
        A. E. Taylor, Aristotle (New York: Dover Publications,
        Inc., 1955), pp. 29-30.

10.   Kapp, pp. 77-78.

11.   Posterior Analytics 81^{a}40-^{b}5.   Hugh Tredennick, trans. (Cam-
        bridge: Harvard University Press, 1960).

12.   Ibid., 72^{a}11.

13.   Randall, pp. 45-46; Taylor, p. 38.

14.   Post. Anal. 81^{b}5-9.

15.   Ibid., 71^{b}33-72^{a}5.   For a detailed discussion of this point
        see Richard McKeon, "Aristotle's Conception of the Develop-
        ment and the Nature of Scientific Method," Journal of the
        History of Ideas, VIII (January, 1947), 3-44.

16.   While this appears to be a strange distinction, it does seem
        warranted by the Aristotelian texts.   "Induction" refers to
        Aristotle's general investigative procedure.   "Proof by in-
        duction" refers to enumerating the particulars which support
        a generalization.   "Syllogism by induction" refers to Aris-
        totle's theory of complete enumeration which he reduced to
        syllogism at Prior Analytics 68^{b}15-29.   See Kapp, pp. 77-
        78.

17.   Topics 103^{b}1-7; 108^{a}15-17; 108^{b}10-12; 113^{b}27-30; Pr. Anal.
        68^{b}15-29.

18.   Topics 108^{a}15-17.

19.   Kapp, p. 78.

20.   Post. Anal. 100^{a}3-9.   It should be added, as noted before,
        that in grasping this universal premise, the individual passes

      from what is prior and better known to him to what is
      prior and better known in nature.

21.   Met. 1019^{b}ff.; 1048^{a}31-35; for Aristotle's definitions of po-
      tentiality and actuality.
22.   De Anima 418^{a}4-6.
23.   For an interesting discussion of this relationship see John
      Anton, Aristotle's Theory of Contrariety (London: Routledge
      & Keegan Paul, 1957), pp. 125ff.
24.   Met. 1025^{b}25ff.; 1035^{b}33; 1042^{a}28.
25.   De Anima 425^{b}22-25. J. A. Smith, trans., The Basic Works
      of Aristotle, ed. Richard McKeon (New York: Random
      House, 1951). On the relation between the sense organ and
      sense object, Anton observes, "The organ, in order to as-
      similate, must possess powers that enable it to undergo
      such changes as to respond to the dynamic configuration of
      the sensible objects.... Both the sensing organ and the
      sensible object have qualitative properties; or to put the
      matter differently, the qualities exist in both the object and
      the knower. The object, however, is in a given moment
      what it happens to be; and its qualitative state is determi-
      nate at the time it is sensed. Then, it is not the object
      but the perceiving organism that has to make the response
      and produce within itself by means of the process of sensa-
      tion a situation which in its structural and formal determi-
      nateness will be identical in kind with the stimulus." An-
      ton, p. 125.
26.   De Anima 418^{a}14-17.
27.   Ibid., 429^{a}28-29. Aristotle emphasizes this point by refer-
      ring to the soul as the place of forms.
28.   Ibid., 429^{a}13-17.
29.   See G. R. G. Mure, Aristotle (London: Ernst Benn, Ltd.,
      1932), p. 115; for a more detailed discussion of this point.
30.   Taylor, p. 81.
31.   McKeon, 26. See Post. Anal. 99^{b}15-100^{b}17; especially
      100^{b}9-10.
32.   Post. Anal. 100^{a}14-^{b}4.
33.   Physics 247^{b}4-7. R. P. Hardie and R. K. Gaye trans.,
      The Basic Works.
34.   This is to say, "independent" induction leads man to knowl-
      edge of an arche. This type of knowledge cannot be had
      apart from "independent" induction and is necessary for
      demonstrative syllogism to proceed.
35.   Both Cope and McBurney adopt such a position. Neither
      seems aware of Aristotle's bifurcated notion of induction.
      This could account for their confusion in treating example.
      See E. M. Cope, An Introduction to Aristotle's Rhetoric
      (Cambridge: Macmillan and Co., 1867), pp. 105-106;
      McBurney, 58-59.
36.   Pr. Anal. 68^{b}38-69^{b}19.
37.   Ibid., 69^{a}3-8. Trans. Hugh Tredennick (Cambridge: Har-
      vard University Press, 1960).
38.   It is not unfair to suspect that Aristotle's zeal for explaining

example in terms of syllogism is much the result of the
work in which the explanation appears. His concern in
Prior Analytics is to make the case for his brainchild,
syllogism. Elevation of its importance and all-inclusive nature is what one would expect. This is not to say we should
dismiss his remarks but, perhaps, temper them.

39. Rhet. 1357^{b}28-37.

40. It is interesting to note that in both instances the movement
of example seems to conform to the self-persuasive movement which Bitzer contends is in enthymeme. The audience
is aiding the speaker in constructing the argument since the
review of previous occurrences joins them with the speaker
in recognizing the like genus of these occurrences. As such
it shares, with enthymeme, the distinction of being a self-
persuasive entity since the audience itself is supplying the
relationship. The recognition in the independent mode that
the exemplified is of a like genus as the examples is the
parallel of the recognition in enthymeme that the conclusion
results from jointly formed premises. Recognition in the
supportive mode that thus and so examples give thus and so
premise parallels the effects of premises supplied by probability and sign.

10. A NOTE ON THE MEANING OF πιστισ
IN ARISTOTLE'S RHETORIC*

by Joseph T. Lienhard, S.J.

Two recent articles have treated the meaning of pistis in
Aristotle's Rhetoric; the first, William M. A. Grimaldi's "A Note
on the Πίστεις in Aristotle's Rhetoric, 1354-1356,"[1] was countered
by G. H. Wikramanayake's "A Note on the Πίστεις in Aristotle's
Rhetoric."[2] Grimaldi, who confines his study to the crucial opening chapters of the Rhetoric, proposes three meanings for the
word pistis. The first (a)--to follow his designation--is, "source
material, or the subject-matter capable of inducing in an audience
a state of mind called πιστις, or belief, if employed correctly."[3]
He assigns this meaning to pistis in the expressions πίστεις ἄτεχνοι
and πίστεις ἔντεχνοι, and identifies the latter as ἦθος, πάθος, and
πρᾶγμα.[4] The second meaning (b) is, "the method or technique
whereby one utilizes the material, gives the matter form, so to
speak, and produces the state of mind, pistis, in the audience."[5]
Here he locates ἐνθύμημα and παράδειγμα, the instruments of probable argumentation directed toward κρίσις. The last meaning (e)
is "the state of mind produced in the audience."[6] The key concept
of (a) is matter, the "source material" or "subject-matter" for
bringing the audience to pistis. In (b), form is the operative word,
taken not as distinct from matter but as having already informed
the matter; pistis here is the argument as ordered for presentation.
The idea of effect is essential to (e). In short, he distinguishes
pistis as matter, as form, and as effect.

Grimaldi's theory of the meaning of pistis is rooted in a
specific interpretation of Aristotle's rhetorical theory; his interpretation may be summarized thus; pistis as matter (ethos, pathos,
pragma) is ordered by pistis as form (enthymeme and example) to
produce pistis as effect. Grimaldi refuses to separate ethos and
pathos, as non-logical or quasi-logical proofs, from some third,
logical proof. Instead, he calls the third member pragma, and
makes it only an aspect of the proof, "the logical, rational, intellectual aspect of the subject under discussion."[7] The three pisteis,
then (ethos, pathos, pragma), are sources which "are integrated
and made into effective rhetorical demonstration"[8] by enthymeme

---

*Reprinted by permission of the author and of The Johns Hopkins
Press, from American Journal of Philology 87 (1966), 446-454.

and example. This theory is grounded in a philosophy of language which denies that discourse can be purely logical, rational, and intellectual (to use Grimaldi's terms), in no way revealing the speaker or touching the auditor affectively. Grimaldi implies such a philosophy of language in a footnote: "It appears that attention should also be called to the fact that in the Rhetoric Aristotle recognized as Plato did in the Phaedrus that we accept propositions and make judgments as human beings with the whole complex of intellect, will, emotions, feelings coming into play."[9]

When he says that pistis as form is a technique for utilizing the material, he brings ethos and pathos under the control of enthymeme and example. He sees this universal application of enthymeme and example as the rhetorical counterpart of Aristotle's tenet that deductive and inductive reasoning are essential to all demonstration.

Two questions must eventually be asked about this theory: first, whether the texts proposed by Grimaldi (or any texts) show a distinction between pistis as matter and pistis as form; secondly, whether the linguistic thesis that discourse is not only denotative but also reveals the speaker and affects the auditor (an acceptable modern view) is really Aristotle's.

Wikramanayake wrote in refutation of Grimaldi. He treats the use of the word pistis throughout the Rhetoric. The word, he says, has two uses relevant to Aristotle's theory: it may mean (a), "the state of mind produced in the audience,"[10] or (b), "the means whereby the state of mind called πίστις is produced in the audience."[11] It should be noted immediately that Wikramanayake's definition (a) corresponds word for word with Grimaldi's (c). Wikramanayake also seems to believe that his definition (b) corresponds with Grimaldi's (b). The idea, however, of some means whereby the state of mind called pistis is produced in the audience, Wikramanayake's (b), is really a note common to two of Grimaldi's definitions, namely, (a) and (b). Grimaldi's words are almost the same in each case: of (a) he says, "source material ... capable of inducing in an audience a state of mind called πίστις or belief...";[12] of (b), "the method or technique whereby one ... produces the state of mind, pistis, in the audience."[13] So Wikramanayake has failed to see, or has chosen to ignore, Grimaldi's distinction between (a) as matter and (b) as form.

Wikramanayake's interpretation is rooted in a different synthesis of the Aristotelian rhetorical theory. Because he has not recognized this, some of his criticisms of Grimaldi are invalid as presented. He writes, for instance, that "nowhere in the Rhetoric is πίστις used unambiguously in this sense [i.e., Grimaldi's (b), pistis as form]. As examples of this usage Grimaldi refers to 1355 b 35, 37ff.; 1356 a 1, 13; and 1356 a 21. But the word can bear the meaning (b) [of Wikramanayake] in all these passages."[14] Grimaldi would readily admit that it does, but would point out that this note is common to both his definitions (a) and (b), and that Wikramanayake has not hit the salient point. The second criticism, [15] that Aristotle uses other words when he wants to refer to "source material" or "sources," leads nowhere without a demonstration that the words are Aristotle's only terms for "source."

The synthesis of Aristotle's theory offered by Wikramanayake is rooted in the word pistis in his sense (b), which he translates "proof."[16] There are, he says, two classes of proofs; inartificial (atechnoi) and artificial (entechnoi). Moreover, there are three kinds of artificial proofs: ethical, which depend on the character of the speaker; emotional, which produce a certain disposition in the hearer; and logical. This last he studies at length. Wikramanayake, following the traditional interpretation of the Rhetoric, places enthymeme and example here under logical proofs.[17] In Grimaldi's view, ethos, pathos, and pragma are three constituent parts which are organized into one proof by enthymeme or example. For Wikramanayake, ethos and pathos stand on their own as proofs; parallel to them there is another kind of proof, logical, which has two species: enthymeme and example. Ethos and pathos require no further organization, and enthymeme and example do not involve the speaker's character or effect an emotional reaction in the audience, but are pure demonstrations by reason. This theory is based on a philosophy of language which admits the possibility of merely denotative discourse.

One criticism of this theory must be made immediately, although a little out of order: if ethos and pathos are on the same level with enthymeme and example, and yet separate from them, it is possible for the speaker to inspire confidence in his own character or produce a disposition in the auditors apart from the deductive and inductive processes of rhetorical reasoning; such a use of ethos and pathos seems to be precisely that condemned by Aristotle in the first chapter of the Rhetoric as ἔξω τοῦ πράγματος (1354 a 15).

An attempt to examine the text of the Rhetoric in the light of the controversy can be begun by narrowing the problem. There are several senses of the word pistis which are clearly recognizable and not directly involved in the dispute. These may be listed here.

At 1375 a 10, pistis means "a pledge of good faith," as Wikramanayake notes.[18] This use is not relevant to Aristotle's theory.

In the part of Book III in which Aristotle treats τάξις, the arrangement of the speech, pistis is a technical term for that part of the speech in which the proofs are set forth, as distinguished from the πρόθεσις, the exposition (cf. 1414 a 35ff.). Pistis, always in the singular, is used with this meaning at 1414 a 36; 1414 b 8, 9; and 1418 a 18.

In the same section, pistis, in the plural, means one argument within the probatio. It is so used at 1414 b 10, 11; 1416 b 34; 1417 b 21; 1418 b 6, 8, 23. The sense of the word in Book III is quite distinct from its sense in Book I, and the later use does not elucidate its meaning in Book I.

As Grimaldi and Wikramanayake both recognize, pistis may refer to the state of mind produced in the audience. The meaning appears in the verb πιστεύω (1356 a 19) and the compound ἀξιόπιστος (1356 a 5). The same sense is found in the noun form occurring at 1367 b 30, 1377 b 25, and 1394 a 10. In each instance, the noun is singular.

But the most important and controversial occurrences of the word remain to be discussed, those which are the cause of the disagreement in the two articles summarized earlier. A study must first decide whether pistis in these texts can be univocal. If it is apparent that it cannot, the next step will be to determine how many meanings it does have, and illustrate them from the text.

The question whether the word is univocal can be decided from a juxtaposition of two texts. One is 1355 b 35 (Wikramana- yake's basic text); τῶν δὲ πίστεων αἱ μὲν ἄτεχνοί εἰσιν αἱ δ' ἔντεχνοι.[19] The other is 1356 b 6ff.; πάντες δὲ τὰς πίστεις ποιοῦνται διὰ τοῦ δεικνύναι ἢ παραδείγματα λέγοντες ἢ ἐνθυμήματα, καὶ παρὰ ταῦτα οὐδέν.... But before a comparison of the texts can be made, one problem concerning the second must be settled. Wikramana- yake says that the meaning of pistis in this text is doubtful, and it can mean either (a) or (b)--that is, the state of mind or the means.[20] But a reading of the rest of the sentence proves that it cannot mean (a). After οὐδέν the passage continues: ὥστ' εἴπερ καὶ ὅλως ἀνάγκη ἢ συλλογιζόμενον ἢ ἐπάγοντα δεικνύναι ὁτιουν, ... ἀναγκαῖον ἑκάτερον αὐτῶν ἑκατέρῳ τούτων τὸ αὐτὸ εἶναι.[21] In the clause begin- ning ὥστ' εἴπερ, which compares rhetoric and the methods of dia- lectic and science, the counterpart of the phrase τὰς πίστεις ποιοῦνται διὰ τοῦ δεικνύναι is δεικνύναι ὁτιοῦν, "to demonstrate some- thing," not "to convince somebody." Therefore pisteis in 1356 b 6 refers to some means for producing belief.

This established, the argument may be resumed. In the first text cited, there are many pisteis: some, the atechnic ones, are named; Aristotle does not name the entechnic pisteis, but describes the means by which (διὰ οὖ) they are produced.[22] In the second text, he states that the speaker may use enthymeme or example to prove something, but that these two exhaust the possi- bilities. Now there cannot be both many pisteis and only two, if pistis is univocal. Therefore it must have more than one meaning.

If pistis cannot be univocal, it remains to determine how many meanings it does have, and what those meanings are. Gri- maldi's view of the matter appears defensible; a further demonstra- tion of it from the text will be attempted.

In the first of the quotations given above (1355 b 35), the pisteis which are many in number are divided into atechnic and entechnic. Aristotle goes on to describe the entechnic pisteis in detail. The paragraph following the quotation resumes the general treatment of the entechnic pisteis in the phrase ἐπεὶ δ' αἱ πίστεις διὰ τούτων εἰσί (1356 a 20f.), and continues in a tone which makes it evident that pisteis here means "the matter of a proof," before it is put into form. The sentence begins: ἐπεὶ δ' αἱ πίστεις διὰ τούτων εἰσί, φανερὸν ὅτι ταύτας ἐστὶ λαβεῖν τοῦ συλλογίσασθαι δυναμένου...; that is, since the (entechnic) proofs are (provided) through these (namely, through the ethos of the speaker [1356 a 2, 5] through some disposition of the auditor [a 3, 14], and through the λόγος 23 [a 3f., 19]), clearly it is the task of one who can form syllogisms to take those (pisteis) in hand.... Therefore the pisteis as presented in the paragraph 1356 a 1-20 still require organization into syllogistic (in the context, enthymematic) form. It should be noted that this is said of all three εἴδη of the pisteis, and not only of the "logical" ones (1356 a 1). The conclusion is that pistis in this context refers to the matter of proof, which as yet lacks organization.

The same text suggests that the pisteis from each of the three entechnic classes are factors contributing to the formed proof, rather than independent proofs, for when Aristotle speaks of ethos he writes that pistis is provided through ethos ὅταν οὕτω λεχθῆ ὁ λόγος ὥστε ἀξιόπιστον ποιῆσαι τὸν λέυοντα (1356 a 5ff.). The implication is that ethos (taken technically) is conveyed to the audience in logos as in a vehicle, rather than as some separate proof.

The other sense of pistis is demonstrated in the second of the texts cited earlier, in which Aristotle states that all men prove (τὰς πίστεις ποιοῦνται) their points through enthymeme and example, and that besides these, there is no other way (1356 b 6). This establishes that these two pisteis, of which one is inductive and the other deductive, exhaust the forms of proof. The text 1356 a 20f., also cited above, makes it clear that syllogism (i. e., enthymeme) organizes the entechnic pisteis. That Aristotle here pairs enthymeme and example very closely should not be forgotten, since he sometimes stresses enthymeme to the neglect of example, as in the following text, which also illustrates pistis in the meaning, "the form of the proof": ἐπεὶ δὲ φανερόν ἐστιν ὅτι ἡ μὲν ἔντεχνος μέθοδος περὶ τὰς πίστεις ἐστίν, ἡ δὲ πίστις ἀπόδειξίς τις, ... ἔστι δ' ἀπόδειξις ῥητορικὴ ἐνθύμημα ... (1355 a 3ff.). Pistis and enthymeme are often associated; for example: [ἐνθύμημα] ὅπερ ἐστὶ σῶμα τῆς πίστεως (1354 a 14f.); or: περὶ δὲ τῶν ἐντέχνων πίστεων [οἱ τεχνολογοῦντες] οὐδὲν δεικνύουσιν, τοῦτο δ' ἐστὶν ὅθεν ἄν τις γένοιτο ἐνθυμηματικός (1354 b 21f.).

In this way, the distinction between pistis as the matter for proof and pistis as the form of a proof imposed upon its matter is demonstrated.

Six senses of pistis have been proposed, five of them relevant to Aristotle's rhetorical theory; the question of their mutual
relations must now be raised. When one studies the text in its
natural order, it becomes apparent that Aristotle varied the meaning of the word with the context, and was careful to give clear in-
dications every time the context changed. For example, the word
occurs seven times before Aristotle begins (at 1355 b 35) to define
the atechnic and entechnic pisteis, namely 1354 a 13, 15; 1354 b
21; 1355 a 4, 5, 7, 28. All these instances are in the introductory
first chapter. Although the meanings of pistis here can be read
back from the later uses, one must admit that these instances
alone would not suffice for the construction of a clear distinction
between pistis as matter and pistis as form. It is interesting that
Grimaldi draws on only one of these seven occurrences for an example, and that after his point is made. [24] The conclusion to be
drawn is that pistis here is used in a rather general sense, because Aristotle is not yet speaking of the technical pisteis of rhetoric.

The discussion of the atechnic and entechnic pisteis (1355 b
35-1356 a 33), examined above at length, yields the clearest instances of pisteis as matter. The word is used four times, at
1355 b 35; 1356 a 1, 13, and 21. This meaning is resumed in the
long discussion of ethos and pathos which occupies parts of Books
I and II. Pistis in this sense recurs at 1363 b 4; 1365 b 19;
1366 a 9, 18, 27; 1375 a 22; 1377 b 12, 18; 1388 b 30; 1391 b 24;
1393 a 23; 1403 b 7, 9.

The last two instances occur in a résumé; otherwise, the
discussion of ethos and pathos ends at 1393 a 23ff., with a text
quite relevant to the present purposes: λοιπὸν δὲ περὶ τῶν κοινῶν
πίστεων ἅπασιν εἰπεῖν, ἐπείπερ εἴρηται περὶ τῶν ἰδίων. εἰσὶ δ' αἱ κοιναὶ
πίστεις δύο τῷ γένει, παράδειγμα καὶ ἐνθύμημα.... The second occurrence of pisteis in this text obviously has the same meaning as the
word has in 1356 b 6, and in 1358 a 1--that is, pisteis as form,
or enthymeme and example. These two references are within the
section devoted to enthymeme and example. Again Aristotle carefully separates the usages.

When pistis means the state of mind produced, it occurs in
the singular, or in a verbal or adjectival form. The instances in
which it refers to the probatio and its parts are restricted to a
well-defined section in Book III, that is, 1414 a 29 to the end. [25]

Therefore, in its five significant meanings, the word pistis
refers in one way or another to the proof, which is simply the
means of inducing belief in the audience. So Wikramanayake is not
wrong in his definition. Only, it is maintained here that it is possible to render the meaning of the word more precise; and if the
evidence presented is accepted, then Wikramanayake must be held
wrong in some of the conclusions he draws. Under Aristotle's
hand, the word shifts its meaning as the topic under discussion

changes; the meaning varies enough to allow separate definitions, but not enough to lose the note of "proof" in any of the occurrences.

NOTES

1. Grimaldi: A. J. P., LXXVIII (1957), pp. 188-92.
2. Wikramanayake: A. J. P., LXXXII (1961), pp. 193-6.
3. Grimaldi, op. cit., p. 189.
4. Ibid.
5. Ibid., p. 190.
6. Ibid.
7. Ibid., p. 189.
8. Ibid., p. 191.
9. Ibid., p. 189, n. 4.
10. Wikramanayake, op. cit., p. 193.
11. Ibid.
12. Grimaldi, op. cit., p. 189.
13. Ibid., p. 190.
14. Wikramanayake, op. cit., pp. 193f.
15. Ibid., p. 194.
16. Ibid., p. 193.
17. Ibid., pp. 194f.
18. Ibid., p. 193.
19. All citations are from the text Aristotelis Ars Rhetorica, ed. W. D. Ross (Oxford, 1959).
20. Wikramanayake, op. cit., p. 193.
21. Ross correctly brackets ἢ ὁντινοῦν after ὁτιοῦν. Both cannot remain, and no MS omits ὁτιοῦν. Ὁντινοῦν yields no sense in context, despite Cope's defense of it. See E. M. Cope (ed.), The Rhetoric of Aristotle with a Commentary (Cambridge, 1877), I, p. 36, n.
22. In the first two clauses beginning διά (1356 a 4f.: διὰ μὲν οὖν τοῦ ἤθους; a 14: διὰ δὲ τῶν ἀκροατῶν), words such as αἱ πίστεις πορίζονται (cf. 1356 a 1) should be understood.
23. Probably to be taken as meaning "logical or rational elements."
24. Grimaldi, op. cit., p. 192, where he cites 1354 a 15.
25. It might be helpful to list in order all the places at which the word pistis and certain of its significant derivatives occur. All have been mentioned above.

Book I:	Book II:
1354 a 13, 15, b 21	1377 b 18, 25
1355 a 4, 5, 7, 28, b 35	1388 b 30
1356 a 1, 13, 19, 21, b 6	1391 b 24
1358 a 1	1393 a 23, 24
1363 b 4	1394 a 10
1365 b 19	Book III:
1366 a 9, 18, 27	1403 b 7, 9
1367 b 30	1414 a 36, b 8, 9, 10, 11
1375 a 10, 22	1416 b 34
1377 b 12	1417 b 21
	1418 a 18, b 6, 8, 23.

11.   THE ARISTOTELIAN TOPICS*

by William M. A. Grimaldi, S. J.

While the influence of the Aristotelian topoi has been rather
extensive in our western tradition, particularly in literature, it
does seem that their methodology has not been fully understood.
A number of factors have contributed to this: the absence in Aristotle of a forthright and formal discussion of what he has in mind, [1]
the neglect of the methodology after Aristotle, [2] a partially misdirected emphasis given to the method by Cicero, one of the first to
concern himself with the topics, [3] and the continuation of the Ciceronian interpretation by Quintilian with whom it passed into the
Middle Ages and the stream of our western tradition. [4]

The rather truncated form in which the topics have come to
us has been rather unfortunate since there has been lost along the
way the far richer method of discourse on the human problem
which they provide.   Seen as mere static, stock "commonplaces, "
stylized sources for discussion on all kinds of subject matter they
have lost the vital, dynamic character. given to them by Aristotle,
a character extremely fruitful for intelligent, mature discussion of
the innumerable significant problems which face man.   Indeed their
genesis within an intellectual environment which included among
other things discussions on φύσις and νόμος related problems of the
First Sophistic, on the nature of justice, goodness, virtue, reality,
etc., of the Platonic dialogues, of education and political science
of Isocrates' discourses, seems to give a clue to their nature.

In his understanding of τόπος it would seem that Aristotle
was attempting to validate a mode of intelligent discussion in the
area of probable knowledge comparable (but not equal) to that enjoyed in the area of scientific knowledge (i. e., the certain knowledge of metaphysics) and, even more than that, to enlarge where
possible the subject of scientific knowledge.   And in this last sense
the topical method would not only be a propaideutic for scientia[5]
but also an assistant discipline.

Even though this idea of the topoi as a formal discipline
and an integrated methodology concerned with both the form and the

*Reprinted by permission of the author and of Fordham University
Press, from Traditio 14 (1958), 1-16.

content of discussion in the field of probable knowledge was lost
shortly after Aristotle, as it would seem, it is interesting to note
that in one form or another the topoi have influenced our western
tradition.   Understood in a rather static sense as "rhetorical invention" they have enjoyed a dominant, and one would have to say
a frequently creative, role in the literature of the West.   Curtius
gives abundant evidence for this but he has missed, it appears,
the vitality of their contribution.   This quality was seen by R.
Tuve in her study of one phase of English poetry. [6] She notes with
insight that it was in the area of the topics that the faculty of the
imagination was thought to be most active: "Thinking of the ad-
juncts of something has provided the pattern for innumerable short
poems, and for innumerable longish images within poems...." And
there is surely no need to comment upon the importance of the im-
aginative faculty or the pervasive presence of metaphor and image
in all significant poetry.   Vico had an idea similar to Miss Tuve's
in mind when he wrote De nostri temporis studiorum ratione, but
he was more concerned with the possible exclusion of the whole
area of probable knowledge.   Apparently he feared that the rejection of the topical method would encourage that attitude of mind
which does not examine all the possible aspects of a problem.   In
our own day this neglect of "problem thinking" (as opposed to "system thinking") could well limit our quest for truth.   No subject is
fully exhausted until intelligent queries can no longer be raised.
The critical examination of subject matter was one phase of the
topical method.   Another aspect of the method as Aristotle worked
it out was the inferential phase, i.e., how one may legitimately
advance by deductive reasoning the material gathered by the topoi.
And here we have the topoi as sources of inference.   Relatively
little has been done with these latter topics, but R. Weaver[7] has
developed from them a way of analysis whose application to prose
literature could bring to light the currents of thought influential in
various periods of our western tradition.   In the course of a rather discerning study of the topical argumentation of Burke and
Lincoln he remarks: "the reasoner reveals his philosophical position by the source of argument which appears most often in his major premise because the major premise tells us how he is thinking
about the world. "[8]

        Aristotle in his topical methodology combined both the ele-
ments just mentioned.   His dominant concern in the topical method
appears to be that of problem thinking, but thinking informed by intelligent procedure.   It does seem that in the whole area of the
problematic, the probable, and the contingent, it is his desire to
enable one, as far as this is possible, to reason as intelligently,
as accurately, and as precisely as one can do in the areas of certain, scientific knowledge.   This becomes possible when one is in
a position to examine the material of the problem with precision
in order to determine it with all the accuracy permissible.   After
this one must be able to develop and enlarge this material by discursive reasoning to further conclusions.   The kind of formal

reasoning used, since one is engaged with the contingent and the probable, will generally be that which relies upon forms and principles of discursive reasoning which are usually considered to be, and are accepted as self-evident principles. The topics are the method devised to supply both elements. There are the "particular topics," varied aspects (i.e., sources) under which the subject may be studied for a clearer understanding. And secondly there are the "general topics," forms of inference, in which to develop this understanding to further conclusions.

Thus Aristotle presents us with a dynamic method, [9] not a mere static listing of likely materials readily usable in discussion, or, as the topoi have been called, "opinion surveys."[10] For Aristotle the τόποι are the methodology of Dialectics, the area of probable knowledge, just as in the Analytics we are given a methodology for the area of certain knowledge, scientia.

In view of the fact that any methodology concerned with language must occupy itself with the form and content of statements, (propositions, to use Aristotle's word),[11] it is possible to see where misinterpretation has arisen. Many commentators, from Cicero on,[12] have fastened upon the content (the particular topics) and then reduced the topics to the mere mechanics of invention, i.e., ways and means of developing and enlarging upon a theme. In more recent studies,[13] though not exclusively, the formal element has been stressed. While this captures the axiomatic character of the general topics, it neglects entirely the non-axiomatic, non-propositional character of the particular topics as they are found in the Topics and the Rhetoric.

In other words, the τόποι, which are the sources for intelligent discussion and reasoning in dialectic and rhetoric,[14] are concerned with both the material and formal element in such discussion. As sources for the content of discussion (the ordinary meaning of loci communes: persons, places, things, properties, accidents, etc., the περιστάεις, or aspects of the subject pertinent to discussion) they ultimately provide the material by means of which general or particular propositions are enunciated. As sources for the forms of discussion[15] they are axiomatic forms, or modes of inference, in which syllogistic (or what is called "enthymematic" in the Rhetoric) reasoning naturally expresses itself. Neither aspect can be neglected. For, granted that the τόποι are concerned with propositions (a point obvious to one acquainted with the Topics and the Rhetoric), it must not be forgotten that propositions consist of terms which must be clearly defined and determined before they can be used in meaningful discussion, or in intelligent, convincing, although probable, inference. There must be a precise apprehension of the subject as far as is possible, and there must be reasonable, inferential modes in which to develop the subject further. In the methodology of the topics Aristotle was apparently concerned with both ideas.

In what follows an attempt will be made to justify this distinction from the Rhetoric. It is generally admitted[16] that we must go to the Rhetoric for a relatively clear explanation of the term τόπος, and more than this, one can clearly show from the Rhetoric a definite distinction in the τόποι, and how Aristotle has developed this idea of the τόποι.

The idea of τόποι, as far as one can decide historically, does not seem to originate with Aristotle. On the other hand he does seem to have isolated and formulated the technique or method which was at work in the collections of τόποι which were probably on hand. His apparent purpose was to arrive at the general method underlying discussion,[17] not to burden the mind with the kind of lists of specific subject headings and arguments for various occasions, which had probably been collected. And in this is the genius of his topical method.

When we turn to the pre-Aristotelian τόπος to make a brief review of the history of the idea, we find nothing quite similar to the meaning Aristotle gives to the term.[18] The ordinary use of the word is primarily one of local designation and we find this common in Plato[19] and Isocrates; and in the latter it is very frequently conjoined with χώρα.

There are, however, four passages in Isocrates which are germane to one aspect of the Aristotelian idea of τόπος as the place to go for material concerning one's subject, or for a clarification of it--the Aristotelian ὑπάρχοντα.[20] In Philip 109 the τόπος is the γαθὰ τῆς ψυχῆς, a topic peculiar (τόπος ἴδιος) to Heracles, and one, as Isocrates says, πολλῶν μὲν ἐπαίνων καὶ καλῶν πράξεων γέμοντα. These γαθὰ (see also Helen 38) are τῇ ψυχῇ πρόσοντα, which is again an echo of the ὑπάρχοντα idea of Aristotle.[21] In Panathenaicus 111 we have τόπος as material for discussion, and the same use in Helen 4.[22]

Demosthenes[23] gives further evidence that τόπος was used in his time and quite rather substantial evidence that not only were such ἴδιοι τόποι known and used, but that writers frequently called them καιρούς rather than τόπους before Aristotle's time. These καιροί for the most part concerned themselves with determining the nature of, and examining in detail, not merely such words and ideas as the good, the useful, the right, the beautiful, the possible,[25] but also other ideas such as war, government, peace, etc.[26]

Such is the more direct evidence which is found on the pre-Aristotelian use of the word τόπος in a way that is at all similar to Aristotle's. Indirect evidence for the pre-Aristotelian existence of the idea in the manner in which Aristotle understood it is twofold: the testimony of Aristotle himself and later writers, and the fairly abundant evidence of Aristotle's τόποι at work in various pre-

Aristotelian writers.

In the Rhetoric Aristotle cites on a number of occasions previous authors or technographers who have employed the particular topos of which he is speaking.[27] One conclusion that may be drawn from this is that the methodology of the topics as Aristotle understood it was being used, even if the term τόπος was not employed to identify it. And actually in the Topics 105 b 11ff. Aristotle suggests the listing of key ideas on life, on the good, a procedure which we have reason to believe was introduced by earlier rhetoricians. For Cicero[28] and Quintilian[29] mention Protagoras and Gorgias as those who were the first to present such "communes locos,"[30] while Doxopater[31] speaks of a tradition which has Corax devising τοὺς τῶν προοιμίων τόπους.

Were one, however, to question this commonly accepted tradition, it still remains true that the actual use of Aristotle's method of particular and general topics is rather convincing. Aside from Aristotle's illustrations of his topics by citations from earlier writers, the general topics have been exemplified from the same source rather frequently by Spengel in his commentary[32] and by Palmer.[33] The particular topics have not been so fortunate, quite possibly because they were not considered τόποι.[34] Why this should be, is strange in view of the fact that the Aristotelian τόπος was certainly understood in the sense of "particular topics" by Cicero, Quintilian and Plutarch[35] among others. Furthermore we find Gorgias continually using such particular topics in his Palamedes[36] and in 22 we find some of them mentioned: τὸν τόπον, τὸν χρόνον, πότε, ποῦ πῶς. Aristotle himself[37] when speaking of the particular topics connected with honor speaks of the importance of τὸ ποῦ and τὸ πότε (τόποι καὶ καιροί) and we also get both of these in the Phaedrus 272a with a slightly different reference. In the Meno we find the particular topics for ἀρετή.[38] And this same process can be seen at work in Prodicus' efforts at definition, or the specification of a term, e.g., pleasure.[39] Further citation does not seem necessary, for, as Radermacher says (and he is speaking of what have thus far been called here "particular topics"): "non potest esse dubium quin de sedibus argumentorum, quae τελικὰ κεφάλαια vocantur, velut de iusto, utili, honesto, pulchro, possibili in scholis sophistarum iam ante Aristotelem sit disputatum."[40]

It would seem, then, that the idea of both particular topics and general topics, or topics to supply one with the material for propositions, as well as topics to supply one with ways of putting this material in a form of inference, was operative prior to Aristotle. Further it does appear that collections of τόποι were made which were concerned for the most part with material and with lines of argument specific to a definite, limited problem or case.[41] These would be the materials and the arguments to be used when a similar problem arose. The process as can be seen is rather static and similar to the study of case law. Aristotle's contribu-

tion was to derive and describe the method at work, [42] and he may
have kept the name τόποι for the method since it describes the
process: these are the places from which originate both the material and the formal elements in all dialectical and rhetorical discussion.

It is in the Rhetoric that a distinction in the τόποι is made
and a clue given to the nature of the methodology which Aristotle
has in mind.   A similar division does not exist in the Topics but
it appears to be operative there. [43]

At 1358 a 2-7 of the Rhetoric the whole question of particular topics (ἴδιοι τόποι or εἴδη) and general topics (κοινοὶ τόποι) is
introduced.   Here we are told that though it is almost universally
disregarded there is a distinction of major importance with regard
to enthymemes (the rhetorical syllogism), a distinction similar to
that which is true of the dialectical syllogism.   For "some enthymemes belong properly to Rhetoric, as some syllogisms belong
properly to Dialectic; other enthymemes are peculiar to other arts
and faculties, either existent or still to be formulated."[44]

A possible commentary on this passage is, perhaps, Soph.
El. 170 a 20-b 11.   The best may be (as Aristotle himself suggests) the section in the Rhetoric which immediately follows:
1358 a 9-28.   Here Aristotle says that the dialectical and rhetorical syllogisms (10-11) are those formed on the basis of the τόποι.[45]
These τόποι are then divided into the κοινοί (12) which would represent the sources of enthymemes and syllogisms κατὰ τὴν ῥητορικὴν
... καὶ ... διαλεκτικὴν μέθοδον (5f.), and the εἴδη (or ἴδια [17] or
ἴδιοι τόποι [28] on analogy with what is quite definitely κοινοὶ τόποι
in the same line) which are the sources of enthymemes and syllogisms κατ᾽ ἄλλας τέχνας καὶ δυνάμεις (6-7). [46]   Aristotle continues[47]
by calling the particular topics peculiar to each subject εἴδη, while
the general topics peculiar to Rhetoric and Dialectic are called
τόποι, [48] a distinction repeated at 1403 b 14 where he sums up the
discussion of Books I and II. [48a]

Aristotle then proposes to discuss the εἴδη, [49] or particular
topics,   and it is in his presentation of them that a distinction between them and the κοινοί becomes quite apparent. [50]   The eidos,
or particular topic, could be called a "material topic"[51] in the
sense that it offers the matter (ὕλη) for the propositions.   It presents one with sources, or focal points, to be examined in order
that one may derive all the material pertinent to the subject, i. e.,
the ὑπάρχοντα of the subject which are necessary for intelligent
statement.   These εἴδη belong to the subject in itself and in all of
its diverse relations.   They represent the varied particular aspects
of an individual subject which can throw light upon the subject and
the field of knowledge which it represents. [52]

To understand the point of view presented here one has
merely to read Aristotle's discussion of the εἴδη for deliberative

(cc. 4-8), epideictic (cc. 9-12) and forensic oratory (cc. 13-15) in
Book I, or those for pathos (cc. 2-11) and ethos (cc. 1, 12-17) in
Book II. Their character is that which has just been described,
and, more than that, one can hardly put aside the fact that Aristotle considers these εἴδη to be τόποι when he himself sums up his
discussion of them with the words: ὥστε ἐξ ὧν δεῖ φέρειν τὰ
ἐνθυμήματα τόπων (1396 b 31-2). The same idea is repeated at
1419 b 15-29. And at 1380 b 30-1 he says of the εἴδη that he has
been discussing relative to πάθος: ἐκ τούτων τῶν τόπων.[53]

These εἴδη, or particular topics, then, are the sources to
which one has recourse to develop an understanding and thorough
knowledge of the subject. As Aristotle says quite simply at 1396 a
5-b 19: to reason intelligently upon a subject, you must reason
ἐκ τῶν περὶ ἕκαστον ὑπαρχόντων (b 2).[54] As a matter of fact, when
reading 1396 a 4-b 21, it is impossible to avoid the conclusion that
not only do the εἴδη offer factual material on the subject, but also
they are considered to be τόποι.[55]

The εἴδη then, are the sources for informative, factual material upon the subject of discussion. Since this material, when
derived from the εἴδη, will usually appear as an enunciation with
respect to the subject, it follows that the εἴδη give us particular
propositions which can be used in enthymematic reasoning on the
subject. In that sense the εἴδη become particular propositions or
statements on the subject under discussion.[56] Yet the kind of statement which they give, does not directly implicate the ultimate and
essential truths about the subject, although it may approach them.
Hence it is, as Aristotle says, that these εἴδη do not put us in
contact with the special principles (ἀρχαί) of the subject.[57] A
study of the references on the εἴδη cited above from Books I and
II[58] will reveal that one could hardly construct a science of government, criminal law, or psychology from the εἴδη presented. Rather the purpose of these particular topics is to enable one to speak
intelligently, but not scientifically, upon the subject under discussion. Enthymematic reasoning based upon them is valid, and only
valid, for the subject to which they belong.[59]

In this respect the εἴδη differ, as topics, from the κοινοί
τόποι.[60] These latter transcend the various subjects which rhetoric may treat. They are valid for all subjects and thus particularly exemplify the nature of rhetoric as a dynamis.[61]

This brings us to a very fundamental characteristic of the
κοινοί τόποι emphatically stressed by Aristotle,[62] namely, that these
κοινοί τόποι are universal and transcend all the fields of knowledge
to which rhetoric may legitimately apply itself.[63] Here, then, we
have a kind of topic which is essentially different from the εἴδη.
Particular topics are confined to and closely related to their own
specific subject matter[64] and are valid sources of information on
that matter alone.[65] The κοινοί on the contrary, have no such
substrate,[66] and are valid sources for enthymematic reasoning

upon any subject. [67] Hence it is, that, no matter how much a particular topic is universalized, the result will never be a κοινὸς τόπος as Aristotle understands that term in the Rhetoric. For an ἴδιὸς τόπος is always specific in its nature and confined to one subject: general or particular. [68]

Any topic, and such are the εἴδη, which is grounded in the particular subject matter of a specific branch of learning and is productive of knowledge in that area, [69] cannot transcend this discipline and include others. But the κοινοί transcend the individual disciplines. This difference in the topics translates itself into what have been called in this paper "particular topics" (εἴδη), or sources of information upon the subject matter to be discussed, and "general topics" (κοινοὶ τόποι), or sources for modes of reasoning by enthymeme: forms of inference most suitable for the enthymeme.[70]

A closer study of what Aristotle has to say of these κοινοί in the passage under discussion[71] and in chapter 23 of Book II appears to justify this division. In the first place the κοινοί are universal and belong properly to Rhetoric in so far as Rhetoric is a δύναμις περὶ ἕκαστον τοῦ θεωρῆσαι το ἐνδεχόμενον πιθανόν[72] and in so far as it is not ἐπιστήμη. [73] Thus Rhetoric does not possess any peculiar ὑποκείμενον, [74] and neither do the κοινοὶ τόποι. [75] And so we can understand why Aristotle, for whom Rhetoric is a dynamis just as Dialectic, lays stress upon the μεγίστη διάφορα in the section 1358 a 2ff. which is so frequently discussed by the commentators. This "difference" resides for him in the fact that there are enthymemes peculiar to Rhetoric as a discipline: κατὰ τὴν ῥητορικὴν μέθοδον. If Rhetoric possesses no particular subject matter of its own, such enthymemes could only be syllogistic forms derived from universal propositional statements which are modes for probable argumentation and reasoning. As he says in the Sophistici Elenchi:[76] there are certain general principles common to all the sciences which even the unlettered can use. In themselves they are known to everyone, for they are natural ways in which the mind thinks. Such in a way are the κοινοὶ τόποι. As general axiomatic propositions they are valid forms of inference by themselves. Further, they may also be applied to the subject matter presented by the εἴδη to permit one to reason enthymatically with this material. [77]

It would appear, then, that the κοινοὶ τόποι are logical modes of inference which generally obtain the matter for their inference from the εἴδη. [78] And as further confirmation that they are general, formal topics, i.e., forms of reasoning, it should be noted that study of the twenty eight κοινοὶ τόποι[79] shows that they are universal[80] and that they apparently fall into one of three inferential and logical patterns:[81]

    a) antecedent-consequent, or cause-effect: VII, XI, XIII,
            XIV, XVII, XIX, XXIII, XXIV.
    b) more-less: IV, V, VI, XX, XXV, XXVII.
    c) some form of relation: I, II, III, VIII, IX, X, XII, XV,

XVI, XVIII, XXI, XXII, XXVI, XXVIII.

One could undoubtedly argue about the terms used for classification, or the distribution of the κοινοί among them. The point of interest, however, is that, no matter how they are classified, these κοινοί τόποι reduce themselves to modes of inference. [82] They always assume a form of reasoning which leads the mind from one thing to another. Expressed quite simply they would resolve themselves into the proposition: if one, then the other. And this last statement acquires new significance when, knowing the close relation between the rhetorical syllogism (enthymeme) and the κοινοί τόποι, [83] one reads: "All Aristotelian syllogisms are implications of the type "if α and β then γ"...."[84] If, further, consideration is given to Aristotle's identification of these κοινοί τόποι with the στοιχεῖα of rhetorical syllogisms, there appears to be no doubt that for Aristotle the general topic is a form of inference and represents the source of enthymemes: κατὰ τὴν ῥητορικὴν μέθοδον.

At 1396 b 20-22 Aristotle summarizes his discussion of the εἴδη and makes a transition to his section on the κοινοί τόποι. He introduces the new subject with words "but let us speak of the στοιχεῖα of enthymemes." From 1358 a 31-2 one would expect him to say as commentators hasten to point out: let us speak of the τόπους τοὺς κοινοὺς ὁμοίως πάντων. Having used στοιχεῖα somewhat unexpectedly, Aristotle immediately clarifies the word with: στοιχεῖον δὲ λέγω καὶ τόπον ἐνθυμήματος τὸ αὐτό. And lest there be any doubt that by τόπος here he means the κοινοί τόποι, he says that these τόποι are καθόλου περὶ ἁπάντων. Thus one can be fairly certain that the τόποι here are the same as the general topics of 1358 a 32: τοὺς κοινοὺς ὁμοίως πάντων.

Aristotle has now specified these κοινοί τόποι as στοιχεῖα. But what is meant by calling them στοιχεῖα? At 1403 a 17-18 we read: "By stoicheion and topos I mean the same thing; for a stoicheion and topos is a general class under which many enthymemes fall." The Greek here: εἰς ὃ πολλὰ ἐνθυμήματα ἐμπίπτει describes στοιχεῖον (and so τόπος) as a larger category which contains many enthymemes. This at once recalls Theophrastus' definition of τόπος as: ἀρχή τις ἢ στοιχεῖον ... τῇ περιγραφῇ μὲν ὡρισμένος (i. e., of determinate form) ... τοῖς δὲ καθ' ἕκαστα ἀόριστος (i. e., indeterminate with respect to the individual matter to which it is applied). [85] Of this definition Bocheński writes: "pour Théophraste le τόπος est une formule logique légitime qui sert à former les prémisses de déduction...."[86] But this is precisely what the κοινοί τόποι are: forms of inference by enthymeme, any one of which may offer a form for inference on various subjects. As Waitz says of a passage in the Analytics 84 b 21 which is parallel to 1403 a 17-18: "In Topicis στοιχεῖα vocat quae alio nomine τόπους appellat, universa quaedam argumenta, ex quibus cum veritatis quadam specie aliquid vel probetur vel refellatur."[87]

Before concluding, a word should perhaps be said about the

Topics. First of all it should be noted that this formal distinction
between εἴδη and κοινοὶ τόποι is not found as such in the Topics.
Yet, as was said earlier, both ideas appear to be operative there.
For in the Topics Aristotle is concerned with determining as accurately as possible the meaning of things by specifying the various
ways in which this meaning can be determined (the εἴδη), and further, establishing these ways to determine meaning, i. e., focal
points from which to examine the subject, he employs time and
again the reasoning of the general topics (κοινοὶ τόποι) as we find
them in the Rhetoric. [88]

In the Topics Aristotle says that a problem can be considered from four primary aspects: definition, property, genus,
accident. [89] The effort in Books 2-7 is to examine the nature of
these categories and what must follow with respect to a thing, if
it comes under one of them. This examination is done by the
τόποι, and the analysis is determined by the very nature of the
category. For example: there are certain ways (τόποι) in which
one can further determine the nature of a genus and consequently
certain statements which can only be made about it--and they are
not valid for an accident. They are ways--determined by reality--
in which one must think about the subject. This kind of analysis
is a vital, logical one, grounded in the metaphysical reality of the
subject, and one engages in it in order to discover as far as possible the true nature of the subject. This was what was meant by
saying that these particular topics are not mere mechanical lists
of terms to be tried on a subject, no Procrustean bed to which
the subject is fitted; rather we have here a method of analysis ori-
ginating in the ontological reality of the subject. [90]

In the Rhetoric, however, as I understand it, Aristotle
would appear to enlarge the method of the particular topics owing
to an apparent awareness that a thing may be conditioned and altered by its situation; in other words, that the time, place, the
circumstances, the character, the emotional involvement, may vitally affect the total meaning of a thing in a given situation. Thus
these and other elements were introduced, and yet they are not entirely absent from the Topics as is seen in 111 b 24ff.; 112 a 24ff.;
118 a; 146 b 20ff.; 150 b 34-151 a 1.

As for the κοινοὶ τόποι they frequently appear in the Topics
as the method whereby one may establish the special focal points
(particular topics) from which a subject may be studied. In this
use they appear in the same form and fulfil the same function as
modes of inference which they have in the Rhetoric. That is to
say, that they are ways in which the mind naturally and readily
reasons, and that they are independent, in a way, of the subject
to which they are applied, and may be said to be imposed as forms
upon this material in order to clarify and determine it further. [91]
Thus it is that we will at times find the general topics functioning
in the Topics as a method to help in the determination of various
particular topics to which one should have recourse. [92]

It is only in the Rhetoric, however, that a clear distinction
between particular and general topics appears, and its presence
would seem indisputable. The distinction may be ignored, but if
the texts cited in this paper are studied, one is forced either to
reject the unity of the Rhetoric, or to question the text as one that
has been confused by later editors, or to seek an interpretation
which keeps in mind the character of the topics as they are met in
the Topics; further, it is an interpretation which appears to be demanded by the text of the Rhetoric as we possess it, and it seems
to express the method Aristotle had in mind when he proposed a
way of human discourse for the whole area of the contingent and the
probable. In summary, then, it is porposed:

> a) that the εἴδη are particular topics concerned with the
> specific content and meaning of the subject under discus-
> sion. They enable one to acquire the factual information
> pertinent to the matter which in turn permits one to make
> intelligent statement upon the subject;
> b) that the κοινοὶ τόποι are general topics, i. e., forms
> of inference into which syllogistic, or enthymematic, rea-
> soning naturally falls. As modes of reasoning they may
> be used for the εἴδη of various subjects which specifically
> differ (1358 a 13-14: διαφεσόντων εἴδει), and when they
> are applied to the εἴδη they effect syllogistic or enthyme-
> matic argumentation. 93

NOTES

1. The Port-Royal logicians rejected the Topics as "des livres
    étrangement confus. " Bocheński, La logique de Théophraste
    (Fribourg 1947) 122, claims that Aristotle never gave us the
    meaning of τόπος, while Solmsen, Die Entwicklung der aris-
    totelischen Logik und Rhetorik (Berlin 1929) 164 maintains
    that Rhet. 1403 a 18-19 is Aristotle's only genuine state-
    ment on the essential character of the term. (All citations
    from the Rhetoric are from Roemer's edition, Teubner
    1923).
2. Theophrastus, of course, wrote on the topics, and apparently
    Straton continued the work (D. Laert. Straton 5. 3). Collec-
    tions of τόποι for prooemia and epilogues apparently existed
    in the 4th century (PW Suppl. 7. 1066. 54ff.). For the gene-
    ral trend in rhetoric between Aristotle and Cicero see ibid.
    1071-1089; and on the topics see Volkmann, Die Rhetorik
    der Griechen und Römer (Leipzig 1885) 199ff., 299ff., 322ff.
3. He himself found Aristotle's work somewhat obscure (Topica
    1); W. Wallies, Die griechischen Ausleger der aristotelischen
    Topik (Berlin 1891) 4, and E. Thionville, De la théorie des
    lieux communs (Paris 1855) 9 would agree with this, for they
    believe that Cicero's work in this field has nothing more in
    common with Aristotle's than its title. This is too severe,
    just as Viehweg, one of the latest to consider the topics,

Topik und Jurisprudenz (Munich 1953) 10, is a bit too san-
guine in his opinion that Cicero's work will help us to understand the Aristotelian topics. The diversity of Cicero's remarks, however, implies at times that he may have seen
into the nature of Aristotle's topics; on this question see B.
Riposati, Studi sui 'Topica' di Cicerone (Milan 1947); his
bibliography, 15-30, is a good one for a study of the general problem.

4. See the pertinent chapters in E. Curtius, European Literature
and the Latin Middle Ages (New York 1953).

5. Top. 101 a 34ff. All citations from the Topics are from I.
Strache-M. Wallies (Teubner 1923).

6. R. Tuve, Elizabethan and Metaphysical Imagery (Chicago 1947)
c. XI. 3.

7. R. Weaver, The Ethics of Rhetoric (Chicago 1953) cc. 3, 4.

8. Ibid., 55.

9. Top., 100 a 18.

10. K. Burke, A Rhetoric of Motives (New York 1950) 56. On
57f. he does see a difference in the topics: there are the
"commonplaces" just mentioned, and then "another kind of
'topic'"; this other kind, from his description of it, is actually the general topic as presented in this paper.

11. For Aristotle the topics are the sources for the προτάσεις and,
as 1358 a 10-35 and 1377 b 16-24 would indicate, this
means sources for both their content and form.

12. Thionville, op. cit. c. vi, traces briefly the development from
Cicero to Marmontel. R. Nadeau gives some attention to
this area in a recent article "Hermogenes on 'Stock Issues'
in Deliberative Speaking," Speech Monographs 25.1 (1958)
59-66.

13. Solmsen, op. cit. 163-6; Riposati, op. cit. 21ff.; E. Hambruch, Logische Regeln der platonischen Schule in der aristotelischen Topik (Berlin 1904) 31; Thionville, op. cit., 30ff.

14. Rhet. 1358 a 10-35; 1377 b 16-24.

15. 1358 a 12-17.

16. Viehweg, op. cit. 9; Solmsen, op. cit. 163-4; Thionville, op.
cit. 30f.

17. Top. 100 a 18f.; 102 b 35-103 a 5.

18. As Solmsen, op. cit. 156 remarks: the Aristotelian idea is
something new; he discusses the term in general 151-175;
see also F. Schupp, "Zur Geschichte der Beweistopik in der
älteren griechischen Gerichtsrede" Wiener Studien 45 (1926-
7) 17-28, 173-85.

19. See Ast, Lexicon Platonicum sub τόπος; this is also true of all
the pertinent references in Diels, Die Fragmente der Vorsokratiker⁶ (Berlin 1952), with the exception of the Cicero and
Quintilian citations which will be seen later.

20. See Top. 105 b 12-8 for the idea, and 112 a 24ff. and Rhet.
1396 a 34ff. where Aristotle says that what he was trying to
do in the Topics was to determine the ὑπάρχοντα.

21. Solmsen, op. cit. 167 mentions these two references and he
tries to connect the Helen citation with his idea of the Aris-

totelian τόπος as "Formprinzip, " or a propositional, axiomatic topos. This appears no more possible here than Thionville's attempt, op. cit. 55-77, to formulate many of the τόποι in the Topics as propositional, axiomatic statements, a process of which he must say: "j'ai dù parfois retrancher, parfois interpreter, parfois changer la forme, " 63.

22. In Panathenaicus 88 the use is ambiguous: it may mean the subject previously under discussion, but it more probably indicates the place in his speech at which he digressed.

23. In Aristogeiton 76 (ed. Dindorf-Blass, Teubner 1888).

24. L. Radermacher, Artium Scriptores (Vienna 1951), see the notes on 48-9, 224. It has been called to my attention by A. E. Raubitschek that this use of καιρούς may throw new understanding on the nature of Theophrastus' πολιτικά πρὸς τοὺς καιρούς, on which see PW Suppl. 7.1517. 31ff.

25. What later rhetoricians called the τελικὰ κεφάλαια, see Radermacher, op. cit. 226 note to 62.

26. See the scholiast to Thucydides 3.9.1 (ed. Hude, Teubner 1927) where we find Thucydides doing this very thing for δημηγορία; or see Anximenes 19 (ed. Spengel) where various meanings of δίκαιον and ἄδικον are given. Syrianus examines συμφέρον in this manner and introduces the examination thus: ἐξετάσομεν δὲ τὸ συμφέρον διὰ τόπων ἕπτα (Rademacher, op. cit. 227); I mention Syrianus here since Radermacher in his note is of the opinion that the τόποι may be quite old.

27. E. g. 1399 a 15-7; 1400 a 4-5; 1400 b 15-7; 1402 a 15; and see Radermacher, op. cit. 221 note to 48.

28. Brutus 12.46.8 (ed. G. Friedrich, Teubner 1893).

29. Institutiones Oratoriae 3.1.12 (ed. E. Bonnell, Teubner 1891).

30. Solmsen, op. cit. 167-8 discusses the Cicero text.

31. Radermacher, op. cit. 34.

32. E. g. ad 1398 a 30ff; and see note of Radermacher, op. cit. 57 and 223 note to 52; and comment of Solmsen, op. cit. 166.

33. G. Palmer, The ΤΟΠΟΙ of Aristotle's Rhetoric as Exemplified in the Orators (Diss. Univ. of Chicago 1934).

34. Marx, "Aristoteles' Rhetorik, " Sb. Gesellschaft der Wissenschaften zu Leipzig 52 (1900) 281ff. does not consider the εἴδη (i. e., ἴδιοι τόποι) to be topics, nor does Solmsen, op. cit. 17, 34ff. 165 and note 3.

35. Quaest. conviv. 616 c-d (ed. Bernardakis): Plutarch remarks that to appreciate the social position of dinner guests who differ in so many ways--ἡλικία, δυνάμει, χρεία, οἰκειότητι-- one would need τοὺς Ἀριστοτέλους τόπους. These are particular topics. We also find such particular topics in the scholiast on the Staseis of Hermogenes (ed. Walz IV 352. 5ff.); the scholiast calls them τόποι and finds them used in a work by Lysias.

36. Diels, Vorsokratiker⁶ II 294ff.

37. 1361 a 33f.

38. Radermacher, op. cit. 49 number 27 with note.

39. Ibid. 68f., numbers 7-11 with notes.
40. Ibid. 226 note to 62.
41. Navarre, Essai sur la Rhétorique grecque (Paris 1900) speaks
     of collections of τόποι that were made, 60ff. 124ff. 166-74.
42. As Navarre, ibid. 166 says in comparing the treatment of ἤδη
     in the Rhetoric and in the Παρασκευαί attributed to Lysias:
     "l'ouvrage de Lysias n'était pas un traité théorique, mais
     un recueil de modèles (τόποι γεγυμνασμένοι)." As far as can
     be judged (see Navarre 166-74), these collected topoi appear
     to be concerned with stock offense and defense tactics for
     typical situations, not for an intelligent discussion of the
     problem, which was what Aristotle had in mind: Top. 101 a
     25ff.; Rhet. 1354 a 11ff. In the Soph. El. 183 b 36ff. Aris-
     totle himself criticizes the formulaic quality of these collec-
     tions.
43. Cf. infra 14.
44. Jebb's translation. In the interpretation of this text, I agree
     with Maier, Die Syllogistik des Aristoteles II 1 (Tübingen
     1900) 497 note 1. Spengel in his commentary 71 (1867 edi-
     tion) and Solmsen, op. cit. 15 note 1 substantially agree.
     The minor variant readings admitted by Spengel together
     with Vater (Animadversiones ad Aristotelis librum primum
     Rhetoricorum [Halle 1794]) are not substantial, once the
     correct antithesis of the sentence is understood: μέν setting
     off 4-6 against the δέ of 6-7. In the light of the context 9-
     28, this gives the idea of general and particular topics.
     Such a distinction is also seen in Anonymus, Commentaria
     in Aristotelem graeca 21.6 line 27 and Stephanus, ibid. 267,
     lines 1-23; but I would not accept their identification of the
     general topics.
45. Solmsen, op. cit. 15 note 4 appears more correct on the
     meaning of περὶ ὧν than Cope-Sandys (Cambridge 1877) I 49.
46. It appears that τόποι are divided into κοινοί (12) and ἴδια (17).
     The neuter case is noted by Spengel in his commentary sub
     linea. I do not see any insurmountable problem in it, in
     the light of the neuter κἀκεῖνα (21) referring to κοινοὶ τόποι.
     See also Roemer, "Zur Kritik der Rhetorik des Aristoteles,"
     Rhein. Mus. 39 (1884) 506 on similar instances at 1395 a 11,
     1355 b 35. Confirmation of this division seems to be present
     in 1358 a 21-32. Maier's note, op. cit. 497-8 does not ap-
     pear correct in its exclusion of the notion of τόπος from the
     ἴδια; this would also be true for Solmsen, op. cit. 14ff.;
     Marx, op. cit. 281 note 2, 283 and 296 (if I read him cor-
     rectly) would understand ἐνθυμήματα or εἴδη with ἴδια. On
     the contrary it would appear that the ἴδια, as they are pre-
     sented here, are not only τόποι but are general enough to
     be "loci ex quibus quasi conspiciatur via quam insistere de-
     beamus ut et adversarium refutemus et quod nobis placeat
     evincamus," as Waitz describes topos, Aristotelis Organon
     (Leipzig 1844) 438.
47. 1358 a 30-31.
48. Ibid. 32.

48a. 1403 b 13-14: εἴρηται δε καί τὰ ἐνθυμήματα πόθεν δεῖ πορίζεσθαι·
     ἔστι γὰρ τὰ μὲν εἴδη τῶν ἐνθυμημάτων, τὰ δε τόποι.

49. Ibid. 32-3.

50. Thus Süss, Ethos (Leipzig-Berlin 1910) 170, would seem
     wrong in saying that Aristotle has not given us any sharp
     and satisfactory division between εἴδη and τόποι.

51. Spengel, Ueber das Studium der Rhetorik bei den Alten (Mu-
     nich 1842) 22ff. makes such a distinction. It may appear a
     quibble but "sources for material" seems better than "ma-
     terial proofs" (materielle Beweise). For it would appear
     that the "proof" is the enthymeme and that the εἴδη offer
     material for inferential argument by syllogism or enthymeme,
     whereas the κοινοί τόποι present forms for inference by syl-
     logism. There would be no objection to calling the κοινοί τόποι
     which are sources for formal reasoning by syllogism or enthy-
     meme "formele Beweise" as Spengel does.

52. See 1396 b on the use of ἴδια; and Stephanus, Commentaria
     Graeca 21.268 lines 12-15.

53. Marx admits that there are εἴδη for deliberative, forensic,
     epideictic oratory, but only τόποι for the πάθη and ἤθη.
     This forces him to say on 1396 b 28-34 that a "Redaktor"
     has confused the words and incorrectly brought them togeth-
     er, op. cit. 299,307. Solmsen on the other hand, op. cit.
     170 note 2 with his interpretation of τόπος, has a far diffe-
     rent problem: he cannot understand how any of these εἴδη
     can be called τόποι by Aristotle: it is "prinzipwidrig."

54. The note of Cope-Sandys, op. cit. II 228-9 indicates what is had in
     mind here. These εἴδη are always specific to the subject
     but may be particular or general, see 1396 b 11-9, with
     which compare Isocrates, Philip 109. This idea I find fre-
     quently present in the Topics, e.g., 105 b 12-8: one can
     discuss the idea of "good" in itself, or that which consti-
     tutes "the good" in this specific subject.

55. 1396 b 28-34 undoubtedly refers to the section on the εἴδη in
     Books I and II, and they are called τόποι here. This is
     made more probable still by the contrast between τρόπος
     at 1396 b 20 and 1397 a 1. Here Aristotle contrasts the
     method already presented in the first two books, of seeking
     source material for enthymemes (a method called τοπικός,
     see Spengel in his commentary sub 1396 b 20) with the me-
     thod which he now intends to take up, namely the method of
     the κοινοί τόποι. See also Riccobono, Paraphrasis in Rhe-
     toricam Aristotelis (London 1822) 206, who writes on
     1396 b 28ff. and 1358 a 12ff.: "Constat igitur locos accipi
     aut latius aut strictius. Primo modo loci comprehendunt
     etiam formas [his translation for εἴδη].... Secundo modo
     distinguuntur a formis."

56. 1358 a 31.

57. Ibid. 23-26.

58. Cf. supra 9f.

59. 1358 a 17-21.

60. See Stephanus, Commentaria Graeca 21.267, lines 34ff.

61. 1358 a 12ff.; 1355 b 25ff.

62. 1358 a 2-7.
63. Ibid. 10-14.
64. Ibid. 17-18.
65. Ibid. 18-19.
66. Ibid. 22.
67. Ibid. 15-16.
68. See note 54.
69. 1358 a 17-26.
70. E. Havet, Etude sur la rhétorique d'Aristote (Paris 1846) 34,
    expresses the distinction precisely: "En un mot, les τόποι
    ne sont que des formes logiques, ... τὰ εἴδη, au contraire,
    ce sont les observations, les faits ou les idées, qui font la
    matière du raisonnement, et sans lesquels les formes sont
    vides." In essence the idea of a distinction is found in
    Throm, Die Thesis (Paderborn 1932) 42-6; Jebb in an ap-
    pendix to his translation of the Rhetoric (Cambridge 1909);
    Lane-Cooper, The Rhetoric of Aristotle (New York 1932)
    xxiv.
71. 1358 a 2-7.
72. 1358 a 2-7, 14ff.; 1359 b 1-16.
73. 1355 b 25-34; 1359 b 12-16. Spengel's long note in his com-
    mentary on 1355 b 26 acquires, it seems, a greater signifi-
    cance in the light of this relation between rhetoric as a
    dynamis and the κοινοί τόποι.
74. 1355 b 31-34.
75. 1358 a 21-22.
76. 172 a 29-b 1.
77. Aristotle at 1397 a 23ff. gives an example. Here we have
    the κοινὸς τόπος from correlative terms. As we know, in
    true correlatives what is predicable of one is generally
    predicable of the other. As a general axiomatic proposition
    (assuming A and B to be correlatives) we may say: If A is
    x, then B is x. Aristotle applies this general form to the
    question of taxes (26-7). But he calls attention to the fact
    that it cannot be used indiscriminately and that before it can
    be applied to a subject (justice is his example) one must
    carefully determine the meaning of the terms (29ff.). Such
    a determination must come from the εἴδη before the κοινὸς
    τόπος of correlative terms can be used.
78. Spengel apparently has this in mind when he writes that the
    function of rhetoric is to work up the special proofs of the
    εἴδη and combine them with the formal to make the subject
    of discussion universally understood, Ueber das Studium (n.
    51) 22: "... ihr [Rhetorik] liegt ob, die Beweise, welche
    die einzelne Wissenschaft gibt, zu verarbeiten, mit den
    formellen zu verbinden, und den Gegenstand zur allgemeinen
    Kenntriss zu bringen.
79. As found in c. 23 of Book II.
80. Spengel in his commentary sub 1397 a 1 maintains that some
    are not universal, i.e., common to all rhetorical argument;
    also Cope, An Introduction to Aristotle's Rhetoric (London
    1867) 129.

81. The Roman numerals refer to Roemer's numbering in his text.
82. Solmsen, op. cit. 163 and note 5 says well: "Die als Bei-
    spiele beigebrachten ἐνθυμήματα der Rhetorik sind durchaus
    in sich geschlossene Gedankengänge ... und verhalten sich
    zu den τόποι, die sie illustrieren, in der Tat wie die πολλά
    zum formbestimmenden ἕν."
83. Cf. supra 8, and 1358 a 10-17.
84. J. Lukasiewicz, Aristotle's Syllogistic (Oxford 1951) 20, see
    also 2.
85. And see Alexander, Commentaria graeca II 2 p. 5 lines 21-
    28.
86. Bocheński, op. cit. 122. Bocheński (and also Solmsen) does
    not think that the Theophrastean τόπος is the same as the
    Aristotelian; Throm, op. cit. 43 and Thionville, op. cit.
    30-35 consider it Aristotelian. And Bonitz and Ross on
    Met. 1014 b note that τόπος as στοιχεῖον would be "an argu-
    ment applicable to a variety of subjects." Top. 163 b 18-
    164 a appears to express a similar idea.
87. Waitz, op. cit. 362.
88. I believe that Thionville, op. cit. 74 sees this process at
    work but does not recognize it.
89. Top. 101 b 15ff.
90. In the Topics, then, many of the τόποι are focal points for
    the analysis, criticism, and evaluation of terms, all within
    the framework of the four categories. For instance at 132
    a 22-4 it is by these τόποι (διὰ τῶνδε σκεπτέον, ἐκ τῶδε
    θεωρητέον) that we determine a thing as a property. Another
    summary expression of the method appears at 153 a 6-28,
    on definition: to be a true definition a genus and differentia
    must be present, and to ascertain whether these are on
    hand, certain places (τόποι) must be examined. In this re-
    gard Solmsen's (op. cit. 156) observation on the origin of
    the τόποι is of significance to me, although I am confining
    it to the particular topics. He sees the genesis of the Aris-
    totelian topoi in the attempt to specify one's subject, and
    traces their probable origin to the elenchic dialectic of the
    Socratic-early Platonic τί ἐστι questions. In general it does
    seem true (and a passage like Top. 152 b 36-153 a 5 would
    appear to strengthen this) that Aristotle is concerned with
    specifying the meaning of terms, and a meaning grounded in
    the metaphysical reality. In this sense his method may well
    have had in mind what Hambruch (op. cit. 29) says was the
    aim of one of Plato's dialectical methods: "die Bildung
    eines festgefügten und wohlgegliederten Begriffsystems...."
91. In this regard Hambruch's attempt to discover the genesis of
    the methodology of Aristotle's topics appears valid in its
    general outline. He finds it (op. cit. 8-17) in the logical-
    metaphysical rules for Platonic διαιρεσις, e.g., ἅμα καὶ
    πρότερον φύσει, πρός τι ὄντα, μᾶλλον καὶ ἧττον. This last rule
    is called the κοινὸς τόπος of the more-less in the Rhetoric
    and is set down in this axiomatic form (1397 b 12-14): τοῦτο
    γάρ ἐστιν, εἰ ᾧ μᾶλλον ἂν ὑπάρχοι μὴ ὑπάρχει, δῆλον ὅτι οὐδ' ᾧ

ἧττον. As I see it, Hambruch's rules are the same fundamental sort of rules which were discovered independently to
be at work in the general topics (see _supra_ 13).

92. E.g., in 114 b 38ff. he uses κοινὸς τόπος IV; in 116 a-b, XI,
XIII, XVII; in 119 a 37ff. I and II are employed, and they
are described as: μάλιστα δ'ἐπίχαιροι καὶ κοινοὶ τῶν τόπῶν;
in 124 a 15ff we find III, and in 154 a 12-22 he speaks of
the general effectiveness of these topics that are τοὺς
μάλιστα κοινούς.

93. In terms of this distinction it is interesting to note that if a
rough analogy is drawn between rhetoric as a part of practical philosophy and _scientia_ as a part of speculative philosophy we seem to have something of a parallel between the
principal elements leading to ἐπιστήμη in one instance, and
to πίστις in the other:

i) ἀρχαι {	κοιναί - ἀξιώματα		through which syl-
			logism and induc-
	ἴδιαι - θέσεις	ὁρισμοί	tion effect knowl-
		{	edge
		ὑποθέσεις	

ii) ἀρχαί {	κοιναί - τόποι	through which en-
		thymeme and ex-
	ἴδιαι - εἴδη	ample effect belief.

Furthermore it would follow that there is not in the _Rheto-
ric_ a double enthymeme theory as Marx, _op. cit._ 281ff. and
Solmsen, _op. cit._ 14f. would suggest, but rather a single
theory which considers the enthymeme a unit composed of
εἴδη and κοινοὶ τόποι.

12. ARISTOTLE'S CONCEPT OF FORMAL TOPICS*

by Donovan J. Ochs

In his Rhetorica, [1] Aristotle defines a topic by saying, "I am designating a topic and an element as the same. For an element (στοιχεῖον) and topic is that under which several enthymemes fall. "[2]

From this statement many scholars have attempted to define a rhetorical τόπος. Ernest Havet, for example, contends that "topics are only logical forms. "[3] King, [4] Roberts, [5] McBurney, [6] and Cooper[7] favor "lines of argument" as the best descriptive term. More lyrical than the foregoing is the definition advanced by Wilson and Arnold. [8] They define topics as a "system that can draw one's thoughts to the best hunting ground where ideas suitable to a particular speaking assignment can be found. " Baldwin calls topics, "headings, "[9] and Freese[10] gives a literal definition as "a place to look for a store of something, and the store itself; a heading or department, containing a number of rhetorical arguments of the same kind. " Jebb[11] asserts that "τόπος means the place in which a thing is to be looked for in the memory. " Grote, more expansive but less clear than any of the foregoing, declares:

> Locus (τόπος) is a place in which many arguments pertinent to one and the same dialectical purpose, may be found--sedes argumentorum. In each locus the arguments contained therein look at the thesis from the same point of view; and the locus implies nothing distinct from the arguments, except this manner of view common to them all. [12]

Grimaldi is more cautious than Grote and prefers a functional definition of topics as "sources for rhetorical demonstration by enthymeme. As such they are loci, both particular and general, to which one must have recourse in constructing probable argumentation in an effort to produce πίστις. "[13]

Of these diverse views, none is incorrect; rather, they show the difficulty in defining an Aristotelian rhetorical topic in general

---

*Reprinted by permission of the author and of the Speech Communication Association, from Speech Monographs XXXVI (1969), 419-425.

terms.   Some insight into the causes of this difficulty is provided
by Hill:

> Aristotle makes no attempt to relate specific premises
> to probabilities and signs, nor probabilities and signs to
> either specific premises or common topics. And some
> enthymemes seem to be derived directly from (common)
> topics as in 1358 a 27 and 1402 a 33. If it were not for
> statements like these, it might be possible to interpret
> Aristotle as meaning by topic a group of premises and
> say that premises were drawn from topics. But he says
> plainly that sometimes enthymemes themselves are drawn
> from topics. And in the latter passages topics are said
> to form enthymemes. The notion of topic seems to con-
> tain in itself both the material and the formal elements
> of a logical system.[14]

Clearly, then an attempt should be made to determine what
Aristotle considered a rhetorical topic to be. A complete explication would need to encompass not only Aristotle's formal systems
of topics but the several kinds of material topics as well. This
essay, however, will focus solely on τόπος as it refers to the
twenty-eight basic forms of the demonstrative enthymeme in the
first draft of Aristotle's Rhetorica. Rather than interpreting topics
as merely different containers or receptacles for the rhetorical syllogism, this essay argues that topics, as elements, are the primary, indivisible, and inherent components from which enthymemes
are to be constructed. In addition, this essay argues that Aristotle's rhetorical topics do not constitute a logical system of invention.

Few scholars still maintain that the Rhetorica is a unified
treatise[15] on the art of "discovering in any given case the available means of persuasion. " Such discrepancies as the two theories
of the enthymeme, the inclusion of ethical and pathetic proofs, and
most of Book III seem to indicate that the Rhetorica which we have
is probably a series of additions and modifications. Assuming that
parts of the Rhetorica were written at different times, one must
determine which parts were composed in what sequence and at what
dates.

In order to visualize the probable schedule followed in the
composition of the Topica and Rhetorica, the following time line
provides a synthesis of relevant studies.

-Aristotle enters Academy
  at age 17   368-367

                    362   -criticizes rhetoric in the
                              Gryllus[16]

                    360   -begins his collection of
-Plato writes the Phaedrus[17]   topics and begins lecturing

                                       on rhetoric in competition
                                       with Isocrates[18]

                     359-357   -Aristotle begins Topica[19]

                                       -first draft of Rhetorica
                                       (I. i; II. xxiii; II. xxiv; II. xxv;
                                       II. xii-xvii)[20]

                     351-347   -first expansion of Rhetorica
                                       (II.ii-xiv; II. xix; III. i-xii)[21]

                                       -second expansion of Rhetorica (II. xv; III. xiv-xix)[22]

-Plato dies   348-347

                     344   -Sophistical Elenches and
                                       Topica VIII written[23]

                                       -three expansions of Rhetorica[24]

-Aristotle dies   322

Several important observations may be made on the basis of this time line. First, Aristotle's theory of topics--both dialectical and rhetorical--preceded his development of the syllogism of logic and the rhetorical enthymeme from probabilities and signs. His first draft of the Rhetorica included his definition and defense of rhetoric as an art (1354 a 1-1355 b 15), the twenty-eight basic forms of the demonstrative enthymeme, the forms of the apparent

enthymeme, and the topics of refutation (1397 a 1-1403 a 11). Not until the first expansion of this work, near the end of his residence at the Academy, did Aristotle add the genera-materials (εἴδη) and the "commons" (κοινά). [25]

Aristotle's theory of dialectic as it first appeared in the Topica has been summarized in this way:

> Dialectic reasons from ἔνδοξα, from opinions commonly held. Its arguments are perfectly valid, and do not break any of the laws of logic (77 a 26ff.; 172 a 33). But it has not, like the sciences, particular premises of its own, it involves no special knowledge of any particular branch of learning (77 a 26ff.; 100 b 20). The only premises which it uses are such as seen probable "either to all men or to men or to philosophers" (100 b 20). It has no particular subject matter, but discusses any and every type of problem (77 a 31ff.; 172 a 11ff.). In its

discussions it uses a large number of general methods
and principles, which the <u>Topica</u> expounds in detail.[26]

Dialectical topics, the "general methods and principles" of
which Lee speaks above, have been variously estimated to number
between 287 and 382.[27] They are presented as rules, and are organized according to what were later called the predicables. Books
II and III treat the topics of the predicable "accident," IV those of
"genus," V of "property," and VI and VII those of "definition." An
example of the topical rule of "genus-species" will help clarify what
Aristotle understands as a dialectical topic.

> Since of all those things of which the genus is predicated,
> one of its species must necessarily also be predicated,
> and since all those things which possess that genus, or
> derive their description from that genus, must also possess
> one of its species--for example, if knowledge or musical
> knowledge or one of the other kinds of knowledge will be
> predicated of him, and if a man possesses knowledge or
> if the description which he has derived from his knowledge,
> then he will also possess grammatical knowledge or musi-
> cal knowledge or one of the other kinds of knowledge, or
> will derive his description from one of them, being called,
> for example, a 'grammarian' or a 'musician.'[28]

What we have in this τόπος of "genus" is a convenient "rule
of thumb" for the dialectician. As a device for locating and analyzing how a specific kind of predicate (i.e., one that is classed
as a "genus") may be attributed to a subject, it is useful both in
accepting and in rejecting a statement. Knowing the topical rule
that "of whatsoever a genus is predicated, one of its species must
also be predicated," enables a dialectician to look for and test
premises--his own or his opponent's--against this "genus-species"
relationship. In brief, a dialectical τόπος is a modal pattern, and
as pattern it is primarily concerned with the logical class to which
a term belongs. Moreover, as a τόπος it is a purely formal relationship because the connection between "classes of terms" is not
characterized by any special sort of content. We can conclude,
therefore, that τοποί <u>are formal patterns of relationships existing
between classes of terms</u> in the <u>Topica.</u>[29]

The best recent scholarship dates the first draft of the
<u>Rhetorica</u> between 359 and 357 B.C., and if we limit ourselves to
the content of this first draft we are presented with a unique type
of rhetorical topic. In Chapter i of Book I Aristotle complains
that his predecessors in the art of persuasion have said nothing
about enthymemes, which are, he declares, "the body of proofs"
(1354 a 14-15). An enthymeme[30] is described both as a "rhetorical demonstration" (ἀπόδειξις ῥητορική: 1355 a 6) and as a "kind of
syllogism" (αυλλογισμός τις: 1355 a 8). The relationship of the
enthymeme to dialectic is then specified by saying that "every kind
of syllogism comes within the scope of dialectic, either generally

or in part" (1355 a 8-10). In other words, Aristotle sees the enthymeme as closely related to dialectic, and dialectic involves a
systematic study of the classes of terms that occur in propositions
and of the relationships between these classes of terms.

Still restricting ourselves to the first draft of the Rhetorica
we encounter an early notion of rhetorical topics in II. xxiii-xxv.
Aristotle previews his discussion of the twenty-eight topics of enthymemes in these words: "Now let us speak of their elementary
forms (στοιχεῖον). By the elementary form of an enthymeme I
mean the place (or class) to which it belongs."[31] Since a topic is
equated with an "element" twice in the Rhetorica (1397 b 21 and
1403 a 17-18) and many times in the Topica,[32] the meaning and
implications of this term are significant.

In the Metaphysics (1041 b 30ff.) Aristotle refers to "elements" in this way:

> An element, on the other hand, is that into which some-
> thing is divided and what inheres in it as material; for
> example, "a" and "b" are elements of the syllable.[33]

Elsewhere in the Metaphysics (1014 b 15ff.) he elaborates the many
associated meanings of the term:

> An element means the first inherent component out of
> which a thing is constructed and which cannot be analyzed
> formally into a different form; for example, the elements
> of speech are the parts of which speech consists and into
> which it is ultimately divided, whereas they cannot in turn
> be divided into other forms of speech different from them
> in kind. If an element is divided, its parts are of the
> same kind; as a part of water is water, whereas a part
> of a syllable is not a syllable.... By transfer of meaning
> people call an element whatever, being single and small,
> has many uses ... whatever is most general (καθόλου)
> comes to be called an element. ... What is common,
> therefore, to all the meanings of 'element' is that it is
> primary and inherent.[34]

We can, therefore, compress Aristotle's notion of an "element" into that which is the primary constituent, indivisible, single,
small, capable of many uses, and inherent. For Aristotle an element is the same as a topic, and further, a "topic is that under
which several enthymemes fall." (1403 a 17-18.) By diagraming
the two enthymemes that are inherent to the topic of opposites we
can understand more clearly Aristotle's notion of "topics as elements." His examples are: "It is good to be temperate, for it is
bad to be intemperate," and "If war is the cause of the present
evils, we must correct them by peace."

Example A:

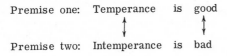

Premise one: Temperance   is   good

Premise two: Intemperance   is   bad

Example B:

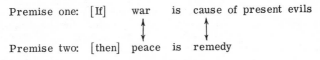

Premise one: [If]   war   is   cause of present evils

Premise two: [then]   peace   is   remedy

The "element" shared in common by both examples is, of course, the relationship of "opposition" between the terms of the premises. Each instance of opposition is formally the same, i.e., a given term is juxtaposed with its commonly accepted opposite. The topic is indivisible (one of Aristotle's properties of an "element") since the relationship between any of the opposing terms cannot be analyzed further.[35] Combinations of premises, therefore, in which this element of opposition exists between terms, can be said to belong or inhere to the enthymematic topic of opposites.

Aristotle's original draft included twenty-eight of these elemental topics (1397 a 7-1400 b 15). Whether they constitute a logical system has been the crux of much controversy. McBurney, for example, contends that "there can be little question that we do have a list of methods of reasoning and types of inference in these topics."[36] Grimaldi also views these topics as "essentially logical processes."[37] Hill, however, argues that there are no principles of logic contained within them.[38] In fact, translators and commentators are agreed on only one point--these topics do not provide the orator with premises for rhetorical argument.

The cause of these disparate views seems to be the difficulty of making any generalization about the twenty-eight τοποί. Aristotle himself is partially the cause of this difficulty. In the first place, his statements of the various topics are incomplete. By this I mean that a complete statement of a topic should include: (1) a definitive statement of the relationship between termini--which apparently can be terms (e.g., the topic from proper names), premises (e.g., the topic from inducements and deterrents), and actions (e.g., the topic from previous decisions); (2) a pattern or model for the form of the argument (e.g., topic #12: "another topic consists in taking separately the parts of a subject: as in the Topics--what sort of motion is the soul? It must be this kind or this kind"); and (3) an example or illustration of the pattern. These three components, requisite for the complete presentation of a topic, are not given for topics: 11, 13, 16, 19, 23, and 28.

Before we could correctly designate Aristotle's rhetorical topics as a "logical system, " we would need to posit the axioms on which the system is based.   There is, however, nothing in the presentation of these topics which resembles the principles of non-identity, excluded middle, or non-contradiction that are the axioms of the syllogism.   We do not have, therefore, a logical system in the enthymematic topics of the first draft of the Rhetorica.

Additional difficulty is caused by Aristotle's inclusion of several of the dialectical topics, namely, 1, 4, 7, 8, 9, 12, 13, 17, and 24.   Apparently the dialectician and the rhetorician can share these nine topics, but are we to conclude that the remaining topics are, in some way, unique to rhetoric?   If so, in what way are they especially suited to that art?   The topic of definition, shared by dialectic and rhetoric, focuses on the relationship between two terms; the topic of proper names, peculiar to rhetoric alone, does the same.

For Aristotle, then, a dialectical topic is a relational principle enabling a person to locate and analyze the ways in which a specific predicate may be attributed to a subject.   Aristotle's list of rhetorical topics, however, is an amalgam of miscellaneous molds into which rhetorical arguments usually are cast.   The title of each topic specifies a type of relationship, and the relationship can exist between terms, between propositions, or between past, present, and future events.   And, it is this elemental relationship, not the termini, that gives rise to the classification of arguments.

NOTES

1.   Bibliographies for Aristotle and Rhetorica are available in Wilhelm Kroll, "Rhetorik, " Paulys Real-Encyclopädie der classischen Altertumswissenschaft, VII. 1062ff. ; Charles S. Rayment, "A Current Survey of Ancient Rhetoric, " Classical Weekly, LII (1958), 75-91; Paul Gohlke, "Ueberblick Ueber die Literatur zu Aristoteles (bis 1925): Teil I: Ethik, Politik, Rhetorik, Poetik, " Bursians Jahresbericht der Klassischen Altertumswissenschaft, CCXX (1929), 265-328; H. S. Long, "A Bibliographical Survey of Recent Work on Aristotle, " Classical World, LI (1958), 96-98, 117-119, 160-162, 167-168, 193-194, 204-209.   An industrious compilation of important editions, translations, paraphrases, and commentaries for the Rhetoric is appended to Forbes Iverson Hill, "The Genetic Method in Recent Criticism on the Rhetoric of Aristotle" (unpubl. Ph.D. diss., Cornell University, 1963).   Of equal value is the bibliography in William M. A. Grimaldi, S.J., "The Enthymeme in Aristotle" (unpubl. Ph.D. diss., Princeton University, 1953).
      I have used the texts of Aristotle as they are edited in the Scriptorum Classicorum Bibliotheca Oxoniensis.   Translations are mine unless otherwise noted.

Among the myriad of secondary source materials, I have found the following to be of exceptional value: J. L. Stocks, "The Composition of Aristotle's Logical Works, " Classical Quarterly, XXVII (1933), 115-124; A. E. Douglas, "The Aristotelian Συναγωγὴ Τεχνῶν after Cicero, Brutus, 46-48, " Latomus XIV (1955), 536-539; Friedrich Solmsen, "The Aristotelian Tradition in Ancient Rhetoric, " American Journal of Philology, LXII (1941), 35-50, 169-190; by the same author, Die Entwicklung der Aristotelischen Logik und Rhetorik (Berlin, 1929); also, E. M. Cope, The Rhetoric of Aristotle with a Commentary, ed. John Edwin Sandys, 3 vols. (Cambridge: Univ. Press, 1877); George Kennedy, The Art of Persuasion in Greece (Princeton: Univ. Press, 1963); and Lane Cooper, The Rhetoric of Aristotle (New York: Appleton-Century-Crofts, Inc., 1932).

2. Rhetorica 1403 a 17-18. Solmsen, Die Entwicklung, p. 164, maintains that this is Aristotle's only genuine statement on the essential nature of the term.

3. Ernest Havet, Etude sur la Rhétorique d'Aristote (Paris: Jules Delalain, 1846), p. 34; "En un mot, les τόπος ne sont ques des formes logiques. "

4. Donald B. King, "The Appeal to Religion in Greek Rhetoric, " Classical Journal, L (1955), 365.

5. Aristotle, Rhetorica, trans. W. Rhys Roberts in Vol. II of The Works of Aristotle, trans. into English under the editorship of W. D. Ross (Oxford, 1924).

6. James H. McBurney, "The Place of the Enthymeme in Rhetorical Theory, " SM, III (1936), 59, 61. McBurney does, however, interpret "lines of argument" as "methods of reasoning. "

7. Cooper, The Rhetoric of Aristotle, p. xxv.

8. John F. Wilson and Carroll C. Arnold, Public Speaking as a Liberal Art (Boston: Allyn and Bacon, 1964), p. 96.

9. Charles Sears Baldwin, Ancient Rhetoric and Poetic (Gloucester, Mass.: Peter Smith, 1959), p. 14.

10. Aristotle, Rhetorica, trans. John Henry Freese (Cambridge, Mass.: Harvard Univ. Press, 1939), p. 482.

11. The Rhetoric of Aristotle, trans. R. C. Jebb (Cambridge, Mass.: Univ. Press, 1909), p. 143.

12. George Grote, Aristotle (London: John Murray, 1880), p. 293.

13. Grimaldi, "The Enthymeme, " p. 116.

14. Hill, p. 30.

15. Cf. C. Brandis, "Ueber Aristotles' rhetorik und die griechischen Ausleger derselben, " Philologus, IV (1849), 1-47. Brandis terms the Rhetorica "ein Werk aus einem Gusse. " See also, L. Spengel, Ueber die Rhetorik des Aristoteles (Munchen, 1851); Cope, Rhetoric; Solmsen, Die Entwicklung, and his "Drei Rekonstruktionen zur antiken Rhetorik und Poetik, " Hermes LXVII (1932), 133-154; Kennedy, The Art of Persuasion, pp. 84-85; and Hill, "The Genetic Method. "

Werner W. Jaeger published his definitive study, Aristoteles: Grundlegung einer Geschichte seiner Entwicklung at

Berlin in 1923. Working from the supposition that as Aristotle matured he would tend to move away from Plato's
theories, Jaeger demonstrated that the Metaphysica--former-
ly considered a linguistically and philosophically unified
treatise--was composed at markedly different periods in
Aristotle's life. Friedrich Solmsen performed a similar
analysis on Aristotle's logical work in Die Entwicklung, op.
cit. A useful condensation of Solmsen's study is provided
by J. L. Stocks, "The Composition of Aristotle's Logical
Works, " op. cit.

16. Quintilian, II.xvii.14; Kennedy, pp. 83ff.

17. The reader who wishes to pursue further the relationship of
the Rhetorica to Plato's treatises should consult the follow-
ing articles by Everett Lee Hunt: "Plato and Aristotle on
Rhetoric and Rhetoricians, " Studies in Rhetoric and Public
Speaking in Honor of James Albert Winans (New York, 1925),
pp. 3-60; "Dialectic: A Neglected Method of Argument, "
QJS, VII (1921), 221-232; "An Introduction to Classical
Rhetoric, " QJS, XII (1926), 201-204; see also Edwin Black,
"Plato's View of Rhetoric, " QJS, XLIV (1958), 361-374; A.
E. Taylor, Plato: The Man and His Work (New York, 1927);
G. M. A. Grube, Plato's Thought (New York, 1938); Karl
Mras, "Plato's Phaedrus und die Rhetorik, " Wiener Studien,
XXXVI (1914), 295-319 and XXXVII (1915), 88-117.

18. Cf. Hill, p. 150 and W. Jaeger, Aristotle, p. 1.

19. Pamela M. Huby, "The Date of Aristotle's Topics and Its
Treatment of the Theory of Ideas, " Classical Quarterly, XII
(1962), 72-80.

20. Hill, pp. 153, 158; Kennedy, p. 84; Solmsen, Die Entwicklung.

21. Hill, pp. 160, 163.

22. Hill, pp. 165ff., 172ff.

23. J. L. Stocks, p. 118.

24. Hill, pp. 178-180.

25. Hill argues (pp. 160-161) that since Isocrates was teaching
more than ἤθη and τοποί, Aristotle had a motive for admitting specific premises (εἴδη) with political content. Furthermore, "a great dichotomy was thus created between proofs
according to topical forms and proofs from special fields.
But no sooner was an enthymeme from premises admitted
than, according to Solmsen's analysis, it became evident to
Aristotle that there are some premises common to all subjects and to all three kinds of speeches. This is the origin
of the "commons" II:xix which Solmsen interprets as "common premises" κοιναί προτάσεις .

26. H. D. P. Lee, "Aristotle's Account of First Principles, "
Classical Quarterly, XXIX (1935), 123. See George Grote,
Aristotle, pp. 262-278, for a clear discussion of dialectic.
Also, Jaeger, pp. 370ff. And, Brother S. Robert, F.S.C.,
"Rhetoric and Dialectic: According to the First Latin Com-
mentary on the Rhetoric of Aristotle, " New Scholasticism,
XXXI (1957), 484-498. Grimaldi, "The Enthymeme in Aris-
totle, " p. 66, summarizes the essential difference by stat-

ing, "Dialectic is in its own way quite frequently speculative in that it moves from probable opinions, or generally accepted facts, to probable conclusions based on the same. But as I said rhetoric moves from the conclusion itself which is assumed, and attempts to produce πίστις with respect to this conclusion."

27. Otto Bird, "The Tradition of the Logical Topics: Aristotle to Ockham," Journal of the History of Ideas, XXIII (1962), 310: "According to Regis, Aristotle states no less than 337 topical rules: 103 for accidents, 81 for genus, 69 for property, 84 for definition. In the enumeration that Lucius gives of them in his 1619 edition I count 287 while Buhle in his 1792 edition counts 382. On any count there are a great many."

28. Aristotle, Topica 111 a 31-111 b 10, trans. E. S. Forster (Cambridge, Mass.: Harvard Univ. Press, 1960).

29. Cf. Sophistical Refutations 184 a 2; Grote, pp. 262-263. Also, Alexander Aphrodisias, In Aristotelis Topica Libri Octo (Berlin, 1891), p. 126. Alexander expands the definition which I am using by defining a topic as "a sort of principle ἀρχή or basic form στοιχεῖον from which we draw the first principles for each particular case (having determined our intention); it is defined in outline (for either it circumscribes common things, that is, universals, which make the most authoritative syllogisms, or such common things can be derived from it by logical demonstration), but with respect to particular facts it is indefinite."

30. Cf. James H. McBurney, "The Place of the Enthymeme in Rhetorical Theory"; Grimaldi, "The Enthymeme," and "A Note on the πίστεις in Aristotle's Rhetoric," American Journal of Philology, LXXVIII (1957), 188-192; Earl W. Wiley, "The Enthymeme: Idiom of Persuasion," QJS, XLII (February, 1956), 19-24; Charles S. Mudd, "The Enthymeme and Logical Validity," QJS, XLV (December, 1959), 409-414; and Lloyd F. Bitzer, "Aristotle's Enthymeme Revisited," QJS, XLV (December, 1959), 399-408.

31. Jebb's translation of 1387 b 19-24.

32. Cf. Topica 121 b 11; 128 a 22; 143 a 13; 151 b 18.

33. Richard Hope, Aristotle's Metaphysics: Newly Translated as a Postscript to Natural Science (New York: Columbia Univ. Press, 1952), p. 168.

34. Ibid., pp. 90-91. A similar definition of "elements" may be found in Physics 195 a 16.

35. Hill, p. 57. Otto Bird, "The Tradition of the Logical Topics," p. 309: "The example, 'but whatever is in the species is necessarily in the genus: thus if man is good, then animal also is good (Topica 111 a 18),' is an enthymeme. Furthermore, the warrant for it might well be described as being contained in many arguments, since it can serve as warrant for any similar argument from species to genus."

36. McBurney, p. 61.

37. Grimaldi, "The Enthymeme, " p. 162: "We find that we have
     again a form modeled on the same logical process of rela-
     tion--it is a mode of inference which enables us easily to
     argue in an elliptical, or shortened syllogistical form. "
     Emphasis mine. Cf. Ibid., pp. 121ff., 127ff. Also, Ken-
     nedy, The Art of Persuasion, pp. 101ff.
38. Hill, pp. 69ff.

13. ARISTOTLE'S RHETORIC ON EMOTIONS*

by William W. Fortenbaugh[1]

Should the account of emotion given by Aristotle in his
Rhetoric be dismissed as a popular treatment that avoids precision?
I think not and in this paper want to argue that the Rhetoric's treatment of emotion is important not only for rhetorical theory but also
for ethical theory and philosophical psychology. Nevertheless there
is a considerable body of scholarly opinion that looks upon this
treatment of emotion as superficial.[2] The Rhetoric's contribution,
we are told, does not lie in the analysis of individual emotions but
rather in the fact that emotional appeal is promoted to a mode of
persuasion coordinate with character and proof or apparent proof.
Whereas previous authors of rhetorical treatises had treated emotional appeal as part of the prooemium and the epilogue, Aristotle
considered emotional appeal independently of particular portions of
an oration. He conceived of emotional appeal as a tool that could
be employed throughout an oration for the purpose of persuading
the audience.[3] But when Aristotle came to discuss the individual
emotions he did not break new ground. True to the method that he
himself proclaimed appropriate to rhetoric,[4] he did not seek exactitude but contented himself with what was generally acceptable.

There have been, of course, scholars who gave Aristotle's
treatment of emotions a higher rating.[5] But these scholars are,
I think, a minority whose opinions have been without their proper
influence. Accordingly, I want to focus upon and to re-evaluate
Aristotle's treatment of individual emotions. My approach will be
in two parts. In the first part, I shall argue rather generally that
the Rhetoric's analysis of individual emotions did receive the close
attention of Aristotle and so should not be passed off as popular
and imprecise. In the second part, I shall argue that the Rhetoric's
account of emotion enjoys a threefold significance, because it looks
upon cognition as an essential element in emotion. First, by making cognition an essential part of emotional response, the Rhetoric
offers an answer to Academic debate concerning the relationship of
emotion to cognition. Secondly, in pointing out the involvement of
cognition in emotion, the Rhetoric makes clear that emotions can
be reasonable and that emotional appeal need not be a matter of

*Reprinted by permission of the author and publisher, from Archiv
für Geschichte der Philosophie 52 (1970), 40-70.

charms and enchantments. And finally, this emphasis upon cognition helps to distinguish emotions from bodily drives and so helps
to develop an adequate moral psychology.

1. Let us begin with some concessions. It is true that
the Rhetoric explicitly disclaims exactitude in analysis and definition (1359 b 2-8, 1360 b 7-8, 1366 a 32, b 24, 1369 b 31-32) and
that in one important case (pleasure, 1369 b 33-35), the Rhetoric
offers a definition that is rejected by the Nicomachean Ethics. It
is also true that when the Rhetoric comes to consider happiness,
it offers a disjunctive definition and then adds that nearly everyone
would agree that one or more members of the disjunction constitutes happiness (1360 b 14-18). These points may be admitted.
But it would be unreasonable, I think, to conclude that the analyses and definitions given in the first two books of the Rhetoric are
simply popular and in no way represent Aristotle's own views. [6]
Take the case of happiness. Here Aristotle does not offer a tidy
definition. He satisfies himself with a definition that may be considered sufficient (1366 b 24, 1369 b 31) and appropriate to the
occasion (1359 b 5, 1366 a 21, b 24). But--and this is the important point--when he claims the assent of nearly everyone, Aristotle
is primarily thinking of the members of the Academy. He is not
especially concerned with people in general. He is concerned with
his audience in the Academy and with the various views on happiness that were being advanced in the Academy. In other words,
he offers a disjunction that is meant to cover the various views or
at least the most important views under debate in the Academy.
This is, of course, an old point. [7] But it must be emphasized,
because it shows that in lecturing on rhetoric, Aristotle's thoughts
are very much focused upon the Academy and the views being advanced by its members. This is not to say that Aristotle is totally
unconcerned whether his disjunctive definition of happiness finds
acceptance outside the Academy. But it is to say that Aristotle's
primary audience is within the Academy and that his definitions and
analyses may be expected to reflect the interests and opinions current within the Academy.

Rather similar remarks can be made concerning the Rhetoric's definition and analysis of pleasure as a movement of the soul
and an intense and perceptible settling down into the natural state
(1369 b 33-35). Aristotle's treatment of pleasure is not oriented
toward the ordinary man. [8] It takes its impetus from the Academy.
In the case of pleasure, however, Aristotle does not offer a disjunctive definition that might satisfy all or most members of the
Academy. [9] Instead, he offers a particular view of pleasure that
was made prominent within the Academy by Speusippus' polemic
against Eudoxus[10] and is familiar to us through Plato's Philebus
and Timaeus. Still, Aristotle does not simply report the view of
other members of the Academy. He seems to modify and supplement the view and so to make it his own. [11] I do not want to
press this point. It cannot, I think, be established firmly that at
the time of writing this portion of the Rhetoric Aristotle accepted

without reservation the view of pleasure as a kind of motion. It
is perhaps likely that he did. At least the view is found not only
in the Rhetoric but also in another early work, Book VII of the
Physics.[12] It is, of course, possible that in two different works
Aristotle offered a view to whose truth he was indifferent, but it
is more likely that he offered the same view on two separate occasions, because he found the view more or less acceptable. On
the other hand, this same view of pleasure as a kind of motion is
treated negatively in still another early work, the Topics (121 a
27-39). In order to illustrate a particular method for rejecting
alleged genera, Aristotle introduces the proposition that motion is
the genus of pleasure and argues that because pleasure is neither
locomotion nor alteration nor any other specific kind of motion,
pleasure cannot be a motion. It is, of course, difficult to be certain of Aristotle's attitude toward any particular example in the
Topics. He may think that this argument against pleasure as a
kind of motion is a telling argument, or he may not.[13] Perhaps
we may say that Aristotle introduced this particular argument
against pleasure as a kind of motion because it was current in the
Academy. He illustrated argumentation concerning genera by drawing upon the Academic debate over pleasure. Like other members
of the Academy he was able to criticize the view of pleasure as
motion, but he was also prepared, on occasion, to advance the view,
perhaps because he found the view on the whole acceptable or at
least better than any other view current in the Academy.

Concerning the analyses of happiness and pleasure more
could be said. We could study at length these two analyses and
then go on to investigate other analyses and definitions offered in
Book I of the Rhetoric. Perhaps, however, we have said enough
to make us hesitate before dismissing the Rhetoric's analyses as
mere popular treatments. Perhaps we have raised the suspicion
that the analyses and definitions presented in the Rhetoric are serious efforts that should be seen within the context of Plato's Academy. If so, let us begin to focus upon the treatment of individual
emotions in Book II of the Rhetoric, considering first an old objection to taking the treatment as a serious effort deserving close
study. The objection is philological in nature: Aristotle introduces
the definitions of individual emotions with the word ἔστω ("let [it]
be" 1378 a 30, 1380 a 8, b 36, 1382 a 21, 1383 b 12, 1385 a 17,
b 13), and this word is a sign that the definitions are of only a
popular nature. Aristotle, it is argued, begins his definition of
anger with the words "let anger be" (1378 a 30) and thereby indicates the provisional nature of the offered definition.[14] But is this
argument as strong as it is old? Certainly the use of ἔστω in
definitions is a characteristic of the Rhetoric[15] and on occasion,
it is possible that Aristotle uses this word to indicate the tentative
nature of an offered definition. The disjunctive definition of happiness begins with ἔστω (1360 b 14) and this may be a sign that the
offered definition is meant to cover the several Academic views
without making precise which view or combination of views captures
the essence of happiness. But it should be observed that when

Aristotle returns to a definition introduced by ἔστω he may give no
indication that the definition is less than his own.[16] Moreover, at
least one definition introduced by ἔστω cannot be described plaus-
ibly as a popular definition. This is Aristotle's definition of rhetoric: let rhetoric be a faculty of considering in each case the possible means of persuasion (1355 b 25-26). Here, Aristotle seems
to be giving us his own definition of rhetoric. He neither follows
the lead of Plato's Phaedrus nor adopts the view of rhetoric current among professional rhetoricians. Aristotle ignores Plato's insistence upon becoming a philosopher (Phdr. 261 A 4) and being
gifted in division (Phdr. 263 B 7, 266 B 3-C 9, 270 B 4, 271
C 10-D 5, 273 D 8-E 4). Moreover, Aristotle's emphasis upon
the persuasive (1355 b 11, 15-16, 26, 32-33) seems discordant
with Plato's emphasis upon truth in comparison with the persuasive
and plausible (Phdr. 259 E-262 C, 272 D-273 E) and with Plato's
insistence that knowledge of truth is not a separable preliminary
but a part of rhetoric (Phdr. 260 E 6).[17] Aristotle, it seems, is
not following the leader of the Academy. Yet neither is he following the view of professional rhetoricians. For these men considered
rhetoric to be the art of effecting persuasion. Among professional
rhetoricians the art of rhetoric was oriented toward successfully
achieving persuasion. Gorgias called rhetoric the artificer of persuasion (πειθοῦς δημιουργός, Plato Gorgias 453 A 2)[18] and in this
definition seems to have been followed by Isocrates (Quintilian,
Instit. Orat. 2.15.4).[19] For professional rhetoricians, success
was essential to rhetoric; for Aristotle, success was not essential.
Modifying the current view, Aristotle explicitly denied the necessity
of success. Instead he suggested viewing rhetoric as the faculty of
observing and discovering the possible means of persuasion (1355 b
10-14, 25-26; cf. Topics 101 b 5-10).[20]

It may be, of course, that this definition of rhetoric is to
some extent deficient or incomplete and that ἔστω helps to point out
this inexactitude. , Perhaps the definition does need further qualification, for it contains no stated limitation upon the kinds of persuasion with which rhetoric concerns itself. There is a need to
add a qualifying in oratione.[21] The rhetorician is not concerned
with every possible means of persuasion but only those means that
involve speech. Aristotle himself would acknowledge the need for
this qualification. He had after all, studied the Gorgias and so
would be familiar with Gorgias' suggestion that the great benefit of
rhetoric is the ability to persuade with speeches (Gorg. 452 E 1).
But to acknowledge that the Rhetoric's definition is in this way incomplete is not to say that it is popular or merely thrown out by
way of example. On the contrary, it is simply to admit that this
definition, like most definitions and analyses in the Rhetoric, aims
at being sufficient and appropriate to the occasion (1359 b 5, 1366
a 20-21, b 24, 1369 b 31).

Sometimes Aristotle's interest in a definition may even lead
him to seek an exactitude beyond that claimed for rhetoric. Consider his definition of goodness. This definition begins with an ἔστω

(1362 a 21) and lists various marks of goodness.   In a certain
sense the definition is popular.   As in the case of happiness, so
here, everybody would endorse one or more of the enumerated
marks of goodness.   But while the several marks of goodness
would be generally accepted, they would also be accepted by Aristotle.   The definition includes nothing that is contradicted by the
Ethics.   Further and perhaps more significant, Aristotle extends
the definition to cover not only things good in themselves but also
things good as means.   This is not a sign of indifference or care-
lessness on the part of Aristotle.   The goods as means are all
carefully grouped together (1362 a 27-29) and important terms are
explained (1362 a 29-34).   Instead of tolerating impression, Aristotle pursues his analytical interest and elucidates two philosophically important terms.   First he explains "follows" by drawing a
distinction between following simultaneously and following subsequently.   Then he illustrates three different senses of "productive."
A thing may be productive in the way that being healthy is productive of health, or in the way that food is productive of health, or
in the way that taking exercise is productive of health.   The example of being healthy producing health is of especial importance.
For the example recurs in the Nicomachean Ethics (1144 a 4, 1174
b 25) and introduces Aristotle's own notion of a formal cause. [22]
Without overstating our case, we can, I think, say that Aristotle
is interested in this definition.   If he is presenting a definition
that is generally acceptable either within the Academy or possibly
outside the Academy as well, he is not doing so independently of
his own views.   An initial ἔστω, it seems, need not imply a popular definition unrelated to Aristotle's own philosophical commit-
ments.

     In respect to the treatment of individual emotions we can be
fairly certain that the definitions offered are not just examples
thrown out by way of illustration.   Aristotle was well aware that
emotion affects judgment (1354 b 8-11, 1356 a 15-16, 1377 b 30-
1378 a 5, 19-20).   He recognized the importance of emotional appeal and treated persuasion "through the hearers" (1356 a 14) as a
special mode of persuasion coordinate with persuasion "through
demonstration" and persuasion "through character."   For Aristotle
a correct understanding of emotion was an essential part of the art
of rhetoric.   Each individual emotion, he tells us, must be analyzed in three ways.   The condition of men prone to an individual
emotion, the objects of an individual emotion, and the grounds for
an individual emotion must all be grasped.   If the orator's understanding of individual emotions is deficient in any of these three
areas, then he will be unable to arouse emotional response (1378 a
23-26).   In other words, the ability to control emotional response
depends upon correctly understanding the nature of individual emotions, upon knowing the conditions favorable to, the objects of, and
the grounds for individual emotions. [23]   In respect to the individual
emotions, Aristotle was not indifferent to the truth of his definitions and analyses; he was not going to be satisfied by mere popular opinions.   For Aristotle was well aware that a mastery of emo-

tional appeal belongs only to the man that has investigated and come to understand what characterizes and what causes individual emotions (1356 a 21-25). [24]

Although the definitions of individual emotions may begin with ἔστω, these definitions are to be taken seriously. Aristotle is not throwing out popular definitions without regard to their truth or adequacy. This is not, however, to say, that the offered definitions are precise in every detail. Such an assertion is too easily refuted by the De Anima. For in this treatise, Aristotle criticizes the rhetorical or, as he styles it, the dialectical definition of anger. [25] Nevertheless, it is important to notice that the De Anima does not reject the Rhetoric's definition of anger. It simply (and predictably) suggests that this definition of anger falls short of standards appropriate to physical investigation. The definition is not erroneous, but it is incomplete. For while it does give the form of anger, it makes no mention of matter or a bodily correlate. On the other hand, anger cannot be defined adequately simply by reference to a bodily correlate. Neither the dialectician who defines anger as a desire for retaliation nor the materialistic student of nature who defines anger as boiling of blood around the heart (De An. 403 a 30-b 1) offers a definition that satisfies the requirements of natural philosophy. A competent student of nature will construct his definition from both of these definitions (De An. 403 b 7-9). [26] It is clear, therefore, that the definitions of anger and other emotions given in the Rhetoric are not so much rejected by the De Anima as supplemented. They are accepted and completed. [27]

We have been arguing that the occurrence of ἔστω in a definition is not in itself grounds for dismissing a definition as something popular and philosophically unimportant. We have acknowledged that the treatment of individual emotions is incomplete but have argued that this deficiency can be pinned down and does not constitute grounds for dismissing the Rhetoric's treatment of emotions as a popular account of little philosophical significance. We now approach the treatment of individual emotions and inquire concerning their significance untroubled by the occurrence of ἔστω. But before moving on to the treatment of individual emotions, I would suggest that ἔστω is not used in the Rhetoric to mark the tentative nature of definitions. Rather, it is used as part of and possibly to emphasize the deductive method that Aristotle employs throughout large sections of Books I and II of the Rhetoric. Within the Academy Plato had criticized severely current rhetorical methods and had called for a new and philosophical rhetoric. If rhetoric was to be taught in the Academy, it had to acquire at least the appearance of scientific method. Toward this end, Aristotle imposed a demonstrative method both upon his discussion of particular premises in Book I and upon his discussion of emotions in Book II. He organized his material deductively, laying down definitions and drawing necessary conclusions. [28] But for Aristotle it was not simply a matter of giving rhetorical instruction a scientific

air.   At this period in his career Aristotle was very much interested in logical method.   The introduction of example and enthymeme into the art of rhetoric is a clear sign of this interest.
Aristotle had recently spent considerable time upon treatises devoted to logical method and was probably still at work upon these
treatises. [29]   He was prepared, therefore, to bring a deductive method to rhetorical instruction.   It is not surprising to find in the
Rhetoric a vocabulary and method that recall the Analytics.   In
particular, it is not surprising to find Aristotle using ἔστω to lay
down a definition or premise from which he draws necessary conclusions. [30]   The vocabulary and method are common in the Analytics. [31]   Of course, in the Analytics the premises introduced by
ἔστω are illustrative and are not advanced as propositions of philosophical importance.   Indeed, letters may be used instead of formulated propositions (e. g., An. Pr. 30 a 37-b 2.   An. Post. 75 a 6-
7, 9-11).   But this does not imply that in the Rhetoric definitions
introduced by ἔστω are merely illustrative and popular in nature.
For the cases are not identical.   In the Analytics Aristotle is primarily investigating logical method.   In the Rhetoric Aristotle is
using logical method to investigate the materials with which a rhetorician must be acquainted.   In the investigation of logical method
Aristotle will be satisfied with premises that illustrate the method
under consideration.   In the investigation of emotions he will not
be satisfied with illustrative premises.   For in this investigation
Aristotle is not illustrating his logical method.   Rather he is using
his logical or deductive method to elucidate the nature of individual
emotions.   It is, then, a mistake to think that the occurrence of
ἔστω in the Rhetoric is a mark of Aristotle's disinterest in offered
definitions.   ἔστω occurs as part of Aristotle's deductive method
and is quite compatible with a lively interest in the material under
consideration.

        2.   In the preceding section we have argued that the Rheto-
ric's account of emotions should not be dismissed automatically as
popular and of little philosophical importance.   In this section we
shall ask what is the significance of this account both for the philosophy of mind and for the development of rhetorical and ethical
theory.   Let us start by looking at the Rhetoric itself.   Here, at
the beginning of Book II we find Aristotle introducing his treatment
of emotion with the following statement: Emotions are that on account of which men so change as to differ in judgment and which
are attended by pain and pleasure, for example anger, pity, fear,
all other such and their opposites (1378 a 19-22).   This initial
statement, we may suspect, is not offered as a final and precise
definition of emotion.   For it is too wide and can include physiological disturbances such as headaches and stomach-aches that are
accompanied by pain and that do affect judgment.   Qualification is
needed. [32]   In this respect Aristotle's immediately following remarks are important.   It is necessary, he tells us, to analyze
each emotion in three ways.   In the case of anger, for example,
we must distinguish how men prone to anger are disposed, at
whom they are accustomed to be angry and on what grounds (1378

a 19-24). The mention of objects ("at whom, " τίσιν) and grounds
(ἐπί ποίοις) is important; it strongly suggests that Aristotle does
not dissociate cognition from emotion. Unless Aristotle is confused, he does not conceive of emotions simply as inner (mental
or bodily) feelings or sensations. [33] For if he did conceive of emotions as mere sensations, he could not explain how emotions have
objects and grounds. Stomach-aches, headaches, and other (bodily)
sensations are not justified. They lack objects and grounds altogether. It is thoughts and beliefs that have objects and it is the
occurrence of these cognitions in emotional response that explains
why we can ask a man at whom he is angry and whether his anger
is reasonable. Instead of viewing emotions simply as particular
kinds of inner (mental) feelings or sensations that impel a man to
behave in certain characteristic ways, Aristotle, we may suspect,
includes cognition within his conception of emotion.

The accounts of individual emotions confirm this suspicion.
Consider anger. Aristotle begins his treatment of this emotion
with a definition: let anger be a desire for revenge accompanied
by pain on account of an apparent insult to oneself or one's own,
the insult being unjustified (1378 a 30-32). The mention of apparent
insult within the definition is important. The appearance of unjustified insult is for Aristotle an essential part of being angry. Whenever a man is angry, he thinks or believes or imagines that someone has done something and has done it unjustly (1378 a 30-b 1,
1379 b 11-12). His anger always involves the thought of unjust
treatment. For anger does not occur when men think that they
suffer justly. As Aristotle explains, they do not think they
suffer unjustly; and anger was (said to be) this (1380 b 16-18).
More precisely, anger was defined in part by reference to apparent
insult, so that part of being angry is thinking oneself unjustly
treated. The thought of outrage is essential and whenever this
thought is not present, neither is anger.

Similar remarks can be made concerning Aristotle's analysis of other individual emotions. Fear, for example, necessarily
involves the thought or belief of imminent danger. Fear is defined
as a pain or disturbance resulting from the appearance of imminent evil (1382 a 21-22). The thought of impending danger is essential, so that a man cannot be afraid unless he thinks himself
threatened. Aristotle makes this quite clear when he argues in
the following manner: If fear is associated with the expectation of
suffering something destructive, it is clear that no one is afraid
who believes nothing can happen to him. No one is afraid of those
things that he believes cannot happen to him, nor of those persons
by whom and at those times when he thinks he cannot suffer harm
(1382 b 29-32). The thought or imagination of imminent danger is
part of the definition of fear, so that it is obvious and a matter of
conceptual necessity (1382 b 33) that whenever men are afraid they
think they can suffer harm. The thought of impending harm or
destruction is essential to being afraid.

For students of philosophical psychology, Aristotle's analysis of emotional response is in itself interesting. His emphasis upon cognition and its necessary involvement within emotional response may be said to anticipate debate among contemporary philosophers.[34] Of equal interest and of more immediate importance to this paper is the way Aristotle's analysis relates to and indicates his answer to debate current within the Academy. For philosophical debate concerning the involvement of cognition in emotional response is not new. On the contrary, the debate was lively within the Academy and is reflected in Plato's Philebus and Aristotle's Topics. In the Philebus, Socrates finds himself constrained to discuss the relationship of cognition to emotion and other kinds of pains and pleasures, when Protarchus balks at calling pleasure and pain true or false. Protarchus allows that opinion (δόξα) may be true or false but refuses to admit that pleasure and pain, fear and expectation can be properly called true or false (36 C 6-D 2). At first Socrates tries to win over Protarchus by pointing out similarities between opinion on the one hand and pleasure and pain on the other. Socrates' argument proceeds smoothly enough until he tries to establish that pleasures and pains, like opinions, can be mistaken. To establish this, Socrates argues that pleasures often occur together with (μετά 37 E 10) false opinion. Socrates' choice of words is unfortunate. Protarchus construes "with" as simple concurrence. He conceives of the opinion as something external to the pleasure[35] and so objects that in such a case the opinion would be false but no one would call the pleasure false (37 E 12-38 A 2). Refused an easy victory, Socrates undertakes a more exhaustive study of opinion and its relationship to pleasure and pain. He gives a rather graphic description of our thought processes and finally argues that just as opinions may lack a basis in reality, so pleasures and pains may be without grounds (ἐπί 40 D 8). And what is true of pleasures and pains in general is, of course, true of painful emotions such as fear, anger and the like. They may be without foundation and so said to be false (40 E 2-4). Protarchus agrees and does not object when a little later Socrates says that true and false opinions "fill up" pleasures and pains with their own affection (42 A 7-9). Opinion is so intimately connected with pleasure and pain that it can infect them with its own condition.

The Philebus certainly makes clear that Plato saw an intimate relationship between emotion and cognition. But the Philebus does not make precise the relationship,[36] and we may guess that the relationship was still a matter of lively debate within the Academy.[37] We get some idea of this debate from the Topics. Cognition, it seems, was generally considered essential to emotional response. But in what way was cognition essential? There seems to have been a difference of opinion. Take, for example, anger. The Topics allows that the thought of outrage is essential to being angry (127 b 30-31). But in what way is it essential? Is it the genus of anger? Apparently not, for pain which is a more likely candidate is not the genus (127 b 26-32).[38] Can we say, then, that anger is pain with (μετά) the thought of outrage (151 a 15-16)? Not without clarification.   After the Philebus and Protarchus' (mis-)understanding of the preposition "with, " we cannot simply define anger as pain "with" thought of outrage.   We must go on and make precise how we are using "with. "   For "with" can be construed in the following ways: "and" (150 a 4), "made up out of" (150 a 22), "in the same receptacle" (150 b 35), "in the same place" (150 b 36) and "in the same time" (150 b 36).   But in none of these senses, the Topics argues, is anger correctly defined as pain with the thought of outrage.   What the definition really wants to show is that the pain of anger occurs on account of (διά) such a thought (151 a 16-17).   The Topics, it seems, prefers a causal definition: anger is a desire for revenge on account of (διά) apparent insult (156 a 32-33), and in this preference agrees with the Rhetoric (1378 a 31) and reflects Aristotle's own contribution to the Academic debate.

To this Academic debate concerning the relationship between cognition and emotion, Aristotle brought his own logical skills. Agreeing with other members of the Academy that cognition and emotion are intimately connected and wishing to make clear the kind of connection that joins cognition to emotional response, [39] Aristotle opted, I think, for a connection that is both essential and causal.   Drawing upon his logical studies and in particular the Posterior Analytics, Aristotle seems to have analyzed cognition as the efficient cause mentioned in the essential definition.   In the Posterior Analytics Aristotle had insisted that questions of essence (τί ἐστι) and questions of cause (διὰ τί ἐστιν) are one and the same.   (An. Post. 90 a 14-15, 31-32, 93 a 3-4, cf. Metaph. 1041 a 28-29) and had illustrated this principle partly by reference to the eclipse of the moon.   This stock example is especially clear and also relevant to our enquiry.   For an eclipse has an efficient cause that is included in the essential definition.   What is an eclipse? asks Aristotle.   It is a deprivation of light from the moon by the obstruction of the earth.   What is the cause of an eclipse, or why does the moon suffer eclipse?   Because light fails owing to the obstruction of the earth (An. Post. 90 a 15-18).   For Aristotle knowing the essence of an eclipse involves knowing the efficient cause (An. Post. 98 b 21-24).   The obstruction of the earth is essential to the occurrence of an eclipse and so is mentioned in the definition of an eclipse.   The efficient cause of an eclipse is part of the formal cause, [40] so that any definition of eclipse that fails to mention the obstruction of earth is to that extent imperfect (Metaph. 1044 b 13-15).   In stating the essential nature of an eclipse we must give a definition that "shows why" (An. Post. 93 b 38), we must give "an account of the cause" (Metaph. 1044 b 15). We must define an eclipse as a deprivation of light on account of obstruction and so make plain that the obstruction of the earth is both essential to an eclipse and also the efficient cause of an eclipse.

The case of emotional response is, I think, similar.   Cognition is both essential and the efficient cause and so is mentioned in a definition that "shows why. "   Just as Aristotle analyzes an

eclipse by considering the total situation including the efficient
cause, so Aristotle analyzes the entire emotional response including the thought or belief that moves a man to respond in a particular sort of way.   He looks upon some sort of cognition as both essential to and also the efficient cause of emotional response.   This
comes out quite clearly in Aristotle's treatment of anger.   The
thought of outrage is essential to anger so that the absence of such
a thought entails the absence of anger (1380 b 16-18).   It is also
the efficient cause of anger.   Being wronged produces anger (1383
b 6-7).   A man is moved to anger by a slight.   For even a trifling
slight such as a forgotten name can produce anger (1397 b 33-34).
Outrage or more precisely the thought of outrage[41] is for Aristotle
both essential to anger and also the efficient cause of anger.   It is,
therefore, included in the definition that "shows why."   And it is
just this kind of definition that Aristotle offers when he says, "Let
anger be (ἔστω) a desire for revenge on account of (διά) apparent
insult" (1378 a 30-31).   It is simply not true that when Aristotle
defines the individual emotion of anger he avoids ἐστι and employs
ἔστω, because the former term signifies the essence (τί ἐστι) in
the domain of truth while the latter introduces a definition that is
merely sufficient and plausible in the domain of opinion.[42]   Rather
Aristotle gives us an essential definition that captures both the essence (τί ἐστι) and the cause (διὰ τί).   He is following the practise of the Posterior Analytics and giving definitions that "show
why."   His definition is not a popular throwout.   It is well formed
and meets standards advanced in the Posterior Analytics.

We could go on and study each individual emotion, pointing
out that some kind of cognition is both essential to and the efficient cause of each individual emotion.   In the case of fear, for
example, we might point out that Aristotle's definition is a causal
definition.   By including the appearance of imminent danger within
the definition (1382 a 21-22), Aristotle forms a definition that
"shows why."[43]   And this "account with the cause" permits him to
argue that necessarily such things are fearsome as appear to
possess destructive power (1382 a 27-30).   Fearsome things (that
is, those things that inspire or arouse the emotion of fear) are
necessarily things that appear to be harmful, because fear is by
definition a pain or disturbance due to the appearance of imminent
danger.   Perhaps, however, we have gone far enough to say with
some confidence that the definitions and analyses of individual emotions given in the Rhetoric are not popular definitions and analyses
to whose truth Aristotle was largely indifferent.   On the contrary
the treatment of individual emotions given in the Rhetoric is Aristotle's own treatment.   Moreover, it indicates Aristotle's own
answer to the Academic debate concerning the relationship of cognition to emotional response.   Cognition is not simply concurrent
with (μετά) emotional response.   It is essential to and the cause of
emotional response.   This answer is characteristically Aristotelian
and should be recognized as such.   This is not to say that the account given in the Rhetoric is written specifically to answer the
Academic debate.   It is not.   The Rhetoric investigates emotion

because it must instruct the orator in persuasion "through the hearers." Still, the Rhetoric's account presupposes and reflects Aristotle's own answer to the Academic debate. It makes clear his own view that may have been worked out and fully stated in the Diaireseis. [44] That work has not survived. But the Rhetoric has, providing us with a rather clear indication of how Aristotle explained the relationship between cognition and emotional response.

Aristotle's analysis of emotion and in particular of the essential involvement of cognition in emotional response is an important contribution to philosophical psychology. It is also important for rhetorical and ethical theory because it makes clear that emotions are not blind impulses. When a man responds emotionally, he is not the victim of some automatic reflex. On the contrary, he is acting according to his judgment. When a man becomes angry, he takes revenge because he thinks himself insulted. He is prepared to explain and justify his action by reference to an insult. He may, of course, be mistaken. He may think himself insulted when he has not been and when it should be clear to him that he has not been. In this case his anger is unreasonable and criticized as unjustified. But he may not be mistaken in thinking himself insulted. He may be correct in his belief and also have good reason for his belief. In this case the man's anger is reasonable. Upon request he can state his reason for being angry, point out that his anger is not based upon some momentary fantasy, and perhaps add that he is prepared to abandon his anger any time his beliefs are shown to be false or doubtful. His anger is reasonable in that it is justified by the particular situation and also is open to reason in that it can be altered by reasoned consideration.

Emotional responses can be intelligent and reasonable actions. This is important for rhetorical theory and may explain in part at least why Aristotle not only recognized persuasion "through the hearers" as an effective means of persuasion but also dignified it by assigning it a position coordinate with persuasion "through demonstration." Persuasion "through the hearers" is not to be confined to the prooemium and the epilogue, for emotions can be aroused and allayed by reasoned argumentation. When an orator demonstrates that danger is imminent, he is arousing fear in the audience. His reasoned arguments lead the audience to conclude that danger threatens. The hearers think their lives threatened, become frightened, and begin to think about their own safety. Fear makes them deliberate (1383 a 6-7). Such men are not the victims of some irrational force that compels them to act as they do. On the contrary, their action is both intelligible and intelligent. Their fear is based upon a reasoned consideration of the situation and so is reasonable. Moreover, it may be allayed in the same way that it was aroused. Further deliberation may convince the hearers that danger is not imminent and so lead them to abandon their fear and become confident. The same is true of anger. When an orator demonstrates that a particular man has acted in an outrageous and insulting manner, he excites anger in the audience. Further deliberation, however, may lead to an abandoning of this anger. If subsequent reasoning shows that a benefit and not an outrage has occurred, the audience will shift from anger to gratitude. The response will be intelligent and reasonable. The hearers are responding according to reasoned judgment and are not the victims of some external power. In particular, they have not abandoned their anger because of some charm or enchantment such as that advertized by Thrasymachus (Phdr. 267 C 7-D 1). Enchantments are outside the sphere of reason. They may cause or compel a man to behave in a particular way but such behavior should not be confused with emotional response, reasonable or unreasonable.

This is an important point. For it helps us to understand the importance of Aristotle's analysis of emotion. As long as emotion went unanalyzed it was possible to look upon emotional appeal as a kind of persuasion distinct from and hostile to reasoned argumentation. In the absence of an examination of emotion that made clear the involvement of cognition in emotional response, it was possible to think of emotional appeal primarily as a kind of charm or enchantment that overcomes the hearer, that works upon him in the manner of a drug.[45] This comes out quite clearly in Gorgias' Helen. Here emotion is depicted as something that happens to an individual. It is like a disease (νόσημα) in that its victims suffer a misfortune (ἀτύχημα) and are outside the sphere of praise or blame (19). Emotional response is not so much an action as an unfortunate affliction that may be induced or caused in an individual. Emotional appeals are like drugs (φάρμακα 14) that work upon the patient. They may be administered in a systematic or rational manner, but they do not depend upon judgment and the patient's reason.[46] Like a noxious potion they work upon the patient, drugging and bewitching him (14). They have the power to charm (θέλγειν 10) their victim. He is overcome by wizardry (γοητεία 10) and so cannot be held accountable for his behavior. He may be said to suffer misfortune but he cannot be said to do wrong (15).

As long as this view of emotional response and emotional appeal went unchallenged it was natural to oppose the arguments of reason to the inspired incantations (Hel. 10) of emotional appeal. We can understand why Gorgias made Padamedes tell the jury of Greek leaders that he would not try to arouse their pity but rather would try to instruct (διδάσκειν) them in the truth (Pal. 33). Similarly we can understand why Plato made Socrates reject emotional appeal in favor of instruction (Apol. 35 B 9-C 2). Looked upon as an affliction divorced from reason, emotional response was naturally opposed to reasonable behavior. It was Aristotle's contribution to offer a different picture of emotional response. Following the lead of Plato's Philebus and subjecting individual emotions to careful analysis, Aristotle developed a view of emotion that made clear the necessary involvement of cognition in emotional response and so made clear that emotional responses may be reasonable and unreasonable. Far from being hostile to reason, emotions are amenable to reason so that an orator can arouse and allay emotion while

presenting reasoned arguments.   By demonstrating that no unjust
outrage has occurred, the orator allays anger and by demonstrating
that the defendent is an innocent victim, he excites pity.   It is to
Aristotle's credit that he pointed out the occurrence of judgment in
emotional response and promoted persuasion "through the hearers"
to a position coordinate with persuasion "through demonstration. "

It remains to speak briefly about the importance of Aristotle's analysis of emotion for ethical theory. [47]   In picking out for
analysis πάθη that are distinguished by the involvement of cognition,
Aristotle was marking off those πάθη that are fundamental to his
own bipartite or moral psychology and so of especial importance to
his ethical theory.   More precisely, in picking out and analyzing
those πάθη that essentially involve some kind of thought or belief
or imagination, Aristotle was picking out emotions and distinguishing them from bodily drives or directed dispositions such as hunger
and thirst.   Plato's tripartite psychology had not drawn this distinction clearly and so had not provided an adequate psychology for
ethical theory.   Hungers and thirsts are bodily drives, and in general do not depend upon a particular kind of cognition.   When men
are hungry, it is not normally because they think that something
is the case.   Rather they have an empty stomach.   Their hunger
is explained not by reference to certain beliefs but by reference to
physiological causes.   In contrast emotions are explained by reference to thoughts and beliefs.   They involve an assessment of the
particular situation and so may be reasonable and unreasonable.
Unlike bodily drives, emotional responses are normally open to
criticism and are important for understanding moral virtue.   As
Aristotle saw, the morally virtuous man is one who is properly
disposed toward emotional response (EN 1105 b 19-1106 a 13, cf.
1104 b 13-14, 1106 b 16-17).

Let me expand this point.   It is, I think, true that the bipartite psychology employed by Aristotle in his ethical and political
writings was developed in Plato's Academy. [48]   Bipartition may be
spoken of as "a Platonic distinction."[49]   Still, we must guard
against an oversimplified view of this development within the Academy.   It is not enough to say that bipartition arose from tripartition by bringing together the θυμοειδές and the ἐπιθυμητικόν[50] and
to argue that this join was encouraged by the ambiguous position of
the θυμοειδές[51] and prepared for in the Timaeus by the connection
of tripartition with the dichotomy of an immortal and mortal soul. [52]
It is, of course, true that the ambiguous position of the θυμοειδές
between the λογιστικόν and the ἐπιθυμητικόν seems to have depended
largely on the political structure of Plato's ideal state and that
whenever such political considerations receded into the background,
the θυμοειδές could be thought of in terms of an emotion like anger
and joined with the ἐπιθυμητικόν to form the emotional side of man.[53]
It is also true that the distinction between an immortal and mortal
soul does encourage a bipartite view.   Even though this dichotomy
of an immortal and mortal soul is not conceptually identical with
the dichotomy of moral psychology, [54] it does help to prepare for

this dichotomy. Still, the move from tripartition to bipartition was not simply a matter of undoing the special status of the θυμοειδές and collapsing the two lower faculties into a single psychic faculty. The move to bipartition also required an alteration or clarification of the status of the ἐπιθυμητικόν. For the ἐπιθυμητικόν is frequently (though not exclusively) connected with bodily drives that are not emotions. Yet it is emotions with which the ἐπιθυμητικόν must be associated, if it is to join with the θυμοειδές in making up the emotional side of man, which is for Aristotle at least the sphere of moral virtue.

This point may be developed by reference to the Timaeus. Here we find the ἐπιθυμητικόν connected with hunger and other bodily needs (70 D 7-8) and quite indifferent to reason (71 A 3-5, D 4). While the θυμοειδές listens to reason, the ἐπιθυμητικόν does not. It must be held down forcibly (70 A 5-6). It is like a wild beast feeding at a manger (70 E 4-6). The ἐπιθυμητικόν is associated with hunger. But hunger is not an emotion such as anger and fear. It is a directed disposition or bodily drive that may be either held down or satisfied, but is not open to reason in the way that emotions are. For hunger does not depend upon an appraisal of the situation but rather arises on account of physiological causes.

The ἐπιθυμητικόν, it seems, is associated with bodily drives. This may be made clearer by considering sexual desire. For in the Timaeus sexual desire is treated in a manner similar to hunger. Both are depicted as animals (70 E 4, 91 A 2); both are presented as bodily conditions immune to reason. In the case of men, sexual desire is caused by marrow in the region of the genitals (91 A 4-B 7). In the case of women sexual desire is touched off by protracted periods of barrenness (91 B 7-C 7). In neither case does the desire depend upon an assessment of the situation. In both cases the desire is caused by bodily factors, so that relief comes not through reasoned argument but through intercourse and reproduction (91 C 7-D 5). And if sexual desire does not depend upon an appraisal of the situation, neither does an excess of sexual desire. Sexual intemperance does not depend upon false assessments. It results from fluidity of marrow and porosity of bone. It deserves treatment and not censure (86 C 3-E 3).

In the Timaeus hunger and thirst and sexual desire are not treated as emotions. They are depicted as bodily drives or directed dispositions that are not on a par with emotions such as anger and fear. There is merit in this analysis. The behavior of a hungry man is quite different from the behavior of an angry man. We respond to the former by meeting his need; we respond to the latter with reasoned argument. We give a hungry man food to calm his stomach and to alleviate painful sensations. We do not offer him reasoned arguments to alter his judgment. With appropriate qualifications something similar could be said about meeting the need of a man afflicted with sexual desire. My purpose, then, is not to criticize the account of hunger and sexual desire that is

presented in the Timaeus. Rather I would emphasize that this account is an account of bodily drives and not of emotions. The
Timaeus associates the ἐπιθυμητικόν with bodily drives and not with
emotions, and this association creates difficulties for simply joining together the ἐπιθυμητικόν and the θυμοειδές to form the emotional
side of man. Despite the fact that the Timaeus introduces a dichotomy between an immortal and mortal soul and groups together
the θυμοειδές and the ἐπιθυμητικόν within the mortal soul, the
Timaeus does not (without significant qualification) prepare the way
for the dichotomy of bipartition. For bipartition is primarily a
moral psychology. It is a psychology that is useful in ethical discussion because it enables one to distinguish between deliberate actions that are preceded by reasoned deliberation and emotional responses that involve perception and assessment but are not preceded by reasoned deliberation. 55 Both kinds of action are intelligent. The agent is responsible and can give reasons that explain
and justify his behavior. In contrast the behavior that results from
a directed disposition is hardly action at all. The victim of acute
hunger explains his behavior not by citing reasons (how he sees the
situation) but by citing bodily causes. He is driven and impelled.
He is, as the Timaeus (86 B 1-87 B 9) points out, hardly a moral
agent. His behavior falls outside the dichotomy of bipartition; it
is like involuntary disease, not like human action. 56

A word of caution is called for. The Timaeus' treatment
of the ἐπιθυμητικόν may be considered special. For the Timaeus
maintains a tripartite psychology even in sections of the dialogue
that are marked by an obvious biological interest. The ἐπιθυμητικόν
is closely connected with bodily nourishment and even assigned to
plants. 57 The concern of the Timaeus with bodily drives or directed dispositions such as hunger, thirst, and sexual desire may
be thought to reflect the physiological interests of the dialogue. Directed dispositions may be assigned to the ἐπιθυμητικόν and in a dialogue like the Timaeus such an assignation is not surprising. But
it would be a mistake to think that such directed dispositions constitute the entirety of the ἐπιθυμητικόν. For as the Republic makes
clear, the ἐπιθυμητικόν has many forms (πολυειδία 580 D 11). It is
connected with avarice (553 C 5, cf. 590 B 6) which does not depend upon a physiological cause but upon an evaluation (554 A 2,
B 2). Avaricious men are not driven to grasp at profit in the way
that hungry men are driven to grasp at food. Their appetite is not
caused by a physiological disorder but based upon an erroneous assessment. Yet their desires and actions are referred to the
ἐπιθυμητικόν. Indeed, in one passage the appetitive faculty is even
labeled money-loving and gain-loving (φιλοχρήματον, φιλοχερδές, 581
A 6-7, cf. 553 C 5). 58

The ἐπιθυμητικόν is not a simple faculty. It includes a
thrifty element (560 C 7), a niggardly and avaricious aspect, that
cannot be construed as a directed disposition similar to hunger and
thirst. Still, it is true to say that the desire for food and drink
and the desire for sexual relations are for Plato central cases of

appetition and of especial importance for understanding the
ἐπιθυμητικόν. In the Republic, Plato calls hunger and thirst most
clear cases of ἐπιθυμία (437 D 3-4) and then proceeds to use thirst
as an example in establishing the existence of the ἐπιθυμητικόν,
that faculty whereby the soul feels sexual passion, hungers, thirsts,
and feels the flutter of other desires (439 D 6-8). And later when
Plato wants to show how unreal are the pleasures of the ἐπιθυμητικόν,
he uses hunger and thirst as examples (585 A 8). Hunger and
thirst and sexual drive are central to an understanding of the
ἐπιθυμητικόν. They are paradigm cases of appetition but they are
not emotions. They are directed dispositions resulting from bodily
causes. 59

We can, I think, say that tripartition failed to draw a clear
distinction between emotional responses and bodily drives. Tripartition did not pick out clearly that class of πάθη that are marked
by the involvement of cognition, that are characterized by grounds
and objects. This is not to say that Plato never saw the importance
of this class of πάθη. He did and in the Philebus focused his attention upon "anger and fear and longing and grief and desire and
emulation and envy and the like" (47 E 1-2). But it is to say that
bipartition could not develop out of tripartition simply by joining together the ἐπιθυμητικόν and the θυμοειδές. It was first necessary
to distinguish emotional responses from bodily drives, to focus upon
those πάθη that necessarily involve cognition and so can be reasonable or unreasonable. 60 And it was to Aristotle's credit that he
followed the lead of Plato's Philebus and pressed forward with an
exhaustive analysis that was important not only for philosophical
psychology and rhetorical theory but also for ethical theory. In
analyzing emotional response, Aristotle was turning his attention
toward those πάθη that are amenable to reason (EN 1102 b 30-1103
a 1) and are the domain of moral virtue (EN 1105 b 19-1106 a 13).
He was developing a moral psychology that would serve him well in
ethical and political investigations. 61

NOTES

1. At the outset I want to acknowledge my debt to the National
    Endowment for the Humanities and to the Center for Hellenic
    Studies. Their support enabled me to read and work upon
    this topic. I am especially grateful to the Director of the
    Center for Hellenic Studies, Professor Bernard Knox, and
    to the Junior Fellows (1967-1968) for discussing with me
    points made in this paper. I am also indebted to Professors
    Glenn R. Morrow and Charles H. Kahn who have made most
    helpful suggestions that I have endeavored to incorporate in
    this paper. Any mistakes or deficiencies remaining in the
    paper are, of course, entirely my own failing.
2. See, for example, C. Brandis, "Uber Aristoteles Rhetorik
    und die griechischen Ausleger derselben, " Philologus 4
    (1849) 27, Handbuch der Geschichte der griechisch-römischen

Philosophie (Berlin: Reimer, 1860) 3. 1. 192.   Brandis
argues that Aristotle's treatment of emotions is concerned
only to describe their modes of expression (Ausserungsweisen).   According to Brandis, Aristotle is concerned neither
with giving an exhaustive treatment of emotions nor with
pinning down their place in inner experience.   Instead Aristotle follows his general procedure (see below, note 4),
avoiding precision and presenting common opinion.   Brandis
is followed by E. M. Cope, An Introduction to Aristotle's
Rhetoric (London: Macmillan, 1867) 13-14, Aristotle's
Rhetoric (Cambridge: University Press, 1877) 2. 8 and by
E. L. Hunt, "Plato and Aristotle on Rhetoric and Rhetoricians" in Studies in Rhetoric and Public Speaking in Honor
of James Albert Winans (New York: Century, 1925; reprinted with identical pagination by Russell and Russell,
New York, 1962) 57-58.   Both Cope and Hunt see Aristotle's
discussion as an imprecise and popular treatment of the way
emotions "express themselves outwardly, " of their "external
manifestations" (Brandis' Ausserungsweisen).   L. Cooper,
The Rhetoric of Aristotle (New York: Appleton-Century,
1932) xx describes Aristotle's treatment as "a popular account. "   M. Dufour, Aristote, Rhetorique (Paris: Société
d'Edition "Les Belles Lettres, " vol. 1, 1932 and vol. 2,
1960) 2. 20-21 says that the definitions of individual emotions
are of an oratorical and contingent character, that the traits
that serve to define the emotions are taken from current
opinion.   G. Kennedy, The Art of Persuasion in Greece
(Princeton: University Press, 1963) 95, note 92 cites without comment Hunt's (58) assessment of Aristotle's analysis
as "a popular and inexact discussion of the external manifestations of, character and emotions. "   See also the
"Rhetoricus Philosophicus" who passes over Aristotle's
treatment of emotion, calling it "the usual material on man-
ipulating the emotions of the hearer to the speaker's advantage" (Philosophy and Rhetoric, 1 [1968] 51).

3.   It is generally accepted that Aristotle's recognition of emo-
     tional appeal as a mode of persuasion coordinate with char-
     acter and proof is new and important.   See F. Solmsen,
     "Aristotle and Cicero on the Orator's Playing upon the Feel-
     ings, " Classical Philology 33 (1938) 393-394; D. L. Clark,
     Rhetoric in Graeco-Roman Education (New York: Columbia,
     1957) 75, 80; Kennedy (above, note 2) 94.   The goal of this
     paper is not so much to emphasize the role Aristotle assigns
     to emotional appeal as to emphasize his analysis of individu-
     al emotions.   It is the latter which needs to be re-evaluated.

4.   For the view that Aristotle did not think exactitude appropriate
     to rhetoric and so did not strive for precise definitions and
     analyses when treating the subject matter of deliberative,
     epideictic, and judicial oratory (1. 4-14), see Brandis "Uber
     Ar. Rhetorik" (above, note 2) 4, 27-29, Handbuch (above,
     note 2) 185-192; Cope, Introduction (above, note 3) 11-14; Hunt
     (above, note 2) 51-52; E. Zeller, Aristotle and the Earlier Peri-
     patetics, translated by Costelloe and Muirhead (New York:

Russell and Russell, 1962) 296; C. S. Baldwin, Ancient Rhetoric and Poetic (New York: Macmillan, 1924) 15-16; Sir David Ross, Aristotle 5th ed. (London: Methuen, 1960) 272; A.-J. Festugière, Aristote, Le Plaisir (Paris: Librairie Philosophique J. Vrin, 1936) LXII-LXIV; R. Gauthier and J. Jolif, L'Ethique à Nicomaque (Louvain: Publications Universitaires, 1959) 2.781, note 14; I. Düring, Aristoteles (Heidelberg: Winter, 1966) 139-140, 144, 148. Perhaps I may single out Hunt's position both because it is forcefully stated and, I think, widely read. Hunt argues that for each of the three branches of oratory: deliberative, epideictic, and forensic oratory, Aristotle offers a cursory treatment of the usual subject matter: "a superficial political science," "a conventional ethics," and "a very loose and inexact criminal jurisprudence" (51). After pointing out that the definition of pleasure is repudiated in the Ethics, Hunt concludes that "the ethical conceptions of the Rhetoric are the conceptions of the man in the street." It is not in his rhetorical writings but in his political and ethical writings that Aristotle made an effort to attain concepts that could withstand criticism (52).

5.   Th. Gomperz, Greek Thinkers, translated by G. Berry (New York: Scribner, 1912) 4.436 speaks of the exhaustiveness and great strength and depth of the Rhetoric's treatment of emotions and character. M. Heidegger, Sein und Zeit (Tubingen: Niemeyer, 1963) 138 credits Aristotle with the first systematically executed investigation of emotions that has come down to us. F. Solmsen, The Rhetoric and the Poetics of Aristotle, Modern Library (New York: Random House, 1954) xvi sees in the Rhetoric "a precise and carefully worded definition" for each emotion. See also Solmsen, "Aristotle and Cicero" (above, note 3) 393-394. While P. Aubenque, "La définition aristotélicienne de la colère," Revue Philosophique 147 (1957) 300-317 emphasizes (correctly) that the definitions advanced in the Rhetoric do not satisfy the standards of natural philosophy (see below, note 26), nevertheless he is quite clear that the definitions do give the form of individual emotions and deserve serious attention.

6.   See G. Lieberg, Die Lehre von der Lust in den Ethiken des Aristoteles, Zetemata 19 (München: Beck, 1958) 23-27. Lieberg argues that the definitions in Books I and II of the Rhetoric are offered as serious definitions and not simply popular opinions. Lieberg sensibly allows that in particular instances Aristotle may be following someone else's view. But when he does so, he adopts the view as his own.

7.   See J. Burnet, The Ethics of Aristotle (London: Methuen, 1900) 1, note 1 and 3, note 3; Festugière (above, note 4) LXIII. According to Burnet and Festugière all four members of the disjunction can be connected with the Academy. The first definition belongs to a particular class of definitions under study in the Academy (Topics 150 b 27). The second definition relates to Definitions 412 B 6 and may

originate from Philebus 20 C ff. as well as definitions of
happiness attributed to Speusippus and Xenocrates. (See
Burnet 3, note 3). The third definition seems to be associated with Eudoxos, while the fourth alludes to Xenocrates.
Whether or not we follow Burnet and Festugière in every
detail, we must admit that tney are correct in referring the
definition of happiness to discussion within the Academy.
The Rhetoric's definition of happiness is not simply in accord with common opinions (Brandis, "Uber Aristotles'
Rhetorik" [above, note 2] 4, Handbuch [above, note 2] 186).
Rather the definition is in accord with opinions common in
the Academy. The definition of happiness takes its thrust
and formulation from the Academy and so can be expected
to satisfy nearly everyone in the Academy.

8.   See, for example, Hunt (above, note 2) 52 who first points
      out that the Rhetoric's definition of pleasure is repudiated
      in the Ethics and then concludes that "the ethical conceptions
      of the Rhetoric are the conceptions of the man in the street."

9.   According to Brandis "Uber Aristoteles' Rhetorik" (above,
      note 2) 27, Aristotle offers an account of pleasure and pain
      as movement not because he totally endorsed the Platonic
      notion, but because he was concerned only with an easily
      understandable explanation that avoided raising disputed points,
      I agree with Brandis in allowing the possibility that Aristotle
      set forth a view about which he had reservations. But I find
      it difficult to imagine this particular view avoiding contro-
      versy. Even if the dispute between Speusippus and Eudoxus
      was for the most part over and even if this view of pleasure
      had been advanced by Plato, it is unlikely that opinion with-
      in the Academy had formed a consensus in favor of this
      view. Topics 121 a 27-39 is, I think, a clear echo of con-
      tinuing debate within the Academy. See also An. Pr. 25 a
      9-12.

10.   The view of pleasure as a perceptible process toward one's
      natural state is attributed by the Nicomachean Ethics (1152 b
      12-15) to those who deny altogether that pleasure is good.
      This group of persons is represented most especially by
      Speusippus. See Festugière (above, note 4) LXII; R. Gauthier
      and J. Jolif (above, note 4) 2.777, 785, 788.

11.   The Rhetoric's definition of pleasure should be compared with
      the view set forth at Philebus 31 D 8-9, 42 D 5-6, 46 C 6
      and Timaeus 64 D 1-2, 65 A 1. Lieberg (above, note 6)
      27-42 examines in detail the dependence of the Rhetoric upon
      the Philebus and shows how Aristotle adopted with some mod-
      ification the physiological conception of pleasure as a return
      to one's natural state. According to Lieberg, Aristotle's
      interest in the Platonic precedent coupled with his attention
      to and modification of particular details (e. g., replacing the
      pronoun αὐτῆς or αὐτῶν [Phil. 31 D 8, 42 D 5] with his own
      term ὑπάρχουσαν [1369 b 34-35]; developing or adding to the
      Platonic position so as to recognize a highest form of plea-
      sure that occurs after the return to the natural state [1370 a

4-5]) makes evident that the Rhetoric's account of pleasure should be taken seriously, that Aristotle is not simply trotting out a popular or current opinion but is concerned with establishing his own conception of pleasure.

12. See Physics 246 b 20-247 a 19. At 247 a 16 Aristotle connects pleasure with a particular kind of motion, ἀλλοίωσις or alteration. Düring, Aristoteles (above, note 4) 119, note 7 recognizes that the conception of pleasure advanced in the Rhetoric fits that found in Physics VII 3. Düring also thinks that Rhetoric 1370 b 27 has wording similar to Physics 247 a 7-8. For similar wording I would point to 1370 a 29, 33-34 and 247 a 9.

13. I. Düring, "Aristotle's Use of Examples in the Topics" in Aristotle on Dialectic, edited by G. E. L. Owen (Oxford: Clarendon, 1968) 210 takes this passage as a rejection by Aristotle of Plato's opinion that pleasure is a kind of motion. I respect Düring's judgment but cannot myself justify so positive a stand. On the general relationship between the Topics and Rhetoric see J. Brunschwig, Aristote Topiques (Paris: Société d'Edition "Les Belles Lettres," 1967) 1. XCVI-CIII.

14. The view that Aristotle used ἔστω in the Rhetoric specifically to introduce imprecise and popular definitions goes back at least as far as L. Spengel Specimen Commentariorum in Aristotelis Libros de Arte Rhetorica (München: Libraria Scholarum Regia, 1839) 16-17. Spengel was followed by Brandis, "Über Aristotles' Rhetorik" (above, note 2) 28, note 42 and Cope, Aristotle's Rhetoric (above, note 2) 1. 73, 97, 188, 2. 8. See also Dufour (above, note 2) 1. 39, 46, 47, 54, 2. 20, 21. Festugière (above, note 4) LXIII, Aubenque (above, note 5) 305, and Düring (above, note 4) 140.

15. For ἔστω in Book I, see 1355 b 25, 1360 b 14, 1362 a 21, 1363 b 7, 1368 b 6.

16. See 1363 b 13 and 1364 b 17 where Aristotle refers to the definition of goodness by saying simply "we call" and "has been defined."

17. With Phdr. 260 E 6, see R. Hackforth, Plato's Phaedrus (Cambridge: University Press, 1952) 120, note 2. For a general discussion of Aristotle's divergence from Plato see Dufour (above, note 2) 1. 11-14, Hunt (above, note 2) 49-59.

18. Cf. Plato Philebus 58 A 7-B 2, Republic 365 D 4 and Quintilian, Inst. Orat. 2. 15. 18 The label "artificer of persuasion" may have originated before Gorgias in the circle of persons around Tisias and Korax. See L. Radermacher, "Artium Scriptores: Reste der voraristotelischen Rhetorik," Sb. Ak. Wien 227. 3 (1951) 30; B ii 13.

19. According to Sextus Empiricus adv. Math. B 62, Isocrates said that orators practice nothing else than the science of persuasion (ἐπιστήμη πειθοῦς).

20. On Aristotle's rejection of success as an essential feature of rhetoric see Quintilian Instit. Orat. 2. 25. 13: Quidam recesserunt ab eventu sicut Aristoteles dicit: rhetorice est

vis inveniendi omnia in oratione persuasibilia.   See also
Cope, Introduction (above, note 2) 28-33.

21.   See Quintilian Instit. Orat. 2. 15. 6-13 where Quintilian criticizes those persons who define rhetoric by reference to persuasion without delimiting the kind of persuasion with which
rhetoric is concerned.   In what appears to be a carelessly
written passage (2. 15. 13), Quintilian first adds a qualifying in oratione to Aristotle's definition of rhetoric and then
seems to criticize Aristotle for failing to add this qualification.   See Cope, Introduction (above, note 2) 34.

22.   Cf. Metaph. 1070 a 21-23, b 28.   The proper interpretation
of EN 1144 a 4 and 1174 b 25 has been a matter of considerable discussion.   For a survey of the literature see
Gauthier and Jolif (above, note 4) 2.542-547, 839-841.

23.   Gomperz (above, note 5) 435 gets this correct when he says
that "this triple knowledge is the preliminary condition for
the rousing of emotions by oratory."

24.   It should be emphasized that when Aristotle discussed the individual emotions he was providing his pupils not only with
an interesting exercise in philosophical psychology but also
with a mode of persuasion.   In analyzing the nature of individual emotions, Aristotle was providing the knowledge necessary for successfully arousing and allaying emotion (1355 b
21-25, 1378 a 24-26).   This close tie with a mode of persuasion seems to be lacking in the discussion of particular
premises (εἴδη or ἴδιαι προτάσεις 1358 a 31) that occupied
so much of Book I.   In discussing the particular premises
Aristotle is primarily providing materials for persuasion
"through demonstration."   He is not elucidating a mode of
persuasion but rather supplying materials for enthymemes.
(Of course, the discussion of virtue is also connected with
persuasion "through character" [1366 a 25-27, 1378 a 15-17]).
These materials, it might be argued, may be popular opinions.   For if an orator is to be persuasive he cannot use
controversial premises.   His demonstrations must begin from
generally accepted premises.   (Cf. 1357 a 12-13 and Plato,
Phdr. 259 E 7-260 A 4, 272 D 2-273 A 1).   This argument
has some force as long as it is directed at the discussion
of particular premises in Book I.   But it loses its force
when transferred to the discussion of emotions in Book II.
For in discussing emotions Aristotle is primarily concerned
with a mode of persuasion.   He is no longer supplying "fill-
er" for the enthymemes of deliberative, epideictic and judicial oratory.   Instead he is conveying an understanding of
individual emotions that is fundamental to mastering persuasion "through the hearers."   The definitions of individual
emotions are not external to a method that can be mastered
independently of the definitions.   While it is possible to
master persuasion "through demonstration" without mastering
any particular set of premises, persuasion "through the
hearers" cannot be mastered apart from an understanding of
individual emotions.   While the former mode of persuasion

belongs to the man who is able to "syllogize," the latter
mode belongs to the man who is able to investigate and so
understand the nature of emotional response (1356 a 21-25).
The definitions and analyses of individual emotions are not
external to the mode of persuasion but rather what a man
learns when he learns the mode. See A. Stigen, The Structure of Aristotle's Thought (Oslo: Universitetsforlaget,
1966) 371.

25. Clearly the dialectician's definition of anger as a desire for
returning pain (De An. 403 a 30-31) is to be connected with
the Rhetoric's definition of anger as a desire for revenge
(1378 a 30). See Cope, Introduction (above, note 2) 13,
Aubenque (above, note 5) 304, 311, and D. W. Hamlyn,
Aristotle's De Anima (Oxford: Clarendon, 1968) 80.

26. Cope, Introduction (above, note 2) 13 suggests that the natural
philosopher's definition of anger as a boiling of blood around
the heart "endeavors to penetrate into its (anger's) true nature and to state what it (anger) is." This is overstatement.
The De Anima is quite clear that neither definition is sufficient. Aubenque (above, note 5) 314 tacitly corrects Cope
when he says that the competent natural philosopher pene-
trates most deeply into the knowledge of anger, not because
he knows the matter, but because he grasps how and why
such matter is such form. In other words, competence in
natural philosophy demands a knowledge of both form and
matter.

27. There is no reason to think that Aristotle ever shelved the
treatment of emotions given in the Rhetoric. The evidence
of the De Anima suggests the continuing importance of this
detailed (if incomplete) treatment. Moreover the mention
of Deiopeithes (1386 a 14) indicates that Aristotle was still
using and adding to this portion of the Rhetoric at least as
late as 341 B.C. While most of the treatment of emotions
was probably written during Aristotle's residence in the
Academy, revision and addition may have occurred considerably later, possibly after 335 B.C. (Düring, Aristoteles
[above, note 4] 120.)

28. See, for example, the Rhetoric's treatment of goodness. First
Aristotle offers a definition of goodness that begins with ἔστω
(1362 a 21) and enumerates several marks of goodness. After pausing to clarify two terms Aristotle resumes with the
phrase "these things having been laid down" (1362 a 34) and
proceeds to draw necessary (ἀνάγκη 1362 a 34, b 3, 7, 10)
inferences. See Solmsen "Aristotle and Cicero" (above,
note 3) 393 who neatly characterizes Aristotle's method in
dealing with emotions: "Throughout these chapters Aristotle
is anxious to base every assertion either on the definition itself, one of its component parts, or on something previously
deduced from the definition." Cf. Solmsen The Rhetoric and
Poetics (above, note 5) xvi.

29. It seems fairly certain that Aristotle composed the relevant
portions of the Rhetoric either concurrently with or soon after

the Analytics.   See Düring (above, note 4) 119 with note 7,
Kennedy (above, note 2) 85, F. Solmsen, Die Entwicklung
der Aristotelischen Logik und Rhetorik, (Berlin: Weidmann,
1929) 223.

30.   See above, note 28.   For another example consider Aristotle's
analysis of anger.   He begins with the words "Let anger be
(ἔστω) a desire for revenge" (1378 a 30), and after complet-
ing the definition of anger resumes with these words "If
anger is this, then it is necessary (ἀνάγκη) that...." (1378
a 32-33).   It may be noticed how Aristotle's procedure
agrees formally with that recommended by Plato in the
Phaedrus.   A λόγος should begin with a definition (263 D 2-
3) and subsequent portions should be arranged according to
a certain necessity (ἀνάγκη 264 B 4, 7).   But it would be
false to suggest that Aristotle's immediate inspiration is this
portion of the Phaedrus.   For here Plato is concerned primarily with the organic unity of a λόγος (264 C 2-5) and
possibly with the method of division (265 D 3-266 B 1) that
he calls dialectic (266 C 1, Phil. 17 A 4).   In proceeding
deductively (see Solmsen quoted above, note 28) Aristotle is
not primarily influenced by the Phaedrus but by his own
Analytics.   In his use of ἔστω Aristotle seems to be drawing on the vocabulary of the Analytics (see below, note 31)
and in defining the individual emotions he seems to be offering causal definitions that meet the standards of the Posteri-
or Analytics (see below, section 2) and that may have been
worked out in his own Diaireseis (see below, note 44).

31.   ἔστω occurs in the Analytics both in connection with whole
premises and in connection with single terms.   The following list is only a sample: With premises An. Pr. 25 a 14;
30 a 37, b 9; 31 a 5, 10, 24; An. Post. 75 a 6, 9; 81 b 30;
94 b 14; 98 b 26; 99 a 31; with terms An. Pr. 30 b 33;
An. Post. 78 a 31, 40, b 24; 84 b 9; 87 b 8; 93 a 29; 94 a
28; 98 a 9, b 5, 12; 99 b 3.   The plural ἔστωσαν also occurs: An. Pr. 27 b 12, 23.   Professor Morrow has called
my attention to the fact that ἔστω is also commonly used in
Euclid's Elements to introduce the first premise of the
"given" in a demonstration.   ἔστω is part of the vocabulary
of demonstration and as such had already been used by
Aristotle not only in his Analytics but also in his Rhetoric.

32.   It may be instructive to compare this initial statement concerning emotion with the definition of rhetoric given in Book
I (1355 b 25-26).   Both need qualification.   In both cases
Aristotle passes over without mention a qualification that had
been insisted upon by Plato.   We have noted already (above,
in section 1) Aristotle's failure to add a qualifying in oratione
to his definition of rhetoric although he was familiar with
Plato's Gorgias and the suggestion that rhetoric is the ability to persuade with speeches (452 E 1).   The failure is
hardly serious.   Aristotle's audience within the Academy
would understand an in oratione, if Aristotle failed to make
the qualification explicit.   The same is true of Aristotle's

initial statement concerning emotion. It needs a qualification that had been made already by Plato and that would be supplied by Aristotle's audience. For in the Philebus (46-48) Plato had distinguished itches and tickles, hunger and thirst from emotions such as "anger, fear, yearning, grief, emulation, envy and the like" (47 E 1-2). The former group he had referred to the body (more accurately, itches and tickles are referred to the body, while hungers and thirsts are referred to both the body and the soul [46 B 8-C 4, 47 C 1-E 3]) and the latter group to the soul. Aristotle's audience, like Aristotle himself, would be familiar with the Philebus' distinction and so prepared to add a qualifying "psychic" to the initial statement concerning emotions.

33. Cope (above, note 2) 2.7 may err when he distinguishes between emotions proper and other "feelings or affections of like nature, such as the appetites, hunger and thirst." According to Cope, the appetites involve bodily pleasures and pains, while emotions involve mental pleasures and pains. Cope is correct to distinguish between appetites and emotions, but his statement of the difference is insufficient, if not erroneous. For in speaking of "feelings or affections of like nature," he suggests too great a similarity between emotional response and bodily upset. We are encouraged to think that being angry is like feeling pangs of hunger. In both cases a man experiences unpleasant sensations. Only in the case of anger the sensations are mental and not bodily. Sensations may be part of emotional response, but they are not the whole of it. For as Aristotle sees, the involvement of cognition in emotional response is of especial importance for distinguishing emotional responses from bodily upsets and the occurrence of particular kinds of cognition in emotional response is important for differentiating between particular kinds of emotional responses.

34. Aristotle's emphasis upon the necessary involvement of thought or belief in emotional response may be compared with the similar position of E. Bedford ("Emotions," Proceedings of the Aristotelian Society 57 (1956-1957) 281-304) and contrasted with the view of G. Pitcher ("Emotion," Mind 74 [1965] 326-346). Pitcher offers a Wittgensteinian analysis according to which certain kinds of cognition are characteristic of but not essential to particular kinds of emotional response.

35. See R. Hackforth, Plato's Examination of Pleasure (Cambridge: University Press, 1958) 69, 77. Protarchus' "view is that the 'mistakenness' is something lying outside the pleasure, a wrong opinion held concurrently with the feeling" (69). Perhaps it should be noted that Protarchus does not claim the view as his own. When Socrates congratulates him on his defense of pleasure, Protarchus modestly replies that he is merely saying what he hears (38 A 5). Perhaps we may add "in the Academy." It is convenient to refer to this argument as Protarchus' view or, as I shall soon do, Pro-

tarchus' (mis-)understanding, but we should remember that
Protarchus does not claim the view as his own.

36. "With" (37 E 10) only gets Socrates into trouble. "Follows"
(38 B 9) needs qualification, while "fills up" (42 A 9) is a
metaphor that may avoid but does not solve the problem.

37. When Socrates finishes his account of envy and begs off giving a similar account of fear, love, and the other emotions,
he wins Protarchus' consent by promising to continue the
discussion tomorrow (50 C 10-E 2). This promise may be
a dramatic device to enable the dialogue to move on to new
material, but it may be viewed also as a genuine reflection
of discussion within the Academy. For emotions together
with other kinds of pleasures and pains were a subject of
current and lively debate among members of the Academy.
When Plato makes Socrates promise to consider the subject
again tomorrow, he would seem to be both reflecting and
encouraging debate within the Academy.

38. Brunschwig (above, note 13) 1.109, n. 1 rejects ὀλιγωρίας at
127 b 31 as a gloss on the grounds that the passage is concerned with determining the genus of anger, and while
ὑπόληψις is a genus, ὑπόληψις ὀλιγωρίας is not one. Whatever text we adopt, it remains true that this passage in conjunction with 151 a 15-16 and 156 a 32-33 reflects debate
within the Academy concerning the relationship between emotion and cognition in general and anger and thought of outrage in particular.

39. It should be emphasized that Aristotle is clarifying or advanc-
ing the Academic discussion. He is not overthrowing previous work. This is particularly true in regard to the
Philebus. This dialogue had not made precise the exact
relationship between cognition and emotion but it had emphasized an intimate relationship. Certainly Aristotle had
learned much from studying this dialogue. We have already
noticed a close relationship between the accounts of pleasure
in the Philebus and in the Rhetoric (above, section 1 and
note 11) and have suggested that the Rhetoric's initial statement on emotions assumes certain distinction already made
in the Philebus (above, note 32). We may add that there is
close agreement between the accounts of envy given in the
Philebus and Rhetoric. Both works agree in calling envy a
pain (48 B 8, 50 A 7; 1386 b 18, 1387 b 23), in emphasizing the grounds (ἐπί) that explain an envious man's emotional response (48 B 11, 49 D 3, E 9, 50 A 2, 5; 1386 b 19,
1387 b 22-23, 1388 a 25), in pointing out that envious men
are delighted at the misfortune of a neighbor or peer (48 B
11-12, 50 A 2-3; 1386 b 32-1387 a 3, 1388 a 24-27), in
associating envy with bad character (49 D 6-7, 1386 b 33-
1387 a 1), and in dissociating envy from the fearsome (49
A 7-C 5; 1386 b 20-24). These similarities indicate, I
think, the influence of the Philebus upon Aristotles' treatment of envy. This is not to say that Aristotle simply re-
wrote the account of envy given in the Philebus. But it is

to say that even if Aristotle did not borrow directly from
the Philebus, he did borrow indirectly through discussion in
the Academy.

40. On the efficient cause as an element in the formal cause and
in the essential definition, see Sir David Ross, Aristotle's
Prior and Posterior Analytics (Oxford: Clarendon, 1949)
640; Aristotle's Metaphysics (Oxford: Clarendon, 1958)
2.223, 235.

41. Anger may be caused by the mere appearance of outrage. Of
course, when outrage actually occurs, it is natural to refer
to the outrageous act as the efficient cause. We may compare An. Post. 94 a 36-b 8 where Aristotle introduces the
Athenian attack upon Sardis as the efficient cause of the
Persian Wars. Since the attack actually occurred, it is
natural to pick out this attack as the efficient cause that
moved the Persians to retaliate. Nevertheless, actual outrage is not essential to anger. Only the thought or imagination of outrage is essential, so that whenever a man is
moved to anger he thinks or imagines himself insulted.

42. Cf. Dufour (above, note 2) 1.39: "ἔστι signifierait l'essence
(τὸ τί ἐστι) dans l'ordre et le domaine de la vérité. ἔστω
introduit une formule seulement suffisante et plausible dans
l'ordre et le domaine de l'opinion. "

43. The fact that here (1382 a 21) Aristotle employs the preposition ἐκ and not διά (as in the case or anger, 1378 a 31) is
not significant. Even in the Posterior Analytics Aristotle
does not control carefully his use of prepositions. He uses
διά to introduce the question of causation and to speak of
definitions that "show why" (90 a 15, 93 b 39). But in giving causal definitions Aristotle does not insist on using διά.
In the case of the eclipse, Aristotle may use ὑπό to introduce the efficient cause (90 a 16, 93 b 7, Metaph. 1044 b
14), or he may avoid a preposition by using a genitive absolute (90 a 18), or he may omit other elements in the definition and give the efficient cause in the nominative case
(93 b 7, cf. Rhet. 1380 b 17-18 where Aristotle states that
fear was (said to be) this, namely the thought of unjustified
suffering).

44. It is, I think, likely that Aristotle first worked out his views
on emotions in his Diaireseis and then incorporated these
views into his treatment of individual emotions given in the
Rhetoric. The account of emotions presented in the Diaireseis was probably not restricted to a formal division or simple list. It probably divided or analyzed (διαιρεῖν, Rhet.
1378 a 22) each emotion in respect to the condition of the
emotional man, the object of his emotion, and the grounds
for his emotional response. On the Diaireseis, see H. v.
Arnim, Das Ethische in Aristoteles Topik, Sb. Ak. Wien
205.4 (1927) 91-94, F. Dirlmeier, Aristoteles, Eudemische
Ethik (Berlin: Akademie Verlag, 1962) 242, 259, 356-357;
Aristoteles, Magna Moralia (Berlin: Akademie Verlag,
1958) 300-302. It should be added that it is at least debat-

able whether or not Aristotle wrote a Diaireseis. The fact that the catalogue preserved by Diogenes Laertius (5. 23, number 42) mentions a Diaireseis in seventeen books cannot be taken as certain proof. See P. Moraux, Les Listes Anciennes des Ouvrages d'Aristote (Louvain: Éditions Universitaires, 1951) 83-86. The Eudemian Ethics (1220 b 10-12, 1221 b 34-35, 1234 a 26) refers to Diaireseis concerning emotions, faculties, and dispositions. Since most scholars now accept the Eudemian Ethics as a work of Aristotle earlier than the Nichomachean Ethics, it may seem that these references in the Eudemian Ethics settle the issue. But it would be a mistake to claim that there remains no room for doubt. Those who follow Moraux and think that the Diaireseis mentioned by Diogenes Laertius are pseudo-Aristotelian compilations may well think that the mention of such collections by the Eudemian Ethics is a sign that this treatise is not genuine.

45.   While both Thrasymachus and Gorgias spoke of charms and enchantments, neither seems to have investigated the nature of emotional responses like pity and fear. Such an investigation was left for Aristotle. See Solmsen "Aristotle and Cicero" (above, note 3) 392, 404; C. Segal, "Gorgias and the Psychology of the Logos, " Harvard Studies in Classical Philology 66 (1962) 121, 133.

46.   Segal ([above, note 45] 115-117) points out correctly that for Gorgias and Thrasymachus the ability to control emotion was τέχνη. Like a doctor the skillful orator proceeds systematically and may be said to operate in an artful manner. But it is the orator who acts in a rational manner. The audience is conceived of as a patient upon whom the orator works. Gorgias seems to emphasize this when he speaks of the soul suffering its own suffering (πάσχειν, πάθημα, 9). This repetition of the idea of suffering in both verb and cognate accusative is emphatic and may recall the preceding mention of violent physical suffering (7). (See Segal 105.) For Gorgias being overcome by emotion is analogous to being raped.

47.   Once again we must allow the possibility that Aristotle wrote a Diaireseis which included a study of emotion (see above, note 44), and which may have had a more immediate effect upon Aristotle's ethical theory than the account of emotions given in the Rhetoric. Still, the account given in the Rhetoric would reflect the study included in the Diaireseis. Moreover, in the Rhetoric Aristotle makes quite clear that rhetoric and ethics have common interests and that rhetoric is a kind of offshoot of ethics in so far as it studies character and emotion (1356 a 20-27, 1359 b 8-12). We are, I think, encouraged to look for relationships between the Rhetoric and Aristotle's ethical theory.

48.   See D. Rees, "Bipartition of the Soul in the Early Academy, " Journal of Hellenic Studies 77 (1957) 112-118.

49.   F. Solmsen, "Antecedents of Aristotle's Psychology and Scale

of Beings, " American Journal of Philology 76 (1955) 150.

50. Arnim (above, note 44) 7, cf. Plutarch, Moralia 442 B.

51. F. M. Cornford, "Psychology and Social Structure in the Re-
     public of Plato, " Classical Quarterly 6 (1912) 246-265; R.
     Hackforth, "The Modification of Plan in Plato's Republic, "
     Classical Quarterly 7 (1913) 265-272; Rees (above, note 48)
     114.

52. Rees (above, note 48) 113; H. J. Kramer, Arete bei Platon
     und Aristoteles (Heidelberg: Carl Winter, 1959) 146-147.

53. Even Republic 439 E 5 suggests such a join.

54. R. Heinze, Xenocrates (Leipzig: Teubner, 1892) 140-142;
     J. Burnet (above, note 7) 63, note 1, criticized by Rees
     (above, note 48) 113, note 30.

55. The dichotomy is not absolute. Emotional response may fol-
     low upon and be controlled by reasoned argumentation. We
     have already noticed that the reasoned arguments of an ora-
     tor may lead an audience to judge that danger is imminent
     and so to become frightened. Similarly an individual per-
     son may reflect upon his situation, conclude that his life is
     in danger, and become frightened. Still, emotional responses
     are frequently (perhaps all too frequently) not preceded by
     any kind of deliberation. A man simply assesses his situa-
     tion in a certain way and acts appropriately. His action is
     not preceded by deliberation, but it is intelligent and is open
     to evaluation. His emotional response may be said to be
     proper or improper. And it is the mark of a morally virtu-
     ous man that his emotional responses are correct. Cf. EN
     1117 a 17-22 where Aristotle describes the most courageous
     individual who is fearless in the face of sudden danger. He
     responds properly on account of his virtuous character (ἕξις)
     and not as a result of deliberation (λόγισμος). For further
     discussion of this passage and in general of Aristotle's con-
     ception of moral virtue see my article "Aristotle: Emotions
     and Moral Virtue, " forthcoming in Arethusa 2 (1969).

56. On involuntary disease as a misfortune, see Gorgias, Helen
     19, discussed above, this section.

57. On the general problem of adapting tripartion to biological in-
     vestigation see Solmsen (above, note 49) 153-157, 160-161
     and cf. M. J. O'Brien, The Socratic Paradoxes and the
     Greek Mind (Chapel Hill: University of North Carolina,
     1967) 170-171.

58. Here in Book IX of the Republic each of the three faculties is
     said to have its own ἐπιθυμίαι (580 D 8), so that the appeti-
     tive faculty cannot be called without awkwardness the
     ἐπιθυμητικόν. See the note of J. Adam, The Republic of
     Plato, 2nd edition (Cambridge: University Press, 1963) 342-
     343.

59. Cf. Rep. 439 D 1-8 and the comment of R. C. Cross and A.
     D. Woozley Plato's Republic, A Philosophical Commentary
     (London: Macmillan, 1964) 122.

60. This is not the only reason why bipartition could not arise by
     simply combining the θυμοειδές and the ἐπιθυμητικόν. An ad-

ditional reason is the fact that the θυμοειδές and the
επιθυμητικόν together did not cover the entirety of man's emotional side.   Shame is an important emotion and is assigned
by the Topics (126 a 8) to the λογιστικόν.   This assignation
is in agreement with Republic 571 C 9 and in possible disagreement with Phaedrus 253 D 6, 254 A 2, 256 A 6.   (See
Arnim [above, note 44] 68-71 and O'Brien [above, note 57]
167-169).   Whatever the proper assignation of shame it
seems clear that tripartition was not well suited for picking
out the emotional side of man.   It was necessary to start
over and group together emotions, including shame (Rhet.
1383 b 11-1385 a 15), that involve cognition and are marked
by grounds and objects (Rhet. 1378 a 23-24).

61.   For further discussion of emotion, moral psychology and
moral virtue, see my "Aristotle and the Questionable Mean-
Dispositions, " Transactions of the American Philological Association, 99 (1968), 203-231; "Aristotle: Emotion and
Moral Virtue, " Arethusa 2 (1969), 163-185; "On the Antecedents of Aristotle's Bipartite Psychology, " Greek Roman
and Byzantine Studies, 11 (1970), 233-50; "Aristotle: Animals, Emotion and Moral Virtue, " Arethusa, 4 (1971) 137-
65; and "Zu der Darstellung der Seele in der Nikomachischen
Ethik I 13, " Philologus.

14. ARISTOTLE'S CONCEPT OF METAPHOR IN RHETORIC

by William J. Jordan*

Unlike much of Aristotle's rhetorical theory, his concept of metaphor has received relatively little attention from contemporary rhetorical theorists. Traditionally, rhetoricians have either overlooked or have not been concerned with Aristotle's psychological aspects of metaphor, as Kennedy observes that "none of the later Greek or Roman accounts seem to share Aristotle's philosophical concern with the psychological bases of figures of speech."[1] Osborn's recent discussion of metaphor likewise denies a psychological consideration of Aristotle's concept of metaphor. According to Osborn:

> The emphasis in Aristotle remains primarily upon the linguistic character of metaphor, and the reasons for this emphasis again lie both in the natural tendency of early theory to stress the most obvious characteristics of the figure, and in the conceptual framework which placed the figure under the canon of Style. Moreover, there is no explicit acknowledgment in these observations that the psychological dimension of metaphor is an integral component of its occurrence, an essential part of its being. Certainly the Aristotelian definition does not at all suggest such an essentiality.[2]

While the Aristotelian definition, alone, may not suggest a psychological orientation to metaphor, the context of his statements concerning metaphor in both the Rhetoric and Poetics provides support for the thesis that Aristotle's concept of metaphor is essentially psychological in that it identifies semantic and structural characteristics which affect reader and listener behavior. The following analysis seeks to reconstruct Aristotle's concept of metaphor, identifying his particular emphases on the psychological elements of the rhetorical metaphor.

*Mr. Jordan is Associate Professor of Speech and Theatre at Texas Tech University. This essay is based upon a portion of his doctoral thesis, "A Psychological Explication of Aristotle's Concept of Metaphor," directed by Dr. Ronald H. Carpenter at Wayne State University.

Characteristics of Metaphor

Aristotle's statements which indicate his concern with semantic characteristics of metaphor consider the relationship between words and meanings.   While the term word (λόγος) is quite
common in Aristotle's writings, and refers to meaningful speech
sounds or their written counterparts, his term for meaning varies.[3]
In addition to using the term meaning, Aristotle refers to "mental
experience" or "images in the thinking soul."   Aristotle argues
that words denote meanings when he refers to spoken words as
"the symbols of mental experience and written words are the symbols of spoken words.   Just as all men have not the same writing,
so all men have not the same speech sounds, but the mental experiences, which these directly symbolize, are the same for all,
as also are those things of which our experiences are the images."[4]
That is, for the speakers of a language, most words will be used
to refer to a specific set of things, objects, concepts or referents.[5]
The common meaning accompanying the generally accepted usage of
a word may be considered its denotation.   What the word names is
its referent.   The meaning, however, according to Aristotle, is
neither the denotation nor the referent but the mental experience
which the word evokes in a listener.   From this basis Aristotle's
statements concerning metaphor may be considered as part of a
semantic construct.

Aristotle's statements which indicate his concern with structural characteristics consider relationships between words.   Aristotle makes comparisons between words and groups of words in
terms of their frequency of occurrence in the language and their
length.   These statements provide a basis for considering the structural characteristics of metaphor.   After establishing the distinction in Aristotle's writings between semantic and structural characteristics of words, this discussion considers the specific characteristics which distinguish metaphor from literal language.

Buckley sees a distinction in Aristotle's writings between
two classifications of word characteristics, a semantic class and
a structural class.   Each class may be subdivided into two species
of words.   According to Buckley;

> κύρια are words in general use, opposed to γλῶτται out-
> landish expressions. οἰκεία, words in their primary and
> literal acceptations [are] opposed to μεταφοραί....   Many
> words are κύρια which yet are not οἰκεία.   In fact, of
> the three divisions the οἰκεία are necessarily the fewest;
> since the proper and original designations of individual
> objects cannot extend to a number sufficiently great to
> answer all the purposes of language; the resources of
> which must therefore be augmented by metaphorical trans-
> fer. [6]

These classifications may be diagrammed as discrete categories.

Semantic Class	Structural Class
literal words, οἰκεῖα	words in general use, κύρια
metaphors, μεταθοραὶ	unfamiliar words, γλῶτται

This distinction explains Aristotle's identification of "the regular [κύρια] and proper [οἰκεῖα] terms for things," by emphasizing that words have both semantic and structural aspects. [7]

This distinction has been ignored by Cope who says that κύρια and οἰκεῖα are virtually the same. [8] Welldon concurs: "There seems to be practically no difference in meaning between 'proper' and 'special' names; they are the names employed in ordinary speech." [9] Gillies, however, seems to support Buckley's distinction: "κύρια are words ordinary and appropriate, in opposition to γλῶτται and πεποιημένα foreign and new coined words: οἰκεῖα are proper words, in opposition to metaphors." [10] Aristotle's use of κύρια, which Roberts translates in the following context as "Clearness is secured by using the words (nouns and verbs alike) that are current and ordinary," also suggests that Aristotle was concerned with a distinct structural element. [11]

It should be noted that these two classifications are not mutually exclusive. A literal word may be either familiar (in general use) or unfamiliar. Likewise, a metaphor may be composed or either familiar or unfamiliar words. This interrelationship of the semantic with the structural aspects of metaphor is central to Aristotle's concept of the effective metaphor.

Semantic Characteristics

Semantically, metaphor differs from literal language in that it denotes a new or unique meaning. According to Aristotle, "ordinary words convey only what we know already; it is from metaphor that we can best get hold of something fresh." [12] Aristotle provides the following example of metaphor denoting new meaning. "When the poet calls old age 'a withered stalk,' he conveys a new idea, a new fact, to us by means of the general notion of 'lost bloom,' which is common to both things." [13] This basic semantic nature of metaphor, the denotation of new meaning, can be attributed to the semantic characteristics which distinguish metaphor from literal language.

Semantically, metaphor differs from literal language in terms of its conceptual denotation and in some cases its sensory denotation. These may be thought of as cognitive discrepancies in that they are based on both the listener's and the speaker's knowledge of how things and ideas are related.

Conceptually, for Aristotle, "metaphor consists in giving the thing a name that belongs to something else; the transference

being either from genus to species, or from species to genus, or
from species to species, or on grounds of analogy. "14 Words
used as metaphor denote either a) a specific meaning instead of a
more general literal meaning (genus to species), b) a general meaning instead of a more specific literal meaning (species to genus),
c) a different specific meaning instead of a literal specific meaning
(species to species), or d) an analogous meaning instead of a literal meaning.15 In all of these cases, the cognitive discrepancy
grows out of the metaphor's denotation of a meaning which is different from the literal or ordinary meaning of the words used as
metaphor.

     The second type of cognitive discrepancy described by Aris-
totle as being potentially denoted by metaphor is sensory discrepancy. According to Aristotle, metaphor has a discrepant sensory
denotation when the words used as metaphor denote a referent
capable of expending energy. At the outset, it must be noted that
sensory denotation, as a semantic characteristic, is ancillary to
metaphor. It is not inherent in all metaphor, nor is it unique to
metaphor; other words may also have this characteristic. Sensory
discrepancy is considered here because Aristotle explicitly emphasizes this characteristic when treating metaphor.

     What Aristotle means by sensory denotation or activity
(ἐνέργεια) is best illustrated in his examples. Activity is expenditure of energy.

> So with Homer's common practice of giving metaphorical
> life to lifeless things: all such passages are distinguished
> by the effect of activity they convey. Thus,
>> Downward anon to the valley rebounded the
>> boulder <u>remorseless</u>;
> and
>> The (bitter) arrow <u>flew</u>;
> and
>> Flying on <u>eagerly</u>;
> and
>> Stuck in the earth, still <u>panting</u> to feed on
>> the flesh of heroes;
> and
>> And the point of the spear <u>in its fury</u> drove
>> full through his breastbone.
> In all these examples the things have the effect of being
> active because they are made into living beings; shame-
> less behavior and fury and so on are all forms of activi-
> ty.16

English translations read ἐνέργεια as either "activity" or "actuality"
(except Buckley, who translates this as "personification"). This
suggests that a metaphor which has a sensory denotation is not
limited strictly to visual referents as some translations seem to
suggest.

Apparently activity has been selected by some translators because Aristotle relates metaphorical activity and physical vision in his introduction to his discussion of the sensory metaphor.

> By making them "see things" I mean using expressions that represent things as in a state of activity. Thus, to say that a good man is 'four-square' is certainly a metaphor; both the good man and the square are perfect; but the metaphor does not suggest activity. On the other hand, in the expression 'with his vigor in full bloom' there is a notion of activity; and so in 'But you must roam as free as a sacred victim'; and in
>
> Thereat up sprang the Hellenes to their feet, where 'up sprang' gives us activity as well as metaphor, for it at once suggests swiftness. [17]

Freese translates the first sentence of the preceding passage as "I mean that things are set before the eyes by words that signify actuality."[18] This is a literal rendering of λέγω δη' πρὸ ὀμμάιτων ταῦτα ποιεῖν, ὅσα ἐνεργοῦντα σημαίνει. The other translators, with the exception of Roberts, explain the metaphor, πρὸ ὀμμάιτων, "before the eyes" as denoting things in a state of activity or energy. Roberts explains activity as setting things "before the eyes" of the listener. As a result of this interpretation, Roberts calls the active metaphor a "graphic metaphor," implying that the metaphor is limited to representing visually active referents.[19] As the examples provided by Aristotle suggest, the active or sensory metaphor is not limited to denoting visual activity. Thus, "remorseless," "eagerly," "panting," and "in its fury" as examples of the sensory metaphor are understood better as metaphors which denote expenditure of energy, rather than graphic metaphors. Aristotle even notes that things not in motion may be thought of as capable of expending energy.[20] The example, "with his vigor in full bloom," is not a movement but a state of being which can be sensed. Therefore, the concept of sensory denotation seems to encompass all of the possibilities suggested by such terms as graphic, active, representing actuality or ἐνέργεια.

In describing metaphor, Aristotle suggests that metaphor differs from literal language in its evaluative or affective denotation. This discrepancy is considered affective because it concerns the evaluations which the speaker or listener places upon the referent. According to Aristotle, when the speaker uses metaphor and gives the thing a name that belongs to something else, he necessarily denotes meaning which is more favorable or less favorable than would be denoted by literal language. Aristotle argues that two different words denote different evaluations. "Two different words will represent a thing in two different lights; so on this ground also one term must be held fairer or fouler than another. For both of two terms will indicate what is fair, or what is foul, but not simply their fairness or their foulness, or if so, at any rate

not in an equal degree. "[21]   On this point Aristotle's translators
are in agreement.   Metaphor and the word it replaces meet the
criterion of two different words, for if they were the same in their
denotation, then one could not be metaphor.

According to Aristotle, all possible words whose meanings
can be denoted by other words will differ in the evaluative meaning
which they denote.   Aristotle explains that "it is like having to ask
ourselves what dress will suit an old man; certainly not the crim-
son cloak that suits a young man.   And if you wish to pay a com-
pliment, you must take your metaphor from something better in
the same line; if to disparage, from something worse. "[22]   For example, "Somebody calls actors 'hangers-on of Dionysus, ' but they
call themselves 'artists':   each of these terms is a metaphor, the
one intended to throw dirt at the actor, the other to dignify him.
And pirates now call themselves 'purveyors.'   We can thus call a
crime a mistake, or a mistake a crime. "[23]   Semantically metaphor is more than a word substitution technique.   It is the selection of a word for the purpose of changing the evaluative relationship which exists between the referent and the word which names
it.   All metaphors are evaluative.

Structural Characteristics

Aristotle's concept of metaphor concerns the occurrence of
words within a language and the norms which are descriptive of
their occurrence.   In the Rhetoric, Aristotle's treatment of structural phenomena is inexact and unsystematic.   On the basis of his
observations, Aristotle identifies two structural characteristics
relevant to metaphor.   These characteristics are the frequency of
occurrence of the words which compose the metaphor and the length
of the metaphor.

Aristotle's concern with the frequency of occurrence of words
in speech is evident in his linguistic classification of words into two
subgroups.   The first consists of ordinary words, or κύρια, which
Aristotle defines as those "in general use in a country. "[24]   Due to
their general use, these words would have a relatively high frequency of occurrence.   The second group of words consists of
strange words, or words "in use elsewhere, " or γλῶτται.   Frequency
of occurrence distinguishes κύρια from γλῶτται.   According to Aristotle, "the same word may obviously be at once strange and ordinary, though not in reference to the same people; σίγυνον, for instance, is an ordinary word in Cyprus, and a strange word with
us. "[25]   Strange words are, necessarily, words with a low or no
frequency of occurrence in the language.   Other words which have
a low frequency of occurrence and which Aristotle includes in the
category of γλῶτται are compound words, invented words, lengthened
words, curtailed words, and words altered in form, for all of these
deviate from normal speech. [26]

The Rhetoric recommends that metaphor be constructed from high frequency words. According to Aristotle, the speech of ordinary life, or high frequency words, are of two kinds. "In the language of prose, besides the regular and proper terms for things, metaphorical terms only can be used with advantage. This we gather from the fact that these two classes of terms, the proper or regular and the metaphorical--these and no others--are used by everybody in conversation."[27] Because they are used by everybody in conversation, words used metaphorically can be identified as high frequency words. In addition, Aristotle says that "metaphor ... gives style clearness ... as nothing else can."[28] And clearness is obtained by using high frequency words. Aristotle says that "style to be good must be clear, as is proved by the fact that speech which fails to convey a plain meaning will fail to do just what speech has to do.... Clearness is secured by using the words (nouns and verbs alike) that are current and ordinary."[29] Because metaphor gives style clearness, and clearness is also obtained from words of high frequency, Aristotle asserts that the effective metaphor will be composed of high frequency words.

Limitations

In developing limitations to the invention of metaphor, Aristotle explicitly states that knowing the characteristics which compose metaphor does not guarantee the successful construction of metaphor. Specifically, Aristotle states that "their actual invention can only come through natural talent or long practice; but this treatise may indicate the way it is done."[30] The invention of metaphor, or the way it is done, is accomplished by combining the necessary semantic and structural characteristics in selecting words for discourse. The basic limitation imposed by Aristotle upon the selection process is that the words be appropriate to rhetorical discourse.

By appropriate, Aristotle means that metaphor should denote discrepant meaning which, while differing from literal meaning, also is related to the literal language which the speaker would normally use in the same situation. According to Aristotle, "metaphor must be drawn, as has been stated already, from things that are related to the original thing, and yet not obviously so related."[31] But Aristotle warns against constructing a metaphor which is too discrepant. "Metaphors must not be far-fetched," and "we must draw them not from remote but from kindred and similar things."[32]

Aristotle provides examples of metaphor that are too "far-fetched," or too discrepant. According to Aristotle: "Others [metaphors] are too grand and theatrical; and these, if they are far-fetched, may also be obscure. For instance, Gorgias talks of 'events that are green and full of sap,' and says 'foul was the deed you sowed and evil the harvest you reaped.' That is too much like poetry. Alcidamas, again, called philosophy 'a fortress that threatens the power of law, ' and the Odyssey 'a goodly look-ing-glass of human life, ' and talked about 'offering no such toy to poetry.' "33   While Aristotle's translators seem to object to these metaphors because they are too much like poetry, the point Aris-totle seems to be making is that the potential meanings of the words used as metaphor in these instances were either too dis-crepant from or too similar to the literal words which would de-scribe the same referents. 34   Ideally, then, metaphor should ob-tain some optimal mean of discrepancy although that mean is un-identified in Aristotle's concept of metaphor.

Effects of Metaphor

Whereas the preceding discussion has focused on the speci-fic characteristics of metaphor, this discussion explains how Aris-totle sees those characteristics contributing to a rhetorically func-tional metaphor, one which is potentially advantageous in discourse. Aristotle's concept points to three potential rhetorical advantages evolving from metaphor: liveliness, appetence and pleasure. These advantages evolve from the characteristics which Aristotle attributes to metaphor.   These advantages, in conjunction with the characteristics previously described, constitute a composite expli-cation of Aristotle's concept of the rhetorically functional metaphor.

Metaphor and Liveliness Effects

Aristotle identifies metaphor as evoking new meaning rapidly and with little effort for the listener.   Although Aristotle develops this point with a concept of liveliness, this rhetorical advantage may be described more precisely in terms of the listener's effi-ciency of response.

Aristotle explicitly relates rapid evocation of new meaning to liveliness when he says "both speech and reasoning are lively in proportion as they make us seize a new idea promptly. "35   Stated somewhat differently, words which require little mental effort to understand utilize a characteristic of liveliness which allows the listener "to get hold of new ideas easily. "36   The Greek term for "lively" is αστεΐα which is defined as "of the town, urbane, courte-ous, polite, witty, elegant, neat, and pretty. "37   Translations of αστεΐα read "smart and popular, clever and popular, urbanities, and lively, pointed, sprightly, witty, facetious, clever, and popu-lar sayings. "38   Aristotle's metaphorical use of αστεΐα is not clari-fied by his translators.   From what Aristotle says about liveliness in the Rhetoric, however, "efficiency" seems to be the better term to describe how metaphor evokes new meaning.   While liveliness rather ambiguously describes a characteristic of language, effi-ciency is more descriptive of a behavioral response.

Aristotle identifies metaphor as an efficient symbol when he states that "liveliness is specially conveyed by metaphor."[39] According to what Aristotle says concerning liveliness, a word may be more efficient when it is semantically discrepant with the listener's expectations, when it evokes sensory denotations, and when it is linguistically or structurally frequent and brief.

Metaphor may create the potential advantage of efficiency because it is discrepant with the expectations of the listener. In Aristotle's terminology "liveliness is specially conveyed by metaphor, and by the further power of surprising the hearer; because the hearer expected something different, his acquisition of the new idea impresses him all the more."[40] Aristotle's implication here is that the listener expects literal language. That is, he expects words to be used in consistent ways. Because it is cognitively and affectively different from literal language, any specific metaphor should be unexpected. As a result, when the listener perceives a metaphor, he is either aware of being "deceived" or "surprised," depending upon translators, because metaphorical meaning is unexpected.

Metaphor may be more efficient than other symbols when it has sensory denotations. Although the Rhetoric does not provide a detailed analysis of how the active or sensory metaphor evokes new meaning efficiently, it does suggest that sensory metaphors are more efficient.

According to Aristotle, "liveliness is got by ... using expressions that represent things as in a state of activity," and "activity is movement."[41] The psychological implications of this premise are explained, in part, by Aristotle in his psychological treatise On the Soul. In Aristotle's concept of the physical world of perceivers and referents (as opposed to the verbal world of listeners and words), of all things capable of being perceived, man most readily perceives movement. This is because all states of an object's existence are, according to Aristotle, states of movement. "The objects which we perceive incidentally through this or that special sense, ... we perceive by movement, e.g., magnitude by movement, and therefore also figure (for figure is a species of magnitude), what is at rest by absence of movement."[42] Because movement or its absence is more readily perceived, Aristotle seems to attribute efficiency to metaphors which represent things as moving or capable of moving.

In addition to semantic characteristics, Aristotle suggests that structural characteristics may also contribute to metaphor's potential efficiency.

According to Aristotle, literal words are inefficient in evoking new meaning rapidly and easily. This assumption applies to both infrequent and frequent words when used literally. A structurally infrequent or strange word is not generally understood by a

listener, and a frequent or ordinary word is one whose literal
meaning is not new to the listener. According to Aristotle, "strange
words simply puzzle us; ordinary words convey only what we know
already."[43] Neither of these structural units, when used literally,
evokes new meaning easily or efficiently.

Metaphor, however, may be an efficient source of new meaning, particularly when constructed of structurally frequent words.
According to Aristotle, "it is from metaphor that we best get hold
of something fresh."[44] Two alternatives exist for metaphor. It
can be either an infrequent word used uniquely or a frequent word
used uniquely. Since infrequent words usually have no literal meaning for the listener, he cannot perceive that the word is being used
metaphorically and no new meaning is evoked. This implies that
what may be metaphor for a speaker may not be metaphor for a
listener. When such a situation occurs, Aristotle would suggest
that the meaning is unclear.

To achieve efficiency and still insure clarity, Aristotle recommends using high frequency words in unique ways. According to
Aristotle, "clearness is secured by using the words (nouns and
verbs alike) that are current and ordinary."[45] At the same time
clearness is obtained, the essential discrepant nature of metaphor
also may be obtained by using words uniquely. This is apparently
what Aristotle means when he states that metaphor gives style
"clearness" and "distinction" at the same time.

Related to frequency is the structural characteristic of
length. The shorter the metaphor, the more efficient it should be
in evoking new meaning. Specifically Aristotle states that "the
more briefly ... such sayings [metaphors] can be expressed, the
more taking they are, ... brevity [impresses the new idea] more
quickly"; or "conciseness gives knowledge more rapidly."[46] Aristotle is not concerned here with absolute length of words, but
rather with relative lengths of alternative words, whether it be a
shorter word in place of a longer word, or a shorter passage in
place of a longer passage. As a case in point, Aristotle's major
criticism of the simile is that it is unnecessarily long: "The
simile, as we have said, is a metaphor differing only by the addition of a word, wherefore it is less pleasant because it is longer."[47] The essence of Aristotle's argument seems to be that
words which do not contribute to new meaning impede the efficiency
of the other words which are being used to evoke new meaning.
Thus, by eliminating the unnecessary words within the metaphor,
the length is shortened, and the shortened metaphor may be more
efficient.

Metaphor and Appetence Effects

In Aristotle's concept, metaphor potentially has an effect
on the motivational states of the listener. In terms of a rhetori-

cal advantage, metaphor associates meaning with the desire of the listener to avoid or pursue the referent of the meaning to a greater degree than literal symbols. While Aristotle does not use the term motivation, he does talk about appetence, that faculty "of which desire, passion, and wish are the species."[48] In Shute's analysis of Aristotle's concept, motivation follows perception in that "the presence of sensation always arouses some kind of desire, for what is sensed causes pleasure or pain, and desire is a craving for what is pleasant."[49] As Aristotle would explain motivation theory, "when the object is pleasant or painful, the soul makes a quasi-affirmation or negation, and pursues or avoids the object."[50] Aristotle illustrates how the motives of a person may filter what he perceives in the process of associating meaning and values.

> The faculty of thinking then thinks the forms in images, and ... what is to be pursued or avoided is marked out for it.... E.g. perceiving by sense that the beacon is fire, it recognizes in virtue of the general faculty of sense that it signifies an enemy, because it sees it moving; but sometimes by means of the images or thoughts which are within the soul, just as if it were seeing, it calculates and deliberates what is to come by reference to what is present; and when it makes a pronouncement, as in the case of sensation, it pronounces the object to be pleasant or painful, in this case it avoids or pursues; and so generally in cases of action.[51]

The listener may not make a simple yes-no type of evaluation. Instead, as Shute explains Aristotle's concept of motivation, the process of associating referents with values may be very complex.

> This process of deliberation may be immensely complicated. It may lead to considerations which nullify the claims of the goal. But if it reaches its end, that conclusion is the conclusion of the individual, for the mind is the organism thinking, rather than something apart from it. Thus the conclusion of this mental activity is identical with the actualizing or energizing of the individual in relation to his object, and the overt activity is in progress.[52]

Because of this complexity of the intervening considerations, metaphor is qualified as "potentially" affecting motivation.

Metaphor potentially may affect motivation because it evaluates its referent. As discussed previously, Aristotle states that no two words used to denote the same meaning will evoke the same meaning. The meanings will differ at least in evaluation. Stated another way, metaphor evokes a different evaluation of a referent than does the literal word. The purpose of the evaluation, according to Aristotle, is to identify the referent as being either more

or less pleasant or more or less painful.   Aristotle provides examples of these possibilities.

When metaphor evaluates a referent as pleasant, it identifies it as an object of pursuit for the listener.   Of course there
may be relative degrees of pleasantness.   When the referent is
evaluated as more pleasant than the listener's evaluation, the
referent potentially becomes an object of increased pursuit.   When
the referent is evaluated as less pleasant than the listener's evaluation, the referent potentially becomes an object of decreased pursuit.   Aristotle's example of two terms for a religious title illustrates this.   "So Iphicrates called Callias a 'mendicant priest' instead of a 'torchbearer,' and Callias replied that Iphicrates must
be uninitiated or he would have called him not a 'mendicant priest'
but a 'torchbearer.'   Both are religious titles, but one is honourable and the other is not."53   The religious position of Callias, a
potential object of pursuit, is evaluated as an object of greater
pursuit by the metaphor "torchbearer," and as an object of lesser
pursuit by the metaphor "mendicant priest."   Again, it should be
emphasized that any possible evaluation only potentially affects the
listener.   He may accept the evaluation or reject it.   If he accepts the evaluation, according to Aristotle's explanation of motivation, he should act accordingly.   To the extent that metaphor
may be held responsible for associating the meaning with the pursuit motives of the listener, it may be considered a persuasive
stimulus.

When metaphor evaluates a referent as painful, it is identified as an object for the listener to avoid.   The evaluation may
suggest greater or lesser avoidance of the referent.   Evaluation
which identifies the referent as an object of greater avoidance is
evidenced, says Aristotle, when we call actors "hangers-on of
Dionysus," or say that a thief "plundered his victim," or that
Orestes is a "mother-slayer."54   Evaluation which identifies the
referent as an object of lesser avoidance is evidenced when beg-
ging is described as "praying," when pirates call themselves "purveyors," when a crime is called a "mistake," when a thief is said
to "take" a thing, or when Orestes is called his "father's aveng-
er."55   All of these examples, according to Aristotle, attempt to
change the evaluative meaning of the referent through metaphorical
transfer which identifies the referent as an object to avoid.   To
the extent that the listener accepts the evaluation and avoids the
referent, the metaphor may be considered persuasive.

Metaphor and Pleasure Effects

In addition to describing metaphor as a motivational element, Aristotle suggests that metaphor creates pleasure.   In Aristotle's philosophy, pleasure is a normal or natural state of man
which results from human activity or movement.   In Metaphysics,
Aristotle states that "pleasure in its highest form of speculative

philosophical pleasure, is identical with the highest happiness ...
[and] is represented as the pleasure of the Supreme Being; and because this is the nature of pleasure, all states of activity, waking,
sensation, thinking give the highest pleasure; and to one of these
all other pleasure, as those of anticipation and recollection are
due. "56 Ross concludes from this definition that pleasure "cannot
be a movement.... But it is in fact something complete in itself. "57 Pleasure, then, is a resulting condition or state. Cope
prefers this to the definition found in the Rhetoric which he dismisses as being sufficient enough for the rhetorician, but "both
virtually and actually contradicted" in Aristotle's other writings. 58
In the Rhetoric, Aristotle defines pleasure as both the activity leading up to and the final effect of the listener's achieving a normal
state of being: "We may lay it down that Pleasure is a movement,
a movement by which the soul as a whole is consciously brought
into its normal state of being. "59 When viewed as a natural state
rather than a movement or process, pleasure may be studied more
profitably from a rhetorical viewpoint as a potential effect of metaphor rather than a process.

Metaphor potentially creates a pleasurable state in the listener because it causes the activity of learning to occur. Aristotle
uses the term "learning" to describe a pleasurable experience when
he states that "learning things and wondering at things are also
pleasant as a rule; wondering implies the desire of learning, so
that the object of wonder is an object of desire; while in learning
one is brought into one's natural condition. "60 Acts of imitation
also cause learning because "the spectator draws inferences ('That
is a so-and-so') and thus learns something fresh. "61 In almost
identical terms Aristotle talks about the pleasure derived from
metaphor. "Easy learning is naturally pleasant to all, and words
mean something, so that all words which make us learn something
are most pleasant.... It is metaphor, therefore, that above all
produces this effect. "62 And again, "Well-constructed riddles are
pleasant for the same reason--the solution is an act of learning;
and they are expressed metaphorically, too. "63 Metaphor causes
the listener to learn, and to Aristotle this is a pleasurable experience. The pleasure which can be created by metaphor exists as a
potential rhetorical advantage in Aristotle's concept.

Conclusion

Whereas all symbols may function to evoke new meaning,
Aristotle distinguishes metaphor from all other evocative symbols.
Aristotle's essentially psychological concept of metaphor suggests
that the listener potentially responds to metaphor by constructing
new meaning more efficiently than if the new meaning were evoked
by literal language, by changing his evaluation of the metaphor's
referent, and by deriving pleasure from the metaphor. Both semantic and structural characteristics appear to account for these
effects. This interpretation of Aristotle's concept of metaphor is

pertinent to modern studies of style. Aristotle's essentially psychological emphasis provides a deeply traditional basis for a behavioral study of the rhetorical effects of metaphor. Not only does Aristotle's concept identify those effects, it also identifies stimulus characteristics pertinent to any behavioral study of metaphor.

NOTES

1. George Kennedy, The Art of Persuasion in Greece (Princeton: Princeton University Press, 1963), p. 111.
2. Michael M. Osborn, "The Function and Significance of Metaphor in Rhetorical Discourse, " (unpublished Ph. D. dissertation, The University of Florida, 1963), p. 21.
3. Categories 1a. Unless indicated, all subsequent quotations from Aristotle's works are from the Oxford edition, The Works of Aristotle, 2 Vols., ed. by W. D. Ross, in Great Books of the Western World, Vols. 8-9, ed. by Robert Maynard Hutchins (54 vols.; Chicago: Encyclopaedia Britannica, Inc., 1952). In addition to the Rhys Roberts translation of the Rhetoric in the Oxford edition, additional texts and translations of the Rhetoric have been consulted. These are: Aristotle's Rhetoric (London: Printed by T. B. for Randall Taylor near Stationers-Hall, 1686); Theodore Buckley, Aristotle's Treatise on Rhetoric and the Poetic of Aristotle (fourth edition, London: George Bell and Sons, 1906); Lane Cooper, The Rhetoric of Aristotle (New York: Appleton-Century Crofts, Inc., 1932); Edward Meredith Cope, The Rhetoric of Aristotle, ed. by John Edwin Sandys, (3 vols.; Cambridge: University Press, 1877); Daniel Michael Crimmin, A Dissertation on Rhetoric, translated from the Greek of Aristotle (second edition, London: J. J. Stockdale, 1812); J. H. Freese, Art of Rhetoric (Cambridge, Mass.: Harvard University Press, 1926); John Gillies, A New Translation of Aristotle's Rhetoric (London: T. Cadell, 1823); Richard Claverhouse Jebb, The Rhetoric of Aristotle, ed. by John Edwin Sandys (Cambridge: University Press, 1909); J. E. C. Welldon, The Rhetoric of Aristotle (London: MacMillan and Company, 1886); and G. M. A. Grube, On Poetry and Style: Aristotle (Indianapolis: Bobbs-Merrill Company, Inc., 1958).
4. On Interpretation 16a.
5. As used by Ogden and Richards, "referent" seems to be the most all inclusive term. C. K. Ogden and I. A. Richards, The Meaning of Meaning (New York: Harcourt, Brace and World, Inc., 1923), pp. 9-12.
6. Buckley, Aristotle's Treatise, p. 209.
7. Rhetoric 1404b.
8. E. M. Cope, An Introduction to Aristotle's Rhetoric (London: Macmillan and Company, 1867), pp. 282ff.
9. Welldon, The Rhetoric, p. 230.
10. Gillies, A New Translation, p. 368.

11. Rhetoric 1404b.
12. Ibid. 1410b.
13. Ibid.
14. Poetics 1457b. In Posterior Analytics 96b ff., Aristotle treats genus and species as categories of thought. As such, these may be viewed as inventive "places" from which the speaker develops metaphor. While Osborn recognizes this kind of inventive system in Peacham's The Garden of Eloquence, he overlooks this interpretation of Aristotle's definition; see Michael M. Osborn, "The Evolution of the Theory of Metaphor in Rhetoric," Western Speech, XXXI (Spring, 1967), 123-26. When genus and species are viewed as categories of thought, Aristotle's definition of metaphor does point to an essential psychological dimension.
15. Aristotle's definition of metaphor concerns the generic concept rather than the specific trope Metaphor found in most modern treatments of style. According to Welldon, "the Aristotelian use of μεταφορα is considerably wider than that of 'metaphor' in English. Any transference of a word from its proper or ordinary application to another would be a μεταφορα, whether it involved a comparison or not," The Rhetoric, pp. 232-33.
16. Rhetoric 1411b-1412a.
17. Ibid. 1411b.
18. Freese, Art of Rhetoric, p. 405.
19. Rhetoric 1411b.
20. On the Soul 425a.
21. Rhetoric 1405b.
22. Ibid. 1405a.
23. Ibid.
24. Poetics 1457b.
25. Ibid.
26. Rhetoric 1404b. In Poetics, Aristotle classifies metaphor with deviate forms. "On the other hand the diction becomes distinguished and non-prosaic by the use of unfamiliar terms, i.e. strange words, metaphors, lengthened forms, and everything that deviates from the ordinary modes of speech." Poetics 1458a. This is contradicted in the Rhetoric. "These two classes of terms, the proper or regular and the metaphorical--these and no others--are used by everybody in conversation." Rhetoric 1404b. Metaphor, in rhetoric, is a semantic deviation, a deviation from norms of word usage, while at the same time not deviating from word frequency norms. Perhaps a difference between the poetic metaphor and the rhetorical metaphor is that the rhetorical metaphor attempts to clarify meaning and the poetic metaphor attempts to obscure meaning.
27. Rhetoric 1404b.
28. Ibid. 1405a.
29. Ibid. 1404b.
30. Ibid. 1410b.
31. Ibid. 1413a.

32. Ibid. 1410b; 1413a.
33. Ibid. 1406b.
34. According to Grube, "We should agree with Aristotle that
    Gorgias' reference to Philomela, who in legend was changed
    into a swallow, is frigid. We should also condemn most of
    his other examples, but the Odyssey as a mirror of human
    life rather appeals to us, except that by this time it is a
    cliché. " Grube, On Poetry, p. 75.
35. Rhetoric 1410b.
36. Ibid.
37. See Henry George Liddell and Robert Scott, The Classic Greek
    Dictionary (Chicago: Follett Publishing Company, 1927),
    p. 109.
38. Rhetoric 1412a.
39. Ibid.
40. Ibid.
41. Ibid. 1411b; 1412a.
42. On the Soul 425a.
43. Rhetoric 1410b.
44. Ibid.
45. Ibid.
46. Ibid. 1412b; Freese, Art of Rhetoric, p. 413.
47. Rhetoric 1410b.
48. On the Soul 414b.
49. Clarence Shute, The Psychology of Aristotle (Morningside
    Heights, New York: Columbia University Press, 1941),
    p. 85. This is Shute's summary of the concepts found in
    On the Soul 413b, 414b, and 431a.
50. On the Soul 431a.
51. Ibid. 431b.
52. Shute, The Psychology, pp. 82-3.
53. Rhetoric 1405a.
54. Ibid. 1405a, 1405b.
55. Ibid.
56. This is Cope's interpretation of Metaphysics 1072b in An In-
    troduction, pp. 238-39.
57. W. D. Ross, Aristotle (fifth edition, London: Methuen and
    and Company, 1949), p. 228.
58. Cope, An Introduction, p. 235.
59. Rhetoric 1370a.
60. Ibid. 1371b.
61. Ibid.
62. Freese, Art of Rhetoric, pp. 395, 397.
63. Cooper, The Rhetoric, p. 312.

15. AN ASPECT OF DELIVERY IN ANCIENT RHETORICAL THEORY*

by Robert P. Sonkowsky

In John Bulwer's Chirologia and Chironomia, [1] the fullest
account of rhetorical delivery written in England during the Renaissance, there appear some unusual statements about delivery which
are not found as commonplaces in the other rhetorical writings of
the period. [2] I shall quote these statements because they anticipate
the conclusion of this paper and because they make one begin to
wonder what sort of precedent they have in the ancient period when
the theories of delivery that are Bulwer's ultimate sources were
being developed. Writing on the relationship of what he calls the
"language" of delivery to that of words per se, Bulwer says, "The
Speech and Gesture are conceived together in the mind, " and again
on the same subject, "The gestures of the Hand must be prepar'd
in the Mind, together with the inward speech, that precedes the
outward expression. "[3] The basic conception which supplies a context for these statements is the ancient view of delivery as mentis
index. This involves the principle that rhetorical delivery to be
effective must be sustained by impulses of "natural" emotion; i. e.,
the expressions of the voice and the body must seem unfeigned,
sincere and appropriate, as direct signals from the center of
thought and emotion in the mind; the purpose of training in the art
of delivery is to perfect the natural ability to express these signals;
natura and ars overlap one another just as the gestures and inflec-
tions of conversation or "private" speech are similar and often
identical to those of public speech. The chief criticism of most of
the rules for delivery in ancient rhetoric is directed to their pre-
scriptive nature--as against (the rule of) spontaneity. In this way
the classical tradition provides a retort to such criticism. Bulwer's Chirologia--on the "naturall, " conversational gestures--serves
as a necessary foundation for his Chironomia, the "naturall expressions" perfected by art. [3a] In the quoted statements, however, Bulwer seems not only to embrace this principle but also to imply
that the desired effect of delivery could be ensured in the process
of composing the speech. "It appears ... that not only the sound,
but also the gestures, could be imagined at the same moment when

*Reprinted by permission of the author and publisher, from Ameri-
can Philological Association, Transactions and Proceedings 90
(1959), 256-274.

thoughts were turned into language in the mind. "[4]   Moreover, Bulwer represents rhetorical delivery as a language whose expressions
are as capable of definition as printed words.   The numerous plates
which he uses to illustrate gestures are a kind of dictionary.   When
Bulwer's Renaissance orator composed a speech, a language of delivery seems to have been involved directly in his labors of writing in the same way as the language of words, both of which were
to be expressed together in the spoken performance.   As to whether the ancient orators composed in this way, common sense without the aid of scholarship might tell us that authors such as Demosthenes or Cicero probably consulted their sense of effective delivery and imagined gestures, facial expressions, tones of voice
under the same impulses that inspired suitable words.   Moreover,
since ancient literature as a whole is in its nature and origin an
oral literature, we might suppose it to be true that the ancient
orators suited "the action to the word, the word to the action, " not
merely in delivering a speech but especially in composing it.   The
purpose of this paper, however, is to discuss the evidence as to
whether this method of composition was assumed or even advocated
in ancient rhetorical theory.

      Does Aristotle in the Rhetoric so include delivery within the
art and the actual process of literary composition?   In the Poetics
he makes a conspicuous point of excluding the actor's art[5] as a
separate art from that of the tragic poet. [6]   In Aristotle's day the
tragic poets no longer were accustomed to perform their own plays
(Rhet. 1403B23-24).   The orator, however, combined in a certain
way both the making and the performing of the speech in his art.
Aristotle in his somewhat revolutionary book on rhetoric establishes
delivery as one of the elements of the art of rhetoric as a whole.
Aristotle's method of analyzing the components of rhetoric differs
greatly from that of his predecessors.   They had arranged the
rhetorical material under chapters which corresponded to the partes
orationis (exordium, narratio, etc.) and had discussed the rhetorical techniques that could be employed in each "part" of a speech.
Aristotle on the other hand analyzed the individual components of a
speech which pervade it throughout, the elements common to all
the "parts" of a speech.   These elements are the erga (officia) or
"functions" of rhetoric. [7]   He considers delivery as one of these
along with invention, arrangement and style.   Even with regard to
the orator, however, as opposed to the actor, it may be asked
whether delivery is vitally involved in the composing of a speech,
or if delivery is merely something which is added in a superficial
way in the performance after the artistic labors of composition
have been completed.   Aristotle does not give the same kind of
prominence to the element of delivery in the structure of the rhetorical art as he gives to invention, arrangement and style.   These
form the three main divisions, but he includes delivery within his
discussion of style.   Although he treats delivery quite briefly, one
is able to see its relationship to style.   He says:

      Our next subject will concern style.   It is not enough to

know what to say, but one must also know how to say it
(hôs dei eipein).... Following the natural order we first
investigated ... subject matter as a source of persuasion;
second comes the question of style with which the subject
is set out; the third division is ... delivery (Rhet. 1403B
15-22).

From this we may abstract Aristotle's diaeresis according to which
style and delivery are the two divisions of the "how" to speak. [8]
Moreover, he assumes that there would have been no technical concern for delivery unless the matter of style had come into consideration first (1403B35f.). He also considers delivery a matter
of natural talent[9] and quite independent of technê unless it is involved with style περὶ δὲ τὴν λέξιν ἔντεχνον (1404A15f).

The relationship of style and delivery can be seen more
clearly in Aristotle's discussion of the lexis graphikê and the lexis
agônistikê in Rhet. 1413B3-1414A20. Plato in his Phaedrus had
proposed some requirements to be met by anyone attempting a serious treatment of rhetoric. Among other things he will "classify
the different kinds of speech and kinds of soul according to type
and emotional affinities and go through all the causes involved; he
will match the different types with one another and show what kind
of speech must effect persuasion in a particular kind of soul but
not in another and for what reason."[10] Plato apparently wanted
the rhetorician to classify both the qualities of the soul and the
qualities of the speech so as to compare soul and speech according
to mutual compatibilities. In the famous passage on the emotions
Aristotle says that the speech should create the conditions under
which men feel particular emotions (1380A2f.), but he does not list
the correspondences between the emotions in the soul and the types
of speech. He discusses the types of speech separately from the
analysis of the emotions.[11] However, in the passage on the lexis
graphikê and lexis agônistikê he does to a certain extent pair off
the kinds of style with psychological qualities. The lexis graphikê
is the most precise style (akribestatê). It is to be used in compositions designed for a careful reading with the book in the hands
(en chersin). Presumably this style appeals mainly to the intelligence; it is used in forensic oratory more than in the deliberative
kind (ἡ δὲ δικανικὴ ἀκριβεστέρα) since one is speaking to a single un-
distracted judge whose mind is clear (καθαρὰ ἡ κρίσις). The lexis
agônistikê has two aspects: the êthikê and the pathêtikê. This is
the style of plays that are written for a full performance on the
stage as opposed to those designed for a reading;[12] it is also used
in deliberative oratory. In both of these it is important to play
upon the emotions as well as to delineate character.

In the same passage, however, Aristotle goes beyond the
suggestion of psychological affinities between the style and the audience. He is more concerned with what the styles can do than with
their passive qualities.[13] The ergon of the lexis graphikê is
anagnôsis ("a reading")[14] rather than a full performance employing

delivery on a grand scale.   The lexis agônistikê is described as
hypokritikôtatê, and its ergon is delivery (hypokrisis).[14]   The
styles are a pair of ideal classifications; he recognizes a relative
scale between them, along which, presumably, the two could be
mixed together in varying degrees: "Where there is the most
scope for delivery, there is the least precision (akribeia) of style."
Aristotle tells us that the more carefully something is written, the
better it is suited to a reading without full delivery.   It does not
follow that something written for full delivery is always carelessly
written.   On the contrary, in accordance with the ergon of the
lexis agônistikê some very definite stylistic techniques, such as the
repetition of the same word, are used as vehicles for delivery (ὡς
προοδοπιεῖ τῷ ὑποκρίνεσθαι, 1413B22f.).

So far we have discussed the relationship in Aristotle's
Rhetoric of style and delivery, and some mention has been made
of their psychological affinities.   It will be necessary now to go
behind these things into the influence from Plato and from the older
times before rhetoric had been established by anyone as a technê.
In Aristotle's treatment of delivery after he has said that delivery
is entechnon with regard to style (see above, page 253), he continues as follows:

> For this reason actors with histrionic ability also win
> prizes in their turn, just as orators who excel in de-
> livery; for written speeches (graphomenoi logoi) owe their
> effectiveness more to the expression than to the thought
> (1404A18-19).

There seems at first sight to be no obvious reason for using the
word graphomenoi.   Surely the suggestion of Cope-Sandys (ad. loc.)
that the epideiktikon genos is meant cannot be correct unless Aristotle is inconsistent.   Epideictic in the lexis graphikê is the most
accurately written of the three kinds of discourse and depends the
least upon delivery, the counterpart of style, for its effectiveness
(see above, page 253).   The technical term lexis graphikê must not
be confused with graphomenos logos, which means "a speech that is
written down."   Speeches in the lexis agônistikê can also be graphomenoi.   But why does Aristotle scruple to use this word at all?
Recall that Plato in the Phaedrus had had some rather hard things
to say of the speech that is "written down" (gegrammenos logos
277Dff.).   Plato's strictures on writing are well known, while Aristotle nowhere speaks in disparagement of it.[15]   It is indeed worth
noting that Plato did write his dialogues and that Aristotle published
less during his maturity as he did more oral teaching; thus Plato
and Aristotle seem in a paradoxical way to agree to a certain extent on the question of the value of writing.[16]   However, in respect
to rhetoric as a technê they are found, I think, in disagreement.
Professor James A. Notopoulos[17] has given a pertinent analysis of
the background for Plato's disapproving the invention of writing.
He shows evidence of the struggle that took place in the transition
from oral literature of the Homeric type to literature that was

committed to writing. There was a strong prejudice against "the
encroachment of the written word upon the spoken word" partly because the use of writing tended to destroy the memory, which was
valued highly among the ancient oral peoples. The prejudice
against writing is seen in several places in ancient literature and
is reflected in the myth of Theuth and Thamus, which Plato play-
fully adapts to his argument on writing in the Phaedrus (274E-
275A). Theuth, a "culture hero" like Prometheus, had discovered
numbers, arithmetic, geometry, astronomy and letters. He boasts
to Thamus, King of Egypt, that his invention of letters will aid the
memory of the Egyptians and make them wiser. Theuth replies
that letters will do just the opposite because people who use them
will not practise their memory and will become forgetful; writing
will improve not memory (mnêmê), but reminding (hypomnêsis).
Notopoulos shows that Plato while opposing the use of the written
word advocates a certain kind of memory, "not the memory of the
written word, which is simply a static and retentive memory, but
the creative memory or oral literature." Notopoulos demonstrates
that memory is used in ancient oral poetry of the pregraphic era
as a means in the process of oral composition. Including in his
argument the evidence of Milman Parry's computations of the number and frequency of formulas in the Homeric poems, he points
out that the oral poet memorized a vast and complex system of
formulas in order to compose orally. "There is no place for passive memory in this technique, for the formulas vary in length
and are fused together in the very heat of oral recitation." A
slight qualification is needed here as to the distinction between composition by oral memory and by written memory. Homer and other
oral poets may have used writing as notes or hypomnêmata, in
planning the general direction of a poem.[17a] Conversely while the
orators trained in rhetoric relied primarily on mnemonic systems
for the purpose of "passive" or retentive memory, yet their memorization of commonplaces for use in extempore speaking has a
slight similarity to the memorization and use of formulas in oral
composition. This may dull the edges of the distinction, but it
seems to have been none the less a valid one for Plato who advocates a relatively active kind of memory, used creatively in oral
composition, rather than the written memory of books. He tells
us that the written word is only "an image of the living and breathing word of the philosopher" (Phaedrus 276A). This conviction is
a "reappearance in Plato's philosophy of the old conflict between
memory and letters." The oral dialectician such as Socrates must,
like the poet of earlier times, compose with the aid of oral memory. Since Plato had postulated an art of rhetoric based on dialectic and had criticized the "written" aspect of speech making, it
is highly improbable that Aristotle would have ignored him on a
matter so essential to dialectic. It is, therefore, possible to think
that Aristotle in this passage mentions the dependence of "written
speeches" upon style and delivery not in reference to epideictic
oratory which he has not been talking about, but as a subtle answer to Plato on a matter essential to the whole art of rhetoric. If
so, it is as if Aristotle were saying that written speeches must

differ from oral dialectic for they properly "derive their power
(ischyousi) from the expression more than from the thought (1404A
19)."

Plato in the Phaedrus and Aristotle in the Rhetoric both
want an art of rhetoric based on dialectic; for Aristotle, however,
the correspondence between the two arts was close, but not exact
(ἡ ῥητορική ἐστιν ἀντίστροφος τῆ διαλεκτικῆ [1354A1]).[18] In the oral
composition advocated by Plato the creative use of oral memory
makes composition and performance identical, i.e., the oral poet
or the dialectician speaks his thoughts to his listeners directly
from the workings of his memory without advance preparation held
in writing or in the retentive memory. It is in this sense that
Plato speaks of "the living and breathing word of the philosopher."
How was the orator of the era of the merely retentive memory to
match oral dialectic in liveliness and spontaneity? Aristotle may
already have answered this in part when he spoke of the graphomenoi logoi, i.e., through attention to style and its counterpart,
delivery, in "written speeches" which depend for their effect upon
the expression more than the sense. This will be discussed more
fully below where it will be seen that Aristotle perceived a vital
power in "written" composition that was especially suitable to the
art of rhetoric, in which style and delivery were more important
than in dialectic. First, however, let us ask just how much
prominence "the expression" has over "the thought" in Aristotle's
theory of the two styles. For Plato states his objection to the
written speech in other terms as well as those mentioned above.
He says that writing is like a painting of living creatures (zôgraphia); the creatures stand in the painting as if alive, but if one asks
them a question, they maintain a solemn silence. It is the same
with the written word; the audience has no chance to ask questions
(Phaedrus 275D). Written words cannot defend themselves by argument and cannot adequately convey the truth (276C). This leads to
the question why did Aristotle choose graphikê as the technical
term for the "most accurate style," whose function is "a reading"?
He may have been thinking of Plato's objection to the logos gegrammenos since graphikê pertains to the care taken in the writing (cf.
graphein, 1413B8). At the same time he may have intended to
echo Plato's comparison of the written speech with painting, in
which Plato plays with the words graphê, "writing," and zôgraphia,
"painting" (see above); for graphikê sometimes refers also to painting (e.g., Rhet. 1371B6, cf. Plato Gorg. 450C), and it is altogether possible that Aristotle is taking advantage of the ambivalence
of "graph" in the same way as Plato. If so, Aristotle would seem
to be replying to Plato that instead of defending itself by argument
a written speech can employ the accuracy (akribeia) of the lexis
graphikê and make unnecessary any further clarification by question
and answer. We may support this interpretation by noting in the
same passage an unmistakable comparison between a speech and
painting. Deliberative oratory, which is in the lexis agônistikê, is
compared not to zôgraphia ("painting from life, realistic painting")
but to skiagraphia ("painting in outline, rough sketch"). Aristotle's

basis of comparison is not that both "skiagraphic" painting and deliberative oratory are lifeless and unable to respond to questions,
but that both achieve their effect from a distance where too much
attention to close details would be wasted (1414A7-10). If Aristotle
is making a retort to Plato as the echoes of thought and words suggest, Aristotle implies that it is not proper to demand the dialectical method of question and answer in this style of speaking.   The
function, hypokrisis, of the lexis agônistikê is such that the orator
in a sense can only "answer," as if in reply to his audience who
have not literally asked any questions.   However, it will be seen
that in the Aristotelian rhetorical tradition it is hypokrisis itself
that produces in effect the same identity of composition and performance which was produced by the "living and breathing word" of
oral memory.   So far we have suggested only that in developing a
technê of rhetoric which depends on invention, arrangement, style
and delivery, all conjured in the labors of writing itself, Aristotle
draws respectability to rhetoric from a quarter which Plato had
disparaged.

Plato also disparages in some ways the part played in utterance by the operation of divine inspiration.[19]   Miss Alice
Sperduti[20] has traced the history of the ancient belief in divinity
as the source of literary inspiration from its origin in mythological
period in connection with the divine enthousiasmos of manticism
and the divine mission of the poet in the community.   A key aspect of divine inspiration was its association with the emotional
state of mantic frenzy.   Plato shows his distrust of this in the
Phaedrus as well as in the Ion; he views it largely as a state of
separation from logos.[21]   It is with this in mind that he makes
fun of Phaedrus' apparently inspired reading of Lysias' speech
when Socrates begins his criticism of Lysias' rhetorikon (Phaedrus
234Df.).   To Aristotle, however, in his discussion of to prepon
inspired discourse depends on τὸ ... εὐκαίρως ἤ μὴ εὐκαίρως χρῆσθαι
(Rhet. 1408A36-B20).   An orator may use the techniques of a certain exaggerated style when he "has" his audience and they are
filled with "enthusiasm."   The style of orators who are enthousi-
azontes "is also appropriate to poetry, for poetry is an inspired
thing (entheon)."   A comparison between the divine ecstasy of the
poet and the orator's feeling the emotions which he wishes to
arouse in his audience persists in the later rhetorical tradition;
all the examples of this that I have found pertain largely to the
manner of delivery.[22]   This perhaps was to be expected since
Aristotle fixed delivery as an aspect of rhetoric which is directly
linked with the emotions.   "Delivery is a matter of how to use
the voice for each particular emotion (pros hekaston pathos, 1403B
26f.)."   It must be noted that in linking delivery specifically with
pathos Aristotle does not mean to exclude êthos and logical argument.   He indicates the connection between delivery and êthos and
pathos when he says that the lexis hypokritkôtatê comprises the
êthikê and the pathêtikê (see above, page 253).   It appears that
logical argument also has some need for delivery (διαφέρει γάρ τι
πρὸς τὸ δηλῶσαι ὡδὶ ἤ ὡδὶ εἰπεῖν (1404A10).   Aristotle would include

the expression of cold fact as a possible use of delivery, he would definitely add the expression of character, but apparently he observed that delivery is particularly adapted to the expression of feeling.   In accordance with the doctrine of to prepon, mentioned above, delivery as well as style would express logical argument, êthos, or pathos, giving more prominence to one or the other as the occasion required.   For example, at the appropriate moment an orator might depart so far from logical thought as to speak from inspiration.   Aristotle may have discussed the subject of inspiration in the rhetorical art more fully with his students. 23   In regard to this possibility, since we have soon to mention Aristotle's most productive student, it seems pertinent to note that Aristotle changed his name from Tyrtamus to Theophrastus, a name compounded of theos and phrazô (Diog. Laert. 5. 38).   However, the point has been made that at least from Plato's time divine inspiration began to be associated in a technical way with the emotional feeling and expression of the orator.   If it can be assumed that rhetoric absorbed more influences than those of a linear history of technai going back to Corax and Tisias, one may suggest that some of the elements of inspiration with its frenzied glances, tones, rhythms, postures, emotions were taken over from the more ancient development into rhetoric; that these elements were caught and preserved by Aristotle and others in the technê, especially under the headings of the emotions and delivery.

    Aristotle did not work out a theory of delivery in detail; he left this to Theophrastus. 24   In a way, however, Aristotle had done the ground work.   In his famous analysis of pathê (Rhet. 1378A31-1388B30) and ethê (1388B31-1391B7) he carefully defines each emotion and the types of character and gives shrewd psychological observations in a methodical way.   Professor Friedrich Solmsen has gathered considerable evidence tending to show that no rhetorician from a time after Aristotle, until Cicero, discussed the emotions and character as a primary subject of rhetoric. 25   On the other hand Theophrastus expanded the technical material on delivery, the external expression of the emotions and character.   It is difficult to say why the treatment of the emotions and of character dropped out of rhetorical theory.   It has been suggested that the Stoics influenced the later systems of rhetoric in this way, especially through Hermagoras, with their disapproval of arousing the emotions. 26   It is possible too that there was a practical reason. When Aristotle wrote his detailed analysis of êthê and pathê, he carried out Plato's suggestion that an orator must have an understanding of the psychê.   After that had been done, the orator presumably, in order to master his art, also needed to know the outward signs (signa, charactêres) of the inward motions (kinêsis tês psychês) with which Aristotle had been concerned.   He himself had supplied the hint that delivery should be used pros hekaston pathos and that the lexis hypokritikôtatê (agônistikê) consisted of the êthikê and the pathêtikê.

    If Stoicism influenced the destiny of the rhetorical theory of emotions, some influence may have come from the Stoic view of the natural source of emotional expression in the psychê. According to this view the thoughts and emotions which originated within the psyche through the logos endiathetos were expressed by means of the logos prophorikos. The Stoics defined the logos prophorikos as φωνὴ διὰ γλώττης σημαντικὴ τῶν ἔνδον καὶ κατὰ ψυχὴν παθῶν (Porphyr. De abstin. 3.3).[27] It is possible to consider this conception as the background against which a shift of emphasis in rhetorical studies took place. Plato and Aristotle emphasized "psychology," but Aristotle prepared the way to the study of the outward expressions of the psychê by briefly incorporating delivery into rhetoric. Theophrastus expanded delivery, and the Stoics followed him by including delivery in their rhetorical scheme (Diog. Laert. 7.43). Theophrastus himself may have begun to bring the theory of delivery into harmony with Aristotle's whole analysis of the emotions, but is difficult to say just what Theophrastus contributed in this way since we do not know to what extent Cicero and others who wrote on delivery are indebted to him.[28] At any rate as the amount of material on the techniques of delivery increased, the orators may have gained some practical benefit from this new emphasis even at the expense of neglecting somewhat the study of the emotions which ought to accompany delivery. However, the Hellenistic rhetoricians apparently developed more and more rules of delivery; the pedantic nature of their endless divisions of the kinds of delivery is reflected in a long passage of the Ad Herennium (3.23-27).[29] As they continued to neglect the Aristotelian tradition of the knowledge of the emotions, they seem at the same time to have enfeebled the theory of delivery.

It remained for Cicero to go back to the ratio Aristotelia and to apply his own talents to rhetoric. Aristotle had divided inventio into three kinds of "proofs": apodeixis, êthos, pathos. Cicero in the De oratore is the first author known to have returned to this scheme.[30] He does not discuss exactly the same subject as Aristotle did under êthos; for Cicero this is not the speaker's character but the leniores affectus, a lesser degree of pathos.[31] But by following Aristotle's tripartite division as a pattern he restores to the theory of the emotions the same degree of prominence as in Aristotle's Rhetoric. It is also important to notice how Cicero's approach to the subject of the emotions differs from Aristotle's.[32] Aristotle defines and describes êthê and pathê in themselves so as to give the knowledge needed by the orator for finding his means of persuasion. Cicero does less of this; instead he includes information on the external techniques to be used. He stresses the signa of the leniores affectus and recommends the proper tone of voice, facial expression, language and a certain technique of delivery whereby the orator can give the impression of being under involuntary compulsion when his attack is too vehement (De or. 2.182). Cicero assumes that the orator must have a knowledge of the stronger emotions as well as the techniques of arousing them, for he thinks the orator must himself feel the emotions of his speech in order to impart them to his audience (2.189).

This would not necessarily call for a systematic knowledge but at
least for an empirical knowledge. Even here, however, as one
might expect, Cicero again includes the visible signs of the emotions: e. g. ... neque ad misericordiam adduceretur (iudex), nisi
tu ei signa doloris tui verbis, sententiis, voce, vultu, collacrima-
tione ... ostenderis (2. 190).

    Even if we had no evidence of a traditional connection be-
tween the emotions and delivery, it would not be surprising to find
that Cicero discusses them together; for he tells us that content
and form are not separable and that eloquence is a unity no matter
how it may be divided into chapters for purposes of discussion
(De or. 3. 19-24; 37; cf. Orator 61). Accordingly in the chapter
on style in the De oratore we find that one of the most important
principles is discussed in terms of delivery. Crassus illustrates
the avoidance of satietas in the grand style by describing the delivery of Roscius and Aesopus of some lines of tragedy (3. 98-103).
At the end of the chapter on the techniques of style Cicero reminds
us that style and delivery are traditionally (see above, page 253)
associated under the single rubric of "how" to speak: Haec omnia
perinde sunt ut aguntur (3. 213). He then proceeds in the chapter
on delivery to show how delivery in turn is bound to the emotions
(3. 216). In the Orator he states the relationship of delivery, style
and emotions in a brief passage which could almost stand as a
summary of the three as treated in the De oratore (Orator 55):

> Quo modo ... dicatur, id est in duobus: in agendo et in
> eloquendo.... Vocis mutationes totidem sunt quot ani-
> morum.... Perfectus (orator) ... utcumque se affectum
> videri et animum audientis moveri volet, ita certum vocis
> admovebit sonum.

    This passage will serve in turn to introduce the next sub-
ject of this paper. Cicero seems to be saying something similar
to Aristotle's πῶς (φωνῇ) δεῖ χρῆσθαι πρὸς ἕκαστον πάθος (see above,
page 258). It may seem difficult to believe that Cicero means a
"fixed" (certum, "predetermined") tone of voice for each emotion,
for this would imply that an author creates the delivery of a speech
while in the actual process of composing the language. At this
point in the argument we might accept this interpretation as a factual statement of a principle in the Aristotelian tradition, but we
are fortunate in having the additional assurance of Cicero's fuller
treatment of delivery in the De oratore (3. 213-27). Here he says,
"Nature has assigned to every emotion its own particular facial expression, tone of voice and gesture."[33] He describes the operation of this principle only in the voice but implies that facial expression and gesture operate in the same way (cf. 3. 220 ff.). By
"nature" Cicero does not mean sine arte, but natura ab arte perfecta. [34] Nature and training in the art of delivery together produce and establish a genus vocis for each emotion (3. 215f.). There
are of course many things which we do not know about Cicero's
terminology of the voice and about certain phonetic aspects of the

Latin language, [35] but Cicero explains very plainly the principle of
the general tones that are fixed in the voice.   Another author
might well express his despair of trying to portray the use of the
voice in writing (e. g., the author of the Ad Herennium 3. 27), but
Cicero uses the term genera vocis in an illuminating comparison
with the strings of a lyre. [36]   The sounds of the voice are fixed by
nature and by the control of art in the same way as the strings of
a lyre are set in tune.   The sounds of the voice express emotions
in the same way as the strings of the lyre respond to the touch.
Different emotional impulses (touches) activate different sounds of
the voice (strings).   The sounds referred to are the various qualities of the voice (strings).   Each quality consists of a range of
sounds which is defined by its two extremes (acuta-gravis, cita-
tarda, magna-parva); between each pair of extremes there is a
medium sound.   Each quality so defined is a genus vocis.   From
combinations of the three basic qualities (acuta-gravis, etc.) other
qualities are derived.   Cicero then leaves the comparison with the
lyre and takes up the emotions with a description of the genera
vocis which are bound to each emotion: iracundia, miseratio ac
moeror, metus, vis, voluptas, molestia.   For Cicero each one of
these is a separate, well-differentiated motus animi. [37]   Each genus
vocis is correspondingly defined in exact terms (3. 217-19).   In the
chapter on the emotions Cicero compares the orator's ability to
feel for himself the emotions of his speech with the way in which
the actor feels the emotions of his role and with the way in which
the poet was "inspired" with them when he wrote the play (in scri-
bendo, 2. 193f.).   In the present passage he gives the techniques to
be used to insure a sharp expression of the emotional content of a
speech.   The assumption of Cicero is that before the speech is delivered to an audience the genera vocis are already as much a part
of the speech as the written words.   It is on the basis of this assumption that he is able to illustrate the genera vocis as he does
with quotations from dramatic poetry.   There is nothing unusual
about using quotations in this way; e. g., Aristotle quoted dramatic
poetry to show the stylistic devices in the lexis hypokritikôtatê
(agônistikê) which require certain kinds of delivery (Rhet. 1413B21-
1414A7, see above, page 254).   Similarly Cicero probably means
to demonstrate each genus vocis not only with the meaning of the
quotations but also with the style in which they were written. [38]

It remains only to strengthen the argument of this paper by
adding the support of a few passages on delivery in Quintilian,
whose dependence upon the rhetorical writings of Cicero is conspicuous and well known. [39]   Quintilian too stresses the connection between the emotions and delivery (Inst. orat. 11. 3. 61f.); he clearly
includes êthê and pathê within the province of delivery (commenda-
tione morum, qui ... ex voce ... atque actione pellucent, 11. 3. 154;
movendi ... ratio aut in repraesentandis est aut imitandis affecti-
bus, ibid. 156).   Cicero had said that if the orator did not readily
feel for himself the emotions of his speech, some higher kind of
art (maior ars) would perhaps be required (De or. 2. 189).   Quintilian supplies this art; he suggests that one can kindle his own

emotions by calling to mind <u>phantasiai</u> or <u>visiones</u>, images of the
facts of a case; such <u>visiones</u> are involved in dreams and cause
the poet to write vividly (6.2.29-33). He recommends this for effective delivery when the proper emotion does not come of its own
accord (11.3.62). In discussing the causes of some faults of delivery Quintilian quite incidentally makes a revealing remark concerning the operation of delivery in the actual process of composing a speech. He finds that a fault of delivery derives from the
existence of certain subtle stresses in language which are like
metrical feet; most people gesture on these stresses; the fault is
that when young orators write and when they plan their gestures by
meditating (<u>cum scribunt gestum praemodulati cogitatione</u>), they
compose their speeches according to the way the hand falls on
these subtle stresses (11.3.108f.). Other writers probably take
for granted the activity of delivery in the process of composition.
It is fortunate that Quintilian mentions this, even if incidentally.
Whatever was John Bulwer's immediate source, we now have further confirmation of the existence of ancient precedents for his
statement, "The gestures of the <u>Hand</u> must be prepar'd in the
Mind, together with the inward speech, that precedes the outward
expression."

In this paper we have examined evidence concerning in in-
terpenetration of delivery and literary composition in ancient rhetorical theory. Since this evidence comes largely from rhetorical
manuals, the conclusions pertain in the first place to oratory itself, but they could be extended to all forms of literature in the
same way as the rhetoricians themselves include other forms of
literature in their analyses of style and delivery. The scope of
this paper has been restricted to the development of ancient rhetorical theory itself and to some influences that worked upon it. The
extensions that can be made to ancient literature in practice will
have to be the subject of further research. On the basis of the
evidence pertaining to theory, however, this conclusion may be advanced, that in the Aristotelian tradition, which includes the Theo-
phrastan and the Ciceronian, the techniques of delivery are not
merely something that is added in a superficial way after the process of literary composition has been completed, but something that
is vitally involved in the very labors of composition anticipating the
public presentation. As evidence of this the theoretical interpene-
trations of delivery, style and the emotions have been examined in
the rhetorical tradition. It was suggested in addition that the history of ancient literature before the invention and/or extensive use
of writing and before the technical study of rhetoric made this important aspect of delivery inevitable. From the ancient quarrel of
philosophy and rhetoric, in the form it took between Plato and
Aristotle, evidence was selected tending to show that the rhetorical
delivery of the written speech competed in a certain way with the
spontaneously vivid manner of oral composition; it was also shown
that rhetorical delivery in the Aristotelian tradition lays claim to
something resembling divine inspiration. The beginnings of all
these things are found in Aristotle's <u>Rhetoric.</u> Some inferences

were drawn as to the uncertain period from Aristotle to the author
of the Ad Herennium, chiefly that the theory of delivery suffered
from the absence of the Aristotelian way of studying the emotions.
Cicero revived the study of the emotions and gave new life to the
theory of delivery. His explanation of the genera vocis shows
most clearly how delivery expresses the emotions and how it is involved in composition so as to anticipate the public presentation.
Certain passages of Quintilian serve to confirm these conclusions.

NOTES

1. John Bulwer, Chirologia: or the Naturall Language of the
    Hand. Composed of the Speaking Motions, and Discoursing
    Gestures thereof. Whereunto is added Chironomia; or the
    Art of Manuall Rhetoricke. Consisting of the Naturall Ex-
    pressions, Digested by Art in the Hand, as the Chiefest In-
    strument of Eloquence. (London 1644.) Part 1, Chirologia
    and part 2, Chironomia, were issued together with the same
    title page. "Digested" here means "reduced to order."
    Bulwer's view descends from the ancient conception of de-
    livery as natura ab arte perfecta. See below, pages 258-59
    and 269, and notes 27 and 34.
2. B. L. Joseph, Elizabethan Acting (Oxford 1951) 29.
3. Bulwer (above, note 1) Chirol., 4. Chiron. 142. Cf. Quint.
    Inst. orat. 11.3.62 on the voice as mentis index, and
    11.3.65 on gesture: "animo cum ea (voce) simul paret. "
3a. The title page of Bulwer's work (above, note 1) indicates his
    view of natura and ars. Cf. Ibid. Chirol., 4f. The princi-
    ple of natura ab arte perfecta shows a vigorous continuation
    in rhetorical instruction in this country. See J. A. Winans,
    Public Speaking (New York 1923) 20-49, 468-473; cf. W. M.
    Parrish, "Whatley on Elocution, " The Rhetorical Idiom
    (Ithaca 1958, ed. D. C. Bryant) 43-52; R. H. Wagner "Con-
    versational Quality in Delivery, " Speech Training and Public
    Speaking for Secondary Schools (New York and London 1925,
    ed. A. M. Drummond) 52-62.
4. Joseph (above, note 2) 29.
5. Some actors according to Aristotle performed dia technês, and
    others dia synêtheias (1447A20). The latter is similar to
    the Platonic term empeiria; cf. Bywater, Aristotle on the
    Art of Poetry (Oxford 1909) 102. On the other hand Aris-
    totle polemicizes against Plato to some extent in claiming
    delivery as a technê; see Plato, Rep. 3. 395A-396B, 397A;
    Arist. Poet 1447A18-24; and cf. Gerald Else, Aristotle's
    Poetics (Cambridge [Mass.] 1957) 20-I.
6. He does so most expressly in 1461B26-62A14 where he de-
    fends the tragic form of imitation against the charge that it
    is inferior to the epic form because the tragic actors exag-
    gerate their gestures for the crowd; cf. Else (above, note 5)
    640-42. See Else also, ibid. 24, note 91, for references
    to passages from other works of Aristotle showing that he

thought of the phônê, the chief medium of the actor, as the mere carrier of the logos, the medium of the poet.

7. See Friedrich Solmsen, "The Aristotelian Tradition in Ancient Rhetoric, " AJP 62 (1941) 35-50, 169-90. Cf. Aristotle's similar treatment of the art of poetry in the Poetics 1447A 8-18, and see Solmsen, "The Origin and Methods of Aristotle's Poetics, " CQ 29 (1935) 192-201; Else (above, note 5) 3-16. Both the pre-Aristotelian and the Aristotelian methods of rhetorical analysis persisted in later manuals on rhetoric; these are classified by Karl Barwick, "Die Gliederung der rhetorischen ΤΕΧΝΗ und die horazische Epistula ad Pisones," Hermes 57 (1922) 1ff.

8. Cf. Quo modo ... dicatur id est in duobus: in agendo et in eloquendo (Cic. Orat. 55).

9. esti physeôs; cf. above, note 5.

10. Δῆλον ἄρα ὅτι ὁ Θρασύμαχός τε καὶ ὅς ἄν ἄν ἄλλος σπουδῆ τέχνην ῥητορικὴν διδῷ ... διαταξάμενος τὰ λόγων τε καὶ ψυχῆς γένη καὶ τὰ τούτων παθήματα δίεισι πάσας αἰτίας, προσαρμόττων ἕκαστον ἑκάστω καὶ διδάσκων οἷα οὖσα νφ' οἵων λόγων δι' ἥν αἰτίαν ἐξ ἀνάγκης ἡ μὲν πείθεται, ἡ δὲ ἀπειθει. (Phaedrus 271Af.). It is possible that the introductory sentence of Aristotle's discussion may be intended to echo the above passage: Δεῖ δὲ μὴ λεληθέναι ὅτι ἄλλη ἑκάστω γένει ἁρμόττει λέξις (Rhet. 1413B3f.). It is also possible that the three verbal correspondences may be mere coincidence since Aristotle does not mean γένει ψυχῆς τε καὶ λόγων but only γένει λόγων. He had already dealt with the requirement concerning the psychê in the famous passage on êthos and pathos in Rhet. 1378Aff; see below, page 258. On this point and on the influence of Plato's Phaedrus upon Aristotle's treatment of pathos see the "appendix" in Solmsen, "The Orator's Playing upon the Feelings, " CP 33 (1938) 402-4. For a bibliography concerning the well-known points of contact between the Phaedrus and the Rhetoric see ibid. 402, note 38; cf. W. Rhys Roberts, "References to Plato in Aristotle's Rhetoric, " CP 19 (1924) 342-46.

11. He uses the standard classification of speeches, deliberative, forensic and epideictic in 1358B-1369B, 1414A-1417B.

12. I translate anagôsis "a reading" to avoid the notion of silent comprehension which is usually conveyed by the current use of the word "reading. " Cf. δεῖ εὐανάγνωστον εἶναι τὸ γεγραμμένον καὶ εὔφραστον· ἔστι δὲ τὸ αὐτό (Rhet. 1407B11f.). Concerning the fact that the ancients customarily read orally, "eine vielleicht wenigen bekannte Tatsache, " see Norden, Die antike Kunstprosa 6 and "Nachträge, " pages 1-2.

13. Plato had demanded an account of the pathêmata logôn (above, note 10). Aristotle emphasizes in this passage the erga (poiêmata) or "active functions. "

14. The exact difference between anagnôsis and hypokrisis would be difficult to define; see above, note 12; cf. distinctio vs. pronuntiatio in Maurice P. Cunningham, "Some Phonetic Aspects of Word Order Patterns in Latin, " PAPS 101 (1957)

503, cf. 494, 497f.
15. See W. Rhys Roberts, Greek Rhetoric and Literary Criticism
    (New York 1928) 54-5; cf. Arist. Soph. elen. 1836b-1846;
    see James A. Notopoulos, "Mnemosyne in Oral Literature, "
    TAPA 69 (1938) 476-85; W. C. Greene, "The Spoken and
    the Written Word, " HSCP 60 (1951) 23-24, 45-52.
16. Cf. Greene (above, note 15) 50, 52; Jaeger, Aristotle 317.
17. Notopoulos (above, note 15) 471-76.
17a. Cf. Greene (above, note 15) 31.
18. See Cope-Sandys ad. loc.
19. E.g., Phaedrus 234Df., 245A; cf. ibid. 238D, 241E which
    probably are the passages referred to by Aristotle, Rhet.
    1408B19f., as being in the "enthusiastic" style μετ'
    εἰρωνείας. Cf. Ion; e.g., ὁ θεὸς ἐξαιρούμενος τούτων τὸν νοῦν
    (534C).
20. Alice Sperduti, "The Divine Nature of Poetry in Antiquity, "
    TAPA 81 (1950) 209-40.
21. Cf. Sperduti (above, note 20) 238.
22. Ne hoc in nobis (oratoribus) mirum esse videatur, quid potest
    esse tam fictum quam versus, quam scaena, quam fabu-
    lae? ... Si ... histrio, cotidie cum (versus ex tragoedia
    Pacuvii) ageret, tamen agere sine dolore non poterat, quid
    Pacuvium putatis in scribendo leni animo ac remisso
    fuisse? Saepe enim audivi poetam bonum neminem--id quod
    a Democrito et Platone in scriptis relictum esse dicunt--
    sine inflammatione animorum exsistere posse, et sine quo-
    dam afflatu quasi furoris. Cic. De or. 2.193f.; cf. furiosis-
    sime, Sen. Contr. 10.5.21; phrenetici, ibid. 27; see esp.
    plena deo, Sen. Suas. 3, 6; cf. Kroll, "Rhetorik, " RE Sup-
    plementband 7.1076.26-46.
23. For enthousiasmos as an emotion in the soul and as subject
    to purgation along with pity and fear, see Pol. 1340A2-12,
    1342A6-11.
24. See Kroll (above, note 22) 1075, 23-50; Stroux, De Theo-
    phrasti virtutibus dicendi (Leipzig 1912) 70f.; Maximilian
    Schmidt, Commentatio de Theophrasto rhetore (Halle 1839)
    61.
25. Solmsen (above, note 10) 394-96; Solmsen (above, note 7),
    178. Cicero treats the affectus in De. or 2.48.185-52.211;
    see below (pages 257-58).
26. Solmsen (above, note 7) 178.
27. Cf. Horace, Ars poetica 108-11:
        format enim natura prius nos intus ad omnem fortunarum
        habitum; iuvat aut impellit ad iram aut ad humum mae-
        rore gravi deducit et angit; post effert animi motus inter-
        prete lingua.
    See Kiessling-Heinze ad loc.; cf. G. C. Fiske and M. A.
    Grant, Cicero's De oratore and Horace's Ars Poetica (Madi-
    son [Wis.] 1929) 113.
28. Cf. Athanasius, Proleg. rhet. (ca. saec. IV): θεόφραστος ...
    φησὶν εἶναι μέγιστον ῥητορικῇ πρὸς τὸ πεῖσαι τὴν ὑπόκρισιν, εἰς
    τὰς ἀρχὰς ἀναφέρων καὶ τὰ πάθη τῆς ψυχῆς καὶ τὴν κατανόησιν

τούτων, ὡς καὶ τῇ ὅλῃ ἐπιστήμῃ σύμφωνον εἶναι τὴν κίνησιν τοῦ σώματος καὶ τὸν τόνον τῆς ψυχῆς (Walz, vol. 6, 35f.). Cf. also Kroll (above, note 22) 1075. 34-43; Solmsen (above, note 7) 45f.; H. Caplan, Rhet. ad Herennium 191, note b; H. Rabe, Proleg. syll. 177.

29. Cf. H. Caplan (above, note 28) 194, note c; Kroll (above, note 22) 1075. 48-50.

30. Solmsen (above, note 10) 398.

31. L. Voit, Deinotês, Ein antiker Stilbegriff (Leipzig 1934) 135-40. Cf. Quint. Inst. orat. 6. 2. 9.

32. The most noticeable correspondences between the two treatments in the De oratore and the Rhetoric are those between 2. 206 and 1380B35ff. and between 2. 211 and 1385B13ff. Cf. Solmsen (above, note 10) 397.

33. Omnis enim motus animi suum quendam a natura habet voltum et sonum et gestum (De or. 3. 216). Cf. Philod. 1. 196. 8.

34. Cf. ... sine dubio in omni re vincit imitationem veritas, sed ea si satis in actione efficeret ipsa per sese, arte profecto non egeremus; verum quia animi permotio ... perturbata saepe ita est ut obscuretur, ... discutienda sunt ea, quae obscurant, et ea, quae sunt eminentia et pompta, sumenda (3. 215). For Cicero's conception of natura ab arte perfecta see Fiske and Grant (above, note 27) 83f.

35. But see Cunningham (above, note 14) 481-505.

36. ... totumque corpus hominis et eius omnis vultus omnesque voces, ut nervi in fidibus, ita sonant ut a motu animi quoque sunt pulsae. Nam voces ut chordae sunt intentae quae ad quemque tactum respondeant, acuta gravis, cita tarda, magna parva, quas tamen inter omnes est suo quaeque in genere mediocris; atque etiam illa sunt ab his delapsa plura genera, lene asperum, contractum diffusum, continenti spiritu intermisso, fractum scissum, flexo sono attenuatum inflatum (De or. 3. 216).

37. See quotation above, note 34. Cicero deliberately casts out anything which might blur the distinctions between separate emotions. Today there is often the opposite tendency to lump the whole gamut of human feelings obscurely into two vague groups; in general people say they are either "feeling good/ happy" or "depressed. "

38. Although the terms used by Cicero to describe each genus vocis are specifically applied to delivery in this passage, Cicero and others apply the same terms and their kind to style (genera discendi) as well. See Charles Henderson, Jr., A Lexicon of the Stylistic Terms Used in Roman Literary Criticism (Diss., Chapel Hill [N. C.] 1954) passim. On the intimate connection of delivery with word order see Cunningham (above, note 14) 481-505.

39. See Kroll (above, note 22) 1105. 14-24.

16. STASIS IN ARISTOTLE'S RHETORIC*

by Wayne N. Thompson

     A commonly held oversimplification is the belief that stasis as a rhetorical doctrine began with Hermagoras of Temnos in the late second century B.C. The more accurate appraisal, as Ray Nadeau points out, is that Hermagoras is responsible for the first detailed and systematic treatment but that antecedents are to be found in earlier works, including Aristotle's. [1]

     For antecedents the modern scholar can look profitably at several parts of the Aristotelian corpus. Both Nadeau and Otto Alvin Loeb Dieter[2] have made such analyses, but neither has reported a detailed examination of the Rhetoric as an early source of ideas on stasis. The purposes of the present article are to supplement the studies by Nadeau and Dieter, to compare books i and ii of the Rhetoric with book iii, to characterize stasis as it appears in the Rhetoric, and to examine the relation of the treatment of stasis in the Rhetoric with that by Hermagoras and those who followed him.

Preceding Studies of Stasis in Aristotle's Works

     The only major modern studies of stasis are those of Nadeau and Dieter cited above. What does each of them say about Aristotle as a possible source for the clearly developed doctrine that was to come later?

     Nadeau, although he mentions the Rhetoric as a source for material on stasis, centers his examination on the Topics and apparently the Categories. He mentions the ten categories without identifying specifically the work of that name and then takes up the predicables. In a well-developed paragraph he names the predicables and shows that they "constitute a plan of inquiry which enables one to analyze a subject more easily."[3] He then points out that the "Stoics had a similar fourfold plan for arriving at judgments necessary and basic in the study of matter"[4] and that both

*Reprinted by permission of the author and of the Speech Communication Association, from Quarterly Journal of Speech 58 (1972), 134-141.

the Aristotelian predicables and the Stoic categories correspond
closely to the four stases of Hermagoras. Nadeau presents all of
these ideas with such detail and clarity that further elaboration
here is inappropriate. To summarize, Aristotle's Organon, especially the Categories and the Topics, includes, although not as a
primary feature, an early treatment of the doctrine of stasis.

Dieter in his analysis goes to a different part of Aristotle's
corpus than does Nadeau. He sees the physical sciences, especially the Physics, the Generation of Animals, and the Parts of Animals, as the critical works for gaining a full and true understanding of stasis. Hence, although he refers also to the Organon, the
Metaphysics, and the Nicomachean Ethics, his basic position is that
an understanding of stasis is possible only if one has a sound grasp
of the relevant parts of the Physics and related works. As in
Nadeau's article, the Rhetoric receives only limited attention.

Together, the papers of Nadeau and Dieter provide an excellent summary and analysis of Aristotle's treatment of stasis in
works other than the Rhetoric. As for stasis in this volume, there
has been no significant examination since that of E. M. Cope. [5]

Stasis in the Rhetoric

But how does one decide whether a passage pertains to
stasis? A discussion of definition, for example, is not necessarily
indicative of a concern by Aristotle for stasiastic method. The criteria used in this study are these: (1) Does the content of the passage pertain to the elements that constitute the essence of stasis in
later works--fact, definition, quality, and procedure? (2) Do the
context and the purpose of the passage coincide with those in the
later, fully developed treatments of the doctrine? In particular,
does the reference present a set of options that the defendant may
use in finding the basis for his case? Are these options to be explored successively, and collectively do they constitute a standard
and complete pattern of analysis? [6]

Stasis in Books i and ii. Only two passages in books i and
ii are close enough to pertaining to stasis to justify an application
of the preceding criteria. The first of these is in i.3, where as
part of the general introduction to the Rhetoric Aristotle writes of
the choices that a speaker has in selecting his stand:

> The litigant will sometimes not deny that a thing has
> happened or that he has done harm. But that he is guilty
> of injustice he will never admit. ... So too, political
> orators often make any concession short of admitting that
> they are recommending their hearers to take an inexpedi-
> ent course or not to take an expedient one. The ques-
> tion whether it is not unjust for a city to enslave its in-
> nocent neighbours often does not trouble them at all. In

> like manner those who praise or censure a man do not
> consider whether his acts have been expedient or not. [7]

Whether this passage deserves inclusion in the literature of
stasis is unclear.   In content it includes the issue of fact and several aspects of quality, but at most this is an incomplete system of
analysis when compared with that to be found in later works.   In
purpose there is a similarity with subsequent writings in that both
this passage and those that follow on stasis contain the idea that
the orator has the option of abandoning one issue in favor of taking
his stand elsewhere.   On the other hand, the context does not support the argument that Aristotle in this passage was writing about
stasis.   The reason for the inclusion of these lines has nothing to
do with the analysis of a controversy or the search for the strate-
gic position.   The point that is being made is that each kind of
oratory has its distinctive end.   The sentence that precedes the citation reads: "That the three kinds of rhetoric do aim respectively
at the three ends we have mentioned is shown by the fact that
speakers will sometimes not try to establish anything else. "[8]

Coming closer to meeting the criteria set up for determining
whether a passage is an early form of the doctrine of stasis is a
section in i. 13, but again a full analysis raises questions.   The apparent treatment reads as follows:

> Now it often happens that a man will admit an act, but
> will not admit the prosecutor's label for the act nor the
> facts which that label implies.   He will admit that he
> took a thing but not that he "stole" it; that he struck
> some one first, but not that he committed "outrage";
> that he had intercourse with a woman, but not that he
> committed "adultery"; that he is guilty of theft, but not
> that he is guilty of "sacrilege, " the object stolen not
> being consecrated; that he has encroached, but not that
> he has "encroached on State lands"; that he has been in
> communication with the enemy, but not that he has been
> guilty of "treason. "   Here therefore we must be able to
> distinguish what is theft, outrage, or adultery, from
> what is not, if we are to be able to make the justice of
> our case clear, no matter whether our aim is to estab-
> lish a man's guilt or to establish his innocence.   Wherev-
> er such charges are brought against a man, the question
> is whether he is or is not guilty of a criminal offence.
> It is deliberate purpose that constitutes wickedness and
> criminal guilt, and such names as "outrage" or "theft"
> imply deliberate purpose as well as the mere action.   A
> blow does not always amount to "outrage, " but only if it
> is struck with some such purpose as to insult the man
> struck or gratify the striker himself.   Nor does taking a
> thing without the owner's knowledge always amount to
> "theft, " but only if it is taken with the intention of keep-
> ing it and injuring the owner. [9]

The first of the two criteria is met to a degree. The
descriptions and the examples are easy to connect with the stases
of fact and of definition in later rhetorics. The closing lines on
what "constitutes wickedness and criminal guilt, " however, although
they may appear at first to constitute an early form of the stasis
of quality, are more properly analyzed as pertaining to definition.
The objective is to establish the presence or the absence of a
criminal offense, and the material that follows is a presentation
of the elements that must be included if the definition is to be
satisfied. At most, therefore, this passage is an incomplete version of stasis, limited to two of the four possible stands.

By the second criterion, also, these lines in one respect
deal with stasis. The idea that definition is a means of defense if
conjecture is not arguable is a major characteristic of the doctrine.
As with the passage in i. 3, however, the avowed purpose is unrelated to a search for the resting place of the controversy. Aristotle is not setting forth a method for locating the critical issue,
but instead is clarifying for the reader what "being wronged"
means. The possibility exists, Aristotle is explaining, that the
defendant will reject the prosecutor's label and when this happens
the test of deliberate intent is to be applied. The most that one
can argue, therefore, is that Aristotle knew an incomplete doctrine
of stasis; his intention here is not to present the doctrine for its
own sake as a part of his instruction on invention.

In no place in books i and ii, therefore, does Aristotle
offer stasis as a system of analysis. Moreover, in length, position, and context the only two passages that bear important stasis-
like characteristics are insignificant when viewed in relation to the
total treatment of invention. Aristotle's objective, it should be
remembered, was to provide students with those broad principles
and specific applications that would be helpful to them in preparing
speeches. To fulfill this objective he ranged widely through materials pertaining to the emotions, types of audiences, forms of
reasoning, topoi, and types and sources of ideas. If he had had a
theory of stasis at the time he wrote books i and ii, he surely
would have found in such an extensive treatment of invention a specific place for it. Stasis is such a useful tool in analysis and
speech preparation that it seems unlikely that Aristotle, if he knew
about it, would take it up only inadvertently. Moreover, except
for the passage in i. 3 he nowhere in a preview or a summary refers to stasis as a part of the inventional system.

These considerations, along with those stated earlier, lead
to the conclusion that Aristotle when writing books i and ii did not
have a clear, well-developed theory of stasis and that he did not
appreciate the value to the orator of this doctrine. At most, only
two of the later four stases appear, and they are not named, defined, or given a generalized, philosophic treatment. Their inclusion is incidental to purposes other than those distinctive to a doctrine of stasis. Completely missing is the idea critical to later

rhetorics that <u>stasis</u> is an analytic tool for finding the position on which the controversy depends.

As a final word, the attention to definition has more likely sources than some innerly held, unverbalized doctrine of <u>stasis</u>. The concept of definition is critical to the treatment of demonstration and receives full, systematic development in several places in the <u>Organon,</u> including book vi and part of book vii in the <u>Topics</u>.

<u>Stasis in Book iii</u>.   In book iii, however, the situation is different from that in books i and ii.   Beginning with chapter 14 Aristotle instructs his students in the preparation of the several parts of the speech, and the inclusion in three of these parts of material on <u>stasis</u> suggests that Aristotle had a general conception of this analytic tool.

The first appearance, which is in the section on the preparation of the introduction, meets both of the criteria at least to some degree.   The passage, with a fourteen-line deletion, follows:

> Another way is to meet any of the issues directly: to deny the alleged fact; or to say that you have done no harm, or none to him, or not as much as he says; or that you have done him no injustice, or not much; or that you have done nothing disgraceful, or nothing disgraceful enough to matter: these are the sort [sic] of questions on which the dispute hinges.   Thus Iphicrates, replying to Nausicrates, admitted that he had done the deed alleged, and that he had done Nausicrates harm, but not that he had done him wrong.   Or you may admit the wrong, but balance it with other facts, and say that, if the deed harmed him, at any rate it was honourable; or that, if it gave him pain, at least it did him good; or something else like that.   Another way is to allege that your action was due to mistake, or bad luck, or necessity.   ... You may balance your motive against your actual deed....   Euripides said that his opponent himself was guilty in bringing into the law-courts cases whose decision belonged to the Dionysiac contests. [10]

The first criterion is met in part in that three of the four <u>stases</u> of Hermagoras appear.   The cited lines begin with the possibility of taking a position by denying the fact, and they close with an example illustrating the option of challenging jurisdiction.   In between are a series of suggestions whose function is comparable to that served by the <u>stasis</u> of quality: one may admit the deed, but take a position of defense by pointing out something extenuating in its nature.   The number of options is considerable: harm, harm to the aggrieved, serious harm, injustice, significant injustice, disgrace, significant disgrace, balancing contentions, lack of intent and absence of volition, and worthy motivation.   The passage, thus, serves the function of <u>stasis</u> by setting forth possible posi-

tions.   Though the exposition lacks the completeness and the sharp
purposefulness of later rhetorics, its similarities to full treatments
of stasis are significant.

Likewise, by the other major criterion the passage appears
to deserve to be included in the literature of stasis.   The objective
is that of analysis.   In the summary of the general exposition,
Aristotle writes, "These are the sort [sic] of questions on which
the dispute hinges."[11]

The next part of the speech is the narration, and in three
places Aristotle gives advice that appears to be drawn from a general stasiastic theory.   The first of these, it is interesting to note,
pertains to the introduction to ceremonial oratory, which is the type
to which the doctrine has the least application.   The narration,
Aristotle states, includes both nonartistic and artistic elements.
For advice on invention of the second of these types Aristotle seems
to go to stasis: "The other part is provided by his art, namely,
the proof (where proof is needed) that the actions were done, the
description of their quality or of their extent, or even all these
three things together."[12]   Similar advice appears a few lines later
in a section setting forth what the orator must prove: "That is,
in saying just so much as will make the facts plain, or will lead
the hearer to believe that the thing has happened, or that the man
has caused injury or wrong to some one, or that the facts are
really as important as you wish them to be thought: or the opposite facts to establish the opposite arguments."[13]   Finally, the
same ideas, but with a little more elaboration, are to be found in
iii. 16 in the statement of what the defendant should include in the
narration when it comes his turn to speak: "He has to maintain
that the thing has not happened, or did no harm, or was not unjust,
or not so bad as is alleged.   He must therefore not waste time
about what is admitted fact, unless this bears on his own contention; e.g., that the thing was done, but was not wrong."[14]

From these three passages in iii. 16 one may conclude that
Aristotle's invention possessed some elements that characterize the
theory of stasis.   Foremost, there is a list of possible positions,
though not the same ones as in later rhetorics.   Of the four stases
of Hermagoras, the conjectural clearly is present, whereas definition and procedure (or objection) are missing.[15]   That the quality
of the act is a possible controlling issue is important both to Aristotle and to later rhetoricians, but there is not much similarity in
subparts.   Notably unique to Aristotle is the emphasis on extent or
seriousness as a potential issue.

Furthermore, in function and purpose Aristotle's treatment
is both similar to those of later rhetoricians and different from
them.   The purpose in the Rhetoric, as in Hermagoras and others,
is to set forth a series of positions from which the defendant may
choose.   Missing from Aristotle, though, are the ideas that the
items constitute a systematic and exhaustive scheme of analysis and

that the resting point for the case comes about through the interaction of the pleas of prosecution and defense.

In iii. 17 is still stronger support for the argument that
Aristotle's inventional system included an element that can properly be called stasis. Two passages are pertinent:

> The duty of the Arguments is to attempt demonstrative
> proofs. These proofs must bear directly upon the ques-
> tion in dispute, which must fall under one of four heads.
> (1) If you maintain that the act was not committed, your
> main task in court is to prove this. (2) If you maintain
> that the act did no harm, prove this. If you maintain
> that (3) the act was less than is alleged, or (4) justified,
> prove these facts, just as you would prove the act not to
> have been committed if you were maintaining that. 16

> In political speeches you may maintain that a proposal is
> impracticable; or that, though practicable, it is unjust,
> or will do no good, or is not so important as its propos-
> er thinks. 17

To the ideas in iii. 15 and iii. 16 Aristotle here adds two
points that characterize later treatments of stasis. The options
constitute a series of positions that the defendant is to explore in
turn, and the list of options is said to be all inclusive. Except
for minor features, the nature of the possible issues is the same
as in the preceding chapters--definition and various approaches
to quality, including the topos of seriousness or extent. In other
words, the citation is a system of analysis; and, unlike the passages in books i and ii, the avowed purpose of the exposition is the
presentation of such a system.

Comparison of Book iii with Books i and ii. The treatment
of stasis in book iii when compared with that in books i and ii suggests that the doctrine was much clearer and more prominent in
Aristotle's system of invention when he wrote book iii than it was
when he wrote i and ii. First, stasis-like passages appear six
times in the comparatively short space of three chapters in book
iii but only twice in all of i and ii. Second, the purpose in book
iii is to give advice on analysis and even to set forth a system of
analysis, whereas in i and ii the stasis-like material is in other
contexts. Third, the presentation of the ideas in book iii is sharp-
er and better organized than in i and ii.

The Rhetoric as Compared
with Later Works on Stasis

In the Rhetoric the treatments of stasis are brief, but certain features are so consistent that a characterization is possible.
First, though the stases of definition and procedure appear in the

Rhetoric, they are absent from most passages. Second, most
treatments begin with the possibility that the issue of fact may or
may not be a feasible one for the defendant and continue with a
list of possible positions pertaining to the quality of the action.
Variations occur, but the topoi of quality usually included are
harm (including pain), injustice (including doing wrong), and importance or seriousness. One passage (in iii. 15) takes up as possible defenses the claim that the act was honorable, that it did the
aggrieved good, that the motive was good, and that the action occurred because of a mistake, bad luck, or necessity rather than
because of bad intention. Third, the treatments of stasis in the
Rhetoric are brief and not always highly structured.

When compared with the presentations of Hermagoras and
Hermogenes, the Rhetoric, indeed, is sketchy. The two later
works plainly include four stases, and these form a definite system
of analysis. More clearly than in the Rhetoric, the objective is
the presentation of a comprehensive scheme that serves as a major
inventional feature.

One other noteworthy difference between Aristotle and the
later rhetoricians, beginning with Hermagoras, is the far greater
emphasis of the former on the topos of extent or seriousness.
Two interpretations of this feature are possible. Cope regards
Aristotle's treatment of extent or quantity as the counterpart of
the later stasis of definition on the grounds that the designation
for a crime was dependent on its degree or amount.[18] This analysis ignores the fact that Aristotle raises the question of degree in
several contexts, including harm, injustice, and disgrace, without
any mention of the relation of degree to how a crime is classified.
Aristotle elsewhere, moreover, considers definition and degree
separately, clearly, and in detail,[19] and it seems improbable that
in the passages on stasis he would use the roundabout method of
discussing degree if his real point is defining by classifying. The
more likely interpretation, especially in the light of Aristotle's
awareness of degree as a topos, is that in the treatment of extent
or seriousness Aristotle really means what he says--that in dealing
with the quality of an act one can examine both its aspects and
their degrees. In fact, Cope's own commentary on iii. 17 seems
to support the foregoing view as one of two reasonable possibilities.[20]

Moreover, the inclusion of degree in Aristotle as an aspect
of the stasis of quality is consistent with his sharp differentiation
between a logic for science and a logic for rhetoric. Whereas the
former was dependent on absolute, necessary premises, the latter
provided for probabilities. Whereas the syllogism of science, for
example, required that a premise pertaining to harm be an assertion that the act either was harmful or was not, the logical system
for rhetoric was flexible enough to include degree as a factor affecting persuasiveness.

Why later rhetoricians gave so little explicit attention to extent as an aspect of the stasis of quality is unknowable, but speculation is possible. Perhaps they took their logic from the Organon, even though their treatment of stasis was within the art of rhetoric. Hermogenes, in particular, reasoned through dichotomizing, which is incompatible with the notion that degrees of harm, justice, or anything else are possible.

Discussion and Conclusion

To what extent Hermagoras and those who followed him were indebted to the Rhetoric for the ideas that comprise their doctrine of stasis is impossible to know, but the Rhetoric was a possible source for much that they wrote. This early volume contains the idea that the defendant has a series of options that he can explore in the preparation of his case, and in iii. 17 Aristotle presents these possibilities as a complete system of analysis.   In one place or another the Rhetoric includes the four stases, though never all at any one time.   Though Hermagoras and his successors may have secured a number of ideas from Aristotle, they were not indebted to the Stagirite for the full form of their systems or for many of the details.   They neglected extent as a topos of quality.

The substantial difference between book iii and books i and ii in the treatment of stasis deserves some final comments.   On the relation of book iii to the rest of the Rhetoric there is a range of scholarly opinions.   One view is that it was written later and appended: "It seems pretty plain that, after he had written the two first books of his Rhetoric, there was an interval, and that he did not add on the third book for some time afterwards. "[21]   Sir David Ross shares this view that book iii originally was a separate volume. [22]   J. W. H. Atkins, however, though pointing to differences between book iii and the first two books, concludes that iii is "a component part of the whole. "[23]   George Kennedy, after summarizing evidence for other views, likewise concludes that Aristotle regarded the third book as a part of the whole treatise during at least two stages of its preparation. [24]   Doubts about the genuineness of book iii, all modern scholars seem to agree, have been dispelled.

But if book iii is of the same period as books i and ii, how is the neglect of stasis in the first part of the Rhetoric to be explained? The conclusion of the present study seems to support the opinion that book iii was a separate and later work.   The doctrine of stasis is of so much importance to invention that it is unlikely that Aristotle had it in mind at one time and then at a later date overlooked it.   The more reasonable explanation is that he had no clear, organized theory of stasis when he wrote books i and ii and that between their composition and the drafting of book iii he developed his ideas on this aspect of rhetoric.

Such speculation is plausible, but the major conclusions of this study do not depend on its correctness. (1) The Rhetoric is a source of valuable information on Aristotle as a figure in the history of stasis. The present analysis is a supplement to the earlier essays by Nadeau and Dieter. (2) Stasis is a much more significant inventional factor in book iii than it is in books i and ii. (3) In book iii stasis is a system of analysis whose basic elements are the issues of fact and quality. The most common topoi of quality are harm, justice, and extent.[25] (4) Hermagoras could have secured many of his ideas from the Rhetoric, but many of the details of the two treatments differ and the precise system in the later work is not to be found in Aristotle. In the words of Cope, the legal issues, afterwards called stasis, appear in Aristotle in an "embryo stage" and are "never exactly defined, or employed as a well determined and recognized technical and legal classification."[26]

NOTES

1. "Hermogenes' On Stases: A Translation with an Introduction and Notes," Speech Monographs, 31 (November 1964), 370 et passim.
2. "Stasis." Speech Monographs, 17 (November 1950), 345-369.
3. P. 370.
4. P. 371.
5. An Introduction to Aristotle's Rhetoric (London: Macmillan, 1867), pp. 171, 189-190, 345, 349-350, 355-357, and 397-399.
6. See Nadeau, 375-376.
7. 1358b31-1359a1 (trans. W. Rhys Roberts).
8. 1358b29-31.
9. 1374a1-17.
10. 1416a6-33.
11. 1416a9.
12. 1416b19-22.
13. 1416b36-1417a3.
14. 1417a7-12.
15. Cope regards Aristotle's inclusion of extent as a counterpart of the later stasis of definition. For a comment on this interpretation, see infra.
16. 1417b21-27.
17. 1417b35-37.
18. P. 398.
19. Book vi and part of book vii of the Topics is on definition, and the seventh topos of book ii, chapter 23, of the Rhetoric is definition. The fourth and final topos of book ii, chapter 19, is degree.
21. Alexander Grant, "Aristotle," in Encyclopaedia Britannica: A Dictionary of Arts, Sciences, and General Literature, 9th ed. (Boston: Samuel L. Hall, 1875), II, 517.
22. Aristotle (New York: Barnes and Noble, 1964), p. 274.

23.   Literary Criticism in Antiquity (Cambridge, England: Cam-
        bridge Univ. Press, 1934), I, 135.
24.   The Art of Persuasion in Greece (Princeton: Princeton Univ.
        Press, 1963), pp. 103-104.
25.   Cf. ibid., p. 114.
26.   P. 397.

17. THE ARISTOTELIAN TRADITION
IN ANCIENT RHETORIC*

by Friedrich Solmsen

Quintilian in the course of a somewhat sketchy but nevertheless invaluable account of the history of rhetorical theory informs
us that after the first generations of rhetoricians had gradually
built up the science of rhetoric it split up into two different types
--the one represented by Isocrates and his school, the other by
Aristotle, his pupils and, later, by other schools of philosophy
like the Stoic.[1] In the next paragraph he mentions that a third
type came into being with Hermagoras. We are at liberty to combine this piece of information with that found in Cicero's De inventione, where in the context of a similar historical sketch we
learn that the rhetorical systems of the Aristotelian and Isocratean
schools were fused into a new system by the later theorists qui ab
utrisque ea quae commode dici videbantur in suas artes transtulerunt.[2] Taken together, these passages seem to provide something
like a clue to the history of ancient rhetorical theory, for, even
though Cicero may be considered slightly unfair to the originality
of later writers on rhetoric, it will certainly be worth while to
trace the transformations of the two original systems through the
later stages of ancient rhetoric. I am ready to admit that modern
writers on the development of ancient rhetoric[3] have good reasons
for treating the material along rather different lines; yet by doing
so they deprive themselves of the opportunity of appreciating the
extent to which the two outstanding theorists left their mark on the
subsequent phases of the system.

In this paper I have confined myself to tracing the Aristotelian or, rather, Peripatetic influence on the later theories, partly
because this is nearer to the line of my own studies in the field of
ancient rhetoric, and partly because it seems advisable to attack
this subject first, since for the history of the Isocratean tradition
we lack a starting point of the same solidity and authenticity as
Aristotle's three books on rhetoric.[4] I do not suggest that when
the Aristotelian factor has been brought to light the Isocratean may
be found by a process of subtraction, but I hope that the direction

*Reprinted by permission of the author and The Johns Hopkins
Press, from American Journal of Philology 62 (1941), 35-50, 169-
190.

in which one must look for the Isocratean element will be more
obvious when the first half of the job of analysis has been done.
Moreover, as a result of the investigations of Hendrickson, Kroll,
Barwick, Hinks, and Stroux the material to be used in the reconstruction of the Aristotelian tradition seems to lie more ready at
hand than the corresponding material for the Isocratean. 5   Thanks
are due in particular to Professor Stroux for throwing light on the
relation between Aristotle's system and that of his Peripatetic
disciples, 6 for his conclusions show (in remarkable agreement with
those reached in different fields of the Peripatetic philosophy) that
Aristotle's pupils and successors, while keeping alive the master's
ideas wherever they could do so with a good conscience, made it
their object to fill out gaps which he had left (and frequently indicated as such), to arrange the material more systematically under
certain basic categories, and to increase the amount of empirical
data to be fitted into the framework of these categories.

Before we enter into an analysis of later artes it seems
necessary to form as clear a notion as possible of those factors in
Aristotle's own Rhetoric which are sufficiently original and characteristic to justify our singling them out as his peculiar contributions to the rhetorical system.   It would be an impossible (and for
our purpose a fruitless) undertaking if we tried to enumerate all
those more or less significant details which are or may be new in
his work, and we must content ourselves with pointing out the
basic and truly epoch-making methodical ideas through which he
made of the rhetorical system something very different from what
it had been before.   I am aware that in distinguishing between essential and inessential features in his work subjectivity cannot be
altogether avoided; yet the following account may not be far from
the mark:

1.   Aristotle breaks emphatically with the traditional method
of organizing the rhetorical material under the heading of the partes
orationis (μόρια λόγου): proem, narration, etc.   We gather from
Plato's Phaedrus and from Aristotle himself7 that some teachers
of rhetoric had gone very far in dividing the oration into its parts
and subdividing these parts into their various species; but, if it is
true that the Isocratean school recognized only four parts--proem,
narration, proofs, and epilogue--, 8 we may regard this as a reaction against the other rhetoricians who, as I have said, went much
further.   To maintain that the Isocrateans organized their entire
material under these headings would be hazardous, but there can
be no doubt that this school has left its mark on the theory of the
proem, the narration, and the rest, and there are few Hellenistic
rhetoricians who do not echo certain fundamental Isocratean precepts for them (e. g. that the narration should avoid unnecessary
length, be ἐναργές, πιθανόν. ἡδύ, κτλ.).   Although we are not dealing with the Isocratean tradition, we have to bear these facts in
mind in order to understand Aristotle against the right background.

Aristotle is no less scornful than Plato in castigating the

superficiality of this approach and the lack of a clear conception
of the essential functions of a speech which it betrays. [9] In his
Poetics Aristotle looks on tragedy as a totum et unum and concentrates on those features which are essential to tragedy as such,
i. e. to the idea of tragedy: plot, characters, and the other like
elements.   The external (or quantitative) parts of a tragedy such
as the prologue and episodes he relegates to one chapter (12) and
treats them as a matter of secondary importance. [10]   Similarly,
in the Rhetoric he assigns the "parts of a speech" their place in
the third main section of the work where he discusses "disposition, "[11] but organizes the whole material under categories representing essential qualities or functions of any speech.   In every
speech the orator must seek to prove his point, to produce a definite emotional reaction in his audience, to convey an impression
of the speaker's character.   Also, every speech must have a definite style and a disposition; it is here that the "parts" get their
due, yet even here only the really essential and more or less indispensable ones. [12]   Thus, in opposition to the old τέχνη where
the material was arranged under "proem, " "narration, " "proofs, "
"epilogue, " or even more parts, a new type comes into existence,
consisting of three main parts: Proofs (or material content),
Style, and Disposition.   The "proofs" in the alternative system;
"proofs" are no longer a part but a function of the speech, and
Aristotle's "proofs" are subdivided into the theories of the rhetorical argument, of the emotions (πάθη), and of the speaker's character (ἤθη), since these three factors should combine to make the
speech effective.   We may note that Aristotle draws attention to a
further factor worthy of the same standing in the system as
"proofs, " "style, " and "disposition, " namely the delivery (ὑπόκρισις),
yet he refrains from actually working this out. [13]

   This entirely new approach to rhetoric is, like the new approach to poetry, obviously based on Aristotle's conception of a
thing's organic unity as implying a principle of structure and being
different from a mere accumulation of its parts.   We know this
conception from the Metaphysics[14] where it is an integral phase of
Aristotle's notion of an entity.

   2.   The system of "proofs" (πίστεις) may be called the core
of Aristotle's Rhetoric.   As we have seen, the "proofs" are subdivided into three kinds: the rhetorical argument, the arousing of
emotions, and the speaker's character.   In dealing with the first
Aristotle again makes a new departure: He bases the theory of
the rhetorical argument on his logic, that is on his dialectic and
analytics.   The "enthymeme" which with other rhetoricians had
been merely a particular way of formulating a thought (in other
words, a concept of a stylistic rather than logical complexion)[15]
turns with him into the rhetorical syllogism and has to be constructed in close analogy to the logical syllogism, even though in
formulating it one of the premises may, if self-evident, be omitted.
Similarly the rhetorical παράδειγμα is made to correspond to the
logical induction (ἐπαγωγή). [16]

Moreover, such traditional types of "evidence" as σημεῖον, εἰκός, τεκμήριον which in all probability had never before received a logical foundation are by Aristotle reinterpreted as representing certain definite types of syllogisms. [17] To be sure, some of them have to be regarded as somewhat lax and inconclusive, but the fact that matters is that in Rhet. A 2 Aristotle looks at them from the perspective of his new theory of the logical syllogism as set forth in the Analytica Priora.

The τόποι had before Aristotle been ready-made arguments or commonplaces "into which they expected the speeches of both parties to fall most frequently." [18] They referred invariably to particular subjects in the sense that the orator had his ready-made commonplaces for either enhancing or minimizing, say, the trust-worthiness of the witnesses, the importance of the oaths to be sworn in court, etc. Aristotle compares this instruction to a procedure by which instead of learning the art of making shoes the apprentice receives a great number of ready-made shoes without any suggestion as to how to make them. [19]

He replaces this method by an altogether different system of τόποι, conceiving the τόπος as a "type" or "form" of argument of which you need grasp only the basic structural idea to apply it forthwith to discussions about any and every subject. Once you have grasped the τόπος of the "More and Less" you will be able to argue: If not even the gods know everything, human beings will certainly not know everything; or, Whoever beats his father will certainly also beat his neighbors; or to form any other argument of the same kind, always proceeding from the less likely thing (which has nevertheless occurred) to the more likely. [20] What matters in this system is the "form" of the argument, this being perfectly independent of any particular subject-matter or content. Aristotle in II, 2 enumerates twenty-eight τόποι or "forms" of arguments and in addition nine of paralogisms. [21] Here too we find him constructing the rhetorical argument after the model of his logic, this time that of his Topics where he provides τόποι (of the same kind) for purely logical discussions. Obviously this new Aristotelian concept of the τόπος presupposes a new capacity for abstracting from the material content and for grasping the καθόλου or ἓν ἐπὶ πολλῶν. This is an ability which the previous teachers of rhetoric had lacked; in fact I venture the suggestion that before Plato and Aristotle the Greeks had generally lacked this capacity for abstracting. Whether or not Aristotle's τόποι are more practical than the ready-made clichés of Antiphon, Protagoras, and others is a question which we need not discuss, for, although Aristotle would probably claim superiority for his method in the field of practical application also, yet his primary objective is to elevate rhetoric to a subject of philosophical dignity and standing.

In other chapters Aristotle provides premises for the rhetorical syllogisms. [22] These premises appear in the form of general propositions about the "good" ("a thing which everybody seeks

to attain is good"), the "useful, " the "beautiful, " the "just, " the
"possible, " and their opposites. We have to reckon with the possibility that at Aristotle's time other teachers of rhetoric had also
adopted the course of providing their pupils with general propositions as to what was "good, " "just, " and, more particularly, of
enumerating good, just, desirable things. 23 This may be regarded as a step in the same direction, and yet an important difference lies in the fact that behind Aristotle's procedure there is
a definite logical conception of the nature of the rhetorical argument. His general propositions are really intended to be major
premises in a rhetorical syllogism.

3. We have already referred to the important position of
the three πίστεις or means of persuasion in Aristotle's system. It
was Aristotle who set up the argumentation, the playing upon the
feelings, and the speaker's character as the three factors essential
for the effectiveness of a speech. We know that both earlier and
contemporary rhetoricians included some practical suggestions for
the arousing of pity, indignation, good will, etc. in their treatment of the "parts of the speech, " especially of proem and epilogue. Aristotle's innovation consists not only in his granting to
πάθη and ἤθη a status on a par with the arguments and thereby ele-
vating them to first-rate factors but also in his careful analysis of
the nature of the various emotions and of the conditions under
which they may be either aroused or allayed. 24 The chapters B
12-17 are certainly a very interesting essay on "social psychology,"
if this term may be used for a theory of the customary reactions
of certain social groups or age-groups (the young, the old, the
rich, the noble, etc.). It must be admitted, however, that we are
completely in the dark as to the position of the ἤθη in the conventional rhetorical system before Aristotle. 25

4. Aristotle distinguishes between three different kinds of
speeches, the political speech, the forensic speech, and the laudation. The first deals with the ἀγαθόν, the second with the δίκαιον,
the third with the καλόν; in other words they are related to three
cardinal values. He arrives at these tria genera causarum (as
they are technically called) by a deductive reasoning which is Platonic in form and method. 26 Yet it is also possible to regard the
concentration on these three species as the logical result of the
development of the rhetorical theory and practice in the course of
the fourth century and to suggest that in spite of his deductive efforts the result was for Aristotle something like a foregone conclusion. In these circumstances we welcome the testimony of
Quintilian who tells us that the adoption of this tripartite scheme
by later theorists at large was due to Aristotle's influence. 27 It
may have been his authority rather than his originality which determined developments in this phase of the rhetorical system.

5. In the field of style or diction Aristotle went a long way
towards fixing the "virtues of style, " i. e. the qualities which a
good speech or, more generally, a good piece of prose ought to

possess. He lays down three: clarity, ornateness, and appropriateness (the last being subdivided in accordance with the three
πίστεις).[28] A considerable portion of his more specified propositions and suggestions is arranged under these categories, and there
is also a chapter on Ἑλληνισμός,[29] the correct use of the Greek
language; but the organization of the material under these headings
is by no means complete, and it was left to Theophrastus to put
the finishing touch to his master's work here and to reduce this
whole part of rhetoric to a hard and fast system, along the following lines:[30]

"Virtues of style"
(ἀρεταὶ λέξως)

(1) correct use of the language (Ἑλληνισμός)	(2) clarity (σαφήνεια)	(3) appropriate-ness (πρέπον)	(4) ornateness (κόσμος)
			(a) selection of words (ἐκλογή)
			(b) composition of words (σύνθεσις)
			(c) figures (σχήματα)

Further stylistic categories like ἀστεῖον, ψυχρόν, ὄγκος find
a treatment in <u>Rhet</u>. Γ,[31] and although Aristotle may not have been
the first to use them he is likely to have been original in consti-
tuting their main types and organizing the material which comes
under them. Yet we are not in a position to define the degree of
his originality here; and, as we lack material for a comparison,
any attempt to detect new departures in his theory of the metaphor[32] or other phases of the rhetorical ornament would necessarily lead to guesswork. In a few points his dependence on the Isocratean tradition or, more particularly, the Theodectean τέχνη appears obvious.[33]

It may be well to add a few other points even though they
are slightly less important. In A 2 (1355 b 35) and A 15 (1375 a
22) Aristotle differentiates between those "proofs" which the orator
has to provide by himself and those which do not depend on him
but may be "used" by him to his best advantage. The former are
those which we have already discussed, namely the argumentation,
the speaker's character, the arousing of emotions (pp. 38, 42,
supra); the other class consists of the witnesses, oaths sworn by
the parties before the jury, the laws which are relevant to the case
in hand, documents such as contracts, etc.[34] It is obvious that
the orator cannot "invent" this material; he can at best "use" or,
to put it less euphemistically, twist it according to his purpose,
and Aristotle in fact tells him how to do this. He refers to these

"proofs" as ἄτεχνοι πίστεις, contrasting them with the other kind of proofs which he calls ἔντεχνοι πίστεις. It should be noted that the author of the <u>Rhetorica ad Alexandrum</u> draws a similar distinction although he does not use the same terms. [35]

The definition of the sentence period as a "sentence which has beginning and end in itself" and a certain definite extension in all probability originated with Aristotle. [36] His point is that what he calls "beginning and end in itself" should be secured through the rhythm.   Also his famous distinction between λέξις εἰρομένη and λέξις κατεστραμμένη rests on the fact that the former lacks this quality of having beginning and end definitely marked.   On the other hand it is not essential for Aristotle's conception of the period that it should consist of several κῶλα.

Among the new items which the Peripatetics after Aristotle added to the stock of his system two should certainly be mentioned. The Peripatetic theory of the rhetorical joke or the "laughable" (τὰ γελοῖα) has been reconstructed, mainly with the help of the so called <u>Tractatus Coislinianus,</u> "Demetrius," περὶ ἑρμηνείας, and Cicero's <u>De oratore</u>. [37] Two main sources of the "laughable" appear to have been distinguished; the theory is that it may lie either in the subject matter or in the verbal expression.

Theophrastus was the first to theorize on ὑπόκρισις, the oratorical delivery.   Aristotle had suggested[38] that in working out this part of the system particular attention should be paid to the voice and its modulation, but Theophrastus may have gone further and may have included <u>gestus</u> and the expression of the orator's face (though we cannot say this with certainty since we do not know how closely later authors, especially Cicero, followed him). [39]

I should hesitate to credit Aristotle with any of the notions or precepts of the second part of book Γ (chaps. 13-19), since there are good reasons for assuming that Aristotle in that section is reproducing a system of the alternative "Isocratean" type.   I have suggested elsewhere[40] that the τέχνη from which he borrows was that of his friend Theodectes.   To be sure, Aristotle does not reproduce his source mechanically and there are passages in which he evidently expresses disagreement with the author from whom he derived most of his material. [41] Nevertheless, chaps. 13-19 represent a system of the μόρια λόγου type and, so far from being characteristic of Aristotle's own approach to rhetoric, may rather be regarded as the first stage in the process of fusion between the two rival traditions.

On the basis of the foregoing analysis it should now be possible to form an opinion about the way in which the <u>ratio Aristotelia</u> has left its mark upon the later rhetorical systems.

1 (corresponding to section 1, page 37 <u>supra</u>).   In a paper

published in Hermes[42] Professor Barwick pointed out that the extant artes of the Hellenistic and Imperial era fall into two groups
according to the way in which their authors divide and arrange
their material. Although we have to reckon with a considerable
amount of mutual borrowing, mixing, and combining between the
two types, the basic forms emerge with certainty. The one type
consists of a discussion of proem, narration, proofs, epilogue,
and usually one or several more "parts" of the speech, [43] whereas
the other type is usually a quinquepartite system including inventio,
dispositio, elocutio, actio, and memoria. It is not difficult to
recognize in the former type a continuation of the system which
had been in vogue before Plato and Aristotle and which as we
know was severely criticized by both of them. The other is described by Quintilian as that of the plurimi maximique auctores, [44]
and I think that we have every right to consider these plurimi maximique auctores as following in the footsteps of Aristotle. The first
three sections certainly correspond to his three: Proofs, Style,
Disposition, εὕρεσις (inventio) being merely a new name for that
part of the system in which, as in Aristotle's πίστεις, the material
content of the speech is discussed. [45] The fourth part, ὑπόκρισις
or actio, had, as we have seen (p. 39, supra), been postulated by
Aristotle as a necessary supplement to his tripartite division. It
was supplied in accordance with the master's suggestion by his
faithful pupil Theophrastus. [46] The problem which remains and
which cannot be solved with certainty is this: Who was the first
rhetorician to add memoria (μνήμη) to the Peripatetic system? All
that we may say is that this addition must have been made between
Theophrastus and those authors from whom Cicero and the Auctor
ad Herennium borrow the structure of their artes, since when they
wrote this quinquepartite scheme must have been firmly established. [47] Yet, although the inclusion of memoria (μνήμη) had as
far as we know never been contemplated by Aristotle or Theophrastus, the fact remains that the plurimi maximique auctores have
their place in the Peripatetic tradition.

    Cicero's De inventione was meant to cover the first part of
this quinquepartite scheme, explicit references to which it contains. [48] Thirty years later Cicero adopted the same division of
the rhetorical system for De oratore, dealing in book II with inventio, dispositio, memoria, in book III with elocutio and actio. [49]
Quintilian's Institutio is also based on the Peripatetic scheme; here
the inventio is treated in III, 4-VI, dispositio in VII, [50] elocutio in
VIII-XI, 1, memoria in XI, 2, pronuntiatio (which a plerisque actio
dicitur) in XI, 3. Fortunatianus, Julius Victor, Martianus Capella,
and, on the Greek side, Longinus are the other extant authors
whose artes show the same structure. [51]

    We must add at once, however, that scarcely any ars pre-
sents the Peripatetic system in its true and uncontaminated form.
Compromises with the alternative system are a regular and normal
feature. Cicero in his De inventione and the Auctor ad Herennium
in his (closely corresponding) section on inventio so far from re-

producing an Aristotelian or Peripatetic theory of the πίστεις actually deal with the "parts of the speech": <u>prooemium</u>, <u>narratio</u>,
<u>partitio</u>, <u>confirmatio</u>, <u>refutatio</u>, <u>epilogus</u>.[52] This at least is true
in the discussion of the forensic branch (<u>genus iuridiciale</u>) which
receives far more attention and much fuller treatment than either
of the other branches (see p. 282 <u>supra</u>). In the description of
these others (which is rather sketchy) the "parts" have not been
adopted as a basis,[53] and we are entitled to conclude that the
<u>inventio</u> of these two <u>genera causarum</u> (the laudation and the politi-
cal oration) has suffered less interference from an alternative system, whether "Isocratean" or Hermagorean. The different fate of
these branches is, however, certainly not due to a greater respect
for them in their true Peripatetic form but rather to a neglect of
them and to a general concentration of interest on the <u>genus</u>
<u>iuridiciale</u>. Quintilian also organizes his material for the <u>inventio</u>
of the forensic speech under headings representing the <u>partes</u> (<u>ex-
ordium</u>, <u>narratio</u>, <u>egressio</u>, <u>propositio</u>, <u>partitio</u> in IV; <u>probatio</u> including <u>refutatio</u> in V; <u>peroratio</u> in VI, 1) but refrains from follow-
ing the same method in his discussion of the two other branches,
which is, again, much shorter.[54] A further instance of εὕρεσις
(inventio) based on the parts of the speech is to be found in Longinus' τέχνη.[55]

Wherever the <u>inventio</u> consists of a discussion of the <u>partes</u>
the material available for the "proofs" would naturally find its
place under <u>probatio</u> (or <u>confirmatio</u>, which is only another name
for the same part). As a result this "part" by far exceeds the
others in bulk. Theoretically this material might still be good
Aristotelian or Peripatetic theory; to what extent it actually is we
shall have to discuss under 2. It is clear, however, that the use
of the "parts of the speech" as the principle of structure and organization in the section on <u>inventio</u> constitutes an important departure from the original Peripatetic system; in fact we have to
regard it as a "contamination" with the alternative Isocratean tradition.[56] The only major work that shows no signs of this contamination is Cicero's <u>De oratore</u>.[57] The fusion of the two systems must have taken place some time prior to Cicero's <u>De in-
ventione</u> and the <u>Auctor ad Herennium</u>, and it is not difficult to
imagine that practical reasons determined influential teachers of
rhetoric to blend the two rival systems in the manner which we
have discussed. Cicero's <u>unum quoddam genus est conflatum a
posterioribus</u> is certainly borne out.

We remember that Aristotle himself had borrowed from the
alternative system and discussed the "parts of the speech" under
τάξις, that is to say in the section on <u>dispositio</u>. The later rhetoricians who use the "parts" in the <u>inventio</u> cannot, of course,
discuss them again in the <u>dispositio</u>. Thus they must in the <u>dis-
positio</u> confine themselves to some remarks concerning the length
of each of these parts, the sequence of the points to be made, and
other subjects of minor importance.[58] With them, therefore, the
<u>dispositio</u> tends to assume the form of <u>Addenda</u> to the <u>inventio</u>, and

this may be the reason (or perhaps one of several reasons, as we cannot trace this development with certainty) why the rhetoricians preferred to deal with dispositio immediately after inventio instead of discussing elocutio between them--which would have been in keeping with the original Peripatetic order.

Martianus Capella obviously knew both traditions and was anxious to give each of them its due; in his book on rhetoric (V) he first presents us with a discussion on the lines of the quinque-partite system, refraining from any reference to the partes in the inventio (although he makes extensive use of the status) and treating the dispositio very briefly (30), yet after finishing this he adds a full treatment of the alternative system beginning with the proem and ending with the epilogue (44-53). This is a unique procedure, and it is interesting to see that in the "Aristotelian" part of the book he preserves some elements of that tradition which the majority of rhetorical theorists no longer know.[59] Another curious fact is that he deals with argumentation in both parts of the book but treats it differently.

2 (see p. 280 supra). Aristotle, as we have seen, provided a new basis for the theory of the rhetorical argument by constructing the enthymeme in closest analogy to his logical syllogism. Thus any theory of the argument in a later system that shows a distinctly syllogistic complexion would naturally come under suspicion of Aristotelian influence even though in the details it may be found to diverge from Aristotle. A theory of the kind is in fact included in not a few of the later systems, but it must be mentioned at once that the customary name for the rhetorical argumentation which corresponds to the syllogism is no longer "enthymeme" but "epicheireme"; at least this is the term used by Cicero and Quintilian, and there is every probability that Hermagoras too preferred this name. The difference, however, between "enthymeme" and "epicheireme" is not of a purely terminological nature.[60] For, while Aristotle's enthymeme (like his syllogism) consists of two premises and a conclusion, but may under certain circumstances be reduced to a single premise and the conclusion,[61] the epicheireme has a more complicated form. Its normal type includes no less than four premises and the tendency of the rhetoricians is to regard epicheiremes consisting of less than five sentences as a reduction of this normal type. We learn, however, from Cicero's De inventione[62] that another school of thought, which he considers important enough to justify a lengthy discussion of its view, clung to the old tripartite Aristotelian syllogism; and Quintilian actually reverts to this view, after duly informing us that other authors regard four or five or even six parts of the epicheireme as normal.[63]

In comparing Aristotle's enthymeme with the normal form of the epicheireme we easily realize what accounts for the difference: whereas Aristotle took the premises for granted the later theorists consider it necessary to prove each of them before combining them in the final conclusion. This is again stated in so many words by

Cicero, 64 who points out that the controversy between the champi-
ons of the quinquepartite form of the epicheireme and those of the
tripartite form reduces itself to one simple question: If it is necessary to argue in support of one's premises should these arguments
be regarded as having an existence independent of these premises
and as forming separate parts of the epicheireme or rather as an
integral part of the premises which they support. We need not go
into the details of this discussion, but we may confidently assume
that the epicheireme with its five parts is an outgrowth or extension of the Aristotelian syllogism. In fact Cicero assures us that
this form was favored by omnes ab Aristotele et Theophrasto pro-
fecti and passed from these men to the rhetoricians. 65 The authors
of late artes waver between the enthymeme and the epicheireme and
show a considerable variety with regard to the definition as well as
the place of each of these terms. 66 Some authors include both,
describing the enthymeme as a reduced, the epicheireme as an extended form of the syllogism. We should admit that this description
is reasonable and in keeping with the historical origin of these
forms.

    In De inventione the "epicheireme" is treated on a par with
"Socratic" induction. 67 Cicero's Latin name for the epicheireme
is ratiocinatio, and the distinction in his system between ratiocinatio and induction obviously echoes Aristotle's distinction between
enthymeme and paradeigma, i. e. between syllogism and induction
(ἐπαγωγή). But in De inventione the theory of inductio and ratiocinatio is preceded by a discussion not only of the material of the
argument but also of necessaria and probabilis argumentatio, complexio, enumeratio, simplex conclusio, signum, credibile, compara-
bile, etc. 68 It is not suggested (and it would be difficult to believe) that all these forms should be fitted into the syllogistic procedure or resolved into the epicheireme. Post-Aristotelian rhetoricians obviously added a great amount of material to the old Peripatetic stock. As a result, those writers of artes who were anxious to include as much as they could of the new material found it
increasingly difficult (if they attempted it at all) to bring order,
system, and unity into the great variety of argumentative forms.
It cannot be our aim to unravel the various threads and to write
the history of the locus de argumentatione. Let us rather note with
gratitude that Quintilian is more restrained than some others, since
he concentrates on the loci argumentorum, the exempla (for which
he refers us to Socrates and Aristotle, see p. 288 supra), the epicheireme, and, of course, on the refutation of these forms. 69 Yet
he too separates signa as well as credibilia (σημεῖα and ἐικότα)
from the syllogistic procedure as represented by the epicheireme.
For him they are not even argumenta, though he reports that others
regarded them as a class of the argumenta. 70 To class them under
argumentum, however, is by no means the same (for a rhetorician
of the Hellenistic or Imperial era) as to regard them as a form of
the epicheireme and to describe them along syllogistic lines. Altogether our evidence suggests that hardly any later author followed
Aristotle in his very interesting attempt to understand signa, credi-

bilia, etc. (i. e. τεκμήρια, εἰκότα, σημεῖα) as imperfect and not fully cogent syllogisms.[71] We have to remember that τεκμήρια, σημεῖα, εἰκότα had their place and function even before Aristotle in the legal and (more or less technical) rhetorical practice. They were simply "evidences." Traces of blood are "evidence" of a murder; the fact that someone has been seen on the spot is evidence that he has committed the murder. Early rhetoricians distinguished different types of such "evidence," using the words which they found in common use. It was left to Aristotle to force τεκμήρια, σημεῖα, εἰκότα into the strait-jacket of his syllogism; but, as in the later systems we find them discussed without any reference to the syllogistic epicheireme, we are obviously entitled to infer that Hellenistic authorities considered it wiser not to follow him in this point. We may say that the signa, etc. come to the fore again in their Pre-Aristotelian form even though in passing through the hands of rhetoricians they have naturally become somewhat more technical.

The distinction between necessaria argumentatio and probabilis argumentatio[72] may also be traced back to Aristotle; yet we observe again that Aristotle explained the difference between them from the point of view of the syllogism, whereas later writers discuss them without reference to the syllogistic principle. For the rest, it goes without saying that the theory of the refutatio had to keep pace with that of the argumentatio and became in the same degree more elaborate and complicated.

Aristotle also bequeathed to the later rhetoricians a new conception of the τόπος. As we have seen, his new approach sprang from the idea that instead of providing a great number of ready-made arguments (one and all applying to quite definite and specific subjects or situations) the teacher of rhetoric ought to concentrate on general forms or types of arguments (see pp. 280 supra). To judge from the Roman authors, the question how general a way one should adopt in dealing with the arguments continued to occupy the rhetoricians, and remarks to the effect that it is unnecessary or impossible to provide ready-made arguments for every possible subject on which an orator may have to speak are found in Cicero and Quintilian.[73] We have again to note that in De oratore Cicero keeps very close to what he, with perfect right as it seems to me at least, considers Aristotle's idea. The loci or sedes argumentorum enumerated in II, 163-173 are of the Aristotelian type even though they are not materially identical with Aristotle's τόποι.[74] They are not connected with any definite subject-matter, and yet they are applicable to every subject. On the other hand, certain sections of De inventione contain loci of a more specific type.[75] We read there that arguments may be drawn from circumstances connected either with the person or with the fact under discussion and find a good deal of information about those circumstances which may serve as a basis for impressive arguments. Although it is true that Aristotle investigated the motives leading to crimes and the psychological conditions favoring their perpetra-

tion, [76] the discussion of "circumstances" in De inventione has little
in common with his theory.   The Greek word for circumstance is
περίστασις, and there is evidence that this term played an important rôle in Hermagoras' system of the status (στάσεις). [77] For
this reason (and others) scholars have assumed that the elaborate
theory of the circumstances in the form in which we find it in Cicero's De inventione and in later artes is closely connected with
that of the status and owes much to Hermagoras and to the Stoics
who inspired him.   It may be wise to leave the matter at that without indulging in further guesses about the inventor.   Nor should I
stress the fact that material of the same kind is found in τέχναι of
the fourth century B.C., notably in the Rhetorica ad Alexandrum
under εἰκός. [78]

Quintilian has loci of the general as well as of the more
specialized type. [79] Even in discussing the πίστεις ἄτεχνοι (witnesses, documents, etc.) he proceeds along rather general lines,
although here if anywhere the traditional practice was to provide
ready-made arguments, and even Aristotle had condescended to lay
down in concrete terms arguments both for the strengthening and
for the minimizing of witnesses, etc.   We may wonder, however,
whether Quintilian's teacher Domitius Afer, who wrote two books
on this subject, [80] also confined himself to general points of view
and excluded the customary clichés altogether.   A remark like the
following in Quintilian (V, 10, 20): locos apello non ut vulgo nunc
intelliguntur in luxuriem et adulterium et similia, sed sedes argumentorum shows that the Pre-Aristotelian type of "commonplace"
survived and that Aristotle killed this as little as the traditional
conception of σημεῖα, εἰκότα, etc., or the practice of organizing the
material under the "parts of the speech."   The rhetoricians of the
better type, however, appear to leave these commonplaces alone.

Among the rhetoricians of the Imperial era the Anonymus
Seguerianus stands out as reproducing most closely the Aristotelian
conception and division of the πίστεις:

Also, following Alexander Numenius, he defines the relation between the τόπος and the epicheireme in the true Aristotelian spirit:
τόπος ... ἐστὶν ... ἀφορμὴ ἐπιχειρήματος ἢ ἀφορμὴ πίστεως ἢ ὅθεν ἄν
τις ὁρμώμενος ἐπιχείρημα εὕροι.   His system has rightly been used
as evidence for a revival of the Aristotelian system in earlier
phases of the Imperial epoch, [81] and this revival among the Greeks
is in some way comparable to that on the Roman side for which
Cicero is responsible.   No other Greek rehtorician, however, ap-

pears to be affected by this revival in the same degree as the
Anonymus.

Reverting to the τόποι or loci, we are justified in saying that
they are an almost regular feature in the later artes where they appear in different forms; in some authors they are conceived as
points of view of a general type useful for the argumentation irrespective of its subject.   This appears to be the closest approxima-
tion to Aristotle's original conception.   Yet other authors confine
their loci to a more specified use either by connecting them with
the "circumstances" or by dividing them, according to a scheme
which seems to have been rather popular, into loci ante rem (that
is loci to be used in discussing what happened before the fact, e. g.
before the murder), in re, circa rem, post rem.   Yet, even in
this form they are still "types" of arguments, not ready-made
clichés; in other words they are very different from the "commonplaces" of the rhetorical tradition before Aristotle. 82   To maintain
that it is due to Aristotle that no Hellenistic or Imperial ars (of
which we know) consists merely of an enumeration of such commonplaces would be a gross overstatement of his influence; for the
tendency to give rhetorical precepts a more general form is probably characteristic of the fourth century B.C., as the evidence of
Theodectes and the Rhetorica ad Alexandrum shows.   We should also beware of underestimating the extent to which the τόποι were
affected and their original idea modified by their close connection
(in most of the later systems) with Hermagoras' status.   And yet,
in spite of these considerations, I suggest that whoever among the
late writers of artes thinks in terms of "types" of arguments and
not in terms of concrete, ready-made arguments is in some measure indebted to Aristotle and to his philosophical treatment of the
rhetorical "proofs."

Propositions comparable to the "premises" put forward by
Aristotle (see pp. 280f. supra) occur in the sections on the political
speech and the laudation, which are on the whole less affected by
the innovations of Post-Aristotelian theorists. 83   The old values
which had been allotted to the political speech and the laudation
(καλόν, συμφέρον, ἀγαθόν==honesta, utilia, bona) continue to domi-
nate them and we feel on familiar Aristotelian ground in reading
general propositions referring to honestas or utilitas, for example,
as well as enumerations of specific honesta, utilia, etc.   It should
be noted, however, that these propositions are no longer characterized as premises for rhetorical syllogisms and that propositions
of the kind are also found in the Rhetorica ad Alexandrum.   Yet
the propositions there are less general than Aristotle's, and it was
Aristotle after all who had taught how to define the values as well
as the "goods" classed under them.   In the Auctor ad Herennium
the sections dealing with the laudatio and the political speech include precepts concerning the arrangement and disposition of material in these types of speeches. 84   Evidently this is a concession
to the alternative, "Isocratean," τέχνη .

Generally speaking, Post-Aristotelian theories of the rhetorical argumentation show a curious mixture of Aristotelian and un-Aristotelian features; and we have to admit that the latter have, on the whole, attained a dominating position. Even the most casual glance at the sections on confirmatio (or argumentatio) in the works collected in Halm's Rhetores Latini Minores would satisfy anyone that Hermagoras with his reorganization of the material under the constitutiones carried the day over alternative theories and tendencies.[85] His four basic status and the distinction between λογικὰ and νομικὰ ζητήματα provided the groundwork for almost all later artes. In addition, there is that considerable variety of arguments to be drawn from the place, the time, the motives, and other circumstances of the fact under discussion. Naturally Hermagoras' theory too suffered many alterations; it appears to have been the ambition of every rhetorician to make some new departure in this field, at the very least by selecting and arranging the traditional material differently from his predecessors. The result is that the inventio in most of the late artes reduces to the verge of despair anyone who attempts something in the nature of an historical analysis. I shall be satisfied if I have come near the truth at least with regard to the outlines of the development, and I am under no illusion about the ample chances of error in this field. The Isocratean school does not seem to have left a deep mark on this part of the system but it looks as though some Pre-Aristotelian concepts have been carried along in the stream of the tradition and may occasionally even come to the surface, though on the whole they are buried under the various layers of later origin and it is not easy to recognize them.

3 (corresponding to section 3, page 281 supra). It may be a matter for wonder that Aristotle's theory of the three "proofs" (or, rather, means of carrying one's point) did not become a mainstay of the later systems; but our evidence for the Hellenistic centuries (which is more definite and explicit than usual[86]) suggests that the inclusion of ἦθος and πάθος--the speaker's character and the art of playing upon the feelings--was abandoned by the Hellenistic rhetoricians.[87] How soon after Aristotle this happened it is difficult to say, but one of the usual taunts of the philosophers against the rhetoricians in the late Hellenistic centuries seems to have been this very point--that the rhetoricians had given up the analysis more Aristoteleo of character and emotions. The Stoics, as is well known, generally disapproved of the arousing of emotions, and Hermagoras was influenced by them. In view of his enormous influence on the later rhetorical systems I should think that he was responsible (though not necessarily alone responsible) for the facts that inventio was reduced to a theory of the arguments and that the other two factors disappeared. Naturally, practical suggestions for the arousing of this and that definite emotion continued to find their place in the sections on proem and epilogue. To rescue the theory of πάθος from such a dubious existence and, in a spirit of loyalty to Aristotle, to restore it to its old dignity were again left to Cicero. In De inventione[88] Cicero still follows the Hellenistic tradi-

tion in confining the arousing of emotions to proem and epilogue
and refuses to recognize this as one of the principal functions of
the orator. Yet in his maturer works we find him assigning to
the orator the threefold task probare, delectare, and permovere;[89]
and this new conviction, which must have grown out of his practical experience, is reflected in a readmission of ἤθη and πάθη to a
position on a par with the rhetorical argument. ἤθος, however,
means to him something slightly different from what it had been to
Aristotle; it now denotes the leniores affectus, a lesser degree of
πάθος.[90]

It is probably the result of Cicero's authority that Quintilian
too makes an attempt to give the theory of affectus its due; but it
is a rather unfortunate attempt, the execution being poor because
of the dearth of material.[91] He says in so many words that he
found no more information in his (Hellenistic and early Imperial)
sources, and he obviously did not see his way back to the original
Aristotelian theory.   In later times Martianus Capella on the Roman, and Minucianus on the Greek side return to Aristotle's tripartite system of πίστεις, and certain other rhetoricians also take
the πάθη into account.[92] In fact Professor Hendrickson[93] has
found a considerable body of evidence for a theory that assigned to
the orator a twofold function (instead of the old threefold one) and
divided rhetorical productions or prose in general into works designed to teach and convince and those of a more emotional complexion.   This theory also goes back to the Peripatetic school and
may in the last analysis have grown out of an Aristotelian distinction between two types of style.[94]

4 (corresponding to section 4, page 181 supra).   With regard
to the tria genera causarum (the forensic speech, the political
speech, and the laudation) we have Quintilian's very valuable testimony: nec dubie prope omnes utique summae apud antiquos auctori-
tatis scriptores Aristotelem secuti ... hac partitione contenti fue-
runt.[95] The Aristotelian division was in fact adopted by the
Stoics,[96] and we find it reproduced in the Auctor ad Herennium,
Cicero, Quintilian, Fortunatianus, and Martianus Capella.   On the
Greek side, Alexander is particularly close to Aristotle's wording
and idea; the rhetorician Menander characterizes his theory of the
ἐπιδεικτικόν as covering a third of the whole field, and a glance at
Rabe's Prolegomenon Sylloge will satisfy us that the division persisted even among the Byzantines.[97] On the other hand, both Cicero and Quintilian indulge in some criticism, and the latter informs us that the division was opposed by the maximus temporum
nostrorum auctor.[98] It was in fact an obvious disadvantage that a
good part of the potential field of rhetoric remained outside the division, and remarks to this effect are found in Cicero's De oratore
and Quintilian.   Moreover, the term which Aristotle had used as
the common denominator of eulogy and invective, τὸ ἐπιδεικτικόν,
lent itself to different interpretations, misunderstandings, and, on
the basis of these misunderstandings, again to criticism; this has
recently been interestingly shown by Mr. Hinks.[99] The alternative

procedure, however, that we notice is an almost exclusive concentration on one of these three genera--the forensic.   This tendency which was probably widespread in Hellenistic centuries is, as far as we can judge, typically represented by Hermagoras, whose new system (of the status) fits only the forensic branch while the other two are condemned to a rather obscure existence in a corner.[100] The effect of this development may be studied in De inventione, where the system of the status, though suitable only for the forensic kind, has yet in principle at least been made the basis for the whole section on the content of the speech (inventio).   In the Rhetorica ad Herennium too the forensic branch receives preferential treatment, and some of the later rhetoricians forget the others altogether.   Hermogenes ignored Aristotle's classification.   His own λόγος πολιτικός embraces in effect the forensic and the deliberative--that is political--branch, and his division into λόγος ἁπλῶς πολιτικός and λόγος ἁπλῶς πανηγυρικός would cover the whole Aristotelian field if his λόγος πανηγυρικός were not something very different from Aristotle's ἐπιδεικτικόν.   (To say that the deliberative branch "takes revenge" for the neglect to which it was commonly exposed, "by finding a new and disruptive place within the theory of status itself, "[101] is not quite fair to Hermogenes who is constantly thinking of deliberative--political--speeches and tries to fit them into all his status.)

     5 (corresponding to section 5, page 282 supra).   The history of the Aristotelian (or Theophrastean) "virtues" of style in later rhetorical theory has been admirably written by Professor Stroux.[102] The fourth book of the Rhetorica ad Herennium shows how completely the Theophrastean scheme had been destroyed, and in what a chaotic condition the theory of style found itself before Cicero in De oratore decided to go back to the auctores et inventores harum sane minutarum rerum, that is to revive the old Peripatetic doctrine. In the third book of De oratore a theory of rhetorical diction (elocutio) is put forward which in its outlines and organization corresponds exactly to Theophrastus' scheme (see supra, p. 283).[103]   It is no exaggeration to maintain that but for this revival modern scholars would not have been able to reconstruct the original system.   And yet, if Cicero when he wrote De inventione had carried out his intention of reproducing the entire Hellenistic system, the section on elocutio would in all probability show the same close resemblance to that in the Rhetorica ad Herennium as does the part which he actually worked out.   As he stopped before arriving at elocutio his development from "Asianism" to "classicism" can be traced only in his stylistic practice, and it is only to the later phase that we have a corresponding "classical" theory in De oratore. In Orator, Cicero is preoccupied with the three "characters"; yet in that work too the Peripatetic basis is unmistakable.[104]

     Quintilian, who devotes three and a half books to elocutio,[105] follows Cicero in arranging the material under the four "virtues" and Fortunatianus, Julius Victor, Martianus Capella, and Cassiodorus proceed in principle on the same lines.   In the field of diction, however, a huge amount of new material had accumulated since Theophrastus' time.   Innumerable new "figures," the whole array of τρόποι, and many other recent pieces of theory were claiming a place in this phase of the system, so that we need not wonder that, while the general outlines of the Peripatetic scheme are preserved intact in writers like Quintilian and the others just mentioned, the content of a section like the ornatus continuae orationis (i. e. κόσμος in the σύνθεσις) differs considerably from what Aristotle, Theophrastus, and other Peripatetic writers would have discussed under this heading.   In fact, as far as the material (as distinct from its organization) is concerned, we find a closer reproduction of the old Peripatetic doctrine in "Demetrius," περὶ ἑρμηνείας, although this author, unlike Quintilian, has broken up the Peripatetic structure. [106]

On the Greek side no revival of the old Peripatetic scheme seems to have taken place.   On the contrary, Stroux has ingeniously shown that writers like Dionysius tend to make the ornatus supreme and to give it a monopoly of elocutio, [107] thus abandoning the fundamental idea of the Peripatetic school for which ornatus (κόσμος) ranked with the three other "virtues": correct language, clarity, and appropriateness to subject matter.   Since this is the theory which the Romans beginning with Cicero revive, we note an important divergence between them and their Greek colleagues, who think of style primarily as an "ornament" and tend to ignore the instructive and informative function of language (guaranteed by σαφήνεια)[108] as well as the requirement of a proper relation between style and subject matter, etc. (τὸ πρειπον).

The so-called Atticistic movement is to a large extent controlled by the κριτικοί who either believe in a multitude of stylistic "ideas" to be used in the appraisal and emulation of the great models or put the main emphasis on the three (or, eventually, more) stylistic "characters."   The origin of this stock-in-trade of the later systems does not concern us here.   It suffices for our purpose to note that the Peripatetic school is no longer considered responsible for its introduction and that the essential difference between this approach to style and that along the line of "virtues" has come to be recognized. [109]   It lies, above everything else, in the fact that, while the Peripatetic believers in virtues theorize on style in a general way and provide precepts applicable to every speech (or even every piece of prose), the writers on χαρακτῆρες divide the whole literature of the past into three or four different types and proceed to describe the peculiarities of each of these. In other words, the theorists of the former type recognize only a distinction between good style and bad style, whereas those of the latter know and approve of four different styles and disapprove of another four.

I am far from minimizing this important difference, and yet it is equally important to understand that both the writers dealing with stylistic "ideas" and those discussing the "characters" draw

to a very large extent on material provided for the "virtues" and,
in fact, on the virtues themselves. [110] Thus they too are indebted
to the Peripatetics. Dionysius' "ideas" are, from the historical
point of view, a rather variegated affair, and yet the Peripatetic
stock is clearly discernible (more so, as it seems to me at least,
than in Hermogenes' περὶ ἰδεῶν). It is true that, besides τὸ σαφές,
τὸ πρέπον, etc., we also find the Isocratean ἡδύ, πιθανόν, ἐναργές,
but we shall see presently that later Peripatetics had found a way
of combining these with the original Aristotelian "virtues, " and we
should bear in mind that Peripatetic writers like Demetrius of
Phaleron had been liberal enough to theorize e.g. on χάρις. It
has also been pointed out that Dionysius in discriminating between
good and bad style makes frequent use of the Peripatetic principle
of the "mean" (μεσότης) between two extremes, which helps him also in establishing the supremacy of his εὔκρατος ἁρμονία, the middle
style. [111] As regards the writers on χαρακτῆρες, the Peripatetic
basis of Pseudo-Longinus and "Demetrius, " περὶ ἑρμηνείας is obvious enough.   Three of the "sources of sublimity" (πηγαὶ τοῦ ὕφους)
in "longinus" are identical with the sub-headings of Theophrastus'
κόσμος, namely the right choice of words (ἐκλογὴ τῶν ὀνομάτων), the
dignified composition of words (σύνθεσις τῶν ὀνομάτων), and the "figures" (σχήματα). [112] "Demetrius" makes an even more extensive
use of Peripatetic material.   In discussing the ἰσχνὸς χαρακτήρ (the
tenue genus dicendi) he declares that in this character σαφῆ δεῖ
εἶναι τὴν λέξιν and proceeds to expound such precepts as the Peripatetics from Aristotle onwards provided for clarity, one of their
"virtues" (σαφήνεια): use the common words, avoid ambiguities,
leave the words in their natural order, use plenty of particles,
etc. [113] Another Peripatetic virtue, ornatus, provides him with
material on metaphors, images, new words, compound words, al-
legories, etc., which he uses in his description of the sublime or
magnificent character.   He also draws on this material, though in
a somewhat different manner, in his sections on the two remaining
"characters. "[114] Again, in theorizing on the "composition of
words" in the various characters and in selecting the figures suitable for each of them he proceeds for the most part by dividing up
between them the Peripatetic material for σύνθεσις ὀνομάτων and
σχήματα.

     Instead of pursuing this subject further in detail, let us note
that "Demetrius, " who borrows and hands on so much Peripatetic
material, shows very clearly that this material had suffered--ob-
viously at the hands of the Peripatetics themselves--important modifications, especially through the addition to the old stock of some
new categories which had previously been sponsored by the Isocrateans (we here notice again the conflatio of the two traditions).
Theophrastus is known to have found room in his system of style
for τὸ ἡδύ and τὸ μεγαλοπρεπές, two Isocratean requirements for the
narration which Aristotle himself had rejected as unnecessary.
From "Demetrius" we infer that τὸ πιθανόν and τὸ ἐναργές, [115] two
other Isocratean "virtues" of the narration, were also admitted by
the Peripatetics (after Aristotle's time) and even elevated to the

position of a quality of style in general, whereas the Isocrateans
had confined these to the narration, one of their four "parts of the
speech." Among the more specialized subjects on which the Isocratean school had theorized and which now came to be absorbed in
the Peripatetic system hiatus is probably the most important. Aristotle himself, though dealing at length with the period and its rhythm, had refrained from making any reference to hiatus. He probably knew that the Isocrateans prided themselves on avoiding colli-
sions of vowels but considered it beneath his dignity to pay attention to this newfangled subtlety. His successors, however, did not
share his prejudice.

Yet, although the later Peripatetics compromised with the
rival school, they did not normally surrender vital and axiomatic
features of their master's system. This may be gathered from the
following two passages in "Demetrius" which are probably typical
of the Peripatetic attitude to Isocratean propositions. [116]

"There are people who hold that we ought to talk about little
things in a grand fashion (τὰ μικρὰ μεγάλως λέγειν; this has been
taken as a reference to Isocrates and is in fact more likely to have
been aimed at him than at Gorgias) and they regard this as proof
of surpassing power.... Yet fitness must be observed whatever
the subject be or, in other words, the style must be appropriate."
This "fitness" is τὸ πρέπον, one of the Aristotelian "virtues" which
is here played off against an Isocratean principle. Instead of τὰ
μικρὰ μεγάλως λέγειν the Peripatetics formulate a new principle, with
the help of Aristotle's πρέπον, namely τὰ μικρὰ μικρῶς λέγειν, τὰ δὲ
μεγάλα μεγάλως.

The following passage refers to the question of hiatus: "With
regard to hiatus different opinions have been held by different
people. Isocrates and his followers avoided hiatus while others
have admitted it whenever it chanced to occur and between all vowels (reading πάντα πᾶσιν instead of παντάπασιν). One ought, however,
neither to make the composition noisy as it will be if the vowels
are allowed inartistically to collide just as they fall together ...
nor shun the direct contact of such letters altogether." This is a
good Peripatetic middle course for which several reasons are given,
especially that common parlance (ἡ συνήθεια) does not hesitate to
bring these letters into contact, in words like χιών, and that much
music and euphony would be lost if hiatus were shunned everywhere.

We referred above (pp. 282ff.) to certain other contributions
and new departures made either by Aristotle himself or by his
school and may now add a few brief remarks concerning their fate
in later authors. Quintilian[117] records that the division of proofs
into ἔντεχνοι and ἄτεχνοι was accepted by almost all writers on
rhetoric (illa partitio ab Aristotele tradita consensum fere omnium
meruit). This is borne out by the extant systems, especially by
those constructed on the lines of the quinquepartite scheme. [118]   A
divergent attitude is taken by Cicero in De inventione where he does

not recognize a distinction between these two kinds of proofs and polemizes against people holding that quaestiones, testimonia, etc. artificio non indigere.[119] Some rhetoricians, one may assume from this, considered that ἄτεχνα should find either no place at all or at least no technical treatment in the τέχνη. Cicero's own view (or, more probably, that of a Hellenistic rhetorician whom he follows) is that these proofs are a phase of one particular status, namely coniectura. Yet, in De oratore he has changed his mind and returns to the orthodox Aristotelian distinction between ἔντεχνα and ἄτεχνα,[120] including in the latter category even the leges. This is noteworthy since, as a rule, later rhetoricians diverged from Aristotle in excluding this item. Nor is it difficult to account for this; the devices which Aristotle in his discussion of the ἄτεχνοι πίστεις had provided for the interpretation of the law, the appeal to the lawgiver's intention as against the letter of the law, the defense of the letter against the supposed intention of the lawgiver, etc., have in the meantime received a place in a different part of the system. Hermagoras used material very similar to Aristotle's to build up his νομικαὶ στάσεις;[121] and, as the later rhetoricians adopted his system of στάσεις, it was logical for them no longer to include the νόμος with the rest of the ἄτεχνοι πίστεις.

As for the sentence period, my impression is that hardly any later rhetorician fully grasped the idea behind Aristotle's definition. The general tendency is to treat this subject more "empirically" and less philosophically. Instead of emphasizing (as Aristotle had done) that the period has a beginning and an end "in itself" and that it is the function of the rhythm to mark these, later writers stress the fact that the period consists of κῶλα and κόμματα, a point which Aristotle as we have seen did not regard as at all essential.[122] Cicero in Orator (where he quotes Aristotle in support of his plea for a rhythmical structure of the oration) comes nearer than anyone else perhaps to the original Aristotelian idea.[123]

The sections of "Demetrius" on χάρις and τὸ γελοῖον are, like almost everything else in his treatise, derived from a Peripatetic source; and Cicero's discussion of the rhetorical joke in De oratore II is based on the Peripatetic distinction between the laughable in the subject-matter and the laughable in verbal expression and certainly owes many of the more specific points also to Peripatetic theory. This has been shown by a comparison with the Tractatus Coislinianus the results of which seem valid, even though one might feel that Cicero's own contributions have been somewhat underrated. Quintilian in turn depends on Cicero. Since the Peripatetics, as far as we know, treated this subject in monographs, it was left to later authors (especially the Romans) to locate it in the system. Cicero as well as Quintilian decided to place it close to his propositions about the arousing of emotions, but Kroll rightly says that the place was never definitively fixed.[124]

We know so little of the Peripatetic theories concerning oratorical delivery that it is very difficult to define the extent to which later authors reproduce them.   According to Kroll, Cicero followed Theophrastus closely both in De oratore and Orator;[125] this would mean that not only the precepts referring to the orator's voice (which Theophrastus certainly discussed) but also those covering his gestus and the movements of his body go back to Theophrastus. It is not easy to substantiate this suggestion.   The best argument (which, however, Kroll would hardly use) is that it is generally Cicero's tendency, especially in De oratore, to revert to the Peripatetic authorities.   And we have seen that the Peripatetics were responsible for the inclusion of ὑπόκρισις (actio) in the quinquepartite system.

The quinquepartite system is certainly the most comprehensive put forward in the history of ancient rhetoric, but even in characterizing it thus we are far from doing full justice to its importance.   It is safe to say that through the quinquepartite system and through the tripartite scheme of "proofs" (arguments, emotions, speaker's character) Aristotle and his school provided the rhetoricians with a principle of organization based on the nature and functions of a public speech.   This is the truly philosophical approach to rhetoric; and, though the Peripatetics did not actually kill the rather mechanical alternative system, they at least succeeded in breaking its monopoly.   Next to this contribution, the theory of argumentation and the theory of style are the two major fields where Aristotle's methods and ideas have left their mark.   Oratorical delivery is a somewhat less important subject; and the analysis of the emotions, though revived from time to time, never secured a definite and undisputed place in the system.   While the history of the most important rival tradition, the Isocratean, still remains to be written, we have at least been able to observe how it weakened and to some extent undermined the Peripatetic position in the two most important sections of the rhetorical system, inventio and elocutio.   To this extent Cicero's unum quoddam genus est conflatum a posterioribus is certainly borne out.[126]   In the field of inventio an even more dangerous rival arose in the person of Hermagoras, and it is not too much to say that with the subtle, scholastic distinctions and the elaborate casuistry of his status he carried the day over Aristotle.   Certain Aristotelian features survived, however, indicating that even Hermagoras' triumph was not complete and that on the whole the result was (here as well as in the fields of conflict between Aristotle and Isocrates) a compromise.

If it is asked (and I do not see why this should not be a perfectly legitimate question) who did most to keep alive or revive Aristotelian ideas and concepts, the answer can hardly be doubtful. I should not stress the fact that the quinquepartite system underlies De oratore (for this system was scarcely in danger of being eclipsed) but rather draw attention to the inclusion in this work of ἦθος and πάθος, the revival of Aristotle's conception of the loci argumentorum, the return to the four "virtues" of the diction, and the insistence on the old boundary between inventio and dispositio.

And we may add, as a point of a less technical nature, that Cicero regards a wide range of knowledge and philosophical speculation as prior conditions for successful oratory. [127] These facts lend substance to his claim that in De oratore he renewed the ratio Aristotelia (along with the ratio Isocratea), [128] and I cannot help wondering why the tendency among scholars has been either to ignore or to minimize the importance of this testimony.

NOTES

1. Inst. orat., III, 1, 14f. Professor Harry Caplan has kindly read the manuscript of this paper which has profited by his suggestions.
2. Cicero, De invent., II, 8. Cf. G. L. Hendrickson, A.J.P., XXVI (1905), p. 266.
3. The long felt need for a truly historical treatment of ancient rhetoric has at last been met by Professor Kroll's very valuable article "Rhetorik" in Pauly-Wissowa-Kroll, R.E. (Suppl. VI).
4. See, however, Harry M. Hubbell, The Influence of Isocrates on Cicero, Dionysius and Aristides (New Haven, 1913).
5. In view of the absence of an authentic Isocratean τέχνη a thorough and at the same time cautious analysis of Isocrates' "speeches" from the technical point of view would seem necessary.
6. Joh. Stroux, De Theophrasti virtutibus dicendi (Leipzig, 1912). For the relation between Aristotle and Theophrastus see especially pp. 29-42. Cf. on this point also H. Diels, Abh. Berl. Akad., 1886, pp. 25ff. and G. L. Hendrickson, A.J.P., XXV (1904), pp. 136f.
7. See Plato, Phaedrus 266 d-267 d; Aristotle, Rhet. A 1, 1354 b 16-19. Cf. O. Navarre's admirable reconstruction of these systems (Essai sur la rhétorique grecque [Paris, 1900], pp. 211-327) and see also Hendrickson, A.J.P., XXVI (1905), pp. 250f.
8. Dionysius' testimony (De Lys. 16ff.) is borne out by what we know about Theodectes' τέχνη (see especially the evidence in Rose, Aristotelis Fragmenta, 133 or in Rabe's Prolegg. Sylloge, 32, 216).
9. Rhet. A 1, 1354 b 16-1355 a 1; Γ 13, 1414 b 13-18; Γ 14, 1415 b 4-9. In this paper I take Aristotle's Rhetoric as a unity and a whole without going into the questions concerning the development of Aristotle's theories which I have treated elsewhere (Die Entwicklung d. aristot. Logik und Rhetorik [Berlin, 1929]). From the point of view of the Aristotelian "tradition" these questions seem irrelevant as there is no evidence that they ever bothered later rhetoricians.
10. Cf. my paper on "The Origins and Methods of Aristotle's Poetics," in Class. Quart., XXIX (1935), pp. 192-201.
11. Γ 13-19.
12. See especially Rhet. A 2, 1356 a 1-27 and Γ 1, 1403 b 6-18, 1404 a 8-12 and 13. It has been pointed out by Volkmann

(Rhetorik d Griechen und Römer, p. 17) that the Rhetorica
ad Alex. may be divided into sections dealing with A)
πράγματα, B) λέξις, and C) τάξις, but the fact is that its
author does not seem to have been aware of this. He certainly makes no attempt to establish a rational division of
his subject, still less to deduce the necessity of such a division. Whether or not rhetorical systems before Aristotle
included anything comparable to ad Alex. 2-7 and to what
extent they had gone beyond organizing the entire material
under the "parts of the speech" is a question which we can
hardly attempt to answer. Aristotle's Rhetoric bears the
mark of philosophical reasoning, whereas the average τέχνη
developed out of practical needs and practical habits. To
divide the τέχνη into proem, narration, proofs, etc. is to
follow the way in which anyone however untrained would
state his case before a jury.

13. Γ 1, 1403 b 21-36.
14. See e.g. Metaph. Z 17, especially 1041 b 11-33, where Aris-
     totle insists on the difference between a syllable and the
     letters of which it consists. See also H 2. Cf. W. D.
     Ross, Aristotle (3rd edition, London, 1937), pp. 172f.
15. The evidence for the meaning of the word ἐνθύμημα before Aris-
     totle is not very definite, but on the basis of Isocrates,
     Paneg. 9, Contra soph. 16, Euag. 10 one may form the im-
     pression that any rather elaborate (and elaborately expressed)
     thought could be called by that name (cf. Navarre, op. cit.,
     p. 255); and I see no reason why Isocrates should not re-
     gard e.g. the famous opening passage of the Panegyricus as
     an enthymeme. Quintilian, V, 10, 1 records different
     meanings of the word and mentions that plures favored a
     notion of enthymema which is certainly not Aristotle's. The
     third variety which he mentions seems to have something in
     common with the description of the enthymeme found in ad
     Alex. 11. "Demetrius," περὶ ἑρμ. 30-33 finds it necessary
     to emphasize the fact that an enthymeme is not the same
     thing as a sentence period. See also Quintilian, VIII, 5, 9.
16. The principal passages are Rhet. A 1, 1354 b 3-10; 2, 1356
     a 35-b 25; 1357 b 26-36; 1358 a 1-35; B 20, 1393 a 24-27.
     See also Anal. Pr. B 23f. The necessity of basing rhetoric
     on dialectic had been emphasized by Plato (Phaedrus 265)
     but Plato did not think of dialectic in terms of syllogisms.
17. The Attic orators make ample use of εἰκότα, σημεῖα, τεκμήρια
     (see Antiphon, V, 25, 28, 37, 38, 43, 61, 63 and compare
     the indices for the other orators; see also Thucydides, I,
     1, 3; 2, 6; 3, 3; and passim). I should hesitate to believe
     that all of them would agree with the definitions given to ad
     Alex. 8, 10, 13. For Aristotle's syllogistic construction of
     these forms see A 2, 1357 a 22-b 25 and Anal. Pr. B 27.
18. See Aristotle, Soph. El. 34, 183 b 36-184 a 1; Cicero, Brut.
     46f. Cf. Navarre, op. cit., pp. 124-132; Volkmann, op.
     cit., p. 159, and my Antiphonstudien (Berlin, 1931), p. 39,
     n. 2; pp. 47, 65.

19. Soph. El. 34, 183 b 36-184 a 8.
20. See the τόπος τοῦ μᾶλλον καὶ ἧττον in Rhet. B 23 (1397 b).
21. Cf. on Aristotle's τόποι Georgiana P. Palmer, The τόποι of
    Aristotle's Rhetoric as exemplified in the Orators (Diss.,
    Chicago, 1934). I cannot fully agree with James H.
    McBurney's comments on the relation between the τόποι and
    the enthymeme (Pap. Mich. Ac., XXI [1935], p. 493).
22. Cf. especially chapters like A 6f., 9, B 19. A 10-19 may
    also with some justification be mentioned here. For the
    methodical idea behind the premises (and behind the τόποι)
    see A 2, 1358 a 1-A 3, 1359 a 5. See for comment on
    this section of the Rhetoric my book (see supra n. 9), pp.
    13-27.
23. Ad Alex. 2-6. Aristotle too has some chapters in which he
    enumerates τὰ ἀγαθά or τὰ καλά (A 5; A 6, 1362 b 10-28;
    A 9, 1366 a 34-b 22) and it might be argued that in these he
    is keeping closer to the procedure of the average, unphilo-
    sophical τέχναι.
24. Rhet. A 2, 1356 a 1-33; B 1-18. See for a fuller discussion
    my paper in C.P., XXXIII (1938), pp. 390-404.
25. The most instructive passage is perhaps Aristotle, Rhet. A 2,
    1356 a 10-13.
26. Rhet. A 3, 1358 a 1-13; Aristotle proceeds along lines of a
    strictly dichotomous διαίρεσις; and, as this method is typi-
    cal of Plato rather than of Aristotle, the division of the
    rhetorical λόγοι which we read here may well go back to
    the Academy (cf. Diog. Laert., 3, 93). The peculiar quali-
    ty of Aristotle's procedure ought to have been taken into ac-
    count by D. A. G. Hinks in his important article on the
    tria genera causarum in Class. Quart., XXX (1936), pp. 170-
    176 because it explains some of the things which puzzle him
    and puzzled ancient rhetoricians.
27. See Quintilian, III, 4, 1. The division into three γένη and
    their sub-division into six εἴδη are also found in the so
    called Divis. Aristoteleae §§ 93f. H. Mutschmann in his
    edition (p. xiii) remarks pertinently: quae εἴδη Aristoteles
    a vulgari arte acceperat. Professor Cherniss has drawn
    my attention to these passages.
28. Cf. especially Γ 2, 1404 b 1-8. Γ 2 and 4 come definitely
    under κόσμος, 7 under πρέπον. Cf. Stroux, op. cit.,
    pp. 29-43. Stroux maintains that for Aristotle these vir-
    tues form a unity, but this is one of the few points in his
    book where one may not follow him.
29. Γ 5.
30. See Stroux, op. cit., pp. 9-28.
31. Γ 3, 6, 10.
32. Γ 2, 1405 a 3ff.
33. A definite reference to this work is found in Γ 9, 1410 b 3,
    but it is hard to believe that Aristotle should not have drawn
    on it also for his discussion of the sentence period in gene-
    ral, rhythm, and related subjects. Cf. p. 46 infra.
34. A 15. In some of the earliest extant Attic orations the argu-

mentation consists entirely in an elaborate twisting of the available ἄτεχνοι πίστεις. See my Antiphonstudien (Berlin, 1931).

35. Chap. 8 init.
36. See Γ 9 passim, especially 1409 a 35f. Cf. also Γ 8. Much light has been shed on these theories and some mistaken interpretations have been refuted by Josef Zehetmeier in his valuable dissertation on Die Periodenlehre des Aristoteles (München, 1930, printed also in Philologus, LXXXV [1930], pp. 192-208, 255-284, 414-436).
37. Cf. E. Arndt, De ridiculi doctr. rhet. (Diss., Bonn, 1904) and Mary A. Grant, The Ancient Theories of the Laughable (Madison, 1924). See also Kroll, R.-E., s.v. "Rhetorik," 38f. Cf. infra.
38. Γ 1, 1403 b 26-31.
39. Kroll (R.-E., s.v. "Rhetorik," 36f.) is probably right in assuming that Cicero's discussion of the actio (De orat., III, 213-225; Orat. 55-60) is a reliable basis for the reconstruction of Theophrastus' theory. See also Stroux, op. cit., pp. 70f.
40. Hermes, LXVII (1932), pp. 144-151. Cf. also Barwick, Hermes, LVII (1922), pp. 1ff., 12.
41. See especially Γ 14, 1415 a 24; Γ 16, 1416 b 30.
42. Hermes, LVII (1922), pp. 1-11.
43. This type is represented by Julius Severianus, Apsines, Rufus, and the Anonymus Seguerianus.
44. Quintilian, III, 3, 1. Cf. Cicero, De invent., I, 9: partes ... quas plerique dixerunt. Quintilian (loc. cit.) refers to attempts made by some rhetoricians to add iudicium to these five sections and mentions a number of writers who in some way or other diverged from the orthodox· quinquepartite scheme. According to Diog. Laert., VII, 1, 43, the Stoics had εὕρεσις, φράσις, τάξις, ὑπόκρισις (see Striller, De Stoicorum studiis rhet. [Breslau, 1887], p. 35). I should gather from Diog., loc. cit. and Cicero, De orat., I, 142 that the Stoics and other Hellenistic teachers tried to do justice to both traditions. In the end, a combination was brought about (see infra, pp. 48-50).
45. See for πράγματα Γ 1, 1403 b 19, for εὕρεσις A 2, 1355 b 39 (cf. Plato, Phaedrus 263a). I cannot agree with Barwick's reconstruction of the history of this type of rhetorical system (loc. cit., pp. 39-41) and think that Kroll's discussion (R.-E., s.v. "Rhetorik," 58f.) is more in keeping with the evidence at our disposal.
46. Cf. Diog. Laert., V, 2, 48 and Stroux, op. cit., p. 70. The Stoics evidently (see n. 44) adopted Theophrastus' system.
47. For the place of μνήμη in the rhetorical system see Kroll, R.-E., s.v. "Rhetorik," 58f.
48. See especially I, 9. The Auctor ad Herennium has all five sections.
49. The inventio is discussed in II, 104-306, 333-349; dispositio in II, 307-332; memoria in II, 350-360; elocutio in III, 37-

212; <u>actio</u> in III, 213-225.

50. To be <u>sure</u>, there is a great deal of material in VII that we should hardly expect to find under <u>dispositio</u>, but we have to infer from the first and last sentences of the book that for Quintilian himself the book deals with <u>dispositio</u>. (Radermacher's recent explanation [<u>Gnomon</u>, 1939, p. 100] is not fully convincing.)

51. See for an analysis of these authors (and for references to Cicero's <u>Orator</u>) Barwick, <u>loc. cit.</u>, p. 2.

52. Cicero goes even a step further. He starts by giving a theory of the <u>status</u> (I, 10) for which Hermagoras had set the fashion.

53. De invent., II, 157 (see, however, 155, 177). Cf. <u>Auctor ad Herennium</u>, III, 2, 10.

54. III, 7, 8.

55. This may be gathered from <u>Rhet. Graec.</u> (ed. Spengel-Hammer), II, 182, 20; 208, 5.

56. For the "Isocratean" system see <u>supra</u> p. 37.

57. Cicero does, however, in <u>De oratore</u> make a concession to the Hermagorean doctrine of the <u>status</u>, the basic idea of which is embodied in II, 104. In <u>Part. orat.</u> the <u>status</u> bulk even larger.

58. Cicero's treatment of <u>dispositio</u> in <u>De orat.</u>, II, 307-332 is again an exception since he has not anticipated the discussion of the <u>partes</u> under <u>inventio</u>. To deal with them under <u>dispositio</u> as he does was in keeping with the original Peripatetic procedure (i.e. with his <u>ratio Aristotelia</u>, see my remarks at the end of this article).

59. I am referring to his inclusion of ἦθος and πάθος.

60. For terminological problems cf. especially Quintilian, V, 10, 1ff. See also p. 170 <u>infra</u>.

61. Rhet. A 2, 1357 a 16-21.

62. <u>De invent.</u>, I, 57-66. The <u>Auctor ad Herennium</u> discusses the epicheireme along different lines and shows less interest in its syllogistic form. See on his discussion (II, 28-30) and on the epicheireme in general Kroll, <u>Sitzb. Wien. Akad.</u>, CCXVI, No. 2, pp. 4-17. For Hermagoras cf. Thiele, <u>Hermagoras</u> (Strassburg, 1893), p. 134.

63. Quintilian, V, 13 (especially 5-9).

64. De invent., I, 60f.

65. Ibid., 61. Cf. Kroll, <u>op. cit.</u>, p. 16.

66. Hermogenes describes the enthymeme (περὶ εὑρ., III, 8) as an argument to be used after the epicheireme and as reinforcing it. Apsines (ch. 10) and Minucianus (περὶ ἐπιχειρ., 2, 3) regard the enthymeme and the παράδειγμα as parts or forms of the epicheireme. For the theory mentioned in the text see especially Julius Victor, 9, 11; Fortunatianus, 2, 28; Cassiodorus, 12, 15. Cf. Dionysius Hal., <u>De Isaeo</u>, 16 where he observes that Lysias prefers enthymemes whereas Isaeus favors epicheiremes (Thiele, <u>op. cit.</u>, p. 135).

67. De invent., I, 51-56. For Aristotle see p. 39 <u>supra</u>.

68. I, 44-49.

69. Quintilian, V, 10-14.
70. Ibid., V, 9, 1; 10, 11. Cf. Philodemus, Rhet., I, 248, 369 (Sudhaus).
71. See p. 40 supra. Cf. Kroll, Philologus, LXXXIX (1934), pp. 337, 340. Kroll rightly points out that the division of σημεῖα into such ante factum, in facto, post factum, which is frequently found in later writers, occurs as early as the Rhet. ad Alex. (ch. 13). Thus we get a glimpse of a tradition which continued in spite of Aristotle. Cf. further Volkmann, op. cit. (supra, note 12), p. 155.
72. See e.g. Cicero, De invent., I, 44. Cf. Aristotle, Rhet. A 2, 1357 a 22-b 25.
73. Cf. e.g. De invent., II, 44f.; De orat., II, 117, 130; Quintilian, II, 4, 27; V, 10, 100.
74. See the references to Aristotle in De orat., II, 152, 160. It is generally and probably rightly assumed that Cicero borrows the loci of the De orat. (and similarly those included in the Topica and the Part. orat.) from a contemporary Academic system which in turn shows Stoic influence. See M. Wallies, De Fontibus Topic. Ciceronis (Diss. Halle, 1878); W. Kroll, Rhein. Mus., LVIII (1903), p. 590; P. Sternkopf, De M. Tulli Ciceronis Part. Orat. (Diss. Münst., 1914), pp. 20f. From our point of view, however, the immediate source of Cicero's loci is less important than the fact that he reverts to Aristotle's method.
75. De invent., I, 34-43; II, 17-42 (the points of view mentioned in I, 41 fin.-42 are not very different from the loci of the De orat.). Cf. the shorter and somewhat different treatment of the material of the argumentation in Ad Herennium, II, 3-8. For the distinction between persona and negotium cf. Longinus, p. 182 (Spengel-Hammer) and Rufus, 27-29.
76. Rhet. A 10-12.
77. See especially Augustine, De rhet., 7f. Cf. Thiele, op. cit., pp. 37-44; Kroll, R.-E., s.v. "Rhetorik," 56. Cf. also Volkmann, op. cit., p. 160.
78. Ch. 8.
79. The first set of loci in Quintilian, V, 10 (23-52) refers to persona and res, but in V, 10, 53 he proceeds to an enumeration of less specified loci, refusing to connect them with the status (as other rhetoricians did; see e.g. Neocles in the Anonymus Seguerianus, 170; cf. Sternkopf's judicious discussion, op. cit., pp. 21f.). For the πιστεις ἄτεχνοι see Aristotle, Rhet. A 15, Quintilian, V, 1-7. Aristotle provides τόποι of a rather specific kind in his chapter on the διαβολή (Γ 15) in which he probably borrowed a great deal from Theodectes.
80. See Quintilian, V, 7, 7. Cf. also Quintilian's remark in II, 4, 27.
81. Anonymus Seguerianus, 144ff., 168f., 172ff. O. Angermann, De Aristotele rhetorum auctore (Diss. Leipzig, 1904), pp. 28-59, suggests that the Anonymus is indebted for the Aristotelian material in his τέχνη to Caecilius of Calacte,

since the two authorities on whom he depends, Alexander
Numenius and Neocles, may both have used Caecilius. Angermann comments on a number of "Aristotelian" passages
in Quintilian which show a remarkable resemblance to the
Aristotelian material in the Anonymus. His arguments for
a common source of Quintilian, Alexander, and Neocles are,
on the whole, convincing, though I cannot regard it as proved
that this common source was Caecilius and that he was the
rhetorician who returned to the genuine Aristotelian doctrine
and passed it on to other rhetoricians of the Imperial time.
Ofenloch's collection (Caec. Calact. Fragmenta [Leipzig,
1907]) is based on Angermann.

82.   For the first type see Apsines, 10 and Anonymus Seguerianus,
169-181. Fortunatianus, II, 23, Julius Victor VI, 1-4, and
Martianus Capella, 49 (contrast 21) have the fourfold division
described in the text; but, while the loci ante rem are based
on the περιστάσεις, those circa rem and in re are of a general logical complexion resembling those in Aristotle and the
De oratore. For another combination of these types see
Minucianus, 3 (p. 343, 24 Spengel-Hammer). For the τόποι
in the mediaeval systems see Harry Caplan's very interesting discussion in C.P., XXVIII (1933), p. 75. In this context attention may be drawn to some attempts to use Aristotle's categories as a basis for inventio (Quintilian, III, 6,
23; Longinus, pp. 179-181 [Spengel-Hammer]).

83.   See especially Cicero, De invent., II, 157-178; De orat., II,
342-349; Ad Herennium, III, 2-15; Quintilian, III, 7f.

84.   III, 7-9 and 15. It may be noted that the chapters on the
laudatio frequently include references to Peripatetic divisions
of the "goods," especially to the famous tripartite division
(goods of the mind, of the body, external goods; see e.g.
Ad Herennium, III, 10; Cicero, De orat., II, 342; Part orat.,
38; Quintilian, III, 7, 12). For Stoic influence on Cicero,
De invent., II, 160ff. see Kroll, Philologus, XCI (1936),
pp. 197-205.

85.   One naturally wonders whether Hermagoras' own system shows
any signs of indebtedness to Aristotle. Unfortunately, the
system has in spite of the careful studies of Theile and W.
Jäneke (De statuum doctrina ab Hermogene tradita [Diss.
Leipzig, 1904]) not yet been reconstructed with sufficient
certainty. It is true that Quintilian was in a position to
point to certain semina of Hermagoras' theory in Aristotle's
work (III, 6, 24, 49, 60). Rhet. A 1, 1354 a 26-31, A 13,
1378 b 38ff. are some of the passages which he may have had
in mind, but those which come nearest to Hermagoras
are found in the second part of book III (15, 1416 a 6-9;
16, 1416 b 20-22; 1416 b 39-1417 a 2) where Aristotle himself depends on the Isocratean tradition (see p. 46 supra).
The value of these passages lies in the fact that they put us
in mind of some practical facts which form a background
also to Hermagoras' theory, but Quintilian's fecit deinde
velut propriam Hermagoras viam (III, 1, 16) remains, after

all, unassailable. See, however, for a different opinion
Volkmann, op. cit., pp. 31f.; Navarre, op. cit. (supra,
note 7), p. 265.

86. See Cicero, De orat., I, 87, 201; Philodemus, Rhet., I, 370
(Sudhaus). Cf. also Quintilian (p. 170 infra).

87. See for details C. P., XXXIII (1938), p. 396.

88. See De invent., I, 22, 100ff., 106ff.

89. E. g. De orat., II, 114, 128, 310; Orator, 69; Brutus, 158;
De opt. gen. or., 3.

90. De orat., II, 182-214. Cf. II, 115. See also Orator, 128-
133. It must be admitted that Cicero's analysis of the emotions goes less deep and is less philosophic than Aristotle's.
See for a fuller discussion of these points C. P., XXXIII
(1938), pp. 396-401. For Cicero's practical ψυχαγωγία see
T. A. P. A., LXIX (1938), pp. 542ff. where I have discussed
the reasons why Cicero was more attracted by Aristotle's
Rhetoric than by the Hellenistic systems. For the new notion of ἦθος see L. Voit, Δεινότης, Ein antiker Stilbegriff
(Leipzig, 1934), pp. 135-140. Cf. Quintilian, VI, 2, 8.

91. VI, 2. Cf. especially his remark VI, 2, 25.

92. Martianus Capella, 28, 29; Minucianus, 1. Julius Severianus
discusses the affectus at length and from various points of
view, drawing to a large extent on Cicero's practice (ch.
21 represents a curious attempt to utilize the loci argumentorum in building up an analogous theory for the affectus).
Apsines (306-329 [Spengel-Hammer]) and the Anonymus
Seguerianus (222-239) treat τὰ πάθη in the context of the
epilogue, and the latter has characteristically a reference
(208) to "Aristotle in the θεοδεκτικαὶ τέχναι"; see p. 46
supra. It is certainly not the genuine Aristotelian tradition.
For a reference to Aristotle's tripartite division of the
πίστεις see Dionysius Hal., De Lys., 19 init. I cannot
include in this paper a discussion of the place of ἦθος in
the theory of style.

93. A. J. P., XXVI (1905), pp. 249-267.

94. Rhet. Γ 12, 1413 b 3ff. Cf. Theophrastus' much quoted fragment (Ammonius, In Arist. de interpret., p. 65, 31 [Ber-
lin ed.]).

95. III, 4, 1; cf. ibid., 12.

96. Cf. Diogenes Laert., VII, 42.

97. See Alexander in Rhet. Graec. (ed. Spengel-Hammer), III,
1; Menander, ibid., 331. For the rest of Rabe's index s. v.
δικανικός, ἐπιδεικτικός, πανηγυρικός, συμβουλευτικός.

98. Cf. especially Cicero, De orat., II, 43-51 and 68; Quintilian,
III, 4, 2.

99. D. A. G. Hinks, "Tria Genera Causarum," Class. Quart.,
XXX (1936), pp. 170-176.

100. Namely under the status called qualitas (ποιότης). Cf. Quintilian, III, 6, 56; Thiele, op. cit., pp. 53f., 78 (see also
p. 182 concerning Athenaeus); Kroll, R.-E., s. v. "Rhetorik," 53.

101. Hinks, op. cit., p. 176.

102. See p. 36 supra.
103. See especially III, 148, 187. Elocutio is discussed in III,
     37-212 (though the "excursuses" containing lofty philosophi-
     cal speculations are, of course, foreign to the rhetorical
     theory and have to be considered as Cicero's own addi-
     tion). See for the disposition of this part of the work III,
     37. Cf. Stroux, op. cit. (supra, note 6), pp. 11-28, 54-
     56.
104. It is apparent especially in the inclusion of πάθος and ἦθος
     (128), the reference to the four "virtues of style" as a
     standard of which the Atticists fall short (79), the use
     made of τὸ πρέπον in defining, among other things, the
     proper sphere of each character (70ff.), and the reference
     to Aristotle and Theophrastus as authorities on period and
     rhythm (172, 228).
105. VIII-XI, 1. See for Quintilian and the virtutes dicendi in
     later Roman rhetoricians Stroux, op. cit., pp. 56-64. Cf.
     Fortunatianus, III, 8; Martianus Capella, 31 (Julius Victor,
     20).
106. See my paper in Hermes, LXVI (1931), pp. 241-267. The
     features of the σύνθεσις which the Peripatetic source of
     "Demetrius" had under κεκοσμημένον appear to have been
     rhythm, length of κῶλα, περιαγωγή, εὐφωνία, structure of
     the period, order and arrangement of the words, σύνδεσμοι,
     hiatus.
107. Cf. Stroux, op. cit., pp. 19, 23.
108. Cf. Aristotle, Rhet., Γ 2, 1404 b 2.
109. See again Stroux, op. cit., especially pp. 88-104 and Hen-
     drickson's papers quoted supra, notes 2 and 6. For a
     more conservative view cf. Kroll, R.-E., s.v. "Rhetorik,"
     35; Radermacher, Gnomon, XV (1939), p. 101. For the
     history of the problem see Stroux' first chapter.
110. Cf. again Stroux, op. cit., pp. 72-88 (for the material in
     Dionysius see especially pp. 73f., 77f.), 104-126. I am
     confining myself in the following pages to a few significant
     illustrations of the process.
111. See S. F. Bonner's recent article (C.P., XXXIII [1938],
     pp. 257-266) in which the author proceeds successfully on
     lines indicated by Hendrickson in A.J.P., XXV (1904),
     pp. 125-146.
112. See De Subl., 8 init., 16-29, 30-38, 39-43. Cf. Hans
     Stefan Schultz, Der Aufbau der Schrift περὶ ὕφους (Diss.
     Berlin, 1936), pp. 30ff., 42, 44.
113. "Demetrius," 191f., 196, 199ff. Cf. Cicero, De orat., III,
     48f.
114. Cf. for a fuller treatment my paper in Hermes, LXVI (1931),
     pp. 244-249, 251, 253. The Peripatetic influence in this
     work is recognized also (at least in principle) by Rhys
     Roberts, Demetrius On Style (Cambridge, 1902), pp. 50-
     52 and passim in the notes, and by Radermacher on p. 12
     of his edition (Leipzig, 1901).
115. "Demetrius," 208-222.

116. Ibid., 120, 68-71.
117. V, 1, 1.
118. See, besides Cicero and Quintilian, Julius Victor, VI, 5, 6;
     Martianus Capella, 27, 43; Anonymus Seguerianus, 145f.;
     Minucianus, 1.
119. De invent., II, 47; cf. Quintilian, V, 1, 2.
120. De orat., II, 116-119. Cf. Part. orat., 6, 48, 117 (in 117
     a particular ἄτεχνον, testes, is discussed under the head-
     ing coniectura, which is in keeping with Cicero's decision
     in De invent., II, 47).
121. See Thiele, op. cit., pp. 78-84 and cf. Quintilian, III, 6,
     61. It is possible, as Thiele points out, that Hermagoras'
     own term was νομικὰ ζητήματα (not στάσεις). A detailed
     comparison of Hermagoras' theory and Aristotle, Rhet. A
     15, 1375 a 25-b 25 would seem to be a desideratum.
122. "Demetrius," 10 is a typical passage. Cf. also Aristides,
     II, 507, 6 (Spengel); Anonymus Seguerianus, 242; Quintilian,
     IX, 4, 122ff., especially 125. See also Martianus Capella,
     39. Cf. Zehetmeier, op. cit. (supra, note 36), passim,
     especially pp. 423ff., 434.
123. Orator, 228. Yet cf. 221.
124. E. Arndt (op. cit., supra, note 37) deals with Cicero, De
     orat., II, 217-289 (pp. 25-40) and Quintilian, VI, 3
     (pp. 41-62). See also Roger Pack, C.P., XXXIII (1938),
     pp. 405-410, who proceeds more cautiously. Kroll, R.-E.,
     s.v. "Rhetorik," 38f., emphasizes that in the Orator, un-
     like the De oratore, Cicero connects the ridiculum with
     the genus tenue (see the notes in his commentary on Ora-
     tor, 87-89); Kroll's identification of facetiae and dicacitas
     with χάρις and γέλως is not tenable and has been refuted
     by Miss Grant, op. cit. (note 37, supra), p. 103. See
     also Ad Herennium, I, 10 which has something in common
     with Cicero (Arndt, op. cit., p. 38).
125. De orat., III, 213-225 (much that we read here must have
     originated with Cicero himself), Orator, 55-60. Cf.
     Kroll, R.-E., s.v. "Rhetorik," 36; Stroux, op. cit., p. 70.
126. De invent., II, 8. See supra p. 49 and p. 185.
127. In stressing the need of philosophical penetration Cicero
     agrees with Plato's Phaedrus, whereas the emphasis put
     on extensive knowledge has parallels in Aristotle (see es-
     pecially Rhet. A 4; B 22). Cf. Hans Schulte, Orator,
     Untersuchungen über das Ciceronische Bildungsideal (Frank-
     furt, 1935) and my review of this book in A.J.P., LIX
     (1938), p. 106.
128. Ad Fam., I, 9, 23. See for literature C.P., XXXIII (1938),
     p. 398 (add Kroll, R.-E., s.v. "Rhetorik," 47-50).

NAME AND AUTHOR INDEX

[Aristotle is omitted as his name appears on nearly every page]